An Expanding World
Volume 12

Textiles: Production,
Trade and Demand

AN EXPANDING WORLD
The European Impact on World History, 1450–1800

General Editor: A.J.R. Russell-Wood

Please note titles may change prior to publication

An Expanding World
The European Impact on World History 1450–1800

Volume 12

Textiles: Production, Trade and Demand

edited by
Maureen Fennell Mazzaoui

Routledge
Taylor & Francis Group

LONDON AND NEW YORK

First published 1998 by Ashgate Publishing

Published 2016 by Routledge
2 Park Square, Milton Park, Abingdon, Oxfordshire OX14 4RN
711 Third Avenue, New York, NY 10017, USA

First issued in paperback 2016

Routledge is an imprint of the Taylor & Francis Group, an informa business

British Library CIP data
> Textiles: Production, Trade and Demand.
> (An Expanding World: The European Impact on World History, 1450–1800: Vol. 12).
> 1. Textile industry–History. 2. Imperialism.
> I. Mazzaoui, Maureen Fennell.
> 677'.009

US Library of Congress CIP data
> Textiles: Production, Trade and Demand/edited by Maureen Fennell Mazzaoui.
> p. cm. – (An Expanding World: The European Impact on World History, 1450–1800: Vol. 12).
> 1. Textile industry–History. 2. Clothing trade–History.
> 3. Economic History.
> I. Mazzaoui, Maureen Fennell. II. Series.
> HD9850. 5. T39   1997   96–52046
> 338.4'7677–dc21   CIP

AN EXPANDING WORLD 12

ISBN 13: 978-1-138-25125-0 (hbk)
ISBN 13: 978-0-86078-509-5 (pbk)

Contents

Acknowledgements

The chapters in this volume are taken from the sources listed below, for which the editor and publishers wish to thank their authors, original publishers or other copyright holders for permission to use their material as follows:

Chapter 1: Murat Çizakça, 'Incorporation of the Middle East into the European World-Economy', *Review* VIII (New York, 1985), pp. 353–377. Copyright © 1985 by the Fernand Braudel Center, State University of New York at Binghampton, New York.

Chapter 2: Edmund Herzig, 'The Iranian Raw Silk Trade and European Manufacture in the Seventeenth and Eighteenth Centuries', *Journal of European Economic History* XIX (Rome, 1990), pp. 73–89. Copyright © 1990 by the Banco di Roma, Rome.

Chapter 3: Adrienne D. Hood, 'The Gender Division of Labor in the Production of Textiles in Eighteenth-Century, Rural Pennsylvania (Rethinking the New England Model)', *Journal of Social History* XXVII, no. 3 (Pittsburgh, PA, 1994), pp. 537–561. Copyright © 1994 by Mellon University Press, Pittsburgh, PA.

Chapter 4: Manuel Miño Grijalva, '¿Proto-Industria Colonial?', *Historia Mexicana* XXXVIII (Mexico, 1989), pp. 793–818. Copyright © 1989 by El Colegio de Mexico, A.C., Mexico City.

Chapter 5: Douglas C. Libby, 'Reconsidering Textile Production in Late Colonial Brazil: New Evidence from Minas Gerais', *Latin American Research Review* XXXII, no. 1 (1997), pp. 88–108. Copyright © 1997 by the Latin American Research Review.

Chapter 6: Kang Chao, 'La production textile dans la Chine traditionelle', *Annales: Economies, Sociétés, Civilisations* XXXIX (Paris, 1984), pp. 957–976. Copyright © 1984 by Société de Périodiques Spécialisés, Paris.

Chapter 7: William B. Hauser, 'Textiles and Trade in Tokugawa Japan', in *Textiles in Trade*, Proceedings of the Textile Society of America, Biennial Symposim, September 14–16, 1990 (Washington, D.C., 1990), pp. 112–125. Copyright © 1990 by William B. Hauser.

Chapter 8: Joseph J. Brennig, 'Textile Producers and Production in Late Seventeenth-Century Coromandel', *The Indian Economic and Social History Review* XXIII, no. 4 (New Delhi, 1986), pp. 333–356. Copyright © 1986 by the Indian Economic and Social History Association. All rights reserved. Reproduced by permission of the copyright holder and the publishers, Sage Publications India Private Limited, New Delhi.

Chapter 9: S. Arasaratnam, 'Weavers, Merchants and Company: The Handloom Industry in Southeastern India, 1750–1790', *Indian Economic and Social History Review* XVII, no. 3 (New Delhi, 1978), pp. 257–281. Copyright © 1978 by the Indian Economic and Social History Association. All rights reserved. Reproduced by permission of the copyright holder and the publishers, Sage Publications India Private Limited, New Delhi.

Chapter 10: Kenneth R. Hall, 'The Textile Industry in Southeast Asia, 1400–1800', *The Journal of the Social and Economic History of the Orient* XXXIX, no. 2 (Leiden, 1996), pp. 87–135. Copyright © 1996 by E.J. Brill. Reprinted by permission.

Chapter 11: Carolyn Keyes Adenaike, 'West African Textiles, 1500–1800', first publication. Copyright © 1998 by Carolyn Keyes Adenaike.

Chapter 12: Jan Vansina, 'Rafia Cloth in West Central Africa, 1500–1800', first publication. Copyright © 1998 by Jan Vansina.

Every effort has been made to trace all the copyright holders, but if any have been inadvertently overlooked the publishers will be pleased to make the necessary arrangement at the first opportunity.

*   *   *

The Editor is grateful to a number of scholars for bibliographical suggestions relating to their areas of specialization. These include David Henige, Jean Lee, H. Leedom Lefferts, Yu-sheng Lin, John McCusker, Maurice Meisner, Kären Wigen, Thongchai Winichakul and Jonathan Zeitlin. In addition, several colleagues read and commented on sections of the Introduction: Kang Chao, Daniel Doeppers, John Kaminski, Kemal Karpat, Diane Lindstrom, Steve Stern, Julia Thomas and André Wink. The Editor is especially indebted to Domenico Sella and Jan Vansina for their generous advice and encouragement at every stage of this project.

General Editor's Preface

A.J.R. Russell-Wood

An Expanding World: The European Impact on World History, 1450–1800 is designed to meet two objectives: first, each volume covers a specific aspect of the European initiative and reaction across time and space; second, the series represents a superb overview and compendium of knowledge and is an invaluable reference source on the European presence beyond Europe in the early modern period, interaction with non-Europeans, and experiences of peoples of other continents, religions, and races in relation to Europe and Europeans. The series reflects revisionist interpretations and new approaches to what has been called 'the expansion of Europe' and whose historiography traditionally bore the hallmarks of a narrowly Eurocentric perspective, focus on the achievements of individual nations, and characterization of the European presence as one of dominance, conquest, and control. Fragmentation characterized much of this literature: fragmentation by national groups, by geography, and by chronology.

The volumes of *An Expanding World* seek to transcend nationalist histories and to examine on the global stage rather than in discrete regions important selected facets of the European presence overseas. One result has been to bring to the fore the multicontinental, multi-oceanic and multinational dimension of the European activities. A further outcome is compensatory in the emphasis placed on the cross-cultural context of European activities and on how collaboration and cooperation between peoples transcended real or perceived boundaries of religion, nationality, race, and language and were no less important aspects of the European experience in Africa, Asia, the Americas, and Australia than the highly publicized confrontational, bellicose, and exploitative dimensions. Recent scholarship has not only led to greater understanding of peoples, cultures, and institutions of Africa, Asia, the Americas, and Australasia with whom Europeans interacted and the complexity of such interactions and transactions, but also of relations between Europeans of different nationalities and religious persuasions.

The initial five volumes reflect the changing historiography and set the stage for volumes encompassing the broad themes of technology and science, trade and commerce, exploitation as reflected in agriculture and the extractive industries and through systems of forced and coerced labour, government of empire, and society and culture in European colonies and settlements overseas. Final volumes examine the image of Europe and Europeans as 'the other' and the impact of the wider world on European *mentalités* and mores.

An international team of editors was selected to reflect a diversity of educational backgrounds, nationalities, and scholars at different stages of their professional careers. Few would claim to be 'world historians', but each is a recognized authority in his or her field and has the demonstrated capacity to ask the significant questions and provide a conceptual framework for the selection of articles which combine analysis with interpretation. Editors were exhorted to place their specific subjects within a global context and over the *longue durée*. I have been delighted by the enthusiasm with which they took up this intellectual challenge, their courage in venturing beyond their immediate research fields to look over the fences into the gardens of their academic neighbours, and the collegiality which has led to a generous informal exchange of information. Editors were posed the daunting task of surveying a rich historical literature and selecting those essays which they regarded as significant contributions to an understanding of the specific field or representative of the historiography. They were asked to give priority to articles in scholarly journals; essays from conference volumes and *Festschriften* were acceptable; excluded (with some few exceptions) were excerpts from recent monographs or paperback volumes. After much discussion and agonizing, the decision was taken to incorporate essays only in English, French, and Spanish. This has led to the exclusion of the extensive scholarly literature in Danish, Dutch, German and Portuguese. The ramifications of these decisions and how these have had an impact on the representative quality of selections of articles have varied, depending on the theme, and have been addressed by editors in their introductions.

The introduction to each volume enables readers to assess the importance of the topic *per se* and place this in the broader context of European activities overseas. It acquaints readers with broad trends in the historiography and alerts them to controversies and conflicting interpretations. Editors clarify the conceptual framework for each volume and explain the rationale for the selection of articles and how they relate to each other. Introductions permit volume editors to assess the impact on their treatments of discrete topics of constraints of language, format, and chronology, assess the completeness of the journal literature, and address *lacunae*. A further charge to editors was to describe and evaluate the importance of change over time, explain differences attributable to differing geographical, cultural, institutional, and economic circumstances and suggest the potential for cross-cultural, comparative, and interdisciplinary approaches. The addition of notes and bibliographies enhances the scholarly value of the introductions and suggests avenues for further enquiry.

I should like to express my thanks to the volume editors for their willing participation, enthusiasm, sage counsel, invaluable suggestions, and good judgment. Evidence of the timeliness and importance of the series was illustrated by the decision, based on extensive consultation with the scholarly community, to expand a series, which had originally been projected not to exceed eight volumes, to more than thirty volumes. It was John Smedley's initiative which gave rise to discussions as to the viability and need for such a series and he has overseen the publishing, publicity, and marketing of *An Expanding World*. As

General Editor, my task was greatly facilitated by the assistance of Dr Mark Steele who was initially responsible for the 'operations' component of the series as it got under way; latterly this assistance has been provided by staff at Variorum.

The Department of History,
The Johns Hopkins University

Introduction

Maureen Fennell Mazzaoui

Between 1450 and 1800, both the total output and the volume of long-distance trade in textiles and raw materials destined for cloth production increased exponentially, despite short-term downturns related to political, economic and demographic trends in various regions of the world economy. In pre-modern economies, the processes associated with cloth production supported the single largest occupational grouping outside the agricultural sector, embracing both professional and part-time workers. Textile fibres, dyestuffs and fabrics accounted for a major share of intercontinental commerce. Textiles were also among the principal articles of exchange in regional shipping and overland systems of communication.

Recent scholarship represented in the present collection of essays has been directed toward a reassessment of the participation of Europeans and non-Europeans in the burgeoning textile trade, and of the degree to which expanding maritime contacts affected the internal dynamics of existing and newly emerging production and distribution networks in Asia, the Near East, Africa and the Americas. The volume as a whole reflects an ongoing conceptual shift in the literature away from Eurocentric interpretations of Western dominance toward a more complex picture of successful diversification among many commercially oriented regions of textile production in the early-modern global economy.

In an age of mercantile capital, the integration of discrete regional economies into an international network of commodity and specie exchanges had the potential to effect multiple transformations in the relations between merchants, producers and consumers. However, comparative regional and international dependency theories that posit colonial domination, peripheral development and economic incorporation have tended to distort the dynamic industrial restructuring that occurred within widely varying political and economic systems in a period of expanding global interactions.[1]

In studies of non-European economies, there has been a marked tendency to downplay the role of European trade while devoting greater attention to local and autochthonous factors in explaining changes in the spatial configuration and structural organization of regional textile centers. This re-examination has extended to the factors promoting regional interdependence, the creation of financial linkages between towns and rural areas, and the economic policies of political élites that promoted or retarded the development of specific industrial sectors.

---

[1] Immanuel Wallerstein, *The Modern World-System*, vols. I–III (New York, 1974–89).

Since the appearance of the classic studies of F. Mendels in 1972, and of
P. Kriedte, H. Medick and J. Schlumbohm in 1982, the study of pre-modern
textile production on the micro-economic level has been dominated by the proto-
industrialization debate.[2] In its original formulation, this theory was narrowly
focused on the development of export-oriented rural industries in zones of
subsistence agriculture which gave rise to the extension of the putting-out system,
rapid population growth and an accelerated pace of regional specialization.
Empirical studies of European and non-European regions have challenged the
validity of the model both as an explanation for the rise of modern capitalism
(i.e., a transitional stage between feudalism and modern industrialization) and as
a structural paradigm of pre-modern forms of industry.

European scholars have qualified many of the original premises of the proto-
industrialization theory. Critics have noted the lack of correlation between proto-
industry and population growth and the extension of domestic industry in areas
of both commercial and subsistence farming. Comparative studies of European
proto-industrial regions have highlighted the existence of a gender division of
labour, the coexistence of proto-industrial and artisan modes of production and
the continued control of towns over those sectors of production which required
a highly skilled labour force.[3] An even greater challenge has come from historians
of non-western societies who have questioned the applicability of the European
proto-industrialization model to the widely disparate forms of spatial organization
that occurred contemporaneously within regions characterized by historically
distinct demographic, agrarian and familial structures.[4]

Evidence of contrasting trajectories and historical discontinuities in the
chronology and pace of industrial development within world regions at different
stages of market development has served to undermine earlier notions of linear

---

[2] Franklin F. Mendels, 'Proto-industrialization: The First Phase of the Industrialization
Process', *Journal of Economic History* XXXII, no. 1 (1972) pp. 241–61; Peter Kriedte, Hans
Medick and Jürgen Schlumbohm, *Industrialization Before Industrialization: Rural Industry in the
Genesis of Capitalism* (Cambridge, 1981).

[3] For an overview of the European debate see Maxine Berg, Pat Hudson and Michael
Sonenscher, eds., *Manufacture in Town and Country Before the Factory* (Cambridge, 1983); Pat
Hudson, ed., *Regions and Industries: A Perspective on the Industrial Revolution in Britain*
(Cambridge, 1989); Maxine Berg, *Markets and Manufacture in Early Industrial Europe* (London
and New York, 1991); Sheilagh C. Ogilvie and Markus Cerman, eds., *European Proto-
Industrialization* (Cambridge, 1996); René Leboutte, ed., *Proto-industrialization: Recent Research
and New Perspectives* (Geneva, 1996). On the significance of regional specialization in European
industrialization see especially Sidney Pollard, *Peaceful Conquest: The Industrialization of Europe,
1760–1970* (Oxford, 1981).

[4] For a partial discussion of the international parameters of the proto-industrialization
debate see Pierre Deyon and Franklin Mendels, eds., *VIIIe Congrès International d'Histoire
Economique, Budapest 16–22 août 1982. Section A2: La Protoindustrialisation: Théorie et
Réalité* (Lille, 1982).

evolution in early modern textile production.[5] On both the analytical and empirical levels, the proto-industrialization thesis, even in modified form, fails to account for the plurality of structural forms and the diverse historical outcomes that occurred within textile producing regions of the pre-modern world economy. Proto-industrialization as a transition to modern capitalism is applicable to only one region outside Europe – Tokugawa Japan – albeit in a context radically different from the Western experience. The rise of a modern factory system in the United States in the nineteenth century was not preceded by a proto-industrial 'stage' in the colonial period. Despite the growth of international competition, marginal and inefficient producers often enjoyed a comparative advantage in fragmented regional markets. However, they remained vulnerable to permutations in trade and secular trends affecting patterns of consumption.

Largely ignored in the proto-industrialization debate, the role of demand has commanded increasing attention in the recent literature on early-modern textile history. In an era when expenditures on apparel and household furnishings absorbed a disproportionate share of family income, shifts in fashion, changes in price and consumer purchasing power, as well as differences in networks of distribution and credit and bartering mechanisms had a pronounced impact on the demand for specific types of finished cloth. Sophisticated hierarchies of consumer preferences for particular textures, colours and designs acted as powerful determinants of marketing strategies.[6] The evolution of consumer tastes in increasingly interconnected regional and world markets led to the diffusion of techniques related to dyeing, printing, weaving and finishing, which had formerly existed in relative isolation. Despite a global trade in dyestuffs and extensive experimentation in new techniques, European craftsmen lagged behind their Asian and African counterparts in the dyeing and printing of vegetable-based fibres in durable, bleach-resistant colours. This technological barrier, which was not overcome until the early 1800s, adversely affected the marketing of European cottons and fustians in competition with Indian fabrics in overseas markets.[7]

In the early-modern economy, the largest sectors of European textile production were those devoted to woollen and linen cloth, for which the primary outlets were the Mediterranean and, after 1700, the Atlantic trade. Silks and fustians were also exported to these markets. Despite attempts by the European East India Companies to develop new outlets for European goods, Asian markets

[5] See especially Frank Perlin, 'Proto-industrialization and Pre-colonial South Asia', *Past and Present* XCVIII (1983), pp. 30–95.

[6] See Jane Schneider, 'The Anthropology of Cloth', *Annual Review of Anthropology* XVI (1987), pp. 409–48.

[7] Naomi E.A. Tarrant, 'The Turkey Red Dyeing Industry in the Vale of Leven', in eds., John Butt and Kenneth Ponting, *Scottish Textile History* (Aberdeen, 1987), ch. 3; K.N. Chaudhuri, *Asia Before Europe: Economy and Civilisation of The Indian Ocean From The Rise of Islam to 1750* (Cambridge, 1990), p. 317.

proved resistant to penetration by Western fabrics. The growth of the re-export trade in Asian silks and cottons, which relied on transfers of bullion, permanently altered the consumption habits of consumers served by the new global networks. It also brought new competition and pricing pressure to bear on established textile producers, while simultaneously opening up new sources of raw materials.

Ottoman Empire

The impact of these realignments on the Ottoman textile industry is described by Murat Çizakça (see chapter 1). He highlights the interdependence of European and Levantine markets in which the free flow of goods was determined by market forces and the self-regulating mechanism of competitive pricing. Ottoman provisionist policies aimed at ensuring an adequate supply of affordable goods on internal markets. Protectionist tariffs on imported goods were eschewed, while fiscal levies were placed on exported raw materials and finished products. The government resorted to import-substitution subsidies only to counter shortages of essential goods.[8]

In the seventeenth century, a decline in the purchasing power of some groups of consumers in Levant markets gave rise to a growing preference for lower-priced English broadcloths and Dutch light woollens over Flemish and Italian luxury woollen fabrics. The dynamic growth of English and Dutch cloth exports to the Mediterranean region depended upon aggressive price-cutting realized through technological innovations, efficiencies in processing, and, in the English case, the utilization of low-cost rural labour.[9] Despite shrinking demand and lower profit margins, Italian producers retained their position as the principal suppliers of quality silk fabrics to the Ottoman empire.[10]

In Ottoman markets, imported Dutch and English fabrics and Italian silks were favoured by the élites and the urban middle classes who had been the traditional customers for domestic woollens and silks.[11] At the same time, an increasingly skewed distribution of income fostered the substitution of cheap

---

[8] Mehmet Genç, 'Ottoman Industry in the Eighteenth Century: General Framework, Characteristics and Main Trends', in ed., Donald Quataert, *Manufacturing in the Ottoman Empire and Turkey, 1500–1950* (Albany 1994), pp. 59–68.

[9] Richard T. Rapp, 'The Unmaking of the Mediterranean Trade Hegemony: International Trade Rivalry and the Commercial Revolution', *The Journal of Economic History* XXXV, no. 3 (1975), pp. 499–525. On products and wages in the Dutch woollen industry see Jonathan I. Israel, *Dutch Primacy in World Trade, 1585–1740* (Oxford, 1981), pp. 117, 187–96.

[10] Domenico Sella, *Italy in the Seventeenth Century* (London and New York, 1997), pp. 30, 35, 42.

[11] On the structure of demand in Ottoman markets, based on estate inventories, see Yvonne J. Seng, 'The Market for Domestic and Imported Textiles in Sixteenth Century Istanbul', in *Textiles in Trade*, Proceedings of The Textile Society of America Biennial Symposium, September 14–16, 1990 (Washington, D.C., 1990), pp. 149–57.

cottons for low-grade woollens among the poor. This occurred at a time when heightened European demand for raw materials led to rising prices for raw wool, silk and cotton in internal markets. These combined trends help to explain the varying fortunes of different sectors of the Ottoman textile industry. The once flourishing Salonica woollen industry succumbed to intense competition from superior grades of English and Dutch woollens and, in the lower quality ranges, from cheap cottons.[12] Çizakça attributes the contraction in the silk cloth output of Bursa to a steep rise in the price of Persian and Ottoman raw silk (bid up by increased demand and Safavid monopolistic practices), while the competition of Italian silk fabrics on Levant markets depressed cloth prices. Silk weaving for internal markets, based on domestic sericulture, recovered in the eighteenth century when European producers increased their reliance on alternate supplies of raw silk in Southern Europe, Asia and the West Indies. It was not until the nineteenth century that Ottoman production of silk fabrics gave way to the preparation of reeled silk for export.[13] In an analogous sector, in the Ankara region, the small luxury industry of mohair cloth also regained momentum after exports of mohair, used in the making of Dutch camlets, slowed.

In contrast to the vicissitudes of the woollen and silk industries, cotton production underwent a steady expansion in the provincial towns of Syria, Anatolia and Greece through the end of the eighteenth century as cotton cultivation intensified in response to both European and internal demand. In addition to satisfying the requirements of the Janissaries for uniforms and of the Arsenal for sailcloth, cotton weavers catered to a large and expanding population of impoverished urban dwellers. The decline of the German cotton industry during the Thirty Years' War, imports of raw cotton from the East and West Indies, and the competition of Indian calicoes in European markets after 1700 decreased western demand for Levant cotton, resulting in a cheap and abundant supply on local markets. The widespread network of local cotton spinners and weavers appears to have constituted a formidable barrier to imports of the lower grades of European woollens.[14] A dispersed production of linen and hemp cloth in provincial towns and rural districts also supplied internal markets with ordinary fabrics for everyday use.[15]

---

[12] Cf. Benjamin Braude, 'International Competition and Domestic Cloth in the Ottoman Empire, 1500–1600, A Study in Underdevelopment', *Review* II, no. 3 (1979), pp. 437–54; Suraiya Faroqhi, 'Textile Production in Rumeli and the Arab Provinces: Geographical Distribution and Internal Trade (1560–1650)', in *Peasants, Dervishes and Traders in the Ottoman Empire*, Variorum Collected Studies Series 230 (London, 1986), ch. XII.

[13] Murat Çizakça, 'Price History and the Bursa Silk Industry: A Study in Ottoman Industrial Decline, 1550–1650', *The Journal of Economic History* XL, no. 3 (1980), pp. 533–50.

[14] Domenico Sella, *Commerci e industrie a Venezia nel secolo XVII*, Istituto per la collabourazione culturale (Venice, 1961), pp. 60–1.

[15] Faroqhi, 'Textile Production in Rumeli', pp. 62, 65–7, 71.

Despite the impressive expansion of rural cotton production, the Ottoman textile industry presents few analogies with European proto-industrial models. Evidence for the development of a putting-out system in Ottoman textile production is extremely limited.[16] The extension of mercantile control over spinners and weavers was restricted by the interests of craft guilds, as well as by state control of wages and profits and limitations on the accumulation of private capital.[17]

Iran

The Ottoman evidence presents a nuanced picture of the complex interplay between new global networks and traditional Levantine trading connections that belies simplistic models of peripheral development. A similar analysis can be made for Iran. Although precise data are lacking, it appears that imports of low-priced English and Dutch woollens and Indian cottons had a negative impact on urban cotton and woollen workers whose output was increasingly restricted to cheap fabrics for the military and the lower classes.[18] In contrast, the silk industry, which was oriented toward the luxury market, remained the strongest sector of the economy. Through the early eighteenth century, Safavid Iran maintained its position as a primary exporter of gold and silver brocades and velvets, as well as costly woollen shawls and carpets, to affluent and discriminating consumers in the Ottoman Empire, Russia, India, Southeast Asia, Japan and, to a lesser extent, Europe.[19] In the late

---

[16] Suraiya Faroqhi, 'Notes on the Production of Cotton and Cotton Cloth in XVIth and XVIIth Century Anatolia', *Journal of European Economic History* VIII, no. 2 (1979), pp. 405–17 and 'Labour Recruitment and Control in the Ottoman Empire', in Quataert, *Manufacturing*, pp. 38–9; Cf. Sevket Pamuk, *The Ottoman Empire and European Capitalism, 1820–1913* (Cambridge, 1987), pp. 109–12.

[17] Mehmet Genç, 'The Economy and Changes in Economic Thought in the Eighteenth and Nineteenth Centuries', forthcoming in the Proceedings of the International Conference on *The Ottoman State, Modernism and the Euro-Islamic Synthesis: A Revisionist Approach*, The University of Wisconsin-Madison (June 1996).

[18] Willem Floor, 'Economy and Society: Fibers, Fabrics, Factories', in ed., Carol Bier, *Woven from the Soul, Spun from the Heart: Textile Arts of Safavid and Qajar Iran, 16th–19th Centuries*, The Textile Museum (Washington, D.C., 1987), pp. 23–4. Although limited quantities of fine cotton cloth were imported from Bengal for the imperial court in Isfahan, the bulk of Indian cotton cloth imports consisted of the inferior grades of Gujarat and the Coromandel coast which were destined for consumption by the masses. Om Prakash, *The Dutch East India Company and the Economy of Bengal, 1630–1720* (Princeton, N.J., 1985), p.177.

[19] Persian silk fabrics and carpets purchased by the Dutch and English East India Companies were marketed primarily outside Europe. With the exception of taffetas, which were reputed to meet European standards, Iranian silk textiles were considered inferior in quality, fashion and price to prime Italian and cheaper Indian products. The English trade in taffetas effectively ended with the imposition of the 1701 ban on imports of wrought silks from Iran and India. Floor, 'Economy and Society', pp. 20–3.

seventeenth century, the royal silk manufactories were gradually disbanded in favour of a procurement system in which work was contracted out to specialized guild artisans, with financing for raw materials and piece-wages advanced by the court and leading merchants.[20]

Through the early 1700s, Iran was also the principal source of supply of superior grades of raw silk to European, Ottoman and Indian markets. In the sixteenth century the military and political disruption of the Central Asian caravan routes ended the overland trade in Chinese silk, with the exception of a diminished flow through northern Russia. Exports of Caspian silk, carried by Armenian merchants, were deflected southward via Baghdad to Aleppo and other Ottoman markets, while the bulk of production from the southeastern provinces of Iran was directed toward India.[21] The Levant route remained the primary source of provisioning for European silk manufacturers, despite the attempt by Shah Abbas, in co-operation with the Dutch and English East India Companies, to develop a competing maritime route through the Persian Gulf in the seventeenth century.[22]

In chapter 2 on the Iranian silk trade, Edmund Herzig argues for the development of commercial commodity production promoted by mercantile and landholding élites in response to heavy foreign demand. The intensification of sericulture assured an adequate supply of raw silk for Iran's flourishing handicraft industry, while expanding export capacity. Following the abortive attempt by Shah Abbas to establish a royal monopoly, the Armenian merchants regained control over the silk export trade in which they made substantial capital investments. In a fully monetized trade that may have involved advance contracts, merchants made cash purchases of supplies which accumulated as rents in kind in the hands of the crown, state officials and the local nobility. There was also a limited degree of private trade in raw silk by small-scale itinerant dealers.

In response to the steep and prolonged rise in Iranian silk prices documented by Çizakça, European silk manufacturers increased their reliance on sources of supply in Italy, Spain and southern France. The spread of the hydraulic silk-twisting mill for warp threads (*organzine*) required reeled silk of a uniform consistency, a condition that was best met by Italian silk producers. In the course of the seventeenth century the regions of Piedmont, Lombardy and the Veneto became exporters of semi-processed *organzine* to the expanding industries of

---

[20] Floor, 'Economy and Society', p. 23.

[21] Morris Rossabi, 'The "Decline" of the Central Asian Caravan Trade', in ed., James D. Tracy, *The Rise of Merchant Empires: Long-distance Trade in the Early Modern World* (Cambridge, 1990), pp. 351–70.

[22] Niels Steensgaard, *The Asian Trade Revolution of the Seventeenth Century: The East India Companies and The Decline of The Caravan Trade* (Chicago, 1973), ch. IX; Linda K. Steinmann, 'Sericulture and Silk: Production, Trade and Export under Shah Abbas', in Bier, *Woven from the Soul*, pp. 12–19.

France, Holland and England.[23] Since Persian silk was still the preferred material for the weft, the rapid growth of silk production in France, Holland and England sustained the Iranian silk trade until the early eighteenth century. The subsequent political collapse of the Safavid state in the face of Turkish and Russian invasions led to a sharp decline in Persian sericulture. Iran's once flourishing silk industry contracted to the level of a domestic craft with production destined primarily for internal consumption.[24] From the late seventeenth century onward, imports of inexpensive Bengal reeled silk displaced Persian grades in European markets. There was a concurrent expansion in imports of Bengal silk and cotton piece-goods. After 1700, the introduction to northern Europe of mechanized silk-twisting mills based on Italian designs also increased the demand for Chinese raw silk. However, problems related to the lack of uniformity and the uneven quality of overseas reeled silk were not overcome until the nineteenth century when mechanized reeling was adopted in the areas of production.[25]

British North America

After 1700, the principal overseas markets for British cloth producers and traders were the West Indies and the American mainland colonies. While European immigrants brought advanced implements and techniques to North America, the development of colonial textile enterprises was inhibited by the lack of suitable raw materials and an inadequate supply of labour. The structure of colonial markets and restrictions imposed by mercantilist regulations also discouraged the growth of commercial cloth production.

Exports to American markets contributed to a recovery in the British woollen trade, which had lost momentum in the final decades of the seventeenth century, owing to protectionist tariffs and heightened competition in Northern Europe. In terms of value, woollen cloth constituted the single most important commodity in British exports to America up to 1774. However, in total volume, the most spectacular growth was in linens and fustians from England, Scotland and Ireland, where the expansion of production was favoured by protectionist legislation.

---

[23] Carlo Poni, 'Archéologie de la fabrique: la diffusion des moulins à soie "alla bolognese" dans les Etats vénitiens du XVIe au XVIIIe siècle', *Annales: Economies, Sociétés, Civilisations* XXVII (1972), pp. 1475–96; Paola Massa Piergiovanni, 'Technological Typologies and Economic Organisation of Silk Workers in Italy, from the XIVth to the XVIIIth Century', *Journal of European Economic History* XXII (1993), pp. 543–64.

[24] Floor, 'Economy and Society', p. 24.

[25] Prakash, *The Dutch East India Company*, pp. 54–7, 201–20; Kristoff Glamann, *Dutch-Asiatic Trade, 1620–1740* (Copenhagen and the Hague, 1958), pp. 112–31, 141–51. For English exports of raw silk from Bengal see K.N. Chaudhuri, *The Trading World of Asia and the English East India Company, 1660–1760* (Cambridge, 1978), Appendix 5. For exports of Chinese raw silk see below note 61.

Medium quality goods from these low-cost producers gradually edged out higher-priced continental linens in American markets.[26]

Re-exported Indian muslins and calicoes represented a growing share of British cargos bound for America from 1660 to 1700. Although Indian calicoes were banned from the home market in the 1690s, exports to America continued at stable levels through the early eighteenth century and even accelerated after 1750. The trade in Indian fabrics continued in the hands of American merchants after the War of Independence until about 1820.[27] Beginning in the 1730s, *nankeen* cottons from China were also exported to the North American colonies.[28] The attractive price of fabrics made by low-wage producers in Asia accounts for their wide consumption as staple household and clothing items among all classes of colonial society. Fine muslins, Indian and Chinese silks, specialty items such as Kashmir woollen shawls, and English silk goods and accessories were imported for the luxury market.[29]

The competition of superior Asian products hindered the opening of overseas markets to English cottons. Favoured by protectionist legislation banning dyed, painted and printed Indian calicoes from the home market, British cotton cloth production expanded initially as an import-substitution industry catering to domestic markets. In the middle decades of the eighteenth century, English (and French) producers developed limited outlets for coarse cotton and cotton/linen checks and prints, made in imitation of Indian piece goods, in exports to West Africa and the New World, where it was used for slave

---

[26] N.B. Harte, 'The Rise of Protection and the English Linen Trade, 1690–1790', in eds., N.B. Harte and K.G. Ponting, *Textile History and Economic History* (Manchester, 1973), pp. 75–112 and 'The British Linen Trade with the United States in the Eighteenth and Nineteenth Centuries', in *Textiles in Trade*, pp. 15–23; Patrick O'Brien, Trevor Griffiths and Philip Hunt, 'Political Components of the Industrial Revolution: Parliament and the English Cotton Textile Industry, 1660–1774', *Economic History Review*, ser. 2, XLIV, no. 3 (1991), pp. 395–423; Ralph Davis, 'English Foreign Trade, 1660–1700', *Economic History Review*, ser. 2, VI (1954), pp. 151–66 and 'English Foreign Trade, 1700–1774', *Economic History Review*, ser. 2, XV (1962), pp. 285–303.

[27] Davis, 'English Foreign Trade, 1700–1774', pp. 294–5, 302–3; O'Brien, Griffiths and Hunt, 'Political Components of the Industrial Revolution', p. 399. See also Susan S. Bean, 'The American Market for Indian Textiles, 1785–1820: In the Twilight of Traditional Cloth Manufacture', in *Textiles in Trade*, pp. 43–52. Indian textiles were re-exported from the U.S. to Africa, the Caribbean and South America, mainly for use in slave clothing. Some white cloth was printed in America. Cf. Florence M. Montgomery, *Printed Textiles: English and American Cottons and Linens, 1700–1850* (New York, 1970).

[28] Kang Chao, *The Development of Cotton Textile Production in China*, Harvard East Asian Monographs, 74 (Cambridge, Mass., 1977), p. 81.

[29] Bean, 'The American Market for Indian Textiles, 1785–1820', pp. 46–7. On the silk trade with the American colonies, see Natalie Rothstein, 'Silk in European and American Trade before 1783: A Commodity of Commerce or Frivolous Luxury?', in *Textiles in Trade*, pp. 1–14.

clothing.[30] However, in a recent study, Stanley Engerman has cautioned against ascribing an important role to the transatlantic slave trade in British industrialization, noting that the sustained expansion of British cotton cloth exports to the Americas, as well as to the African market, occurred at a relatively late date in the era of the slave trade.[31] The rapid growth in English cotton cloth manufacture, based on imported American cotton, can only be traced from the 1790s when, as a percentage of total exports, cotton products surpassed woollens and linens.[32]

The intense demand for imports in British colonial America was fostered by rapid economic and demographic growth, a high per-capita income, and the social status associated with fine cloth in a commonality of taste and fashion shared by consumers on both sides of the Atlantic.[33] Other factors favouring imports were a secular downward trend in prices that made many finer goods accessible even to the less affluent, a dense distribution network extending from wholesalers to country peddlers, and the increasing use of credit.[34] The wide availability of affordable imports militated against the establishment of a commercial textile industry in British North America.

Similar factors restricted the production of ordinary homespun. The results of recent research have cast doubt on the once prevalent view of household self-sufficiency in textiles and other consumer goods in the British colonies.[35] In New

[30] Joseph E. Inikori, 'Slavery and the Revolution in Cotton Textile Production in England', *Social Science History* XIII, no.4 (1989), pp. 342–79. For the export of coarse cottons destined for the slave trade from the port of Nantes in the same period, see R.L. Stein, *The French Slave Trade in the Eighteenth Century: An Old Regime Business* (Madison, Wis., 1979), pp. 134–5.

[31] Stanley L. Engerman, 'The Atlantic Economy of the Eighteenth Century: Some Speculations on Economic Development in Britain, America, Africa and Elsewhere', *The Journal of European Economic History* XXIV, no.1 (1995), p. 168.

[32] B.R. Mitchell with the collaboration of Phyllis Deane, *Abstract of British Historical Statistics* (Cambridge, 1962), pp. 293–5; Phyllis Deane and W.A. Cole, *British Economic Growth, 1688–1959*, 2nd edn., (Cambridge, 1967), p. 185; Ralph Davis, *The Industrial Revolution and British Overseas Trade* (Leicester, 1979), chs. 2, 5.

[33] See among others T.H. Breen, 'An Empire of Goods: The Anglicization of Colonial America, 1690–1776', *Journal of British Studies* XXV (1986), pp. 457–99 and 'Baubles of Britain: The American and Consumer Revolutions of the Eighteenth Century', *Past and Present* CXIX (1988), pp. 73–104.

[34] Carole Shammas, *The Pre-Industrial Consumer in England and America* (Oxford, Clarendon Press, 1990) pp. 52–69; See also by the same author, 'The Decline of Textile Prices in England and British America Prior to Industrialization', *Economic History Review* XLVII, no. 3 (1994), pp. 483–507.

[35] Carole Shammas, 'How Self-Sufficient Was Early America?', *Journal of Interdisciplinary History* XIII, no.2 (1982), pp. 247–72 and 'Consumer Behavior in Colonial America', *Social Science History* VI (1982), pp. 67–86; Bettye Hobbs Pruitt, 'Self-Sufficiency and the Agricultural Economy of Eighteenth-Century Massachusetts', *William and Mary Quarterly*, ser. 3, XLI (1984), pp. 333–64. Cf. Breen, 'An Empire of Goods', pp. 483–5.

England, for example, it was common for white, female family members to spin and weave linen, hemp and wool in their own domiciles. Ordinary homespun was used for servants' apparel or basic domestic needs. However, the output of coarse fabrics met only a small part of the total textile requirements of individual households.[36] As Adrienne Hood demonstrates in chapter 3, a different mode of production prevailed in the Chesapeake, where weaving was a by-employment for male craftsmen/farmers working on commission with yarn supplied to them by individual customers. In this region there was a distinct division of labour between female spinners who prepared yarn for personal use, and male weavers.[37] A similar system prevailed in colonial Quebec where male weavers residing in villages or urban centers were the primary producers of cloth used by rural families through the late eighteenth century. A change occurred after 1780 when a sharp increase in the number of rural households owning looms reflected a greater involvement of farm women in domestic production.[38] Nevertheless, the volume of production was insufficient to meet even the minimal needs of households for finished fabric. Only a very limited amount of locally produced cloth ever reached the market. Throughout the North American colonies, homespun was merely a supplement to, never a replacement for, imported cloth.

Even within the parameters of a handicraft system, expansion of production was impeded by mercantilist prohibitions against colonial exports, inferior grades of fibre and the high cost of labour. The low labour-to-land ratio and the absence of seasonal labour cycles in American subsistence agriculture may also help to explain the failure of colonial household production to evolve into a cottage industry.[39]

---

[36] Laurel Thatcher Ulrich, 'Martha Ballard and Her Girls: Women's Work in Eighteenth-Century Maine', in ed., Stephen Innes, *Work and Labour in Early America* (Chapel Hill, 1988), pp. 90–2 and *A Midwife's Tale: The Life of Martha Ballard Based on Her Diary, 1785–1812* (New York, 1991), pp. 77–81.

[37] See also Adrienne D. Hood, 'The Material World of Cloth: Production and Use in Eighteenth-Century Rural Pennsylvania', *The William and Mary Quarterly*, ser. 3, LIII, no.1 (1996), pp. 43–66. On growing agricultural diversification and the expansion of home textile production in the period 1760–1820, see Lois Green Carr and Lorena S. Walsh, 'Economic Diversification and Labour Organization in the Chesapeake, 1650–1820', in Innes, *Work and Labour*, pp. 146, 171, 175–7, 182.

[38] David-Thiery Ruddel, 'Domestic Textile Production in Colonial Quebec, 1608–1840', in eds., B. Lemire and A.D. Hood, 'Surveying Textile History: Perspectives for New Research', Proceedings of the Colloquium at the University of New Brunswick, April 27–29, 1990, *Material History Bulletin* XXXI (1990), pp. 39–49.

[39] Kenneth L. Sokoloff and David Dollar, 'Agricultural Seasonality and the Organization of Manufacturing during Early Industrialization: The Contrast Between Britain and the United States', *National Bureau of Economic Research Working Paper Series*, no. 30, pp. 1–5.

Spanish Colonial America and Brazil

The contrast between the virtual absence of commercial cloth production in British North America and the dynamic growth of regional textile centers in Spanish America reflects fundamental differences between the two colonial territories with regard to physical resources, demography and mercantilist policies. Chapter 4 by Manuel Miño Grijalva surveys the diverse forms of textile production that developed in Spanish colonial America in the context of the proto-industrialization debate.[40]

Spain's monopoly of colonial trade did not benefit her home industries.[41] Recent scholarship has played down the significance of the American market as a stimulus to Spain's early industrialization. The recovery and rapid growth of the Catalan cotton and woollen industries in the seventeenth and eighteenth centuries were predicated not on the trade with America, but rather on the capture of existing markets in the Iberian peninsula where local products were substituted for foreign imports.[42] In contrast to English and French cotton producers, Catalan entrepreneurs were unable to develop overseas outlets for cheap cotton cloth used in slave clothing, owing to the marginal role of Spain in the transatlantic slave trade. The size of the colonial market for inexpensive imported textiles was also limited by the continuance of preconquest traditions of domestic weaving and a preference for indigenous styles of clothing among the substantial Native American population.[43]

The structures of colonial administration facilitated the expropriation of the traditional skills of Indian weavers through the *repartimiento* system. In Mexico and Central America the surplus product of Indian women operating backstrap looms in peasant households was channeled into regional trade by royal magistrates working in partnership with wholesale merchants who distributed raw cotton and collected cloth as rent in kind for sale in distant mining and

---

[40] For a fuller discussion see Manuel Miño Grijalva, *La protoindustria colonial hispanoamericana*, Fideicomiso Historia de las Américas (Mexico, 1993).

[41] Barbara L. Solow, 'Capitalism and Slavery in the Exceedingly Long Run', in eds., B. L. Solow and S.I. Engerman, 'Caribbean Slavery and British Capitalism', *The Journal of Interdisciplinary History* XVII, no. 4 (1987), p. 729.

[42] Josep M. a Delgado Ribas, 'Mercado interno versus mercado colonial en la primera industrialización española', *Revista de Historia Económica* XIII, no. 1 (1995), pp. 11–31; J.K.J. Thomson, *A Distinctive Industrialization: Cotton in Barcelona, 1728–1832* (Cambridge, 1992), pp. 146–7; Jiame Torras, 'The Old and the New: Marketing Networks and Textile Growth in Eighteenth Century Spain', in ed., Maxine Berg, *Markets and Manufacture in Early Industrial Europe* (London, 1991), pp. 93–113.

[43] Delgado Ribas, 'Mercado interno', pp. 24–5; Richard J. Salvucci, *Textiles and Capitalism in Mexico: An Economic History of the Obrajes, 1539–1840* (Princeton, 1987), pp. 19–20; On the policies of the Spanish Crown regarding the slave trade see Franklin W. Knight, 'Slavery and Lagging Capitalism in the Spanish and Portuguese American Empires, 1492–1713', in ed., Barbara L. Solow, *Slavery and the Rise of the Atlantic System* (Cambridge, 1991), pp. 68–71.

agricultural districts. While Indian textiles influenced colonial styles of dress, there was no direct connection between indigenous weaving traditions and the later development of artisanal and entrepreneurial systems of textile production based on imported European tools and techniques.[44]

The growth of colonial textile industries was bolstered by investments in the cultivation of indigenous cotton and dye plants and the introduction of large-scale sheep ranching and sericulture. With the exception of linen production, which only gained importance in the late colonial period, the various sectors of silk, woollen and cotton production underwent notable expansion through the eighteenth century. The early effort to create an integrated silk industry based on domestic sericulture in the Misteca region of New Spain was undercut by extensive imports of Chinese raw silk beginning in the late sixteenth century. Imported thread was used to weave taffetas, brocades, and silk/cotton mixtures, including specialty fabrics such as the *paño de rebozo*. Production was controlled by urban guilds of Spanish artisans in Mexico City, Puebla and Antequera, which employed approximately 14,000 workers in the early seventeenth century.[45]

Domestic silks were purchased by European élites who constituted less than 20 percent of the total population. They were also the primary consumers of imported luxury goods – French silks and linens and Dutch and English woollens, exported through Spain or via the Caribbean, as well as Chinese and Indian silks and fine Indian cottons shipped via Manila – that could absorb the high costs of tariffs and maritime and overland transportation, this last in often primitive conditions.[46]

As Richard Salvucci notes in a recent monograph, colonial woollen and cotton producers filled a niche in the middle to lower ranges of the market, where they enjoyed a comparative advantage. Ordinary broadcloth, a few specialized products and a broad array of coarse woollen and cotton fabrics served the apparel and household needs of urban wage earners, the clergy, the military, mestizo and mulatto labourers, slaves, miners and agricultural workers who represented approximately 40 percent of the population.[47]

---

[44] Robert W. Patch, 'Imperial Politics and Local Economy in Colonial Central America, 1670–1770', *Past and Present* CXLIII (1994), pp. 94–107. See also Guy Thomson, 'The Cotton Textile Industry in Puebla during the Eighteenth and Early Nineteenth Centuries', in eds., Nils Jacobsen and Hans-Jürgen Puhle, *The Economies of Mexico and Peru During the Late Colonial Period, 1760–1810*, Biblioteca Ibero-Americana vol. 34 (Berlin, 1986), p. 170.

[45] William L. Schurz, *The Manila Galleon* (New York, 1939), pp. 364–5. On sericulture in New Spain see Woodrow Borah, *Silk-raising in Colonial Mexico* (Berkeley, 1943), pp. 85–101.

[46] Salvucci, *Textiles and Capitalism*, p. 19. On the importance of Iberian and Spanish American markets for the French linen trade, see Paul Butel, 'France, the Antilles and Europe in the Seventeenth and Eighteenth Centuries', in Tracy, *The Rise of Merchant Empires*, pp. 156–7. On Dutch exports of camlets, Flemish and German linens and woollen fabrics to Spain and Spanish America, see Israel, *Dutch Primacy*, pp. 313–27.

[47] Salvucci, *Textiles and Capitalism*, pp. 19, 57–61.

Miño Grijalva underscores the distinctive structure of the colonial woollen industry. In order to supply American markets with woollen cloth, the crown issued licenses to operators of centralized urban and rural workshops (*obrajes*), which were based on an advanced division of labour. There was a heavy concentration of *obrajes* in the ranching districts of the Valley of Mexico, the Bajío and the Puebla-Tlaxcala region.[48] The *obrajes* offered colonial consumers a substantial choice of inexpensive fabrics which represented attractive alternatives to coarse homespun and to low-priced imports. Sales of domestic woollens were bolstered by shortages of foreign cloth in periods when transatlantic trade was disrupted by warfare.

The *obraje* structure masked a number of weaknesses. Markets remained fragmented owing to prohibitions on inter-colonial trade and the high cost of overland transport. Growth was further restrained by a persistent shortage of free, low-wage labour, leading shop owners to forcibly recruit workers of both sexes from the ranks of slaves, mulattos, mestizos, indentured servants and prisoners. Limited capital investment and the use of coerced labour resulted in low productivity and technological stagnation, while the small labour force of the *obraje* – typically between 40 and 200 workers – allowed few economies of scale. Despite these deficiencies, *obraje* operators benefited from protected markets during the sixteenth and seventeenth centuries. But structural rigidity impeded their ability to introduce new product lines or reduce costs in the face of competition from expanded imports of cheap foreign textiles following the gradual liberalization of trade after 1765. The prosperity of the *obrajes* was further undermined by a shift in consumer preference to cotton cloth in the late eighteenth century.[49]

The woollen output of the *obrajes* was supplemented by household shops run by artisans employing a handful of workers and, to a lesser extent, by weavers working in their own domiciles for the retail or wholesale market. In contrast, a decentralized system of production prevailed in the cotton industry, which was dominated by small household units of professional urban artisans and part-time rural weavers. The commercial production of cotton cloth entered a period of rapid expansion in the last decades of the eighteenth century, when the cultivation of prime grades of cotton in Spain's American colonies was intensified in response to a booming export demand generated by the expanded spinning capabilities of

---

[48] The *obraje*-based woollen industry in Puebla declined in the second half of the seventeenth century owing to the expansion of woollen production in Mexico City and the Bajío. Thomson, 'The Cotton Textile Industry in Puebla', p. 169. On the *obrajes* of Quito which produced quality cloth through the early 1700s, see Kenneth J. Andrien, 'Economic Crisis, Taxes and The Quito Insurrection of 1765', *Past and Present* CXXIX (1990), pp. 107–9.

[49] Salvucci, *Textiles and Capitalism*, pp. 39–45, 57–61, 101–5; Andrien, 'Economic Crisis', pp.108–9.

the Catalan industry.[50] An increased supply of raw cotton stimulated the development of a colonial cotton industry that catered to a growing domestic demand for cheap alternatives to woollens. In the district of Puebla, the commercial production of cotton fabrics became the principal source of employment for textile workers. Specialized merchants financed production by extending credit to large-scale cotton growers, Indian women engaged in spinning, and Spanish and mestizo weavers in the capital and surrounding towns. However, individual artisans still owned their own tools and had recourse to the market for purchases of raw cotton or yarn.[51]

As Miño Grijalva notes, in late colonial Mexico the commercial production of quality silk, woollen and cotton fabrics tended to develop in and around the most important cities which provided access to high density urban markets, mercantile capital and transportation networks for the provision of raw materials and the distribution of finished goods. The role of merchant capital was weaker in New Granada and Peru where the channels of distribution were more localized. Workshops in and around Quito exported quality cloth to Lima and New Granada. However, the bulk of production was represented by rustic woollens and cottons woven for local consumption by Indian women attached to rural *obrajes*.[52]

In the Andean region, economic decline and a reduction in the demand for colonial woollens led to an expansion of cotton production in the eighteenth century. Brooke Larson has studied this development in Cochabamba (Alto Peru) where population pressure and falling agricultural prices in the eighteenth century caused many peasants to diversify into craft activities on a full or part-time basis. A decentralized cottage industry of cheap cotton cloth employed predominantly male weavers, with the assistance of women and children in auxiliary tasks. Raw cotton from the Peruvian coast was supplied by local merchants who also handled the distribution of the region's *tocuyo* cloth. However, there is no evidence of the development of a putting-out system.[53]

---

[50] Salvucci, *Textiles and Capitalism*, pp. 9–31; The Catalan industry had previously relied on imports of inferior Maltese yarn. A gradual expansion of manual spinning in the 1780s was followed by the introduction of mechanical spinning devices in the following decade. J.K.J. Thomson, *A Distinctive Industrialization*, pp. 236–49.

[51] Thomson, 'The Cotton Textile Industry in Puebla', pp. 169–202. See also Jan Bazant, 'Evolución de la industria textil poblana, 1544–1845', *Historia Mexicana*, XIII, no. 4 (1964), pp. 473–516.

[52] Andrien, 'Economic Crisis', pp. 107–10; Miriam Salas, 'Los obrajes huamanguinos y sus interconexiones con otros sectores económicos en el centro-sur peruano a fines del siglo XVIII', in Jacobsen and Puhle, *The Economies of Mexico and Peru*, pp. 203–32; Miño Grijalva, *La Protoindustria Colonial*, pp. 62–7.

[53] Brooke Larson, 'The Cotton Textile Industry of Cochabamba, 1770–1810: The Opportunities and Limits of Growth', in Jacobsen and Puhle, *The Economies of Mexico and Peru*, pp. 150–68.

The development of a dispersed cottage industry in coarse cotton cloth in the slave society of colonial Brazil in the late eighteenth century is traced in chapter 5 by Douglas Libby. Utilizing an official inventory of looms from 1786, he charts the rise and gradual commercialization of the domestic production of cotton homespun in the wake of the decline of gold mining in the Minas Gerais region in the late eighteenth century. Demographic growth and the expansion of domestic demand in an isolated hinterland with primitive transportation provided the basic stimuli to proto-industrialization as a form of import-substitution. At an early stage, women working in their own households, with the adjunct labour of children and slaves, were engaged in spinning cotton and weaving plain white and patterned cloth for domestic consumption. This modest production from predominantly single loom households was seasonal in nature, with the products destined largely for slave clothing. In the late eighteenth century increased output was achieved through a greater allocation of free and unfree female labour to textile activities in response to new marketing opportunities. This development was accompanied by a growing trade in raw cotton and an increasing specialization in spinning within many households. At its height, the system was characterized by a gender division of labour within households of varied size and social composition, consisting of urban and rural as well as large and small producers. As Libby points out, there is no evidence of mercantile investment nor of a putting-out system. However, with a labour force consisting of tens of thousands of predominantly female workers and an annual output of *c*. 2 million metres of cloth, the scale of production approximated that of many European proto-industrial regions. The commercial production of cotton cloth in Minas Gerais was maintained until the middle of the nineteenth century when the industry suffered a steep decline owing to the intense competition of low-priced English cottons.[54]

China

The reliance on bullion in the European trade with Asia was indicative of the weak demand for western goods in Asiatic markets. Asian cloth producers enjoyed a competitive advantage over European exporters by virtue of their access to sophisticated technologies, a highly skilled, low-wage labour force and well-established distribution networks. Socio-cultural norms governing the usages of textiles, as markers of social, political, or ethnic status or as ceremonial objects, also favoured the consumption of the traditional silk and cotton products of the region.[55] The dynamic expansion of Asian textile production and trade from the

---

[54] On the size of the industry of Minas Gerais in the early 1800s see Douglas C. Libby, 'Proto-Industrialization in a Slave Society: The Case of Minas Gerais', *Journal of Latin American Studies* XXIII (1991), pp. 16–31.

[55] Prakash, *The Dutch East India Company*, p. 12.

fifteenth through the eighteenth centuries was attributable to the rapid growth of domestic demand in Asia's large internal markets, as well as to the development of new commercial outlets in overseas trade.

An extensive trade in Chinese silk and Indian cotton fabrics in the China Sea and the Indian Ocean was well established by the fifteenth century. On the eve of European expansion, silk was a primary article of exchange in the tributary trade monopolized by the Ming government. It also figured prominently in the unofficial private commerce carried on by enterprising Chinese merchants who supplied luxury goods to Central Asia, Japan, Southeast Asia and India.[56] In the late Middle Ages, a variety of cotton fabrics from South India were exported to Southeast Asian ports.[57] In the early fifteenth century, Bengali and other Indian cotton textiles were exchanged for Chinese luxury goods in a tribute trade that seems to have been primarily destined for the consumption of the courts and the nobility.[58]

The later European entry into the established networks of intra-Asian trade in direct competition with Chinese, Indian and Malay merchants never affected more than a small portion of the total volume of traffic in finished goods. While the concurrent opening of global maritime routes created new opportunities that were exploited by traditional cloth producers in China and India, the structural changes that occurred within the textile producing areas reflected local responses to internal economic and political forces, as well as to external market conditions.

Following their acquisition of Macao in 1557, the Portuguese assumed the role of middlemen in the silk trade between China and Japan where imports of silk, exchanged for silver, were encouraged by the government to meet aristocratic demand.[59] In the seventeenth century, the Dutch were the primary importers of

---

[56] Lillian M. Li, *China's Silk Trade: Traditional Industry in the Modern World, 1842–1937*, Harvard East Asian Monographs, 97 (Cambridge, Mass., 1981), p. 63; Pin-tsun Chang, 'The First Chinese Diaspora in Southeast Asia in the Fifteenth Century', in eds., Roderich Ptak and Dietmar Rothermund, *Emporia, Commodities and Entrepreneurs in Asian Maritime Trade, c. 1400–1750*, Beiträge zur Südasienforschung, Südasien-Institut Universität Heidelberg, vol. 141 (Stuttgart, 1991), pp. 13–28.

[57] Sanjay Subrahmanyam, 'Rural Industry and Commercial Agriculture in Late Seventeenth-Century South-eastern India', *Past and Present* CXXVI (1990), p.81.

[58] Haraprasad Ray, 'Bengal's Textile Products Involved in Ming Trade during Cheng Ho's Voyages to the Indian Ocean and Identification of the Hitherto Undeciphered Textiles', in Ptak and Rothermund, *Emporia, Commodities and Entrepreneurs*, pp. 81–93. Ray's definition of several cloth terms as referring to ordinary or coarse fabrics is open to question. In his commentary on Ray's paper (p. 476) Stephen T.-H. Chang notes the high valuations placed on some cloths including *so-fu* and *pi-pu* or *pei-pu* which would suggest a trade oriented toward elites. In a private communication to this author, Kang Chao defines *ta-pu* as a very fine, not coarse, cloth while *pei-ti* and *ti-pu* were Chinese transliterations of the Sanskrit *patta* indicating a bolt or long piece of cloth. *Pei-po* and *Tsao-pu* were uncalendered, undyed cloth. Cf. Kang Chao, *The Development of Cotton Textile Production* pp. 4–5.

[59] Li, *China's Silk Trade*, pp. 63–4.

Chinese and Bengali raw silk, as well as Indian textiles, into Japan. However, profits from this trade gradually diminished as a result of bans on the export of precious metals, and efforts by the Tokugawa Shogunate to expand sericulture and cotton cultivation in order to encourage the domestic production of silk and cotton cloth.[60]

Beginning in the late sixteenth century, the most important overseas outlet for Chinese raw silk and cloth was the triangular trade between China, Manila and Spanish America in which a major role was played by resident Chinese communities in the Philippines. Despite declining volumes in later decades, the Manila traffic, subsidized by New World silver, represented the dominant sector of China's silk export trade in the seventeenth century. Modest quantities of Chinese silks were also exported to Europe by the Dutch and English in the late seventeenth and eighteenth centuries.[61]

The growth of interregional and overseas trade fostered specialization in Chinese sericulture and the emergence of marketing networks for raw silk and cloth. As commercial weaving spread into smaller towns and rural areas, the distribution of raw materials and finished products was undertaken by itinerant brokers who sometimes made advances to producers for the purchase of reeled silk. In the cities which were the sites of the Imperial silk weaving factories, the Ming and early Ch'ing dynasties abandoned the traditional reliance on hereditary wage-earning artisans in favour of a procurement system based on formal contracts between the Imperial Silk manufactories and private weaving workshops. Production levels set by the government and guilds were met by mercantile enterprises (*chang-fang* or 'accounting houses') headed by master weavers who functioned as licensed contractors. They distributed looms and government allotments of silk thread to professional (predominantly male) weavers who worked for piece-rate wages in private domiciles or in handicraft workshops which maintained hundreds of looms. In addition to providing working capital, the *chang-fang* coordinated the activities of specialized workshops which controlled the various stages in the processing of reeled silk, from warping to twisting and dyeing. According to Lillian Li, scholarly attempts to equate the *chang-fang* with the putting-out system are misleading, since they fail to take account of the dual private and public functions of the institution. Master weavers acted not as independent entrepreneurs, but as designated intermediaries within an imperial bureaucracy that also included municipal and guild officials.[62]

In contrast to silk production which expanded in response to new opportunities in overseas trade, the spectacular growth in cotton cultivation and

---

[60] Prakash, *The Dutch East India Company*, pp. 122–41.

[61] Li, *China's Silk Trade*, pp. 64–6; Schurz, *The Manila Galleon*, chs. 1, 11 *et passim*.

[62] Li, *China's Silk Trade*, pp.37–61; Cf. E-Tu Zen Sun, 'Sericulture and Silk Textile Production in Ch'ing China', in W.E. Willmott, *Economic Organization in Chinese Society* (Stanford, 1972), pp. 79–108.

weaving in Ming China was fuelled by rapid population growth and a corresponding increase in the domestic consumption of cotton goods. In the late Ming period, locally produced cotton cloth in a variety of weaves became the most widely used clothing material in China. Cottons were preferred over ramie and hemp fabrics for everyday garments. Cotton cloth collected through the tax system formed part of the salaries in kind paid to governmental officials and military personnel.[63]

In chapter 6, Kang Chao compares the organizational structure of silk and cotton production within China. Apart from urban workshops for dyeing and calendering, there is no evidence of handicraft workshops employing wage earners in cotton spinning and weaving, analogous to those that developed in the silk sector. Nor was there any development of the putting-out system, although a limited trade in cotton yarn can be traced in some districts. The processing of cotton required minimum levels of skill and capital investment. It was thus easily incorporated into a system of domestic production in which rural households controlled the entire productive process from the planting of cotton through the sale of finished cloth.

During the late Ming dynasty, population pressure and agrarian restructuring led to the breakup of large estates into small tenant farms. The practice of intensive agriculture on small plots created a pool of surplus labour within farming households, which was deployed in non-agricultural pursuits. The strong social cohesion of the family unit was preserved by allocating the excess labour of dependent female members to spinning and weaving. Production levels exceeding the basic consumption needs of the household were reached by maximizing output, despite low marginal productivity. As Chao indicates, the existence of household production units in which the price of labour fell below its subsistence cost was a powerful institutional barrier to the growth of private workshops employing piece or wage earners. It also served as an impediment to the adoption of labour-saving technology in ginning, spinning and weaving that required fixed capital and a high degree of specialization.[64]

The commercial cloth produced by rural households was marketed through a dense distribution network that included itinerant wholesale merchants operating on the regional level, local collecting agents and retail dealers. Although the bulk of Chinese cotton cloth was consumed in the large internal market, some textiles were exported to Japan during the Tokugawa period and the cloth known as *nankeen* found markets in Europe and the Americas in the eighteenth century.[65]

An elastic supply of labour, a large internal market, and a limited foreign demand for Chinese silk and cotton cloth after the mid-eighteenth century tended

---

[63] Chao, *The Development of Cotton Textile Production*, pp. 19–22.
[64] Cf. Chao, *The Development of Cotton Textile Production*, pp. 28–55.
[65] Chao, *The Development of Cotton Textile Production*, pp. 81–2.

to discourage any efforts to revamp the traditional systems of production. The resistance of the Chinese textile industry to the importation of western technology in the nineteenth century can only be explained by examining the complex bureaucratic and institutional structures that governed cloth production in the pre-modern period.

Japan

Chapter 7 by William Hauser discusses the role of textiles in the economic expansion of Tokugawa Japan (1600–1867). In a period of political consolidation and relative isolation from external influences, commercial agriculture and rural industry developed concurrently in country districts. From the late 1600s, in a move to reduce the country's dependence on Chinese and Indian silk and cotton imports, the Tokugawa Shogunate and provincial governments (*han*) encouraged the expansion of sericulture and cotton cultivation throughout the various domains. The increase in total acreage devoted to cash crops was followed by the rapid spread of silk, cotton and hemp weaving in rural areas. The growth of domestic industries with lower labour costs and the rise of new distribution networks in the countryside effectively challenged the privileges and monopolies of urban guilds. In the late eighteenth century, rural producers steadily increased their market share, to the detriment of urban artisans.[66]

Industrialization in the Japanese countryside did not give rise to regional specialization and/or rapid demographic growth. In Japan where there was virtually no demarcation between agricultural and proto-industrial regions, farming households combined agricultural pursuits with industrial by-employment. Initially peasants processed their own raw materials and sold the finished product to wholesale traders. As new technologies became available, output increased and domestic production became increasingly specialized. Village merchants bought and sold raw materials and semifinished goods on credit. The late Tokugawa period saw the emergence of a putting-out system in which local merchants, drawn from the ranks of large landowners, supplied raw materials and tools to producers and assumed control over the marketing of standardized grades of cloth. By the late eighteenth century, an advanced division of labour was adopted in textile production. Thomas Smith has traced the emergence of 'semi-industrial villages' that created new employment opportunities for wage earners in side-occupations such as ginning, spinning, reeling and weaving. Females working in their own homes, or in handicraft workshops, constituted the bulk of the labour

---

[66] See also William B. Hauser, *Economic Institutional Change in Tokugawa Japan: Osaka and the Kinai Cotton Trade* (Cambridge, 1974) and 'The Diffusion of Cotton Processing and Trade in the Kinai Region in Tokugawa Japan', *Journal of Asian Studies* XXXIII, 4 (1974), pp. 633–49. On sericulture see Tessa Morris-Suzuki, 'Sericulture and the Origins of Japanese Industrialization', *Technology and Culture* XXXIII, no.1 (1992), pp. 101–21.

force. The absorption of the surplus labour of female members of landless and marginal peasant households in proto-industrial enterprises augmented the non-agricultural income of poor families, creating new avenues of social mobility through the combination of tenancy with agricultural labour and by-employment. Cottage-based industries in reeling and weaving survived into the nineteenth century when they were displaced by urban factories. The introduction of a modern factory system was facilitated by the commercialization and monetization of the rural economy under Tokugawa rule.[67]

According to Osamu Saito, the Japanese experience is distinctive in that productivity gains in industry were achieved in a period of population equilibrium. While intense population density in the seventeenth century provided an initial impetus to the introduction of new agricultural technologies and village by-employments, the expansion of rural industry did not provide a strong stimulus to demographic growth. Total population levels remained relatively unchanged after 1725. The commercialization of agriculture on small farms proved compatible with the introduction of industrial occupations based on local supplies of raw materials. However, these developments were not accompanied by increases in household size. Nor was there any significant decline in the age of women at first marriage which might be correlated with higher birthrates. In Saito's view, population stability was an outgrowth of the gender division of labour between male farm work and female by-occupations which reinforced the cohesiveness of traditional peasant families and their close ties to the land.[68]

India

In the seventeenth and early eighteenth centuries, Indian weavers were the primary suppliers of a diverse range of quality cotton goods to discriminating consumers in the global economy. The competitiveness of Indian weavers in international trade was only in part attributable to low-wage labour. Access to prime grades of cotton, superior technical skills in weaving, dyeing and hand printing, and the marketing expertise of Indian merchants contributed to a high degree of product differentiation. A flexible system of production permitted frequent adjustments of the line of products to conform to the tastes of purchasers in distant markets. The bright colours and intricate designs of Indian printed fabrics created new fashion trends in overseas markets, spawning a host of imitations. Among producers, there was considerable regional specialization. Cloth producers were

---

[67] Thomas C. Smith, *The Agrarian Origins of Modern Japan* (Stanford, 1959), pp. 75–80, 108–23, 163–5, 169.

[68] Osamu Saito, 'Population and the Peasant Family Economy in Proto-Industrial Japan', *Journal of Family History* VIII, no. 1 (1983), pp. 30–54. On the implications of industrial by-employment for the position of women see O. Saito, 'Gender, Workload and Agricultural Progress: Japan's Historical Experience in Perspective', in Leboutte, *Proto-industrialization*, pp. 129–52.

heavily concentrated in and around the urban centers of Northern India and Gujarat. The spatial distribution of the industry was different in Bengal and the Coromandel coast where weaving, dyeing and painting activities were spread among numerous small towns and villages.[69]

Following initial contacts in the Middle Ages, the first phase of large-scale expansion of the Indian textile trade in the eastern seas from *circa* 1400 to 1600 was initiated by Indian and other Asian merchants.[70] As Joseph Brennig suggests in chapter 8, the adoption of standardized qualities of certain types of patterned cloth appropriate to the particularized markets of Southeast Asia occurred in this period, before the arrival of the Europeans in Coromandel. These Indian notions of standardization, originally introduced by indigenous merchants, were later extended to the European calico and plain cloth trade.

In the seventeenth century, Coromandel traders faced increased competition when rival European merchants turned to Indian textiles as a substitute for bullion in the spice trade with Southeast Asia. However, the Dutch, English and other European traders captured only a small share of the total volume of cloth exported from the Coromandel coast to Southeast Asia. Indian merchant entrepreneurs disposed of substantial capital derived from ship-building, landholding, tax farming and the holding of bureaucratic offices. They maintained a competitive edge over foreign traders by their in-depth knowledge of Asian export markets, where they had important political contacts. This expertise was coupled with control over Indian weaving, dyeing and painting villages. Owing to these advantages, they continued to play a major role in the Southeast Asian trade, despite lower profit margins on exported textiles.[71]

The reorientation of the Indian textile trade in the second half of the seventeenth century was predicated upon the explosive growth of European demand for calicoes which Brennig correlates to changes in the spatial distribution of the industry and the development of an extensive internal trade in raw cotton. The Dutch and English East India Companies did not maintain direct contact with the weavers, entering instead into contractual relationships with Coromandel merchants who accepted cash advances against future deliveries of cloth. This arrangement represented a change of strategy for the local merchant elites who were simultaneously losing their former political advantages with the expansion of the Mughal empire. In the last quarter of the seventeenth century, the position of the Coromandel merchants was further undermined by stagnating demand in traditional Southeast Asian markets. This downturn was related to the decline of

---

[69] K.N. Chaudhuri, 'The Structure of Indian Textile Industry in the Seventeenth and Eighteenth Centuries', *The Indian Economic and Social History Review* XI (1974), pp. 127–42.

[70] Subrahmanyam, 'Rural Industry', pp. 81–2.

[71] Sinnappah Arasaratnam, 'Merchants of Coromandel in Trade and Entrepreneurship *circa 1650–1700*', in Ptak and Rothermund, *Emporia, Commodities and Entrepreneurs*, pp. 37–51.

the international spice trade and to internal political and economic changes within the Southeast Asian states.[72] After 1690, Coromandel merchants faced new competitive pressures when the Dutch and English substantially expanded their exports of Bengal cotton and silk goods destined for Europe and the re-export trade.[73]

Brennig's article examines the status of members of the weaving castes in late seventeenth century Coromandel. Indian weavers were not part-time agriculturalists but full-time professional male artisans who were specialized in different qualities of cloth or in processes such as dyeing and painting. There was considerable differentiation within this occupational group. While wealthier weavers negotiated directly with merchants, most depended on the intermediary services of head weavers in the village. Despite efforts by the European trading companies to augment the bargaining power of local merchants over the weavers, a putting-out system was never fully implemented in this period. Merchants made cash advances to weavers for the purchase of yarn on local markets. Weavers controlled the means of production and maintained a measure of independence in their relations with merchants who bore the major risks in the transaction.[74]

Brennig's picture of the weaver class relates to a period when the textile industry was at its peak. In chapter 9, Sinnappah Arasaratnam traces the deterioration that occurred in the position of handloom weavers and traditional textile merchants in Southeastern India during the second half of the eighteenth century. Following the acquisition of political power in the interior, the English East India Company acquired a near monopoly in the textile trade with Europe. In an effort to enforce quality controls and drive down prices, the Company replaced merchants and village headmen with its own agents. Despite widespread resistance, full-time weavers were gradually transformed into wage workers who were vulnerable to price increases in raw materials and foodstuffs and to prolonged economic downturns in trade and production.

In a recent study, Sanjay Subrahmanyan has suggested that these changes must be viewed in the context of a more general decline in India's export capacity after 1690. In his view, the causes of this contraction must be sought in political anarchy following the Mughal conquest, disruption of domestic consumption patterns, rising prices of cotton and rice, and a severe famine in the early 1770s.

---

[72] Arasaratnam, 'Merchants of Coromandel', pp. 49–51.

[73] Prakash, *The Dutch East India Company*, pp. 211–12.

[74] See also Joseph J. Brennig, *The Textile Trade of Seventeenth-Century Northern Coromandel: A Study of a Pre-Modern Asian Export Industry*, University of Wisconsin-Madison, Ph.D. Thesis, 1975. Although weavers were full-time artisans, in times of economic crisis they often resorted to alternative employment as seasonal agricultural workers. Cf. K.N. Chaudhuri, 'Proto-industrialization: Structure of Industrial Production in Asia, European Export Trade, and Commodity Production', in Leboutte, *Proto-industrialization*, p. 112.

There is insufficient data to determine the volume of trade in the late eighteenth century. Although the fluctuations in trade require further investigation, his analysis clearly shifts the emphasis from external factors to internal constraints which he sees as contributing to de-industrialization before the beginning of colonial rule and the growth in English cloth imports in the early nineteenth century.[75]

Southeast Asia

Up to the mid-seventeenth century, Southeast Asia was the primary market for Indian textiles from Bengal, the Coromandel Coast and Gujarat. It was also the most specialized. The demand for different varieties of imported cloth in local and regional markets was shaped by clearly articulated preferences for fabrics in specified sizes, textures, designs and colours. Members of the royal entourage and bureaucracy made extensive purchases of Persian and Indian fabrics incorporating native designs.[76] A high level of household consumption of imported textiles and a marked conservatism in style and taste among distinct ethnic and religious groups was related to complex social and cultural conventions that governed the functions of cloth in ritual and daily life.[77] In chapter 10, Kenneth Hall surveys the changes that occurred in the demand for imports and in the patterns of indigenous production and distribution of textiles against the background of regional political and economic changes and fluctuations in the international spice trade. The sixteenth century witnessed a secular shift in habits of consumption away from bark cloth and other native fabrics produced by local peasant women to imported Indian cottons. This trend, which was evident among all classes of society, led to the creation of a mass market for inexpensive cotton textiles traded by Indian, Chinese and European merchants.

A second major realignment took place in the late seventeenth century in response to a slackening demand for pepper in international markets and a reorientation of Indian imports toward higher-priced quality fabrics. The widespread demand for low-priced cottons was met by native producers. The emergence of new weaving centres and regional distribution networks for yarn and plain and finished cloth was accompanied by the spread of cotton as a

---

[75] Subrahmanyam, 'Rural Industry', pp. 104–15.

[76] For extant samples of late Safavid silks woven with Thai designs see Bier, *Woven From the Soul*, exhibition catalogue, no. 48, pp. 228–29. A number of Indian painted and printed textiles with Thai designs have also been preserved. See John Guy, 'Indian Textiles for the Thai Market- A Royal Prerogative', *The Textile Museum Journal* XXXI (1992), pp. 82–96.

[77] Mattiebelle Gittinger, *Master Dyers to the World: Technique and Trade in Early Indian Dyed Cotton Textiles*, The Textile Museum (Washington, D.C., 1982) pp. 137–91; Mattiebelle Gittinger and H. Leedom Lefferts, Jr., *Textiles and the Tai Experience in Southeast Asia*, The Textile Museum (Washington, D.C., 1992), chs. 3,4.

principal cash crop, displacing pepper cultivation in the dry zones of the mainland and the archipelago. The expansion of cotton cultivation was also favoured by administrative centralization and the economic integration of the hinterlands into emerging market networks. Village production was small-scale and carried on primarily by females in peasant households. However, it was both widespread and diversified in its line of products. While court élites continued to consume foreign silk and cotton fabrics, they also sought alternative sources of supply, thus providing a stimulus to local silk cultivation and weaving as well as to the evolution of advanced dyeing techniques for native cotton cloth. The adjustment made by indigenous producers to changing economic conditions contradicts the formerly widespread view of economic stagnation and isolationism in the Southeast Asian region in the eighteenth century.

Africa

The volume of textiles exported to the African continent along the traditional Indian Ocean and trans-Saharan routes continued unabated and may even have increased, although the relative importance of this traffic as a percentage of total trade steadily declined after the sixteenth century. Indian silks and cotton fabrics from Cambay were carried along the established maritime routes linking India and South Arabia to East Africa, where they were exchanged for ivory, gold and slaves. Indian fabrics were in heavy demand as prestige goods used for apparel and home decor in the predominantly Muslim urban centers of East Africa. The Portuguese entry into this traffic in the sixteenth century was supported by a commercial network that extended from Mozambique and other East African coastal centers to Oman and the ports of Cambay and Surat. For the procurement of quality cloth, the Portuguese relied on the Gujarati Banyans who acted as merchant contractors dealing directly with weavers, in return for privileges and concessions in the East African trade. The competition of African and Banyan merchants and the threats posed by Dutch and English expansion in the seventeenth century undermined Portuguese attempts to establish a monopoly over the commerce with Mozambique.[78]

The extensive demand for imported cottons stimulated the expansion of cotton cultivation and the weaving of rough cloth in African centers such as Sena and Paté in the late seventeenth and eighteenth centuries. However, the availability of alternative sources of supply does not appear to have negatively impacted the trade in superior grades of Indian cloth. Following the liberalization of commerce in 1757, imports of Indian fabrics into Mozambique doubled to around 240,000–

---

[78] Luis Frederico Dias Antunes, 'The Trade Activities of the Banyans in Mozambique: Private Indian Dynamics in the Panel of the Portuguese State Economy (1686–1777)', in ed., K.S. Mathew, *Mariners, Merchants and Oceans: Studies in Maritime History* (Manohar, 1995), pp. 301–31.

320,000 pieces per year. This increase paralleled an intensification of the slave traffic to Oman and islands in the Indian Ocean.[79] Portuguese control did not extend to the northern coast of Kenya, or to Tanzania and Zanzibar where the trade remained in the hands of Asian merchants. According to one estimate, cloth from Surat still accounted for 50 percent of total imports into Zanzibar in 1811.[80]

Cloth was the single most important article of commerce in the European export trade to Africa in the pre-modern period. The trans-Saharan caravan routes continued to provide an important outlet for European cotton, linen, woollen and silk fabrics.[81] In the late fifteenth and sixteenth centuries, the Portuguese traded a wide variety of European textiles as well as North African and East Indian fabrics in Morocco and West Africa.[82] Portuguese traders also shipped Cabo Verdean cotton fabrics to West Africa and Brazil through the seventeenth century.[83] However, the greatest growth in the Atlantic cloth trade occurred in the eighteenth century, with the bulk of the increase represented by re-exported Indian cloth.[84] The latter, together with linens from Haarlem and Leiden, represented 57 percent of Dutch exports to Africa in the 1700s.[85] According to some estimates, textiles accounted for approximately 60 percent of all goods exported from French ports to Africa in the late eighteenth century, the bulk of which were either Indian cottons or French imitations.[86] A recent reconstruction of British exports to Africa between 1699 and 1800 suggests that textiles made up more than 65 percent of all goods shipped, with East Indian goods accounting for 40 percent of all exported cloth. After 1780, the aggregate values of cotton cloth exports – English checks and Indian piece goods –

[79] Dias Antunes, 'The Trade Activities of the Banyans', pp. 315–17.

[80] Abdul Sheriff, *Slaves, Spices and Ivory in Zanzibar* (London, 1987), p.84. Cf. p. 44 for the trade in Indian textiles from Gujarat, Muscat and Diu in the second half of the eighteenth century.

[81] Ralph A. Austen, 'Marginalization, Stagnation and Growth: The Trans-Saharan Caravan Trade in the Era of European Expansion, 1500–1900', in Tracy, *The Rise of Merchant Empires*, pp. 312, 314.

[82] John Vogt, 'Notes on the Portuguese Cloth Trade in West Africa, 1480–1540', *The International Journal of African Historical Studies* VIII, 4 (1975) pp. 623–51.

[83] George Brooks, *Landlords and Strangers: Ecology, Society and Trade in Western Africa, 1000–1630* (Boulder, Col., 1993) ch. 8.

[84] Aggregate estimates of the relative distribution of goods imported into Western Africa from Atlantic ports suggest that textiles rose from 50 to 56 percent of the total from the 1680s to the 1780s. David Eltis and Lawrence C. Jennings, 'Trade between Western Africa and the Atlantic World in the Pre-Colonial Era', *American Historical Review* XCIII, no.4 (1988), pp. 936–59.

[85] J.M. Postma, *The Dutch in the Atlantic Slave Trade, 1680–1815* (Cambridge, 1990), p. 104.

[86] Pierre Dardel, *Navires et marchandises dans les ports de Rouen et du Havre au XVIIIe siècle* (Paris, 1963), pp. 138–42. On the manufacture of printed calicoes in Nantes for the African trade see Stein, *The French Slave Trade*, pp. 134–5.

increased relative to woollens and linens, with cottons accounting for 75–80% of total textile exports from Britain.[87] Re-exported East Indian textiles and English cottons also figured prominently in Portuguese exports from Brazil to Angola.[88]

While Guinea cloth and the coarser grades of Indian calicoes, as well as cheap English and French cottons, were important in the transatlantic slave trade, the high valuations of English and French textile cargos bound for Africa belie the notion that Africa was a 'dumping ground for cheap cloth'. Indeed, in variety and quality, the textiles sold in Africa do not seem to have differed significantly from those traded in other major markets.[89]

This point is underscored in chapter 11 by Carolyn Keyes Adenaike. While the most expensive imports were destined for royal use, extensive purchases of quality cloth were made by sophisticated African consumers who expressed a preference for fabrics of specified dimensions, textures, designs and colours that conformed to indigenous tastes and fashions. The heavy demand for printed and dyed Indian cottons spurred European imitations designed specifically for the African market. The total volume of imported cloth increased substantially through the eighteenth century, with the steepest rise registered in Indian fabrics. However, imported cloth was always a supplement to, not a substitute for, native textiles. The rich symbolic and religious significance attached to traditional cloth enhanced its value as a ceremonial object, a form of stored wealth and a preferred medium of exchange in barter, gift giving and formal tribute. In clothing it served as a visible marker of social status and official standing.

Archeological evidence, literary sources and oral traditions all attest to a long history of African cloth production, based on indigenous fibres and dyestuffs. Beginning in the late Middle Ages, there is evidence of the emergence of commercial weaving in various sites along major trading routes.[90] Textiles

---

[87] Marion Johnson, *Anglo-African Trade in the Eighteenth Century: English Statistics on African Trade, 1699–1808*, ed. J.T. Lindblad and Robert Ross, Intercontinenta 15 (Leiden, 1990), pp. 27–8; H.A. Gemery, Jan Hogendorn and Marion Johnson, 'A Tentative Terms of Trade for Africa and England in the Eighteenth Century', in ed., Serge Daget, *De la Traite à l'Esclavage, Actes du Colloque International sur la Traite des Noirs, Nantes, 1985*, Bibliothèque Histoire Outre-Mer, n.s., Études 7–8, vol. I (Nantes and Paris, 1988), pp. 185–92.

[88] Herbert S. Klein, 'Economic Aspects of the Eighteenth-Century Atlantic Slave Trade', in Tracy, *The Rise of Merchant Empires*, pp. 291–3.

[89] Eltis and Jennings, 'Trade between Western Africa and the Atlantic World', pp. 949–50. On cargo valuations see Klein, 'Economic Aspects', p. 292 and Paul Butel, 'France, the Antilles, and Europe, 1700–1900', in Tracy, *The Rise of Merchant Empires*, p. 170.

[90] Philip D. Curtin, *Economic Change in Precolonial Africa: Senegambia in the Era of the Slave Trade* (Madison, Wisconsin 1975), pp. 211–15; Andrea Reikat, *Handelsstoffe: Grundzüge des Europäisch-Westafrikanischen Handels vor der Industriellen Revolution am Beispiel der Textilien*, Studien zur Kulturkunde, 105 (Cologne, 1997), pp. 15–44.

recovered from the Tellem site in Central Mali have been dated from the eleventh through the eighteenth centuries.[91] The continued vitality of medieval sites and the development of new centres of production offering alternatives to imported fabrics are evidence of a sustained surge in demand for all categories of cloth in African societies in the early modern period.

Many sources attest to the high quality of African cloth. European traders expressed admiration for the superior workmanship of many African textiles which were exported as novelties to Europe and the New World.[92] Europeans also participated in the long-distance African textile trade through the 'trust' system in which credit was advanced to local middlemen or brokers against future deliveries of fabrics.[93]

The systems that governed pre-modern African textile production ranged from casual and informal to highly structured arrangements. Narrow strips of homespun were woven by women using simple upright looms. Cloth destined for personal use in large households was made by domestic slaves or by itinerant weavers working with yarn supplied by the customer. Specialized weavers attached to the courts worked exclusively on royal designs and prestigious exchange goods. Standardized lengths of commercial cloth were woven on horizontal looms owned by male handicraft artisans, caste weavers and part-time peasant producers who purchased yarn or received it on credit from cloth merchants. The dyeing of fine cloth was traditionally a separate craft.[94]

The advanced level of technology and organization achieved in African textile production is nowhere better illustrated than in the complex of activities associated with the processing and weaving of indigenous fibers. In chapter 12, Jan Vansina discusses the production of cloth from the leaves of the raffia palm in West Central Africa between 1500 and 1800. Using elaborate dyeing, weaving and embroidery techniques, highly skilled workers produced a diverse line of products ranging from ornamental luxury fabrics, destined for rulers and members of the nobility, to more ordinary varieties intended for daily clothing or accessories. The heavy demand for raffia cloth among all classes of African society gave rise to an extensive export trade from the prime zones of cultivation and production in

[91] Rita Bolland, *Tellem Textiles: Archeological Finds from Burial Caves in Mali's Bandiagara Cliff*, Tropenmuseum/Royal Tropical Institute (Amsterdam, 1991); R.M.A. Bedaux and Rita Bolland, 'Medieval Textiles from the Tellem Caves in Central Mali', *Textile Museum Journal* XIX–XX (1980–81), pp. 65–74.

[92] John Thornton, 'Precolonial African Industry and the Atlantic Trade, 1500–1800', *African Economic History* XIX (1990–91), pp. 11, 18.

[93] A.F.C. Ryder, 'Dutch Trade on the Nigerian Coast during the Seventeenth Century', *Journal of the Historical Society of Nigeria* III, 2 (1965), pp.203–4.

[94] Marion Johnson, 'Proto-industrialization in West Africa', in eds., Deyon and Mendels, *VIIIe Congrès International d'Histoire Economique, Section A2*, I, no. 23, pp. 6–12; Thornton, 'Precolonial African Industry', pp. 13–14.

the kingdom of Congo, the Loango coast, Angola and other areas. Standardized lengths of raffia functioned as a form of currency in an underlying barter economy. Elaborately worked raffia fabrics were also exported as exotic goods to Europe.

According to Vansina, the extraordinarily high level of cloth output achieved by raffia producers in Congo and Loango was comparable to that of many European proto-industrial regions. Turnover was high owing to the perishability of raffia fabrics which lasted, on average, four months. This remarkable level of output was achieved through intense specialization and a gender division of labour between part-time male weavers and women engaged in other tasks. However, there was no capital investment nor any entrepreneurial involvement. In a weakly monetized society which lacked a sophisticated market economy, a putting-out system could not take root. Cloth was distributed through political and administrative channels until the sixteenth century, when Portuguese traders financed a large-scale caravan traffic in raffia products. Vansina attributes the gradual decline in the demand for raffia in the eighteenth century to increased competition from imported European and Indian cloth and from cottons produced in the developing centres of weaving in West Africa. Internal political and economic changes also affected the trade. Nevertheless, the use of plain raffia cloth survived in some areas until the late nineteenth century.

Conclusion

The example of raffia cloth points to a serious lacuna in the current historical literature on pre-modern textile production, which has been almost exclusively concerned with the worldwide commercial expansion of woollen, silk, cotton and linen production. While a number of studies have been devoted to nonwoven fabrics such as knits, lace, felt and knotted carpets, and to certain luxury products utilizing goat hairs of mohair, angora or cashmere, far less attention has been given to other materials which played a major role in regional textile trade and production. In quantitative terms, the most important were fibres derived from the seeds, leaves, stalks or stems of a variety of plants, trees and grasses. These include, among others, raffia, ramie, hemp, jute, sisal, abaca and tree bark. Cloth producers also employed cameloid fibers (camel hair, alpaca and vicuña), feathers, thread spun from cocoons of wild silkworms, as well as a host of other animal and vegetable substances that were used well into the modern era, and in some cases even today, in a broad range of woven and nonwoven fabrics. Each type of fibre required specific processing techniques. Indigenous materials were employed in both luxury and ordinary products that occupied a special niche in the consumption preferences of non-European societies. Trade in these products often extended far beyond the original zones of supply. As Vansina has demonstrated in his study of raffia production, output destined for gift exchange or long-distance commerce could reach proto-industrial levels.[95]

Traditionally, the emphasis in proto-industrialization studies has been on industries linked to international and interregional trade. However, as some contributors to this volume have noted, the quantitative importance of localized production for regional and sub-regional markets should not be underestimated. The growth of domestic demand was a powerful driving force in the expansion of worldwide textile production between 1450 and 1800.

In pre-modern economies within and outside Europe, the coexistence of urban and rural industries was not characterized by a sharp demarcation in organizational forms or in types of production. Centralized handicraft workshops were found in towns and villages. Nor was the production of luxury fabrics, such as silk, confined to the cities. The same is true of the finishing processes of dyeing, printing and calendering. In the countryside, agrarian and social structures influenced the division of labour along gender lines, as did the level of technology and the degree of specialization within households. Studies in the present volume confirm the existence of a variety of demographic behaviors, measured by changes in nuptuality, fertility and population size, within industrial regions. These findings cast doubt on theoretical attempts to establish a positive correlation between proto-industry and population growth.

Industrialization in town and country occurred within the context of economic policies pursued by governments and ruling elites. Within centralized state economies, the recruitment of labour was not always dependent upon the free play of market forces. Wage earners were prevalent in state-sponsored workshops run by intermediaries who coordinated various stages of manufacture. Piece-wages were also paid to household producers working under contract for merchant financiers who operated these same enterprises. As noted above, procurement systems involving royal subsidies were adopted in the Chinese and Iranian silk industries. In its efforts to counter short-term shortages of domestic cloth in internal markets, the Ottoman government sometimes resorted to the mobilization of textile workers in state factories with officially determined wage scales.[96] In Spanish colonial America the crown licensed privately-owned woollen

---

[95] On the importance of bast fibres used in Chinese textile prodction well into the modern era, see Joseph Needham, ed., *Science and Civilisation in China, Vol. 5: Chemistry and Chemical Technology, Part IX: Textile Technology: Spinning and Reeling* by Dieter Kuhn (Cambridge, 1988) pp. 15–59. On the expansion of commercial hemp production in isolated areas of Japan in the seventeenth and eighteenth centuries, see Smith, *The Agrarian Origins*, pp. 77–80. Bolts of fine ikat-dyed ramie cloth for ceremonial use, woven by village women in the Ryukyu islands (Okinawa), were collected as a tax in kind through the nineteenth century. Amanda Mayer Stincecum, 'Textile Production under the Poll Tax System in Ryukyu', *The Textile Museum Journal* XXVII–XXVIII (1988–89), pp. 57–69.

[96] Genç, 'Ottoman Industry', pp. 68–82.

manufactories and subsidized labour costs by providing legal sanctions for the forcible recruitment of wage labourers.

It was Tokugawa Japan which most closely resembled the European pattern of proto-industrial growth. In a period of political decentralization, wholesale cloth merchants, who belonged to the class of large landowners, distributed raw materials and tools to wage earners in handicraft workshops and household units of spinning and weaving in the countryside. The growth of a putting-out system was fostered by the mercantilist policies of independent domains.[97] Elsewhere, with few exceptions, the putting-out system failed to take hold in rural handicraft production, in contrast to Europe where it was the dominant, if far from ubiquitous, mode of industrial organization. Instead, independent peasant producers purchased raw materials and marketed their cloth directly in local markets or they sold it to itinerant merchants who were linked to broader distribution networks. Credit arrangements, when they existed, normally took the form of loans for the purchase of yarn against future payment in finished goods.

According to Chaudhuri, the concept of the putting-out system has been erroneously applied to India, where it was common for merchants to make cash advances to professional weavers against future deliveries of cloth. This arrangement was compatible with the risk-avoidance strategies of both producers and merchants. Weavers required working capital to purchase yarn. Yet, they retained independent control over the productive process. This allowed them to exercise various options. They could contract or expand output through the reallocation of labour resources between industrial and seasonal agricultural work. They could also adjust the product line according to market conditions. The advance contract system enhanced the bargaining position and pricing power of weavers *vis-à-vis* wholesale merchants and local broker/middlemen competing for the same goods. Merchants relied on financial contracts with weavers and brokers in order to secure the timely delivery of large orders of cloth of a specified type, at a predetermined price.[98]

The failure of merchants to assume a direct role in textile production can be traced in part to cultural and institutional factors. In societies where the status of professional merchants, like artisans, was generally low (often below that of peasant landowners), the traditional avenue of social mobility was through office holding and landed investment. For traders aspiring to higher social standing, the principal goal was to accumulate wealth by maximizing short-term profits, without tying up venture capital.[99] Even when there was no cultural or religious aversion to entrepreneurial activities, professional merchants were forced to compete with

---

[97] Tessa Morris-Suzuki, *The Technological Transformation of Japan from the Seventeenth to the Twenty-first Century* (Cambridge, 1994), pp. 20–1, 27–32.

[98] Chaudhuri, 'The Structure of Indian Textile Industry', pp. 151–7.

[99] Chao, *The Development of Cotton Textile Production*, pp. 144–5; Libby, 'Proto-Industrialization', pp. 34–5.

rulers, bureaucrats, nobles and privileged foreign traders for limited resources and commercial opportunities.

The development of industrial, as opposed to commercial capitalism, was thus constrained by the administrative, fiscal and trading policies of ruling élites. Commercial practices were also conditioned by legal institutions, monetary systems and the evolution of credit instruments and financial services. The indigenous legal and financial structures that affected capital formation and investment in trade and production require further investigation.[100]

The early-modern period witnessed the dissemination of the techniques of sericulture, the spread of sheep ranching and the expanded cultivation of textile fibre crops and dyestuffs on a global scale. The simultaneous growth of commercial textile production in the countryside was predicated upon the gradual diffusion of implements and specialized skills from long established to newly emerging centres, and from urban to rural areas. The reception of new technical knowledge depended on existing institutional structures and the degree to which new implements could be integrated into small labour-intensive units of production. However, the reliance on a low-cost rural work force was also an obstacle to the introduction of large-scale labour-saving mechanical devices.[101] While there were small incremental advances and local variations in handicraft tools, the global expansion of cloth manufacturing and trade from 1450 to circa 1750 was not fuelled by major technological innovations. Gains in output were achieved through expanding the labour force, without basic investments in expensive capital equipment that would have permitted economies of scale.[102] This extended period of stasis in textile technology stands in striking contrast to the accelerated pace of inventions in both the medieval and the modern eras. Apart from fabric imitations and experiments in improved dyeing, printing and finishing processes that affected the appearance of many specialized products, there was a dearth of successful mechanical inventions designed to increase factor productivity. In Europe the few devices that did succeed, such as the stocking frame and the ribbon loom, proved adaptable to small-scale household production.[103] In Asian domestic production, there was a

[100] Frank Perlin, 'Financial Institutions and Business Practices Across the Euro-Asian Interface: Comparative and Structural Considerations, 1500–1900', in ed., Hans Pohl, *The European Discovery of the World and its Economic Effects on Pre-Industrial Society, 1500–1800*, Papers of the Tenth International Economic History Congress, Vierteljahrschrift für Sozial-und Wirtschaftsgeschichte 89 (1990), pp. 257–303.

[101] Morris-Suzuki, *The Technological Transformation of Japan*, pp. 34–5.

[102] Chaudhuri, *Asia Before Europe*, p. 313.

[103] D.C. Coleman, 'Textile Growth' in eds., N.B. Harte and K.G. Ponting, *Textile History and Economic History: Essays in Honour of Miss Julia de Lacy Mann* (Manchester, 1973), ch. 1; Trevor Griffiths, Philip A. Hunt and Patrick O'Brien, 'Inventive Activity in the British Textile Industry, 1700–1800', *The Journal of Economic History* LII (1992), pp. 881–906. On technological stagnation in the textile industry of New Spain, see Salvucci, *Textiles and Capitalism*, pp. 42–3, 48, 52–3, 174–5.

notable under utilization of known advanced machinery such as the drawloom, the treadle-operated multiple spindle spinning-wheel, and the large spinning, twisting and ginning frames of Chinese invention which required substantial capital investment and more than one operator.[104] Cultural, aesthetic and gender biases also influenced the choice of technologies as evidenced in the continued use of the backstrap loom among native women in Spanish America and parts of Southeast Asia, and the long dual tradition of horizontal and vertical looms employed respectively by male and female operators in parts of Africa.[105] The geographical dispersion and skill-intensive character of pre-modern industry, the small units of production, and the incorporation of textile processing within the family household economy with its low-cost work force inhibited the adoption of devices that required fixed capital and an advanced division of labour. In the absence of political support for industrial restructuring, an abundant labour supply and institutional inertia proved to be formidable barriers to the introduction of capital-intensive technology and large-scale factory production in the nineteenth century.

Notions of linear evolution have tended to distort the pattern of technological and industrial development in the pre-modern period. The commercial success of handicraft producers using sophisticated traditional technologies was based on specialization rather than standardization. By focusing on a high level of product differentiation, Asian weavers were able to satisfy a varied and elastic demand for quality fabrics in all price ranges in global markets rendered increasingly accessible by efficiencies in transportation and distribution networks.

Nowhere is this more evident than in the sector of cotton production which registered the greatest growth across the period, with the bulk of the advance occurring outside Europe. This was in large part the acceleration of a trend that began in the Middle Ages.[106] Owing to its comfort, easy care, accessible price, and its affinity for colourfast dyes, cotton cloth achieved the status of a mass consumption commodity, displacing linen and lighter woollen fabrics, well before the full impact of the European Industrial Revolution was felt in world markets. As Chaudhuri has noted, the widespread acceptance of Indian cottons in the global marketplace served to chart the demand curve for British entrepreneurs in the

---

[104] K.N. Chaudhuri, *Asia Before Europe*, pp. 313–18; Chao, *The Development of Cotton Textile Production*, ch. III; Needham, *Science and Civilisation*, V, pt. IX, pp. 215–25; See also pp. 410–11 on the abandonment of the multiple spindle silk-twisting frame in favour of hand-twisting in the Ming and Ch'ing periods. Cf. p. 236 for the declining use of the multiple spindle spinning-frame for bast fibre twisting.

[105] On the continued use of the narrow backstrap loom and simple spinning devices in household production in Southeast Asia, see Anthony Reid, *Southeast Asia in the Age of Commerce*, I (New Haven, 1988), pp. 93–4.

[106] Maureen Fennell Mazzaoui, *The Italian Cotton Industry in the Later Middle Ages* (Cambridge, 1981), chs. 1–2.

last decade of the eighteenth century.[107] The ability of British cotton producers to capture existing international markets depended on the lowering of costs though mechanization, and adequate flows of imported raw materials. It also required mastery of advanced techniques of dyeing, printing and finishing, and the creation of an aggregate demand for standardized products of uniform quality.

With the exception of advanced spinning processes, the British model of cotton manufacture was not replicated in other branches of textile production in the early nineteenth century. Within the cotton sector, the divergence of the British mode of mass production from the decentralized forms of organization prevalent in traditional centres of production created new competitive pressures in world trade. After 1800, massive exports of low-priced, standardized cotton goods by British entrepreneurs challenged the near-monopoly position once held by Indian fabrics in international commerce. Moreover, the gradual penetration of British products into regions once served by local producers adversely affected small-scale craft workers in urban and rural centres. Reactions ranged from resistance to adaptation, based on either the rejection or the selective adoption of foreign technologies. Initially, the decline in hand spinning was faster and steeper than the fall in weaving. Despite occupational losses, some handicraft weavers utilizing machine-made yarn survived into the early twentieth century by concentrating on niche products incorporating designs and characteristics preferred by domestic consumers, although their share of the internal market was progressively eroded.[108] As the linkages between agriculture and industrial by-employments were broken, many peasants turned to the production of raw cotton for export.

The experience of regional cotton weavers in the global economy was not necessarily typical of all handicraft activities nor even of all branches of textile production. The continued vitality of many sectors of artisan production after 1800 is stressed in the 'flexible specialization' thesis postulated by Charles Sabel and Jonathan Zeitlin. In their view, decentralized craft industries were not secondary or transitional stages in the growth of mass production, but parallel and independent responses to temporal shifts in trade, technology and market conditions. In this revisionist interpretation of the rise of modern industrialization, centralized political and strategic decision-making is identified as a decisive factor in the adoption of mass production as the dominant industrial model within consolidating national states. The survival of alternative systems of production, based on skilled artisan labour, depended upon diversification of the product line and innovations in design.[109]

[107] Chaudhuri, 'The Structure of Indian Textile Industry', p. 128.

[108] Pamuk, *The Ottoman Empire*, ch. 6.

[109] Charles Sabel and Jonathan Zeitlin, 'Historical Alternatives to Mass Production: Politics, Markets and Technology in Nineteenth-Century Industrialization', *Past and Present* CVIII (1985), pp. 132–76. See also C. Sabel and J. Zeitlin, eds., *World of Possibilities: Flexibility and Mass Production in Western Industrialization* (Cambridge, 1997).

Within the early-modern global economy, the growth and decline of widely divergent systems of textile production occurred concurrently within distinct political and social contexts that determined the relations of production and the nature and scope of entrepreneurial activities. These same institutional and structural factors conditioned the responses of traditional craft-based cloth producers to new technological and competitive challenges in the modern era, giving rise to contrasting experiences and diverse historical outcomes in various regions of the world economy.

Select Additional Bibliography

Arasaratnam, Sinnappah, 'Merchants of Coromandel in Trade and Entrepreneurship circa 1650–1700', in eds., Roderich Ptak and Dietmar Rothermund, *Emporia, Commodities and Entrepreneurs in Asian Maritime Trade, c. 1400–1750*, Beiträge zur Südasienforschung, Südasien Institut, Universität Heidelberg, 141 (Stuttgart, 1991).

Berg, Maxine, *Markets and Manufacture in Early Industrial Europe* (London and New York, 1991).

— and Hudson, Pat and Sonenscher, Michael, eds., *Manufacture in Town and Country Before the Factory* (Cambridge, 1983).

Bezant, Jan, 'Evolución de la industria textil poplana, 1544–1845', *Historia Mexicana* XIII, no. 4 (1964).

Bier, Carol, ed., *Woven from the Soul, Spun from the Heart : Textile Arts of Safavid and Qajar Iran, 16th–19th Centuries*, The Textile Museum (Washington, D.C., 1987).

Bolland, Rita, *Tellem Textiles: Archeological Finds from Burial Caves in Mali's Bandiagara Cliff*, Tropenmuseum/Royal Tropical Institute (Amsterdam, 1991).

Braude, Benjamin, 'International Competition and Domestic Cloth in the Ottoman Empire, 1500–1600, A Study in Underdevelopment', *Review* II, no. 3 (1979).

Chao, Kang, *The Development of Cotton Textile Production in China*, Harvard East Asian Monographs, 74 (Cambridge, Mass., 1977).

Chaudhuri, K.N., 'The Structure of Indian Textile Industry in the Seventeenth and Eighteenth Centuries', *The Indian Economic and Social History Review* XI (1974).

Çizakça, Murat, 'Price History and the Bursa Silk Industry: A Study in Ottoman Industrial Decline, 1550–1650', *The Journal of Economic History* XL, no. 3 (1980).

Deyon, Pierre and Mendels, Franklin, eds., *VIIIe Congrès International d'Histoire Economique, Budapest 16–22 août 1982. Section A2: La Protoindustrialisation: Théorie et Réalité* (Lille, 1982).

Faroqhi, Suraiya, 'Notes on the Production of Cotton and Cotton Cloth in XVIth and XVIIth Century Anatolia', *Journal of European Economic History* VIII, no. 2 (1979).

—, 'Textile Production in Rumeli and the Arab Provinces: Geographical Distribution and Internal Trade (1550–1650)', in *Peasants, Dervishes and Traders in the Ottoman Empire*, Variorum Collected Studies Series 230 (London, 1986), ch. XII.

Floor, Willem, 'Economy and Society: Fibers, Fabrics, Factories', in ed., Carol Bier, *Woven From the Soul, Spun From the Heart: Textile Arts of Safavid and Qajar Iran, 16th–19th Centuries*, The Textile Museum (Washington, D.C., 1987).

Gittinger, Mattiebelle, *Master Dyers to the World: Technique and Trade in Early Indian Dyed Cotton Textiles*, The Textile Museum (Washington, D.C., 1982).

Gittinger, Mattiebelle and Lefferts, H. Leedom, Jr., *Textiles and the Tai Experience in Southeast Asia*, The Textile Museum (Washington, D.C., 1992).

Glamann, Kristoff, *Dutch-Asiatic Trade, 1620–1740* (Copenhagen and the Hague, 1958).

Guy, John, 'Indian Textiles for the Thai Market – A Royal Prerogative', *The Textile Museum Journal* XXXI (1992).

Harte, N.B., 'The Rise of Protection and the English Linen Trade, 1690–1790', in eds., N.B. Harte and K.G. Ponting, *Textile History and Economic History* (Manchester, 1973).

Hauser, William B., *Economic Institutional Change in Tokugawa Japan: Osaka and the Kinai Cotton Trade* (Cambridge, 1974).

Hood, Adrienne D., 'The Material World of Cloth: Production and Use in Eighteenth-Century Rural Pennsylvania', *The William and Mary Quarterly* ser. 3, LIII, no.1 (1996).

Inikori, Joseph E., 'Slavery and the Revolution in Cotton Textile Production in England', *Social Science History* XIII, no. 4 (1989). 342–9.

Kriedte, Peter, Medick, Hans and Schlumbohm, Jürgen, *Industrialization before Industrialization. Rural Industry in the Genesis of Capitalism* (Cambridge, 1981).

Larson, Brooke, 'The Cotton Textile Industry of Cochabamba, 1770–1810: The Opportunities and Limits of Growth', in eds., Nils Jacobsen and Hans-Jürgen Puhle, *The Economies of Mexico and Peru During the Late Colonial Period, 1760–1810*, Biblioteca Ibero-Americana 34 (Berlin, 1986).

Leboutte, René, ed., *Proto-industrialization: Recent Research and New Perspectives* (Geneva, 1996).

Li, Lillian M., *China's Silk Trade: Traditional Industry in the Modern World, 1842–1937*, Harvard East Asian Monographs, 97 (Cambridge, Mass., 1981).

Libby, Douglas C., 'Proto-Industrialization in a Slave Economy: The Case of Minas Gerais', *Journal of Latin American Studies* XXIII (1991).

Mendels, Franklin F., 'Proto-industrialization: The First Phase of the Industrialization Process', *Journal of Economic History* XXXII, no. 1 (1972), pp. 241–61.

Miño Grivalja, Manuel, *La protoindustria colonial hispanoamericana*, Fideicomisio Historia de las Américas (Mexico, 1993).

Morris-Suzuki, Tessa, 'Sericulture and the Origins of Japanese Industrialization', *Technology and Culture* XXXIII, no. 1 (1992).

Needham, Joseph, ed., *Science and Civilisation in China, Vol. 5: Chemistry and Chemical Technology Part IX: Textile Technology: Spinning and Reeling* by Dieter Kuhn (Cambridge, 1988).

Ogilvie, Sheilagh and Cerman, Markus, eds., *European Proto-Industrialization* (Cambridge, 1996).

Perlin, Frank, 'Proto-industrialization and Pre-colonial South Asia', *Past and Present* XCVIII (1983).

Prakash, Om, *The Dutch East India Company and the Economy of Bengal, 1630–1720* (Princeton, N.J., 1985).

Rapp, Richard T., 'The Unmaking of the Mediterranean Trade Hegemony: International Trade Rivalry and the Commercial Revolution', *The Journal of Economic History* XXXV, no. 3 (1975).

Ramaswamy, Vijaya, *Textiles and Weavers in Medieval South India* (Delhi, 1985).

Ray, Haraprasad, 'Bengal's Textile Products Involved in Ming Trade during Cheng Ho's Voyages to the Indian Ocean and Identification of the Hitherto Undeciphered Textiles', in eds., R. Ptak and D. Rothermund, *Emporia, Commodities and Entrepreneurs in Asian Maritime Trade c. 1450–1750* (Stuttgart, 1991).

Reikat, Andrea, *Handelsstoffe: Grundzüge des Europäisch-Westafrikanischen Handels vor der Industriellen Revolution am Beispiel der Textilien*, Studien zur Kulturkunde, 105 (Cologne, 1997).

Ruddel, David-Thiery, 'Domestic Textile Production in Colonial Quebec, 1608–1840', in eds., B. Lemire and A.D. Hood, 'Surveying Textile History: Perspectives for New Research', Proceedings of the Colloquium at the University of New Brunswick, April 27–29, 1990, *Material History Bulletin* XXXI (1990).

Saito, Osamu, 'Population and the Peasant Family Economy in Proto-Industrial Japan', *Journal of Family History* VIII, no. 1 (1983).

Salas, Miriam, 'Los obrajes huamanguinos y sus interconexiones con otros sectores economicos en el centro-sur peruano a fines del siglo XVIII' in eds., Nils Jacobsen and Hans-Jürgen Puhle, *The Economies of Mexico and Peru during the Late Colonial Period, 1760–1810*, Biblioteca Ibero-Americana, 34 (Berlin, 1986).

Salvucci, Richard J., *Textiles and Capitalism in Mexico: An Economic History of the Obrajes, 1539–1840* (Princeton, N.J., 1987).

Schneider, Jane, 'The Anthropology of Cloth', *Annual Review of Anthropology* XVI (1987).

Shammas, Carole, 'How Self-Sufficient Was Early America?', *Journal of Interdisciplinary History* XIII, no. 2, (1982).

—, 'The Decline of Textile Prices in England and America Prior to Industrialization', *Economic History Review* XLVII, no. 3 (1994).

Subrahmanyam, Sanjay, 'Rural Industry and Commercial Agriculture in Late Seventeenth-Century South-Eastern India', *Past and Present* CXXVI (1990).

Textiles in Trade, Proceedings of the Textile Society of America Biennial Symposium, September 14–16, 1990 (Washington, D.C., 1990).

Thomson, Guy, 'The Cotton Textile Industry in Puebla during the Eighteenth and Early Nineteenth Centuries', in eds., Nils Jacobsen and Hans-Jürgen Puhle, *The Economies of Mexico and Peru During the Late Colonial Period, 1760–1810*, Biblioteca Ibero-Americana 34 (Berlin, 1986).

Thornton, John, 'Precolonial African Industry and the Atlantic Trade, 1500–1800', *African Economic History* XIX (1990–1).

Ulrich, Laurel Thatcher, 'Martha Ballard and Her Girls: Women's Work in Eighteenth-Century Maine', in ed., Stephen Innes, *Work and Labour in Early America* (Chapel Hill, 1988).

Vogt, John, 'Notes on the Portuguese Cloth Trade in West Africa, 1480–1540', *The International Journal of African Historical Studies* VIII, no. 4 (1975).

Zen Sun, E-Tu, 'Sericulture and Silk Textile Production in Ch'ing China', in W.E. Willmott, *Economic Organization in Chinese Society* (Stanford, 1972).

1
Incorporation of the Middle East into the European World-Economy

Murat Çizakça

This article addresses itself to a set of questions raised by Immanuel Wallerstein in 1977 related to the incorporation of the Middle Eastern economy into the European world-economy. The main question that this article attempts to answer is the following:

> When does the Ottoman Empire become incorporated into the world-economy? This question involves three subquestions:
>
> (a) What were the processes, both within the Ottoman Empire and within the European world-economy, that account for this incorporation?
>
> (b) Is the "incorporation" a single event, or can different regions of the empire . . . be said to be incorporated at different moments in time?

In this article, based on original Ottoman archival sources, it is argued that the confrontation of the fiscalist and provisionist

*AUTHOR'S NOTE: I regret that I have not been able to consult the latest contribution by Mehmet Genç, "18.Yüzyilda Osmanli Ekonomisi ve Savas," *Yapit,* April-May 1984, No. 4., pp. 52-61, which appeared while this article was in print.

Ottoman trade regime with that of the mercantilist Europe was mainly responsible for "a." It is also shown that the "incorporation" was by no means a single event and that different regions were incorporated at different periods in history, the exact time being determined by the incorporation of the sectors dominating these regions. Generally speaking, however, two stages of Ottoman incorporation are identified: the early incorporation of the period 1550-1650 and the full incorporation of the period 1830-1900.

I. Introduction

During the First International Congress on the Social and Economic History of Turkey, convened in Ankara on July 11-13, 1977 Immanuel Wallerstein put forward several questions concerning the incorporation of the Ottoman economy into the European world-economy.[1]

At the time that Wallerstein asked these questions, I had just completed my Ph.D. dissertation on the fate of the Bursa silk industry (Çizakça, 1978). As the title of my thesis suggests, I was fairly convinced then that I had discovered a pattern to the Ottoman industrial decline. This pattern, it will be argued,

---

1. Throughout this article "Middle East" and the "Ottoman Empire" will be used interchangeably. To quote Wallerstein:

> My own largest area of uncertainty in relation to the Ottoman Empire is whether its peripheralization should be dated from the nineteenth (or late eighteenth century) or from the early seventeenth century.... I believe that the choice has to be made primarily in terms of the real economics of the situation, and only secondarily in terms of the continuity of political forms or of ideological belief-systems. I would therefore put forward as the questions for research the following:

> (1) If the Ottoman Empire can be demonstrated not to be a peripheral zone of the European world-economy in the sixteenth century, why was it not incorporated into the emerging division of labor from the outset, like Poland or Sicily? ...

> (2) When does the Ottoman Empire become incorporated into the world-economy? This question involves three sub-questions:

>> (a) What were the processes, both within the Ottoman Empire and within the European world-economy, that account for this incorporation?

>> (b) Is the "incorporation" a single event, or can different regions of the Empire-Rumelia, Anatolia, Syria, Egypt, etc. — be said to be incorporated at different moments in time?

Incorporation of the Middle East   355

answers Question 2a of Wallerstein. At about the same time, another Ph.D. thesis was completed by Benjamin Braude on the fate of the Salonica woolen industry that confirmed in many ways the pattern I had in mind (Braude, 1979).

Encouraged by Braude's findings and stimulated by Wallerstein's questions I decided to see if the pattern observed in Bursa and Salonica was part of a general phenomenon dominating the entire Ottoman economy. This research, primarily based on the auction prices of the industrial tax-farms registered by the Ottoman tax-farm administration, is now completed, and the data obtained will be instrumental in answering Wallerstein's Questions 2, 2a, and 2b. These answers, however, are limited in the sense that the impact of incorporation of raw materials and manufacturing has been investigated but the problem of agriculture has not. Moreover, this has been done only from the point of view of the changing division of labor.

II. The Process of Incorporation of the Middle East into the European World-Economy

I have demonstrated elsewhere that the Ottoman industry was already under the pressure of European competition at the second half of the sixteenth century.[2] This competition materialized at two levels: in the purchase of the raw materials and in the sale of the final product. Let us first consider the nature of European competition as it related to the Ottoman raw materials.

(c) What were the political consequences of incorporation?

(3) Whenever the Ottoman Empire was thus incorporated, why was it not incorporated as a semiperipheral region rather than as a peripheral region? Once again, this is not an implausible query, as it might be agreed that Russia (and perhaps also Japan), when they were incorporated came in as semiperipheral regions.

The way I would go about answering these queries, had I sufficient knowledge, would be to look at actual production processes and then at trade Patterns (1980: 119).

2. The following summary, unless otherwise stated, is based on Çizakça, 1980.

*Increased importation of Ottoman raw materials to Europe:
demand conditions*

IMPORTS OF RAW SILK TO EUROPE

If we consider the Ottoman exports of raw silk to Europe
first, we note that the European demand for this raw material
increased substantially at the second half of the sixteenth century. Traditionally Italian city states, but also at an increasing
rate England and the Low Countries, were the main source of
this demand. Ottoman raw silk was used mainly as a supplement to the French and Italian silk.[3] This practice spread and
gained momentum as a result of a technical development in
Italy. As the Italian production of Orsoglio "alla Bolognese"
shot up due to the spread of hydraulic mills, more and more
Ottoman silk was needed to supplement the Orsoglio.[4] England and Holland, regular importers of Italian Orsoglio, soon
followed suit and increased their importation of Ottoman silk
in direct proportion to their imports of cheap and excellent
quality Orsoglio.

It is only in this context that we would understand why
imports of raw silk from the Middle East to England increased

3. Because Ottomans were the main exporters of Iranian silk to the West, the
term "Ottoman raw silk" covers the silk produced domestically as well as the Iranian
silk. The exact share of Persian raw silk in total Ottoman exports of silk is difficult to
determine. For an excellent summary of the state of Persian silk production and trade
see Meilink-Roelofsz (1972-74). In the 1620's the total volume of Persian silk
production was about 20,000 bales (probably an overestimation: 1 bale = 200-225 lbs.).
Of these, 6,000 bales were exported to Europe (Dunlop, 1930: LXVI). The export route
was "exclusively" via the Levant (Glamann, 1958: 114-15). Total Persian exports to
Europe were diffused as follows: to Marseille, 3,000 bales; to Venice, 1,500 bales; to
Genova, Luca, Florence, and Messina, 400 bales (Van Dam, 1939: II, 3, 281).
Interdependency of silk markets over the globe is well illustrated by the fact that when,
in 1628, under special circumstances, the English more than doubled their purchases of
Persian silk in Aleppo, prices in Bursa hit a peak (Glamann, 1958: 115-16). Similarly,
when in late 1620's and in 1634 Dutch demand in the Persian Gulf was high (200,000-
240,000 lbs. per season), Bursa prices hit record levels (Çizakça, 1980: 549). It is
probable that behind these record prices in Bursa both supply factors (shortages of
Persian silk in the city) and demand factors (unusually high European demand) played
a role.

4. Orsoglio was used as a warp, Ottoman silk was used in order to make the weft.
Thus, the two products were complementary.

Incorporation of the Middle East   357

by 275% between 1621 and 1721, and also why already in the 1550's 4 million guldens' worth of silk and silk products from Italy and the Levant were imported into the Low Countries. Italian and Levantine silk constituted the second largest item in the overall importation of the Low Countries in this period (Davis, 1970: 202; Brulez, 1970: 36).

IMPORTS OF WOOL TO EUROPE

According to Braude, the real European pressure on Ottoman wool emerged during the second half of the sixteenth century as Italian woolen cloth production increased rapidly. "During the first half of the century Italian demand for wool was mainly oriented towards Spain, but with rapid increases in cloth production soon Balkan wool began to be tapped" (Braude, 1979: 438-39; for Venetian woolens, see Sella, 1968: 108). Lack of trade data between the Ottoman Empire and Italy does not allow us to quantify this statement. However, price trends to be presented below will support the point.

IMPORTS OF MOHAIR YARN TO EUROPE

During the fifteenth and sixteenth centuries mohair yarn was exported to Europe particularly through Italian and German merchants. Yet, the real increase in volume of exports occurred in the early seventeenth century with the entry of English and Dutch merchants into the Mediterranean. This situation is explained vividly by Ralph Davis:

> A second Turkish product also handled through Smyrna was mohair yarn. This was an extremely valuable textile yarn, spun in the villages of central Anatolia from the hair of the Angora goat. It began to come to England in considerable quantities in the 1630s, chiefly for making buttons and buttonholes, and was to some extent substituted for the cheapest Persian silk, Ardasset. The trade grew rapidly in importance so that at the end of the century it was second only to silk (1970: 200).

Ralph Davis has also given us figures that substantiate his point, indicating that between 1621-1634 and 1663-1669 importation of mohair yarn to England had increased by 400 percent (1970).

Moreover, it must be noted here that mohair yarn had become one of the basic inputs of the enormously successful Leiden cloth industry at the early seventeenth century. Thus, the Dutch imports, in all probability even greater than the English, must also be taken into account (Dillen, 1970: 77). Indeed, it is estimated that in the second half of the seventeenth century Dutch merchants bought about 1500 bales of Angora wool in Izmir (Wätjen, 1909: 163).[5]

IMPORTS OF COTTON TO EUROPE

The pattern of European demand for cotton differed substantially from those inputs mentioned above. European demand for cotton in this period was rather low; the most important market, Germany, was wiped out due to the devastation of the Thirty Years' War. Of the four main raw materials imported by the Dutch—silk, wool, mohair, and cotton—the last was the least demanded. The Dutch cottage industry simply did not use cotton. Moreover, Ottoman cotton faced severe competition in the Amsterdam market from the East Indian cotton, which was whiter and more fine (Wätjen, 1909: 202). The English demand for Ottoman cotton also remained stagnant throughout the seventeenth century, probably due to the fact that the British West Indies began to export cotton to England after the 1620's thus undercutting Ottoman cotton (Davis, 1970: 202).

To sum up, European demand for Ottoman raw materials exhibited varying patterns: It rapidly increased for raw silk, wool, and mohair yarn but stagnated for cotton in the period 1550-1650. The implications of this observation will be studied below.

Effects of increased exportation of raw materials to Europe

We saw above that, with the exception of cotton, European demand for basic Ottoman raw materials increased rapidly in

---

5. Thus, the export prohibition of 1645 was obviously not implemented. For details on this prohibition, see Faroqhi (n.d.). I am grateful to the author for allowing me to read her article in manuscript form.

Incorporation of the Middle East   359

the period 1550-1650. Obviously, an interaction between these changing demand conditions and supply would determine the prices of these products. Let us now investigate the impact of changing demand conditions on the raw material prices.[6] We have at hand three price trends for this purpose: silk prices obtained from the Bursa court registers; prices of Ottoman wool in the Balkans; and prices of Ottoman cotton in Amsterdam markets.

CHANGING PRICE STRUCTURE

In response to the increased European demand explained above, the raw silk prices in Bursa increased by 293% between 1550-1570 and 1620-1640 (Çizakça, 1980: 536). Benjamin Braude explains the nature of Balkan wool prices as follows:

> From 1530 to 1610 Balkan wool prices moved in tandem with Venetian cloth output. . . . After some eighty years of correlation, in 1610 Venetian production declined and Balkan wool prices rose. The explanation is not hard to find; other wool purchasers, notably the Dutch and later the French, entered the Ottoman market supplanting the Venetians (1979: 439).

In sharp contrast to the prices of silk and wool explained above, the prices of Anatolian cotton and cotton yarn declined rapidly in the Netherlands after the 1620's. This depression lasted until the 1670's. By contrast, silk prices in Amsterdam (Organizine of Bologna) tended to increase in the same period, both trends confirming the explanations made above (Posthumus, 1934: Diag. VI).

New evidence on the production of raw materials in the Middle East

It has been demonstrated above that European demand increased substantially for Ottoman silk, wool, and mohair, and stagnated for cotton. Prices of these raw materials respond-

---

6. Obviously, European demand was only one component of the total demand for the raw materials. I have made a considerable effort to separate these components (Çizakça, 1980).

360   *Murat Çizakça*

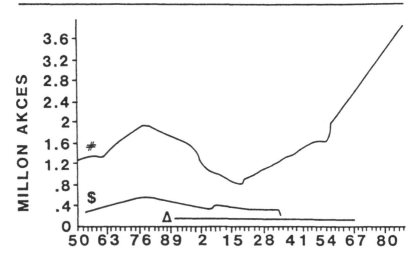

=Bursa silk scale; STokat silk scale; ΔKastamonu silk scale.

Figure 1 Silk Production in Anatolia, 1550-1685

ed accordingly: Prices of silk and wool rapidly increased, whereas cotton prices declined, suggesting that the supply elasticity of silk and wool could not have been great, whereas that of cotton was probably substantial. In view of the developments explained above we would expect that the supply of all raw materials should have increased. Let us now consider this hypothesis.

SILK

The trends of raw material production in the Ottoman Empire can be obtained indirectly by observing the auction prices of relevant tax-farms. This method has been explained already in detail (Çizakça, 1980: 547-48). It should suffice here to note that the trends presented in the following figures do not reflect absolute volumes of production but merely indicate, indirectly, the rate of change over time.

In Figure 1 the production trends of the most important Anatolian centers of silk production, Bursa, Tokat, and Kastamonu, are depicted. The fact that the raw silk production suffered in these towns during the early seventeenth century is

Incorporation of the Middle East   361

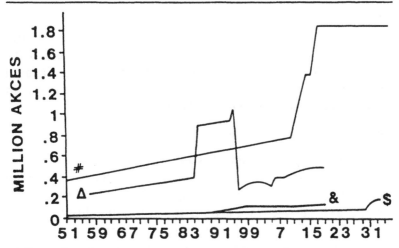

‡Aleppo silk scale; $Aleppo sair silk; &Patras silk scale; ΔMorea silk scale.

Figure 2 Silk Production in Syria-Greece, 1551-1635

understandable. For in this period Anatolia witnessed one of the greatest turmoils of its entire history: the Celali uprisings. The massive destruction on all aspects of economic life in Anatolia has been studied in detail (Akdag, 1975). With near complete chaos prevailing in the countryside we would expect disruption, not only in the Anatolian production of silk, but also in Persian silk supplies.

It is equally noteworthy, however, that while silk supply in Anatolia was declining, it was increasing rapidly in Greece and Syria where the uprisings had not spread. In view of these trends, it could be arued that Persian silk shifted to the southern route via Bagdad to Aleppo, while local production in Greece must have replaced declining Anatolian production.

We can now summarize our findings concerning the Ottoman raw silk production in the period 1500-1700 as follows: In response to the continuously increasing European demand and prices, Ottoman as well as Persian silk supply increased. The increase in supply was continuous in Syria and Greece, but disrupted in Anatolia due to the political turmoil. Yet the production increased rapidly everywhere once peace and order were restored in Anatolia.

COTTON

We are informed by a joint contribution that cotton production was also increasing rapidly in response, particularly, to domestic Ottoman demand. Indeed, İslamoğlu and Faroqhi estimated that the rate of increase of cotton production in Adana region was 142 percent (1979: 413).

WOOL AND MOHAIR YARN

As for the production of wool and mohair yarn we are in complete darkness. Two basic works on the Salonica woollen industry (Braude, 1979; Sahillioğlu, 1973-74) and two on the Ankara (Ergenc, 1975; Faroqhi, n.d.) mohair industry leave us in darkness. Only Sahillioğlu, based on Svoronos, informs us that some 30,000 *okka* of wool was used by the Salonica industry during the eighteenth century. This amount was later increased to 50,000 *okkas* (1973-74: 421). Long-term trends of wool production, like that of silk presented in Figures 1 and 2, may possibly be obtained indirectly by following the auction prices of the "Adet-i Agnam Mukataasi" (Tax-farms of sheep) but this tedious job still awaits an unfortunate Ph.D. student.

At this point it can be argued that increasing prices of silk, wool, and mohair yarn would eventually curb European demand. Yet we know that in the period 1550-1650 this did not occur. This sustained European demand for raw materials notwithstanding rapidly increasing prices has already been explained (Çizakça, 1980: 541-46). So only a brief summary should suffice here: Technological improvements in the seventeenth century, although not so dramatic as in the eighteenth, helped to reduce costs; spread and expansion of rural industries in the West reduced labor costs substantially; in comparison to the western experience, more frequent and violent Ottoman debasements rendered Ottoman products cheaper for Europeans; and finally the chartered companies that benefitted fully from the monopolistic and monopsonistic market structures could afford to purchase Ottoman raw materials despite their rapidly increasing prices. These companies could compensate the losses that they incurred in the Levantine markets by selling the Ottoman raw materials back at home at monopolistic prices.

As it will be remembered, the competition in the purchase of raw materials constituted only one aspect of the European competition. The other aspect of this competition was felt in the sale of the final product. Indeed, in the sale of the final product—that is, cloth—the Ottoman clothier was in direct competition with the European clothes freely imported into the Ottoman markets.

Increased importation of cloth from Europe and its consequences

It has already been shown that the silk industry of Bursa and the woollen industry of Salonica were affected adversely by the increasing importation of European woollens (Çizakça, 1980; Braude, 1979). So it should suffice here to note that these imports could affect Salonica woollens as well as Bursa silks because both light (Flemish Sayettes) and heavy (Suffolk Broadcloth) clothes were imported. Moreover, despite Ottoman debasements, prices of English cloth were definitely declining in the Ottoman markets (Çizakça, 1980: 545-46).

A conspicuous outcome of the penetration of European woollens into the Ottoman markets was the relatively sluggish increase in the prices of Ottoman clothes. Indeed, when compared with the prices of the raw materials, cloth prices increased much less (Çizakça, 1980: 540). This was obviously due to the saturation of Ottoman markets with domestic as well as European cloth.

If we combine these sluggish cloth prices with the much more rapidly increasing raw material prices, the result would be the price scissors. Indeed, Ottoman clothiers were face to face with rapidly increasing raw material prices, and yet were unable to reflect their increasing costs onto the prices of their final product. Ability to reflect increasing input costs onto the output prices depends on the price elasticity of demand for the final product. I argue that increased importation of cloth from

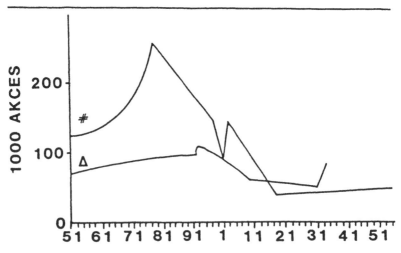

=Stamp tax on silk cloth in Bursa; ΔAleppo dyehouse.

Figure 3   Cloth Production in Bursa-Aleppo, 1551-1651

Europe (European competition at the final product level) rendered the demand for cloth in the Ottoman markets more elastic. With rapidly increasing input costs and elastic demand structure for the final product we would expect a fall in the profitability of cloth production. A fall in the profitability of cloth production, on the other hand, would result in a decline in the production of Ottoman cloth. Let us now test this hypothesis.

New evidence concerning cloth production in the Middle East

SILK CLOTH

We can now examine if the decline of production in the volume of silk cloth observed in Bursa was part of a more general phenomenon. A careful look at Figure 3 reveals that Aleppo, a major center of silk cloth production perhaps even more important than Bursa, follows a trend roughly similar to that of Bursa. Indeed, production of cloth in Aleppo increases from 1550's to 1590's after which we observe a steady and sharp decline until the 1630's.

Incorporation of the Middle East   365

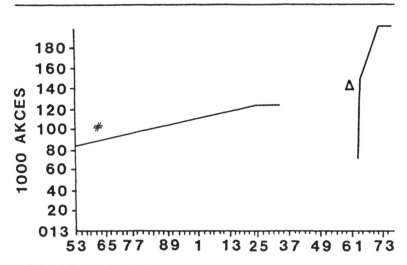

=Tokat dyhouse; ΔIstanbul stamp tax.

Figure 4 Istanbul Stamp Tax—Tokat Dyehouse, 1553-1673

Another center of silk cloth production, Tokat, is represented by two trends (Figures 4 and 5). The first trend is that the auction prices of the dyehouse of Tokat indicate a very slow expansion (an exception), and the second trend (Figure 5) indicates a sharp decline after the 1650's.

A major exception to the generally declining trends of silk cloth production observed so far is the trend of the auction prices of the stamp tax on various silk cloth marketed in Istanbul (Figure 4). A possible explanation of this exception may be as follows: This tax-farm not only dealt with the silk cloth produced in Istanbul (Sandal), but also with imported silk cloth (Atlas). *Atlas,* of course, was also produced in Turkey, but after the 1600's, "almost all of the Atlas, we have found appear to have been of Venetian and European origin" (Dalsar, 1960: 38). As the relative volumes of Ottoman and European silk cloth stamped in this tax-farm are unknown, the rapidly increasing trend observed simply may reflect increased importation of Italian silk cloth. Indeed, if we consider the fact that the silk industry in Venice was one of the few industries to

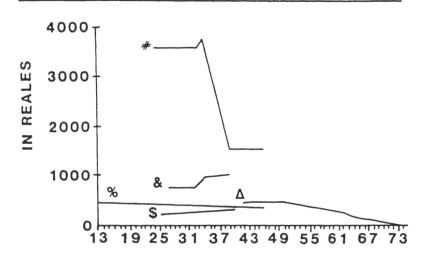

SCungus (Amid) dyehouse; %Rabat (Amid) dyehouse; & Amid cotton cloth; ΔTokat stamp tax.

Figure 5 Cloth Production in Amid-Tokat, 1613-1673

survive the seventeenth century crises, this argument gains strength (Rapp, 1975: 523).

Another declining trend is observed in Amid (Diyarbakir), an important center of trade at the crossroads of major caravan routes between east and west and north and south. Actually, Amid is one of the most interesting centers shown in these figures because it possessed a widespread rural industry. It should be noted in this context that the declining trend observed in Figure 5 represents the auction prices of the dyehouse of the city of Amid, i.e., an urban industry. As for the rural industries spread around Amid, it is difficult to come to a conclusion, for some of them decline and some expand. This inconsistency in the performance of rural industries is understandable. Some of them were isolated small communities producing for the local market and were little affected by international trade. In this context the sharp decline in the production of the city of Amid, much more affected by the international trade, is indeed instructive.

We can now summarize our findings on the performance of silk cloth manufacture in the Ottoman Empire. As expected

Incorporation of the Middle East   367

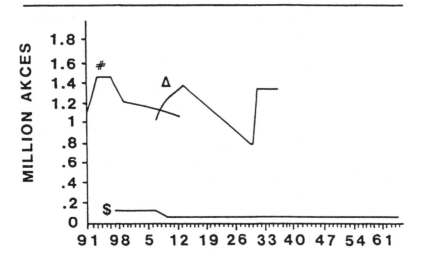

=Ankara mohair press; ΔErzurum alum; SKochisar mohair press.

Figure 6 Mohair-Alum Production in Anatolia, 1591-1661

within the structure of the simple model presented above, production of silk cloth exhibited a generally declining tendency in all major centers of production with the important exception of Istanbul, an exception probably caused by an increase in imported cloth. I argue that this general decline in silk manufacturing was caused, on one hand, by ever-increasing exports of raw silk to Europe and a consequent increase in the cost of the basic input, and, on the other, by importation of cloth from Europe that depressed the final product prices leading to price scissors, declining profitability and, finally, declining cloth production.

WOOLLENS

The above argument also holds for the woollens, as Benjamin Braude has already demonstrated for Salonica and Safed. Let us examine if other centers of woollen cloth manufacturing in the Empire were affected similarly.

In Figure 6 we observe the auction prices of the mohair presses in both Ankara and Kochisar, as well as the alum works of Karahisari Sarki (Erzurum). As we would expect from the model presented above, the mohair production in both cities exhibit declining trends.

COTTON CLOTH—A DIFFERENT PATTERN

The last type of cloth that will be considered here is cotton cloth. Cotton was grown in Greece, Western Anatolia, Cukurova, and Syria and exported to Europe. Germany was probably the most important customer of Levantine cotton. Yet the Thirty Years' War wiped out German industry, and with it the most important source of demand for Ottoman cotton. Moreover, the British West Indies, as well as the Dutch East Indies, began to export cotton to Europe, which displaced Ottoman cotton. Thus, as far as cotton is concerned we have a different pattern than that presented before. With the basic source of European demand collapsing and additional sources of supply emerging from across the Atlantic as well as from Asia, we expect that the Ottoman cotton cloth producer must have enjoyed abundant and cheap raw material supplies. Moreover, with a steadily increasing population, worsening income distribution, and collapsing silk and woollen manufacturing, we would also expect a considerable substitution of cotton cloth for silk and woollens. Under these conditions of abundant supply of the raw material[7] and rapidly increasing internal demand for the final product we would expect a substantial increase in the production of cotton cloth. And this is exactly what we observe in Figure 7. Consider, for instance, the trend of the auction prices of Kastamonu cotton cloth stamp tax-farm. From 1640's onward the trend indicates a continuous and very rapid expansion.

Dyehouse of Istanbul also exhibits a tremendous growth. To be precise, the type of cloth that was dyed in the Istanbul dye-houses is not yet documented. But İslamoğlu and Faroqhi argue that the expansion they observed in Adana cotton production was "clearly a function of increasing demand for cotton in Istanbul (1969: 413). At the end of the sixteenth

---

7. We noted above that cotton production in Adana region increased by 142% during the sixteenth century (İslamöglu and Faroqhi, 1979: 413).

Incorporation of the Middle East   369

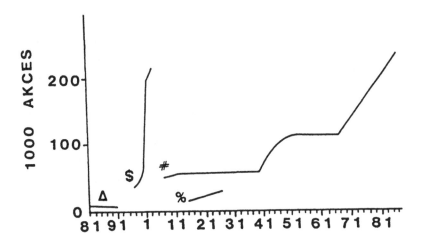

#Kastamonu stamp tax; $Istanbul dyehouse; %Edirne stamp tax for Bogasi;
△Aleppo kirpas-I ham (cotton cloth).

Figure 7 Cotton Cloth Production, 1581-1681

century, Istanbul, with a population of 700,000 to 1 million
inhabitants, had become perhaps the largest city in the world.
Between 1520-1530 and 1580-1600 the population of the city
more than doubled. As mentioned above, this was also a period
of inflation and worsening distribution of income. Under these
conditions it is natural that the impoverished masses should
demand the cheaper cotton products dyed in the city. I argue
that the tremendous expansion observed in Figure 7 reflects
these realities.

In Amid (Diyarbakir), also, we observed rapid expansion
between 1627 and 1639, probably reflecting the above mentioned arguments (Figure 5). Another rapid expansion is observed in the stamp tax-farm of Edirne, where a special cotton
cloth called "Bogasi" was stamped (Figure 7). The only
apparent exception to the otherwise general rule can be observed in Aleppo, where cotton cloth production seems to have
suffered between 1581 and 1591 (Figure 7). Reasons for this
idiosyncrasy are not known to me and need to be studied
specially.

III. Two Stages of Incorporation

We are now at a position to combine the evidence presented above and relate them to the questions of Immanuel Wallerstein. First, let us consider Question 2a, namely: "What were the processes, both within the Ottoman Empire and within the European world-economy, that account for this incorporation?"

The entire argument and the chain of events described so far would not have materialized if international trade between the Middle East and Europe had not proceeded under relatively free conditions. In this context it should be remembered that, with the so-called capitulations, Europeans enjoyed trading rights in the Middle East since Byzantine era, and these capitulations were renewed by the Ottomans (İnalcık, 1971).

Moreover, it must be fully understood that in the sixteenth and seventeenth centuries the foreign trade regimes of the two world-economies differed substantially: Whereas principles of mercantilism were applied in Europe, Ottomans pursued a policy of fiscalism and provisionism. To quote Mehmet Genç: "As a consequence of the system of provisionism the Ottoman state manipulated with only the exportation and usually did not interfere with importation. When the state did interfere with importation it was usually to *encourage* its volume, with fiscalist considerations" (1981). In short, the process of incorporation was initiated by the fact that, whereas Europe protected its economy through a policy of mercantilism, in the Middle East ancient forms of state intervention in the economy prevailed and European mercantilism was not effectively challenged.

Within this framework, as mentioned above, European penetration into the Ottoman markets was facilitated through Ottoman debasements, European chartered companies, low labor costs achieved through the widespread rural industries, technological improvements, and economies of scale. The overall result of these factors was a general change in the trade structure of the Middle East whereby the region began to export more and more raw materials and import manufactured products.

Incorporation of the Middle East   371

Yet the reader must be cautioned here against generalizations; the above pattern describes the fate of the silk and
woollen cloth industries in the period 1550-1650. There are
several exceptions to this pattern. First, as already mentioned,
the cotton sector does not fit into this pattern. Secondly, the
fate of the silk industry and perhaps also the mohair industry
began to follow a different path in the eighteenth century. All
of this relates to Question 2b: "Is the 'incorporation' a single
event or can different regions of the Empire—Rumelia, Anatolia, Syria, Egypt, etc.—be said to be incorporated at different
moments in time?"

In response to this question I would argue that incorporation was by no means a single event: Different sectors of the
Middle Eastern economy were incorporated at different times.
By implication, it can be argued that incorporation of regions
had to follow the incorporation of sectors. Put differently, if
the economy of Bursa was dominated by the silk industry and
Edirne by the cotton industry, these regions would be incorporated when the industries dominating their respective economies were incorporated.

What complicates matters further, however, is the fact that
incorporation was not a linear event. The Bursa silk industry,
for example, appears to have been totally incorporated by the
1650's. Yet Mehmet Genç has observed a definite recovery in
the performance of this industry during the eighteenth century.[8] A similar pattern appears to have existed for the Ankara
Mohair industry. Based on her data concerning the sale of
houses possessing a mohair workshop in Ankara, Soraiya
Faroqhi argues that the Ankara mohair industry was alive and
well during the later seventeenth century (n.d.). The cotton
industry constitutes, once again, an exception. It appears to
have developed in almost a linear fashion until the nineteenth
century.

---

8. Genç has also shown that the exponential growth observed in the auction
prices of the Istanbul Stamp tax-form in Figure 4 had continued in the eighteenth and
nineteenth centuries, whereby the "muaccele" increased from 2,518 kuruş in 1707 to
55,000 kuruş in 1826. A separate research is needed to explain this remarkable
performance of the Istanbul cloth industry.

I would argue that the model presented above can help us to explain this apparently cyclical development pattern. In the case of silk we are informed by Ralph Davis that the demand and supply patterns changed in the eighteenth century. To quote Davis:

> One important use for Levant silk, the making of silk buttons, was being reduced in the early decades of the century by the spreading popularity of cloth and metal buttons. But even within its own field of use, Levant silk was encountering competition from cheaper Bengal silk (1967: 138-39).

Thus, it is clear that the price scissors must have been relaxed in the eighteenth century Bursa silk market, allowing the Bursa silk clothmakers to have access to the raw material no more so eagerly purchased by their European rivals. Indeed, Davis demonstrates clearly how the English demand shifted almost entirely to the Indian raw silk, thus probably initiating the incorporation of the Bengalese economy in the eighteenth century.

As for the recovery of the mohair industry of Ankara, the picture is more complex. On one hand, Ralph Davis informs us that due to a change of fashion (substitution of cloth buttons by metal buttons) English imports of mohair yarn declined during the eighteenth century (1970: 200); on the other, we are informed by Faroqhi that mohair fabrics of Ankara were exported in sizeable quantities to France until the 1730's. This information confirms the model: We have a combination of lucky events whereby the European demand for the raw material is relaxed, on one hand, and, on the other, this demand continues for the final product. Under such circumstances the mohair cloth producers of Ankara must have enjoyed relatively cheap and abundant supply of mohair yarn as well as a healthy demand for their final output. A combination of these happy circumstances was no doubt behind Faroqhi's observation that the industry remained healthy as late as the late eighteenth century (n.d.).

A similar picture is provided to us by Halil İnalcık concerning the Ottoman cotton industries (1979-80). Taking full advan-

Incorporation of the Middle East   373

tage of abundant, cheap, and good-quality domestically produced raw cotton as well as a relatively advanced technology
and skilled labor,[9] this industry successfully resisted not only
European but also Indian competition. Participating fully in
the great epoch of the eighteenth century cotton cloth exportation from Asia to Europe, Ottoman industry flourished in this
period (İnalcık, 1979-80: 13).

The decline of this most successful of the Ottoman industries
can be traced to the later eighteenth century when English
cotton yarn and cloth began to enter into the Ottoman markets.
This process was then greatly enhanced through the well-
known technological achievements of the English industry and
eventually led to the total collapse of the Ottoman cotton
industry in the 1850's. That the Ottoman cotton industry lasted
until the 1850's is a phenomenon by itself. This resilience was
also partially due to the ruthless exploitation of the Ottoman
working class so well documented by Halil İnalcık (1979-80:
46).

To sum up: Incorporation was by no means a single event.
Different sectors were incorporated at different periods in
history. These differences occurred as a result of changing
supply and demand conditions prevailing in world trade. Basically, the eighteenth century appears to have been a period of
recovery for most Ottoman industries. Yet this era was also the
period when European world-economy fully grasped the opportunities offered to it by the world beyond the Mediterranean. Concentration of European energy in these transoceanic
regions appears to have blessed the Middle East with an "Indian Summer," that lasted until the nineteenth century when the
European economic might overwhelmed the Middle East together with the rest of the world. Thus, to answer Question 2 of
Wallerstein, I would argue that the process of incorporation of
the Middle East had definitely begun in the sixteenth century
and would have been completed at the end of the seventeenth

9. As late as the eighteenth century. Edirne dyehouses for cotton cloth were
famous for their secret techniques. French and Dutch entrepreneurs could learn these
techniques only by inviting, secretly, Greek artisans working in these workshops
(İnalcık, 1979-80: 6).

or, at the latest, by the middle of the eighteenth century, had European pressure not been channeled into transoceanic regions. Indeed, when the industrial revolution during the nineteenth century increased, the European demand for Ottoman raw materials and European exports of manufactured products to the Middle East reached unprecedented heights, the Middle East was once again fully hit by the storm, and all of the Ottoman industries, including cotton, were destroyed, thus completing the process of incorporation.

To conclude, I would suggest that the process of incorporation for the Middle East should be viewed as having two stages: the early incorporation of the period 1550-1650, and the full incorporation of the period 1830-1900, the period 1650-1830, in between, being one of recovery induced by the shifting of the European pressure particularly to the Indian Ocean.[10]

Appendix

Documentation

The data for the figures have been obtained from the following sources contained in the Prime Ministry Archives in Istanbul. Abbreviations used are as follows: MAD—Maliye Defterleri, also known as the Maliye'den Mudevver (Finance Ministry Registers); KK—Kamil Kepeci Collection; TD—Tapu Defterleri Collection.

Aleppo: MAD 7146/192-195; 198-199, 200-203 MAD 9834/55; MAD 912/4, MAD 919/8; MAD 300/215; MAD 4383/71; MAD 5604/25 TD 279/62-161, 1-18; MAD 2706/17, MAD 7345/1 MAD 3781/10, MAD 7589/20-26; MAD 9829/25, MAD 6241/6; MAD 4397/

---

10. The later part of the period 1650-1830 (that is, 1700-1830) appears to have witnessed an industrial recovery (Genç, 1975: 273-81). About the earlier part we have no statistics. That the period of full incorporation had to wait until the 1830's is suggested both by Mehmet Genç (1975) and by Halil İnalcık (1979-80: 54).

Incorporation of the Middle East   375

374; MAD 4972/211-226; MAD 4972/136; MAD 993-6;
MAD 9829/47, MAD 12795/14 MAD 22534/1; MAD
657/80; MAD 919/2

Amid: MAD 615/2; MAD 4860/100-206; MAD 1981/74
MAD 3776/39-160; MAD 4383/1-243; MAD 4397/78-
94 MAD 5604/45; MAD 657/130

Ankara: MAD 3985/122; MAD 4088/42-44; MAD 4341/
106

Bursa: MAD 4689/2; MAD 311/2-21; KK 5270; KK
5158/34; MAD 18201/6-20; MAD 6897/?; MAD 5984/
130-133 also; Dalsar (1960: 240, 270, 282, 345, 346.)

Edirne: MAD 4357/109-254, MAD 589/65, MAD 2477/9,
MAD 2957/84

Erzurum: TT 197/1-2; TT468/20 MAD 4383/160-188;
MAD 5604/36 MAD 15935/8; MAD 300/203-235; MAD
4444/26 MAD 3785/10-13; MAD 539/295, KK 2314/3
MAD 3185/8; MAD 615/70; MAD 3781/1

Istanbul: MAD 19354/1; MAD 657/49; MAD 2710/7;
MAD 3185/3; KK 2314/2; MAD 399/4151

Kastamonu: MAD 915/4-98; KK 5158/17-50; MAD 3305/
30 MAD 5270/29; MAD 1850/2-31; MAD
3985/98-107 MAD 5452/?; MAD 2874/47-53; MAD
398/39-76 MAD 5954/82; MAD 5984/130; MAD 16792/7

Kochisar: MAD 398/31-92; MAD 4684/T8; MAD 3985/
104-107 MAD 7299/197; MAD 5452/?; MAD 1850/2
MAD 3305/11-35; MAD 915/12; MAD 18201/5

Morea: MAD 2518/129-97; MAD 461/49-50; MAD 3902/15
MAD 2477/77-136, MAD 624/24; MAD 4357/1-240
MAD 3360/63; TD 884/ 276-491; MAD 624/36

Paleopatras: MAD 4357/1-362; MAD 3360/63-70; MAD
589/4-69; MAD 624/41-104; MAD 2477/70-146

Tokat: MAD 5655/5; MAD 5454/?; MAD 5655/7 MAD
3785/17; MAD 1479/7-36; MAD 4383/228 MAD
4619/5-60; MAD 5597/71; MAD 657/102 TD 287/70-
186; MAD 615/62; MAD 300/230 MAD 5604/38; MAD
4383/95-226; MAD 4619/2 MAD 5597/58; MAD
4397/52-60

376   *Murat Çizakça*

References

Akdag, Mustafa (1975). *Türk Halkinin Dirlik ve Duzenlik Kavgasi Celali Isyanlari.* Istanbul: Bilgi Yayinevi.

Braude, Benjamin (1979). "International Competition and Domestic Cloth in the Ottoman Empire, 1500-1650: A Study in Underdevelopment," *Review,* Win., II, 3, 437-51.

Brulez, Wilfrid (1970). "The Balance of Trade of the Netherlands," *Acta Historiae Neerlandica,* IV, 20-48.

Çizakça, Murat (1978). "Sixteenth-Seventeenth Century Inflation and the Bursa Silk Industry: A Pattern for Ottoman Industrial Decline?" unpubl. Ph.D. diss., Univ. of Pennsylvania.

Çizakça, Murat (1980). "Price History and the Bursa Silk Industry: A Study in Ottoman Industrial Decline, 1550-1650," *Journal of Economic History,* XL, 3, Sept., 533-50.

Dalsar, Fahri (1960). *Türk Sanayire Ticaret Tarihinde Bursa'da İpekçilik.* Istanbul: Istanbul University, Economics faculty publication.

Davis, Ralph (1967). *Aleppo and Devonshire Square.* London: Macmillan.

Davis, Ralph (1970). "English Imports from the Middle East," in M. A. Cook, ed., *Studies in the Economic History of the Middle East.* London: Oxford Univ. Press, 193-206.

Dillen, J. G. (1970). *Van Rijkdom en Regenten, Handbook tot de Economische en Sociale Geschiedenis van Nederland Tidjdens de Republiek.* 's Gravenhage: Martinus Nijhoff.

Dunlop, U. (1930). *Bronnen tot de Geschiedenis der Oostindishche Compagnie in Perzie,* Vol. I (1611-38). 's Gravenhage: Martinus Nijhoff.

Ergenc, Ozer (1975). "1600-1615 Yillari Arasinda Ankara Iktisadi Tarihine ait Arastirmalar," in O. Okyar, ed., *Türkiye Iktisat Tarihi Semineri.* Ankara: Hacettepe Univ. Publication No. 13.

Faroqhi, Suraiya (n.d.). "Mohair Manufacture and Mohair Workshops in 17th Century Ankara," in H. Sahillioğlu, ed., *Festschrift fur O.L. Barkan.* forthcoming.

Genç, Mehmet (1975). "Osmanli Maliyesinde Malikane Sistemi," in O. Okyar, ed., *Türkiye Iktisat Tarihi Semineri.* Ankara: Hacettepe Univ. Publication No. 13.

Genç, Mehmet (1981). "Foreign Trade and Government Policies Towards Industrialization in the Ottoman Empire, 1700-1850," unpubl. paper presented to the International Conference, *Problems and Policies of Industrialization in Opening Economies,* Aug. 24-28, Istanbul.

Glamann, Kristof (1958). *Dutch Asiatic Trade, 1620-1740.* The Hague: Martinus Nijhoff.

İnalcık, Halil (1971). "Imtiyāzāt, The Ottoman Empire," in *Encyclopaedia of Islam.* Leiden: Brill, III, 1179-89.

Incorporation of the Middle East 377

İnalcık, Halil (1979-80). "Osmanli Pamuklu Pazari, Hindustan ve Ingiltere: Pazar Rekabetinde Emek Maliyetinin Rolu," *METU Studies in Development* (special issue), 1-67.

İslamoğlu, Huri & Faroqhi, Suraiya (1979). "Crop Patterns and Agricultural Production Trends in Sixteenth Century Anatolia," *Review*, II, 3, Win., 401-36.

Meilink-Roelofsz, M.A.P. (1972-74). "The Earliest Relations Between Persia and the Netherlands," *Persica, Jaarboek van het Genootschap Netherland-Iran. Stichting voor Culturele Betrekkingen*, No. 4, 1-51.

Posthumus, N. W. (1934). *Nederlandische Prijsgeschiedenis*, deel 1. Leiden: Brill.

Rapp, Richard, T. (1975). "The Unmaking of the Mediterranean Trade Hegemony: International Trade Rivalry and the Commercial Revolution," *Journal of Economic History*, XXXV, 3, Sept., 499-525.

Sahillioğlu, Halil (1973-74). "Yeniceri Cuhasi ve Bayezid'in son Yillarinda Yeniceri Cuha Muhasebesi," *Guneydogu Avrupa Arastirmalari Dergisi*, Vols. II-III.

Sella, Domenico (1968). "The Rise and Fall of the Venetian Woollen Industry," in B. Pullan, ed., *Crisis and Change in the Venetian Economy in the 16th and 17th Centuries*. London: Methuen, 106-26.

Van Dam, Pieter (1939). *Beschrijvinge Van de Oost indische Compagnie*, Vol II, Pt. 3. 's Gravenhage: Martinus Nijhoff.

Wallerstein, Immanuel (1980). "The Ottoman Empire and the Capitalist World-Economy: Some Questions for Research," in O. Okyar & H. Inalcik, eds., *Social and Economic History of Turkey, 1071-1920*. Ankara: Hacettepe Univ. Press, 117-22.

Wätjen, Hermann (1909). *Die Niederlander in Mittelmeergebiet zur Zeit Ihrer Höchsten Mahstellung*. Berlin: Karl Curtius.

2

The Iranian Raw Silk Trade and European Manufacture in the Seventeenth and Eighteenth Centuries

Edmund Herzig

Introduction

From the sixteenth to the early eighteenth centuries much of the silk woven on European looms originated in Iran. This short paper will consider a few of the questions raised by the trade that brought silk from Iran's remote Caspian provinces to the manufacturing industry of early modern Europe. In Iran, the existence of expanding commercial commodity production for distant markets poses serious problems for accepted models of the Safavid state and economy. In Europe, the partial dependence of the silk industry on remote sources of supply had important repercussions: the geographical distribution of the industry was affected by access to raw silk supplies, while its growth was constrained both by the availability of supplies, and by the ability to procure raw materials of the standards required by an increasingly mechanized industry. Before turning to these questions, however, it is necessary to consider first the overall volume of the trade during the period.

The scale of trade

The regular export of Iranian raw silk to Europe began as early as the twelfth century with the establishment of a significant silk industry in central Italy. Lucca and later Florence and Venice all

Edmund Herzig

depended on the Levant for a part of their raw silk supplies, and until the eighteenth century most of the silk exported from the Levant came from Iran. Raw silk was produced in many parts of Iran, but the most important regions for the export to the West were the provinces to the south and west of the Caspian Sea — in particular, Shirvan, Karabagh and above all Gilan.

At first the volume of trade was small: individual consignments were usually of only a few bales, [1] and the annual purchases of even the major buyers did not reach one hundred bales. In the fifteenth century Europe's part in the Levant silk trade was still minor; a large proportion went to the industry of Ottoman Bursa, also the principal market of the time. In the course of the sixteenth century the situation changed, as Aleppo replaced Bursa as the centre of the raw silk trade, and Europeans became the biggest buyers of Iranian raw silk. In the last years of the sixteenth century Venice, the greatest but by no means the only European nation involved, was importing nearly 1,500 bales per annum. Steensgaard, the only historian to have made a serious attempt to calculate the volume of trade, reckoned that in the early seventeenth century Europe imported around 500,000 lb (or some 2,200 bales) of Iranian raw silk. [2]

In the seventeenth century the sources become more numerous, but arriving at a total for the volume of trade is even more difficult, because Iranian raw silk was being brought to Europe via a number of different routes. The principal channel remained the Levant, but there was no longer a single centre. From around 1620 Aleppo faced a growing challenge from Izmir (Smyrna), and by the second half of the century the latter was handling most silk exports,

---

[1] Quantities are given in bales — the unit in which silk was traded. Bales varied greatly in size, depending on the pack animal that was carrying them. Here a standard bale of about 105 kg. has been adopted.

[2] STEENSGAARD, NIELS, *The Asian trade revolution of the seventeenth century,* Chicago, 1973, pp. 160- 162.

though it never succeeded in completely replacing Aleppo. In the second quarter of the eighteenth century, when Iranian silk supplies became sporadic, the merchants turned to Syrian silk, and Aleppo again emerged as the principal centre. Nor were Aleppo and Izmir the only outlets for Iranian silk; occasionally, when Mediterranean shipping was particularly threatened by war or piracy, silk was carried by the overland route through Bursa to Istanbul and across the Balkan penisular to the Adriatic.

Other routes were opened that bypassed the Levant altogether. In the 1620's to 1640's the English and Dutch East India Companies brought considerable quantities of Iranian raw silk to Europe via the Cape route from the Persian Gulf. Then, towards the end of the century, the Russian government agreed to allow the transit of Iranian raw silk from the Caspian port of Astrakhan, along the Russian waterways to the Baltic or White Sea where Dutch vessels loaded it for shipment to Amsterdam.

Reliable data are available for only one of these routes — the Cape route used by the East India Companies — but this was never the most important. For the others, scattered and dubious figures have to be supplemented by the estimates of various more or less informed travellers, diplomats and merchants. The estimates vary wildly — for Iran's total silk export, from 40,000 to 1,800 bales — but they make it possible to arrive at an order of magnitude for the trade, if not at any precise quantification.

The highest estimates, such as the 40,000 just mentioned and the 34,000 bales suggested by the English adventurer Robert Sherley, are unsupported by evidence, and can safely be dismissed. The most commonly cited estimate is Chardin's 22,000 bales (c. 1670) for total Iranian production, [3] but although Chardin is generally reliable on Iran, he seems to have based his figure on that of Olea-

---

[3] CHARDIN, JEAN, *Voyages de Chardin...*, ed. L. LANGLES, 10 vols., Paris, 1811, vol. 4. pp. 162-163.

Edmund Herzig

rius some thirty years before [4] — simply adding two thousand bales
to allow for continuing growth. In fact neither Olearius nor Chardin was personally involved in the raw silk trade, and the estimates
made by those who were are more trustworthy.

The first, in 1618, was that of Barker and Pettus, two English
East India Company agents serving in Iran. They put total silk production (excluding the north-eastern province of Khorasan whose
entire output was consumed locally or exported to India) at
168,000 *man-i shah* (9,300 bales) of which they believed two-thirds,
6,200 bales, was exported to the West. [5] This is a great deal lower
than Chardin's estimate, but high compared with Steensgaard's calculation, especially since Barker and Pettus believed the output
was currently 1,700 bales lower than usual because of war damage
in the silk producing provinces. It seems likely that the Englishmen, like Chardin, erred on the generous side; 1618 was only the
second year of the East India Company's involvement in Iran, so
they may have succumbed to the tendency to exaggeration typical
of the first E.I.C. agents in Iran. Certainly the estimate made by the
Dutch agent, Overschie, in 1637 is much lower, and as Overschie
was probabliy the most experienced European to volunteer an opinion on the subject, his estimate merits serious attention. He calculated that Iran produced a total of only 2,800 bales of silk, 2,100 of
these coming from Gilan. Of the total, 300 bales went to the Turkish market and 1,000 to the domestic industry, leaving 1,500 bales
for export to Europe. Knowledgeable though he was, Overschie
certainly was not a disinterested observer. He was then attempting
to secure for the Dutch East India Company a monopoly in the export of Iranian raw silk to Europe, and his estimate was made in a
report written to persuade his directors that this objective had vir-

[4] OLEARIUS, ADAM, *Vermehrte newe Beschreigung der Muskowitschen und Persischen Reise (1)*, SCHLESWIG, 1656 (reprint Tubingen 1971), p. 601.
[5] FERRIER, RONALD W., "An English view of the Persian trade in 1618", *Journal of the Economic and Social History of the Orient*, vol. 19, part. 2, 1976, pp. 198-199.

tually been achieved. According to Overschie, in the previous year the Dutch had bought a thousand bales and the English 373, leaving only just over a hundred for the Armenians to export via the Levant. [6] But the Company directors were not convinced, and pointed out with unconcealed annoyance that half the silk reaching the Netherlands was still coming via the Levant, where English, French and Italian merchants were finding no shortage of supplies from Iran. [7] It therefore seems certain that Overschie seriously underestimated the scale of trade.

Two other estimates of Iran's total export merit consideration. In the 1660's and 1670's several Armenian silk merchants — the people best qualified of all to talk about the silk trade — came to the Russian court to negotiate the opening of the route through Russia to the silk trade. The delegates several times stated that the annual Iranian silk export was 4,000 loads or 8,000 bales. [8] Some fifty years later, when Peter the Great was preparing for the invasion of Iran's Caspian provinces, an Indian merchant resident in Astrakhan and active in the Caspian trade told Peter's officers that Iran exported 9,000 bales of raw silk to Turkey and the Mediterranean. [9] The fact that these two estimates from independent and well-informed sources are so close certainly lends them credibility, but the Armenians, at least, had a clear motive for giving a high estimate, as they were trying to persuade the Russian government of the enormous customs revenue they would receive by diverting the trade. Despite the large discrepancy between Overschie's 2,800 bales and the eight or nine thousand suggested by the native merchants, these figures have to be taken as outer limits for the investigation.

[6] DUNLOP, HENDRIK, *Bronnen tot de geschiedenis der Oostindisce Compagnie in Perzie,* s'Gravenhage, 1930, p. 612.

[7] *ibid.,* pp. 657, 665-666.

[8] *Armyano-russkie otnosheniya v XVII veke,* ed. V.A. PARSAMYAN, Erevan, 1953, pp. 37, 39, 46, 55.

[9] SOIMONOV, FEDOR I., *Opisanie Kaspiiskago Morya ...,* Saint Petersburg, 1763, p. 108.

Edmund Herzig

The only relatively full series of statistics on the silk trade are for the Dutch and English East India Companies' exports. In the 1620's their average combined export was 670 bales. In the 1630's the figure rose to nearly 1,000 bales, but fell back to around 600 bales in the 1640's, and never amounted to more than a few undred bales thereafter. The largest export was achieved in 1637/8, when the two Companies took 1,873 bales. [10] Figures for the Levant route are very sparse for this period. In 1620 the Venetian consul in Aleppo reported that 4,000 bales had reached the city that year, of which the English had bought 1,400. [11] In 1621, however the English exported only 118,000 great pounds (760 bales). [12] The customs registers of Iskanderun (Aleppo's sea port) indicate an even lower level, giving the total exports by all nations as:

1624/5	544 bales
1626/7	945 bales
1627/8	611 bales
1628/9	1801 bales [13]

It would probably be a mistake to attach too much significance to these figures, since in 1624/5 the port of Iskanderun (Alexandretta) was closed for more than six months after an attack by pirates, and the mid — 1620's were generally difficult years for Aleppo's trade, with the routes interrupted by war. In any case a substantial part of silk exports may already have been passing through Izmir.

Later in the century the data are somewhat richer. In circa 1675 a silk merchant reckoned that Izmir exported 2,900 bales [14] of

[10] SEENSGAARD, *op. cit.,* p. 395 (using a bale of 100 kg.).

[11] *ibid.,* p. 182, DUNLOP, *op. cit.,* p. 11.

[12] DAVIS, RALPH, "England and the Mediterranean 1570- 1670", *Essays in the Economic and Social History of Tudor England,* ed. F.J. FISHER, Cambridge, 1961, p. 125.

[13] KALDY-NAGY, Gy. "Dannye k istorii levantinskoi torgovli v nachale XVII stoletiya", *Vostochnye istochniki po istorii Yugo- vostochnoi i Tsentral'noi Evropy,* vol., 2, ed. A.S. Tveritinova, Moscow, 1969, pp. 327-330.

[14] SAVARY, JACQUES (the elder), *Le parfait negociant,* Paris, 1742-49, vol. 1, part 2, book

The Iranian raw silk trade and European manufacture

Iranian raw silk each year, the English buying 1,000 of these. In the early eighteenth century another estimate put Izmir's export at 2,000 bales, [15] while at the same time Aleppo was said to be handling some 1,400 bales. [16] Scattered figures are available in the Marseilles and London customs records for French silk imports from Izmir, and for English imports from the whole of the Levant. The table below gives these figures converted into 105 kg bales:

	French imports from Izmir[17]	English imports from the Levant[18]
1663 & 1669		1,700
1697-1700		1,400
1701-10	300	1,300
1711-20	300	1,800 D
		2,000 U
1721-30	40	1,600 D
		1,700 U

These figures indicate that the English were much bigger importers of Levant silk than the French — but unfortunately they leave out as much as they include. There are no figures for the Dutch (who were also major importers), or for the Armenians (who

5, pp. 410- 413. He specified the weight of these bales, and they are considerably larger than the 105 kg. bale adopted as standard. In 105 kg. bales the total would be around 4,000.

[15] Pitton de Tournefort, Joseph, *Relation d'un voyage du Levant*, Paris, 1717, vol. 2, pp. 438, 497. Again this is a very large bale. The total is equivalent to some 3,600 105 kg. bales.

[16] Archives du Ministère des Affaires Etrangères, Paris, *Correspondence Politique, Perse*, vol. 5, f. 22.

[17] Ulker, Necmi, *The Rise of Izmir 1688-1740*, unpublished PhD dissertation, University of Michigan, 1974, pp. 83-84. The trade figures given here may be too low, as on p. 116 Ulker cites a different source giving values only for French imports from Izmir that are some three times as great as those given on p. 83.

[18] Based on Anderson, Sonia, *An English consul in Turkey. Paul Rycant at Smyrna, 1667-1678*, Oxford, 1989, p. 160; Davis, Ralph, *Aleppo and Devonshire Square*, London, 1967, pp. 42, 139; and Ulker, *op. cit.*, pp. 86-87. Where they differ they are distinguished by "D" and "U".

Edmund Herzig

were shipping silk to Europe themselves in chartered vessels). Moreover the data cover imports to only two of Europe's major ports. To construct anything approaching a complete picture we would also need the figures for Venice, Livorno and Amsterdam. As it stands, the table represents no more than a large fraction of the total European import of Iranian raw silk from the Levant.

In the later seventeenth and early eighteenth centuries the Cape route had declined, never taking more than a few hundred bales a year in spite of sporadic attempts to revive it. The route through Russia on the other hand grew considerably in import-ance, especially in the 1690's when the Nine Years War inter-rupted the Levant route. Numerous individual consignments of silk recorded in the Russian archives suggest a vigorous trade, but the information is too incomplete to build up annual totals. [19] Con-temporary commentators estimated the volume of silk exported via Russia at one thousand bales a year or more. [20]

Lack of firm data has made it impossible to arrive at a definitive account of the scale of Iranian raw silk exports, but the available in-formation suggests a vigorous and expanding trade. In the early six-teenth century Europe imported only a few hundred bales bales a year. By the early seventeenth century the figure was already more than 2,000 bales, possibly a great deal more. By the late seventeenth and early eighteenth centuries the volume may well have been as great as 5,000 bales, and even the 8,000 suggested by the Armenian merchants is not impossible.

[19] KUKANOVA, NINA, G., *Ocherki po istorii russko-iranskikh torgovykh otnoshenii v XVII-pervoi polovine XIX veka*, Saransk, 1977, pp. 86, 108-110, tables 1-2.
[20] GLAMANN, KRISTOF, *Dutch-Asiatic trade 1620-1740*, Copehagen/The Hague, 1958, p. 126; HANWAY, JONAS, *An Historical Account of the British Trade over the Caspian sea ...*, London, 1753, vol. 2, p. 31.

Silk and the Iranian economy

For Safavid Iran the silk trade was a lifeline. The returns in European silver coin were the only significant source of precious metal, so without silk, the mints would have had no silver to strike coin, and the constant trade deficit with India would rapidly have drained the country of currency. Historians agree on the importance of the silk trade to the Iranian national economy, but the idea of fast-expanding commercial production of raw silk to feed the growing export trade sits very uncomfortably beside accepted notions about the Safavid economy. The agrarian sector is generally depicted as static and geared to subsistence, virtually isolated from the commercial life that animated the towns, and prevented from developing by the grip of exploitative and shortsighted absentee landlords whose only concern was to extract any surplus for their own immediate profit.

The production of raw silk was carried out in villages by peasants who also raised food crops. There was only one silk harvest a year, and from autumn until early spring there was no activity at all in sericulture. Intensive labour was only required for a short period in early summer when, men, women and children all worked together to feed the silk worms several times a day. The silk was wound off the cocoons by a process that required the labour of only one person, and the skeins were then baled together and exported without further treatment. Silk production required very little capital outlay: the eggs were provided from stock; the worms were raised in easily constructed sheds; the winding off process required a large metal basin (the only expensive item) in which the cocoons were softened in hot water, and a simple hand or pedal-powered wooden wheel onto which the silk filaments were wound.

The nature of the production process placed certain obvious constraints on the expansion of production: peasants could not go over to a monoculture of silk because of the seasonal nature of the

Edmund Herzig

activity; and the availability of mulberry leaves to feed the worms, and of labour, limited the level of production within the sericultural season. There is nothing, however, to suggest that the upper limits of capacity were reached in the Safavid period, and such growth as was achieved seems to have come from intensification in the silk-producing regions. There is no evidence that raw silk supplies were diverted from domestic industry to export markets, and attempts to extend sericulture into new regions did not meet with success. This leaves open the questions of how Iranian agrarian production was able to respond positively to the growing demand of the distant European market.

Unfortunately, very little is known about the processes of procurement and marketing in the silk trade. In the Levant, European merchants bought raw silk primarily from the Armenian merchants of New Julfa (the Christian suburb of Isfahan), who transported the silk from Iran. The Armenians' predominance in the trade dates from the end of the sixteenth century, and was considered by contemporaries to be a result of their employment as commercial agents by Shah Abbas I (1587-1629). The Safavid ruling class — the shahs, tribal khans, senior state officials and local nobility — extracted a large share of all surplus agricultural production as rent or revenue. Silk, as a product with a ready market and a high cash price, was a particularly desirable commodity, so it is not surprising to find that the political élite had long taken an active interest in the silk trade. Throughout the Safavid period merchants bought a large part of their silk stocks from shahs, provincial governors, and lesser landholders. In Gilan (the most important province for silk), the main beneficiaries until the late sixteenth century were the local rulers, who retained a degree of independence from the central government, but in 1592 Abbas I crushed the last vestiges of Gilan's independence and a few years later incorporated the province into the crown lands. It is from about this time that the Armenians (his preferred commercial agents) achieved a virtual monop-

The Iranian raw silk trade and European manufacture

oly of the export trade. In 1619 Abbas went a step further and de-
clared the whole of Iran's silk export a royal monopoly, pushing up
prices, playing off the Armenians against the East India Companies' agents, and using his control of the silk trade to threaten the
revenue of the Ottoman Sultan. The Shah's dominance of Iran's
trade appeared so complete to one Italian traveller that he described him as "the greatest, rather the only, merchant in his kingdom". [21] Even after the monopoly was discontinued following
Abbas's death in 1629, the crown still maintained a large share in
the silk trade (over 1,000 bales p.a. in 1634).

The political élite's excessive control and exploitation of economic resources has often been identified as an obstacle to the development of commercial capital and an independent bourgeoisie
in pre-modern Iran, the silk trade being cited as a prime example,
but the flourishing silk export trade of the seventeenth century
hardly supports this view, and the involvement of the crown and
ruling class certainly did not exclude the private commercial sector. Raw silk was sold in local towns by private individuals, described by European travellers as the country people (which probably refers to small local traders rather than the producers themselves). In addition, the major silk merchants went or sent their
agents to Gilan to buy silk in the villages at first hand. It seems
likely, though conclusive evidence is lacking, that they contracted
for the silk before the harvest by making a down payment, and collected the silk and paid the balance in the summer. A point on
which the sources are unanimous is the full monetization of the silk
trade; no-one sold silk without receiving its price in cash. As a result,
in Gilan silver coin was abundant even in the villages, a sharp contrast with most other provinces. The Rasht mint existed almost
solely for the purpose of recoining imported foreign silver into
Iranian currency for use in the silk trade. [22]

[21] VALLE, PIETRO DELLA, *Viaggi*, , Brighton, 1843, vol. 2, p. 41.
[22] SOIMONOV, *op. cit.*, , pp. 189-190.

Edmund Herzig

The big silk merchants were rich and powerful men, each exporting several hundred bales a year. The enormous wealth of the Julfa merchants dispels the notion that commercial capital in Iran was weak. Apart from their own capital, silk merchants won investment from the majority Muslim community (a 1731 partnership contract records an investment of 900 *tumans* by an Iranian nobleman), and even from as far away as Aleppo. [23] Nor were the merchants as politically powerless as has often been supposed. In Abbas I's reign the Julfa Armenians brought effective pressure to bear on the Shah by threatening to hold up the returns from the Levant, and the suspension of the monopoly after his death was partly in response to the representations of prominent silk merchants. An early eighteenth century Russian account draws attention to the great power of the silk lobby in Gilan, where the royal governor could do nothing that threatened the interests of the local merchants and élite. [24] Even under the monopoly, royal control of the silk trade was not complete. There is no evidence, for example, that it was effective outside the crown provinces of Gilan and Mazandarano. The other important silk growing areas, Shirvan and Karabagh, were administered indirectly through governors who appointed and controlled their own officials, so it is unlikely that the monopoly was enforced there. Even in Gilan it did not result in the complete suspension of private commerce, which was permitted on payment of high duties to the crown. [25] Even the East India Companies were allowed to buy from private suppliers when crown stocks failed. [26] Nor did the monopoly itself represent a complete break with existing commercial practices — the crown

[23] KHACHIKYAN, Sh. L., *Nor Jughayi Hay vacharakanutyune...*, Erevan, 1988, p. 121; MASTERS, B., *The Origins of western economic dominance in the Middle East*, new York, 1988, pp. 62-63. A *tuman* was worth about £ 3 10s.

[24] SOIMONOV, *op. cit.*, pp. 189-190.

[25] DELLA VALLE, *op. cit.*, vol. 2, p. 59.

[26] MELINK- ROELOFSZ, M.A.P., "The earliest relations between Persia and the Netherlands", *Persica*, vol 6, 1972-1974, pp. 1-50.

agents found they could only secure the silk harvest by contracting in advance and sending into the villages to pay for the harvest in cash.

The admittedly sparse evidence on the silk trade does not suggest that there was any essential conflict of interest between the merchants and the Safavid ruling class. On the contrary, in some ways the involvement of the latter significantly facilitated trade by gathering and concentrating a substantial part of silk production as revenue, and by the credit it extended to merchants who sold this silk in the Levant either on a commission basis, or against payment deferred until their return. The answer to the question of how Iran was able to substantially increase its output and export seems to lie in the cooperation of mercantile and landholding élites in a system of commercial production whose incentives penetrated as far as the individual producer.

Iranian silk in European industry

For the seventeenth century European silk industry imports from Iran represented a substantial share of raw material supplies. No other Asian source compared with Iran until the mid — eighteenth century. From Bengal, for example, between 1669 and 1718 the Dutch and English East India Companies imported around 1,000 bales per year, and this was several times the level of imports of Chinese raw silk. [27] Comparisons with Europe's own sources of raw silk are more difficult since much was consumed locally, and quantities never recorded in trade figures. For Sicily, however, one of seventeenth century Europe's major raw silk producers, Aymard has suggested an annual export of some five to six hundred

[27] PRAKASH, Om, *The Dutch East India Company and the economy of Bengal,* Princeton, 1985, pp. 217-218; CHAUDHURI, KIRTI N., *The trading world of Asia and the East India Company 1660-1760,* Cambridge, 1978, pp. 533-535; GLAMANN, *op. cit.,* pp. 112-131 *passim.*

Edmund Herzig

thousand Messina pounds, roughly 1,500 to 1,800 bales. [28] Figures
for European consumption are no easier to come by, although in
the mid — eighteenth century Lyons, Europe's greatest single
manufacturing centre, was said to consume 6,000 bales annually. [29]
By either of these indicators, Iran was a very significant supplier to
European industry in this period.

Although Iranian raw silk was imported into Italy, France, Holland and England, it was more important in the northern than
southern countries. The French and Italian industries had easy access to supplies in Sicily, southern France and mainland Italy, and
merely supplemented these with imports from the Levant. England and Holland had no such convenient sources, and the development of their silk industries was more closely connected with
that of their overseas trade. The birth of the English industry has
often been attributed to the influx of protestant refugees from Europe — from Flanders in the late sixteenth century, and from
France after 1685 — but another important factor was the large-
scale importation of raw silk by the Levant Company, which began
in the early seventeenth century when spices could no longer be
profitably imported from the Levant. [30] Later in the century it was
again England and Holland that became involved in the import of
Iranian, Bengal and Chinese silk via the Cape route. It should have
been an advantage to have diverse sources of supply, but in fact it
was difficult to control the level of imports from producing areas
over which the Europeans exercised no direct control, and to
which they were linked by long and vulnerable sea and land routes.
News travelled too slowly, even to the Levant, for information
about market conditions in Europe to be put to effective use in

---

[28] AYMARD, M., "Commerce et production de la soie sicilienne aux XVIe et XVIIe
siecles", *Melanges d'Archeologie et d'Histoire,* vol. 77, part 2, 1965, p. 640.

[29] *ibid.,* p. 610. The total can be broken down by country of origin of the supply: Sicily 1,600 bales; Italy 1,500; the Levant 1,400; Spain 300; Provence, Languedoc, Dau-
phine 1,200.

[30] DAVIS, *Aleppo,* pp. 134-135.

Asia. Throughout the seventeenth century the unpredictable interaction of imports from various sources caused frequent gluts and
shortages on the European market. As a result prices, and hence
profits, in the silk trade were wildly variable — prices fluctuated
more in London than in Aleppo. [31] These diffuculties were generally short-lived, but the Nine Years War of 1689-1697 showed up
the precarious position of the English and Dutch industries. Levant trade was severely disrupted, causing a serious shortage. This
prompted significantly increased orders by the East India Companies for Bengal silk, but political circumstances disrupted supplies there as well. As a result of this double failure, looms were left
standing idle for want of silk. [32]

In the long run Europe did benefit from the diversity of supplies, and when the real crisis for Iranian silk came in the decades
after 1720, with the disintegration of the Safavid state and the Turkish and Russian invasions of Iran, the shortfall in Levant silk was
largely compensated for by increased imports from Bengal and
China. The vulnerability of an industry based on raw material supplies that were outside Eurpean control was a constant incentive to
discover new sources of raw silk, or to increase control over existing ones.

The reliance of the English and Dutch industries on Asian silks
had another far-reaching effect. By the later seventeenth century
silk manufacture in Europe was beginning to be mechanized, with
Italy and France leading the way. In particular the spread of the organzine silk throwing mill led to the exclusive use of that yarn for
the warp threads in all high-quality textiles. England and Holland,
obliged to raise their own standards, had to import increasing
quantities of Italian yarn and use their Asian silks for the wefts of
textiles, and for articles such as ribbons and buttons.

Even after the introduction of the organzine mill into England

[31] *ibid.,* pp. 164-167; PRAKASH, *op. cit.,* p. 209 note 40.
[32] PRAKASH, *op. cit.,* p. 217; GLAMANN, *op. cit.,* p. 126; CHAUDHURI, *op. cit.,* p. 348.

Edmund Herzig

in the second decade of the eighteenth century the dependence on
Italian silk continued; since Levant, Bengal and Chinese raw silks
were not suitable for the new process, Italian raw silk had to be imported. This was partly because of the low quality of Asian silks, but
even more because of their lack of uniformity. [33] Europeans gradually phased out the lower grades in the later seventeenth and early
eighteenth centuries, [34] but even with the higher grades the problems persisted. The Armenian silk merchants were notorious for
mixing low and high grade silks in a single bale to defraud their customers, and Levant silk merchants complained constantly about
the quality of supplies. [35] Furthermore, the Iranian producers
wound the silk in skeins too large to be used on the organzine mills.
That these problems need not have been insurmountable is shown
by the short-lived direct trade established by the English in Gilan
in the 1740's. Their agents found it possible to procure short skeins
of uniformly good silk, [36] but such control could not be exercised
by the Levant merchants buying through Armenian intermediaries. In Bengal, where Europeans were in direct contact with the
producers, the two East India companies made numerous attempts
(with only mixed success) to control quality, even introducing European reeling machines. [37] Some Chinese silks could be substituted for Italian in organzine throwing, but again quality control
was always a problem. [38] In the nineteenth century mechanized reeling was successfully introduced to China — not to increase productivity or reduce costs (it did neither) but to produce raw silk of
the uniform quality required by mechanized industry. [39] Iran's ex-

[33] DAVIS, *Aleppo,* pp. 136-137; CHAUDHURI, *op. cit.,* pp. 346-347.
[34] PRAKASH, *op. cit.,* p. 208; DAVIS, *Aleppo,* p. 140; CHAUDHURI, *op. cit.,* p. 349.
[35] ANDERSON, *op. cit.,* pp. 162-163; ULKER, *op. cit.,* pp. 89-96.
[36] HANWAY, *op. cit.,* vol 2, p. 16.
[37] PRAKASH, *op. cit.,* pp. 111-117; CHAUDHURI, *op. cit.,* p. 350.
[38] *ibid.,* pp. 349-350.
[39] LI, LILLIAN M., *China's silk trade: traditional industry in the modern world, 1842-1937,*
Cambridge (Mass.), 1981, pp. 29-30.

perience was similar: it was not until European companies introduced mechanized reeling in the nineteenth century that Iranian silks again began to play a role in world trade. In the long run the mechanization of the industry dictated that mere access to raw material supplies was no longer sufficient, control over production was also required.

Conclusions

In the long term the trade in Iranian raw silk may appear as no more than an interlude, when European manufacture had outgrown its own raw silk supplies, but before it had established firm control over overseas sources. The final interruption of Iranian supplies through political circumstances probably only hastened their departure from an industry that had already discovered alternative sources, and could no longer tolerate the lack of control over quality and quantity that the long overland route to Gilan entailed. At the time, however, the trade was of immense importance, and was recognized as such by contemporaries. For Iran the trade was vital to the country's monetary and financial stability, and, as this paper has suggested, was responsible for the beginnings of commercial agricultural production (even though those beginnings came to an abrupt halt with the collapse of the Safavid state in the eighteenth century). In Europe, the large-scale import of Iranian raw silk allowed the industry to grow and spread faster than it could otherwise have done in a period before other sources of supply were available. The success of the maritime nations, England and Holland, in securing access to Iranian raw silk gave their textile industries a significant boost. The dependence on Iranian silk may have left them vulnerable to the uncertainties of extended lines of supply, but without it Northern Europe's silk textile industry could hardly have got off to such an early start.

3

The Gender Division of Labor in the Production of Textiles in Eighteenth-Century, Rural Pennsylvania (Rethinking the New England Model)

Adrienne D. Hood

The role of textiles as one of the driving forces of British industrialization has been well studied. Scholars have examined the cotton, woolen and linen branches of the industry, regional variation, details of new technology, and the impact of mechanization on handloom weavers.[1] What has not been so well analyzed is the American experience. Here the research emphasis has been on the transition to industrialization during the post colonial years using New England as a model for the period leading up to this change.[2] The general acceptance of this model has inhibited new investigations into early American textile production with the result that crucial pieces of the industrialization puzzle are missing.

This essay examines the gender division of labor in domestic cloth manufacture in eighteenth-century, rural Pennsylvania to challenge the broad application of the New England experience. It demonstrates that factors other than technology influenced the structure of the textile sector and that there were distinct regional and temporal differences in how the work was organized. These nuances must be recognized before we can appreciate fully the nature and dynamics of industrialization. They are also essential to our understanding of domestic production in early America and the impact of mechanization on local communities.

The studies that do explore the American textile industry were produced by business, economic and labor historians and appeared in two waves, the first, during the early decades of this century and the second, in the last twenty years. The early group was composed of scholars who either sought to understand the evolving mechanization that underlay industrial development, or to shed light on the daily activities of early Americans, particularly women. Writers like William Bagnall, Perry Walton and Arthur Cole concentrated their intellectual efforts on describing the technological history of textile manufacture as it developed in the United States.[3] Rolla Tryon and Victor Clark looked more broadly at all industries, but concentrated substantial portions of their work on cloth production.[4] Less concerned with technology, Alice Morse Earle, Elizabeth Buel and Carl Holliday focused on domestic life and Edith Abbott wrote about women in industry.[5]

The New England Model

It is the interpretations contained in these works, particularly Tryon, Abbott and Earle, that have permeated our subsequent understanding of domestic textile

538   journal of social history   spring 1994

manufacture in the colonial period. Broadly speaking, they suggested that until the advent of technological change in the late eighteenth century, one could look at hand cloth manufacture at any time, or in any region, and find a similar situation. Using New England as the representative example they argued that early American, rural women made some or all of the cloth required by their largely self-sufficient households. This characterization has had a major impact on our understanding of American industrialization and continues to do so as demonstrated by the second wave of scholarly investigation into the topic.

Drawing on the observations contained in these works recent American historians have concentrated their analyses on the period of the transformation from domestic to factory textile production in the late eighteenth and early nineteenth centuries. Topics have focused on the impact of changing technology on workers, the importance of immigrant labor, alterations in social relations and the recruitment of a viable work force.[6] In addition, there has been an increasing focus on the declining status of women as spinning and weaving moved out of the home and into the factory. This latter interpretation relies heavily on the New England model of the earlier generation of historians.[7]

Unfortunately, however, there have been almost no new investigations of American textile manufacture for the period preceding and leading up to these decades of change that reflect the concerns of social history or draw on the new methodologies available to historians.[8] As a result, our understanding remains little altered from the interpretation in Rolla Tryon's seminal work, written in 1917, Household Manufactures in the United States, 1640–1860. More particularly, historians have overlooked several important aspects of early American domestic cloth production: that it grew out of European craft traditions; that spinning and weaving are distinct processes often done by different people; and that there were regional variations in the structure of the craft. The analysis of eighteenth-century, rural Pennsylvanian cloth manufacture that follows shows that the typicality of New England must be reassessed and the difference factored in to our understanding of the consequences of industrialization on American society.

The Need for Re-evaluation

Although colonial historians have not thoroughly reexamined eighteenth-century textile manufacture, recent micro studies suggest that it was a far more complex system than previously thought. Drawing on detailed information contained in the journal of Maine midwife, Martha Ballard, Laurel Thatcher Ulrich argued that in late eighteenth-century New England, weaving and spinning were an integral part of the informal female economy of neighborly exchange and reciprocity. Many households had looms, even more had spinning wheels and young women wove most productively before they were married. That was when a loom might be acquired and daughters would learn to make cloth for their parents, or possibly their own, future families. They might also weave for neighbors in exchange for payment of some kind.[9] This part of Ulrich's argument matches the pervasive interpretation of colonial cloth production: that early American, rural women made much of the cloth required by their families.

But as Ulrich moved back in time, to the late seventeenth and early eighteenth century, she found that cloth making in New England looked quite different. Fewer households had looms, and textile production seemed to belong to an artisan tradition that divided the work along gender lines, with females doing the spinning and skilled male craftsmen responsible for weaving and finishing the cloth.[10] Thus it would seem that the traditional model is not fully applicable even to New England.

Further challenge to the prevalent concept that women wove their household textiles can be found in Jean Russo's examination of the rural Chesapeake economy in the first half of the eighteenth century. Her study of Talbot County, Maryland, demonstrates that contrary to traditional interpretations, specialized craftsmen were firmly rooted in the community and played an integral part in an economy based on a system of local exchange of goods and services.[11] Weavers comprised approximately 7 percent of all artisans from 1690 to 1760 and despite a decline of members in many crafts, the number of cloth makers remained comparatively stable over the period.[12]

Ulrich's and Russo's analyses suggest that in the earlier decades of the settlement of New England and the Chesapeake cloth production was done by skilled male artisans. At some point in New England the gender division of labor changed; more work must be done on the second half of the eighteenth century in the Chesapeake to determine what occurred there. But how do the middle colonies compare?

Pennsylvania as a Test

Pennsylvania's craft traditions have not been studied in the same depth as those of New England, but because its agricultural base and early settlement are so different, it is important to do so in order to test the applicability of the New England model. Not only was this middle colony settled later, but its early immigrants also came from more diverse ethnic and religious backgrounds and established different settlement patterns than their northern counterparts. Moreover, Chester County, which is the focus of this study, has an excellent documentary base with which to explore issues of artisan production.

Chester County

My analysis is drawn from a sampling of 825 of the 5,500 Chester County probate records between 1714 and 1809 that included all records for each of five periods (1715–1718; 1734–1737; 1754–1757; 1773–1776; and 1792–1795); it is further supplemented by a data base of 115 probated loom owners. When combined with available tax list data (beginning with the earliest comprehensive list of 1765) and augmented with evidence in account books, newspapers and court records one can obtain a more complete picture of cloth production than hitherto possible. What we see is a strong European influence on the structure of the local cloth making sector. Artisans combined their craft work with farming,

540   journal of social history   spring 1994

experienced a life cycle similar to their European counterparts, divided the work along gender lines, and relied on an extended labor force. The major change over the period was not in the gender division of tasks as it appears to be in New England, but a shift from the use of bound labor to free wage workers as the latter proliferated in numbers.

Ethnicity

The earliest immigrants came to Pennsylvania from England, Wales, Ireland (Scots-Irish) and Germany. Throughout the eighteenth century, the English dominated the Chester County landscape, comprising approximately two-thirds of the population. In the first decades of settlement the Welsh were the next most populous group, but their numbers declined over the century, while the Scotch-Irish/Irish population grew; the Germans were never a proportionately large group, though they steadily increased (Table 1A)

The county maintained this heterogeneity throughout the eighteenth century in addition to remaining predominantly rural.[13] Similar ratios are reflected in the ethnicity of the probated loom owners, with no indications that one group was more likely to engage in cloth production than another in numbers disproportionate to their population base (Table 1B).[14]

All areas from which the initial settlers originated specialized in some form of cloth production. In England and Wales, although the scale and organization of the industry varied regionally, many rural inhabitants were involved in wool cloth making for a large national and international market. Most of these artisans combined their craft with some other form of income-generating activity; they either farmed their own land or hired themselves out to do agricultural work for others.[15] The Scots-Irish and German immigrants came primarily from rural areas specializing in linen weaving and they, too, were accustomed to combine their craft skills with some form of agrarian income.[16] This tradition persisted in Pennsylvania; the majority of households that owned looms were also involved in agriculture.[17] Despite the ethnic diversity and the different skills and equipment required to process wool and linen, many of the artisans living in eighteenth-century Chester County quickly reproduced and continued to utilize the system of bi-occupational employment with which they had been familiar in the Old World.[18]

Table 1A
Proportions of National Groups in Chester County*

Date	English %	Scots-Irish %	Welsh %	German %	Other %	Total Population (#)
1730	67	12	17	2	2	10,800
1759	59	23	8	5	5	27,000
1782	63	19	7	8	4	34,450

*SOURCE: James T. Lemon, *The Best Poor Man's Country, A Geographical Study of Early South-Eastern Pennsylvania*, (New York, 1972), p. 79, table 14.

Table 1B
Ethnicity of Loom Owners

Date	English %	(#)	Scots-Irish %	(#)	Welsh %	(#)	German %	(#)	Other %	(#)	Total (#)
1717–18	75.0	(3)	—		25.0	(1)	—		—		(4)
1735–37	85.7	(6)	14.3	(1)	—		—		—		(7)
1754–57	53.3	(8)	20.0	(3)	13.3	(2)	13.3	(2)	—		(15)
1773–76	47.4	(9)	36.8	(7)	15.8	(3)	—		—		(19)
1792–95	41.7	(10)	33.3	(8)	8.3	(2)	12.5	(3)	4.2	(1)	(24)
TOTAL	52.1	(36)	27.5	(19)	11.6	(8)	7.2	(5)	1.4	(1)	(69)

SOURCE: Chester County Wills and Inventories, Chester County Archives, West Chester, Pennsylvania. Based on all loom owners (69) from a sampling of 825 inventories.

542   journal of social history   spring 1994

Spinning as Women's Work

Europeans not only combined craft work and farming, they frequently divided the tasks involved in textile production along gender lines. Spun yarn is the raw material required to weave a piece of cloth and its manufacture was primarily women's work, a fact that did not alter with the transatlantic migrations to Pennsylvania.[19] It is clear from a variety of sources that spinning formed a major component of what Laurel Ulrich calls the "female economy," and in Pennsylvania this operated on two levels: some yarn was produced for home consumption only and some was made for commercial purposes. In general, women owned their own spinning wheels, gave them to other females and purchased them. Many received training to acquire the skill, sometimes through formal arrangements, after which they would spin for their own use and/or for wages, regardless of their marital status.

In 1718, almost 30 percent of decedent Chester County households had at least 1 spinning wheel and this number grew steadily throughout the century so that by 1795, 65 percent had one. Female spinning wheel owners mirrored this trend. Although no women were recorded as having wheels in 1718, by 1795 more than 50 percent of female decedents had them.[20] They acquired the tools in a variety of ways. Frequently, husbands bequeathed the household spinning wheels to their wives, either because the women owned them prior to marriage as in the case of Margaret Boyd whose husband, in his 1754 will, gave her "her Little Wheel She brought," or because they had used them during their life together and continued to need them.[21] Some men like Samuel Maxfield, who died in 1774, left his daughters the spinning wheels which had been theirs while he lived.[22]

Women also specified in their wills that their spinning equipment be given to other females. Some, like Mary Sharp of Easttown, kept it within their families by leaving her "grand Children Viz Rachel and Mary the Children of my son Thomas my wooll and flax wheel and Reel ... " in 1779.[23] Others, like Jean Simontown of Tredyffrin, left in 1794, "to [her] Negroe woman Betty and to [her] Negroe Woman Dinah each a Spinning wheel and the Reel & Big Wheel between them."[24]

Another way for women to obtain yarn making equipment was to purchase it for themselves. Several vendue lists that delineate property sold from decedent estates show, for example, that in 1752 Jane Power bought flax, a flax wheel and a reel, and in 1773 Sarah Guthery bought a spinning wheel. Both women were widows of the deceased whose goods were being sold and probably bought wheels that had been theirs prior to their husbands' deaths.[25]

There were a variety of options available for women to learn how to produce serviceable yarn. The most common method was for a mother to train her own daughters in the craft when they were young, for once her children could operate a wheel, the family labor force was extended. Some women were placed as apprentices, with formal indentures to learn the skill from people outside their families. Elizabeth England "put her Daughter Apprentice unto Nathaniel Jefferies of East Bradford ... to Learn to Sew, & Spin." As part of the agreement Jefferies was to teach the girl to read and write and give her "Two Suits of Cloths one intire New."[26] Because he failed to comply with these terms, England took

THE GENDER DIVISION OF LABOR   543

him to court in 1772. This agreement was similar to those drawn up for male apprentices.[27]

Free women trained to spin and with access to the appropriate equipment would have performed the work when they could fit it around other household tasks. If yarn was required for a specific item in a hurry, they might devote a block of time to the work. But unlike weaving, which demanded the full attention of the artisan, spinning could be done at short intervals amid such other household activities as child care, cooking, washing, etc.[28] If the wife of a householder had female help, either indentured servants, slaves, or hired labor, she would relegate the spinning jobs to them entirely or have them assist her with the work. Similarly, any female relatives living in the household would also have helped.[29]

Bound labor offered one way for a family to extend its labor force to assist in household tasks like spinning, especially before 1760. Many of the female slaves and servants coming into, or already living in, Pennsylvania were proficient at the task—clearly a desirable asset in a woman worker. Black women who knew how to make yarn on a spinning wheel had lived long enough in North America to learn these European skills. In 1730, for example, the *American Weekly Mercury* advertised the sale of "a very likely Negroe Woman, who has lived in Philadelphia from her Childhood, and speaks very good English, she can do all Sorts of Housework ... ; she can Knit and Sew, Spin Flax, Cotton, Worsted, and Wool, very well. ... "[30] European female servants whose spinning skills were highlighted originated in places like Holland, Ireland and Scotland.[31] Whether a woman servant/slave spun only wool, or linen, or both, her proficiency with a spinning wheel was a marketable commodity, especially because not all women possessed this skill. After 1760, although the use of bound labor declined substantially, this was not due to a decreased demand, but a change in the nature of the work force. For Pennsylvania householders, the use of free workers meant they had a more elastic labor supply. As a result local female spinners had increased wage earning opportunities.[32]

Both married and single women earned money by spinning commercially. Some went into the homes of others, used their equipment and fiber and were paid a wage for their labor, as in the case of Margaret Rock, who worked "2 Days in the House" of George Brinton and the wife of Harold Chiffrow whom Brinton also hired to spin tow yarn for him.[33] Others worked with fiber they produced on their own farms or purchased from others, spun it at home and sold it, usually to pay for a needed service.[34] Married women customarily disposed of their earnings in this manner while those who were single tended to spend their money on clothing for themselves and were not required to contribute directly to household finances.[35] In most account records, single and widowed women transacted the work in their own behalf, while married women either did so in combination with their husbands, or were totally subsumed under their husband's names.

. Even though some women received special training as spinners and some spun for commercial purposes, in general spinning was regarded as a household task. The only time one sees the designation of "spinster" at this period is in wills and refers to the unmarried status of a woman, not her occupation. Occasionally women were listed on tax lists, but even in the years for which occupation taxes

544   journal of social history   spring 1994

were levied, they were never taxed as spinners. Thus spinning did not have the formal (and therefore taxable) occupational status of such male-dominated crafts as weaving.

What differs between the traditional New England model and the Pennsylvania experience is that spinning was not done only by women for their family's use, though the household may have been a major consumer of the product. It was also done commercially, and wealthier females had the means to liberate themselves from the work by using an extended labor force of female slaves, servants or contract wage workers. Moreover, women's role in cloth making ceased at this point as they handed over their spun yarn to a skilled male artisan whom they paid to weave it into cloth.

Weaving as Men's Work: Joseph Eldridge, Propertied Weaver

Weaving was a more fully commercial activity in Chester County than spinning, with weavers representing approximately 13–20 percent of all taxable artisans between 1765 and 1800—about 1 to 3 percent of the taxable population at this time.[36] The example of one Chester County weaver, Joseph Eldridge, provides insight into how these craftsmen were trained, their use of auxiliary labor and their artisanal life cycle. When followed by a composite portrait of weavers obtained from quantifiable sources, a clear picture of the work lives of these men emerges that is vastly different from the female experience in late eighteenth-century New England.

Eldridge was born in 1765 in Goshen Township where he lived until his death in 1845.[37] Descended from four generations of American weavers, his training and work cycle deviated little from those of his ancestors.[38] Due to the premature death of his mother, Eldridge, while still a boy, went to live with his unmarried uncle James Garrett and learn the weaving business. Over the years Joseph's status changed several times: after serving his apprenticeship, by 1789, at the age of 24, he was a fully trained weaver—an occupation for which he was taxed that year—in addition to being married and having a child.[39] At this point he was living with his wife and young family on his uncle's farm, probably paying for his keep by weaving and assisting his uncle with agricultural work.[40] In 1794 when James died he bequeathed his

> esteemed friend and nephew ... who now liveth with me in the house the whole Plantation or tract of Land and appurtenances that I now live on Situate in the Township of Goshen Containing about one hundred and Fifty acres be the same more or less.... I Also give and bequeath unto my said Nephew Joseph Eldridge the whole of my Stock, farming utensils and household furniture what ever that I am now Possessed of.[41]

The young man, a fifth generation weaver, now had a trade, tools, money inherited from his grandparents and a good deal of property with which to expand his own enlarging household and enter into the next phase of his life cycle.

Three of Eldridge's account books have survived and shed light on his business practices and changing work patterns.[42] The earliest entry is 1786 when Joseph was twenty-three years old, unmarried and childless. As a journeyman weaver, prior to having children and his uncle James's death, in 1794, with the ensuing responsibilities of running a farm, Eldridge produced more cloth than he did later. During this time, he had little help with his weaving; between 1786 and 1789 his annual output averaged approximately 625 yards.

By the late 1790s, however, as a propertied master weaver, increasing agricultural responsibilities left Eldridge with less time to weave himself. Since his own children were too small to help with the craft work, he hired young single men or "freemen" who lived with him to make much of the cloth produced by his workshop.[43] For example, journeyman weaver, Isaac Yarnall, began a year's boarding with Eldridge on April 14, 1795, for which he paid £22/10/0. Like the single female spinners who spent their earnings on personal items, Yarnall bought such things as a sheepskin apron, a silver brooch, yarn for stockings, tobacco, powder and shot and candles from his employer. In return, he wove for half pay and performed a variety of agricultural jobs, for which he received additional wages. At the end of the year, if mutually agreeable, Eldridge and Yarnall could renew their agreement. However, if the young man was in a position to acquire his own property or received a better offer elsewhere, Eldridge would have to find a replacement and enter into a similar agreement with someone new.[44] Operating under this type of arrangement, Eldridge wove only 60 yards himself in 1794, compared to his annual output of 625 yards a decade earlier; his paid worker produced 470 yards of cloth.

As his sons matured, Joseph taught them the skills he had learned from his uncle. By 1809, two sons and a contractual artisan produced about 1,499 yards of cloth among them, more than double what Eldridge had made when he worked alone. The added familial labor freed the older weaver from the necessity of making cloth himself and allowed him to develop further both his agricultural and craft operations. He expanded the latter in 1813, when he acquired a fulling mill, thereby transforming his weaving operation into a small woolen factory that could produce finished cloth for sale.

Eldridge's life as a farmer/weaver paralleled that of his Pennsylvania weaving forebears. He learned his trade from a relative with whom he worked until he acquired his own land (in this case by inheritance). After weaving first for himself and later supplementing his output with contractual, then family, labor, Eldridge was able simultaneously to produce more cloth for sale and to expand his farming activities. Although he utilized contractual workers to assist him while his family was young rather than the bound labor used by earlier generations, Eldridge continued the tradition of training his sons in his craft which they practiced until well into the nineteenth century.[45] An examination of a broader population of Pennsylvania weavers demonstrates that many artisans experienced a life cycle similar to Eldridge.

Life Cycle of Weavers

It took time to acquire the knowledge needed to make saleable cloth. In eighteenth-century Chester County, the two most common methods of obtaining this was through a formal apprenticeship or, as in the case of Eldridge, by working with a family member trained in weaving. Sufficient evidence exists to

546   journal of social history   spring 1994

suggest that apprenticeship occurred regularly throughout the period.[46] Once a young man had acquired the rudiments of weaving, the apprentice assisted his master until he was adequately trained to take over much of the work. At this point, the teacher had several alternatives: if he owned a farm he could devote more time to agricultural work, or if his property holdings were small, he could increase his cloth output by working on another loom in conjunction with his apprentice.[47]

While an apprentice would have been helpful to a weaver with no children or children too young to participate in craft work, the majority of weavers, like Joseph Eldridge, taught their skills to members of their own household, a continuation of European traditions.[48] It is difficult to say if all the male offspring in a family learned to weave, but most would have acquired at least basic knowledge of the trade. Once trained, a son, like an apprentice, was a major contributor to the family's cloth output, retaining some of his earnings until he reached the age of majority when he could set up on his own. Until this time however, he was legally obligated to provide his services to his father.[49] An artisan without his own family, like Eldridge's uncle, might teach his craft to a young relative or seek alternative assistance in the form of bound labor or contractual wage workers.

The most common use of bound labor was in the form of indentured servants, especially in the decades prior to 1770 when there were fewer young, native born artisans available and immigration was active.[50] This type of worker required a cash investment, but many men arriving in Pennsylvania from Europe during the period were already fully trained weavers. As a result, they could be productive immediately and could also be set to work at other household and agricultural tasks.[51] If advertisements for runaway indentured servants are representative of the broader population of this class of people, it appears that the peak decades for servant weavers were the 1730s, 40s and 50s and they were comprised almost exclusively of Irish and English men. There were almost twice as many of the former as the latter though the English were more numerous before 1740.[52] An analysis of the loom owners with servants or apprentices shows that the highest number occurred among married men with no offspring and men whose children were minors (Table 2). The use of bound labor decreased as the population expanded in Chester County, producing a growing number of propertyless young people. As a result a system of short term, contractual wage labor replaced the use of indentured servants.[53]

While some propertyless contract weavers may have had their own equipment, others needed access to the tools of their trade and all required a market for their product.[54] They obtained these by working for landholding cloth makers who owned the appropriate implements and acted as the agents for selling the fabric. Once a propertied loom owner (who usually had been a weaver himself or related to one) could afford to hire journeymen to use his cloth making equipment he was free to perform other work while still sharing the profits from weaving. According to the tax lists, in 1765 there was a ratio of one weaver with property to one without; this changed in 1781 to 2.5 propertyless weavers to one with land, a proportion which was unaltered in 1799.[55] The cloth output could have risen slightly as a result of this since the work may have become more full-time than previously. The increasing availability of workers transformed many landholding weavers from practicing craftsmen to employers, thereby establishing the ground work for a manufacturing sector that appeared in the early nineteenth century.[56] Despite these changes the relations between employer and employed remained much as they had throughout the century.[57]

Trained, native born weavers, then, had the option of working on a short-term, renewable contractual basis, or if they had their own farm they could choose to make all the cloth themselves when agricultural duties permitted, and/or hire someone else to help with the weaving. For many weavers, these options represented consecutive phases through which they passed during the course of their lives—apprentice, contractual worker, property owner—though not everyone was fortunate enough to reach the last stage.

Benjamin Simcock, Inmate Weaver

Benjamin Simcock was another eighteenth-century, Pennsylvania weaver who illustrates the artisan life cycle, though unsuccessfully.[58] Unlike Eldridge, who was propertied and prosperous, Simcock appears in the court records at the end of his life as a pauper. After the death of his parents, Simcock was bound as an apprentice in 1725 at the age of six, to weaver John Lea, who died several years later.[59] Lea's executors then sent the young boy to work for another weaver in East Marlborough where he stayed "two winters & one summer," until his master moved to Philadelphia County and sold him to John Sketchely. Simcock served Sketchely "some more than four years, he then being about 20 years, & worked there a Journeyman Some more than three years." Soon after leaving, Simcock married and went to live as an inmate for the next thirteen years with Sketchely's stepson to whom he "Paid ten Pounds a year ... , Paid all Taxes & Served Parish Offices." At the end of this time, Simcock made the step to which most artisans aspired when he bought a house and lot of his own in Darby Township. For some reason, however, he never lived there and sold it a year later. He was about 33 years old when he next moved to a plantation in Marion County and resumed inmate status for £15 a year rent. Beginning in his early forties, Simcock "broke up housekeeping and ... worked about from Place to Place as a Journeyman Weaver and some time for himself ... " until, at age 69 he presented himself as a pauper to the overseers of the poor to be looked after in Ridley township, the place of his birth. Although Simcock experienced the traditional life cycle of apprentice, journeyman, inmate and even briefly, property holder, without the support of a propertied family or children to assist him, his ability to succeed was not assured.

A Broader Picture

A composite portrait of weavers from an analysis of data contained in wills, after-death household inventories and tax assessments relating to 115 eighteenth-century Chester County loom owners, confirms that the experience of Pennsylvania weavers was very different from our image of housewives producing textiles for their farm families. Moreover it demonstrates that other weavers went through a similar artisan life cycle to Joseph Eldridge and Benjamin Simcock—apprentice, journeyman, and master weaver working for himself (either to accumulate capital or maintain themselves and families).[60]

The most active stages of an artisan's life occurred during his younger years when he was either single, or married with no children or minor ones. This is when, according to tax assessments, the majority of people were identified by the craft they practiced (Table 2).

Forty percent of all people designated as weavers were single men, followed by married men with no children (25 percent), a fact which is not surprising given that many of them would not yet have had the responsibilities attendant on working land (Table 2). Indeed, approximately 75 percent of the men taxed as weavers between 1765 and 1799 did not have sufficient acreage to farm (Table 3).[61] It was during these early stages that Joseph Eldridge's textile production was highest.

The occupancy of either inherited, purchased or rented land usually occurred later in life. Frequently a change in nomenclature signified this new stage in a cloth maker's life cycle; many of the younger men taxed as weavers or who bought property or went to court and were called weavers on deeds and depositions, were designated as "yeoman" or "farmer" in probate when they died.[62] This suggests both a rise in status and that young men spent more time at their craft than they did later (Table 2).[63] Although loom owners of all ages had crops or husbandry tools listed in their inventories, not surprisingly, the highest number were among older men (Table 2). Once a weaver made the transition to landholder, therefore, his time was spent on a wider variety of tasks than previously. It is unlikely that farmer/artisans stopped weaving altogether, however, but spent less time at it, while obtaining the help of younger craftsmen to continue with the work they could no longer do unassisted.

There were several options for propertyless weavers. Single men like Isaac Yarnall, without their own loom, could board with a landholding weaver like Joseph Eldridge, work on his equipment for half pay and help with other farm jobs. Another alternative was to rent a cottage on the land of a more established weaver/farmer or a large entrepreneurial farmer.[64] A cottager or inmate with his own equipment could weave for himself and work for his landlord when needed. Moreover, a married inmate could augment his earnings through the labor of his wife who could also hire herself out to work in addition to keeping a garden to diminish the necessity of buying a lot of food. This is illustrated by George Brinton who kept separate accounts for his male and female cottagers. In 1802–1804 he paid two couples to work for him—the wives for spinning and the husbands for weaving.[65] An inmate with his own equipment, therefore, had more control over the disposition of his time and output and a greater potential to accumulate capital than a freeman weaver who worked on his employer's looms. If a young man did not have a farm when he married, like Benjamin Simcock, he could move into the inmate or cottager category in the hope of eventually acquiring property of his own.

Clearly many weaver/farmers did not work alone, and over a third of the loom owners had more than one loom (Table 2). Despite the size of this piece of

Table 2

Loom Owner Data at Various Life Stages[a]

	Stage 1 % (#)	Stage 2 % (#)	Stage 3 % (#)	Stage 4 % (#)	Stage 5 % (#)	Total
% of loom owners per life stage	8.7 (10)	13.9 (16)	13.0 (15)	29.6 (34)	34.8 (40)	115

	Stage 1 % (#)	Stage 2 % (#)	Stage 3 % (#)	Stage 4 % (#)	Stage 5 % (#)	% of Loom Owners % (#)
Apprentices/ servants[b]	— —	31.3 (5)	25.0 (4)	20.6 (7)	10.0 (4)	17.4 (20)
Weaving shops	— —	6.3 (1)	6.6 (1)	— —	12.5 (5)	6.1 (7)
Called 'weaver'	40.0 (4)	25.0 (4)	13.3 (2)	20.6 (7)	15.0 (6)	20.0 (23)
2 or more looms	30.0 (3)	37.5 (6)	33.3 (5)	38.2 (13)	35.0 (14)	35.7 (41)
Crops/implements	40.0 (4)	68.8 (11)	86.6 (13)	85.3 (29)	85.0 (34)	79.1 (91)

[a]The life stages were based on those used by Mary McKinney Schweitzer, *Custom and Contract: Household, Government, and the Economy in Colonial Pennsylvania*, (New York, 1987), pp. 25–34. They are: 1. a single youth beginning to acquire capital with which to set up his own farm; 2. a married youth with no offspring; 3. a young family with only minor children; 4. a household of people of mixed ages including minors, adolescents and young adults; 5. a household with grown children who were dispersing to set up their own households.

[b]The above categories are not mutually exclusive as some people show up in more than one category.

*Chester County Wills and Inventories, Chester County Archives, West Chester, Pennsylvania. Based on data obtained from 115 Chester County inventories with looms.

Table 3

Land Status Of Weavers*

	1765		1781		1799	
	%ᵃ	(#)	%	(#)	%	(#)
Landholdingᵇ	25.0	(3)	35.2	(6)	18.5	(5)
Nonlandholding						
renters	50.0	(6)	—	—	7.4	(2)
inmates	8.3	(1)	47.1	(8)	37.0	(10)
freemen	—	—	11.8	(2)	37.0	(10)
unspecifiedᶜ	16.7	(2)	5.9	(1)	—	—
Subtotal	75.0	(9)	64.8	(11)	81.4	(22)
Total weavers		(12)		(17)		(27)

ᵃPercentage of all weavers taxed.
ᵇIncludes both land owners and tenants taxed for acreage.
ᶜNo acreage or status assigned.

*SOURCE: Chester County Tax Lists, Chester County Archives, West Chester, Pennsylvania. Based on a tabulation of all taxables in Darby, East Fallowfield, Goshen, East Nottingham, Pikeland, Thornbury and Tredyffrin townships for the years 1765, 1781. The same townships with the exception of Darby (separated from Chester County by a boundary change in 1789) were included in the 1799 run.

equipment, most weavers would have set it up in a room in the house, perhaps the hall.[66] But aside from space requirements, weaving was a noisy and dirty occupation, especially if more than one person worked at a time; thus some weavers housed their tools in outbuildings or shops.[67] Although not all the structures were specifically designated for cloth production—for example, some equipment was in "spring houses"—about 6 percent of the loom owners had designated weavers' shops (Table 2).[68] These independent buildings would have been similar to that listed on the property of David Bailey of East Fallowfield in the 1796 tax assessment: "1 Log house for a Weaver Shop 16 Feet Square;" shops like this could house two and possibly three looms.[69] An examination of the property holdings and life stages of the men with weaver's shops reveals that most were owned by people with larger than average acreage who were in the later stages of their lives (Table 2).[70] This supports the fact that these men hired younger weavers to work for them and probably conducted their weaving operations more along the lines of a small business than when they did the work themselves. This was true throughout the century.[71]

In summary, a weaver's output was highest during his youth when he had few other responsibilities of farm and family. Moving through the life cycle, his role became more supervisory and less productive as he utilized the labor of younger, unpropertied weavers, freeing himself to devote more time to other work. But was weaving in eighteenth-century Chester County the exclusive territory of male artisans or did females also participate in this activity?

Women and Weaving

Because of the strong male bias in eighteenth-century records, it is much easier to examine the role of men in cloth making than that of women. It is difficult, therefore, to know to what extent girls might have participated in learning the requisite skills along with their brothers. There is no doubt that male artisans dominated the craft of weaving in eighteenth-century Chester County, but some evidence suggests that females were not entirely excluded.

Although many women possessed their own spinning equipment, only five could be identified who had looms.[72] In every case, the implements originally belonged to their husbands, or in the instance of Rebecca Davis, her son, who predeceased her. Several of the women only inherited the tools because their children were minors; indeed, Mary Willis's husband left her his estate in trust for their son John. Hannah Shortledge had no children and her husband bequeathed her everything. John Davis willed his property to his brother, but only after the death of their mother; hence the looms in Rebecca Davis's inventory had probably belonged her son. When these women died, if they specified the disposition of the tools, it was to a male relative.[73]

It is almost impossible to know whether or not the women who owned weaving equipment actually used it. If not, it was probably because they had too many other responsibilities or were too old to weave. Females who were daughters and/or wives of weavers were undoubtedly familiar with at least some, if not all the tasks involved in making a piece of cloth. If they had time, they would have helped their fathers and/or husbands with their work. But weaving more than just the simplest patterns demanded concentration and uninterrupted time, both of which would be difficult for women to obtain, especially those who were married and had children.[74] If looms continued to be used after a weaver's death, probably a son, servant or hired person carried on the work.[75] More likely, however, when a wife inherited her husband's equipment, if there was no one in the family to use it she sold it.[76]

The textile sector in eighteenth-century, rural Pennsylvania was vastly different from its New England counterpart. There was a clearly defined gender division of labor that did not alter over the period; the sector was more commercial; and there was a stronger continuation of European craft traditions right up until early nineteenth-century industrialization.

European Traditions

Many Chester County households continued to follow the guidelines set out for the seventeenth-century British housewife who was advised that once she had given her spun yarn to the male weaver she "hath finished her labour: for in the weaving, walking [shrinking], and dressing thereof she can challenge no property more than to entreat them severally to discharge their duties with a good conscience."[77] This was reinforced in Britain through a variety of regulations that prohibited women from weaving. An exception to the exclusion of females from the cloth making and finishing branches of textile manufacture was a widow of a weaver who could take over her husband's work and tools as long as she remained a widow.[78] Similar restrictions existed in other areas of eighteenth-century Europe as well, though there were regional variations.[79]

This structure of women spinning and men weaving commercially in Pennsylvania resembled the experience of British weavers. The stages of apprentice, contractual worker and weaver/farmer paralleled those of apprentice, journeyman, and master found within the English system.[80] Other common features included the existence of bi-occupations—the custom of combining artisanal production with agricultural pursuits; the use of contractual, live-in workers; and the employment of independent artisans who lived in their own cottages and were paid on a daily basis or for doing a specified task.[81] Prior to the industrialization of textile production, therefore, rural Pennsylvanians followed the artisan experience they had known in Europe, and for most of the eighteenth century could confidently expect to move through a clearly defined and familiar life cycle. Glimmerings of change can be seen in the latter part of the century, however, with the growing number of landless cloth makers in the region.[82]

Conclusion: Beyond Gender

This picture of the organization of cloth manufacture in eighteenth-century Pennsylvania is very different from the situation in New England. A further comparison of the two regions suggests that gender is not the only distinction. The scale of domestic textile production was different. Throughout the eighteenth century, Chester County had a ratio of approximately seven households with spinning wheels for every household with a loom, while Essex County, Massachusetts had an average ratio of about three to one.[83] Almost twice as many households in Massachusetts had looms.[84] In addition, the dependency on an extended labor force in Pennsylvania, first through the use of bound labor and later through contract wage workers, does not occur to the same extent or in the same manner in New England.[85] Another important disparity between the two regions is the ratio of males to females in the population: by the late eighteenth century women outnumbered men in Massachusetts, while in Pennsylvania the situation was reversed.[86]

The preceding analysis demonstrates that we must move beyond the past monolithic interpretation of early American domestic textile manufacture. It was a complex process that grew out of its European roots. But we need to know more about the reasons for such pronounced regional differences by exploring the relationship of cloth production to factors such as demographics, agricultural production, and the availability of labor and markets. Moreover a more sustained regional comparison is required to answer a whole series of questions relating to the structure of the textile sector in early North America. Were there areas where women had always been responsible for cloth making and did this represent a break from tradition, and why? Could female weavers expect to experience life cycles similar to their male counterparts? What part did industrialization play in altering the gender roles inherent in cloth making? Was there a difference in the status of male and female cloth makers in the eighteenth and later in the nineteenth centuries? Did women produce the same kinds of cloth as men and

THE GENDER DIVISION OF LABOR   553

were they as skilled? Were they paid equivalent prices for the fabric they made? Did men and women market their cloth in a similar manner?

The issues surrounding the transition of textile production from craft to industry are being addressed gradually.[87] But in North America we must know more about the earlier stages of hand cloth manufacture in order to assess fully the depth of this change. The discussion of the gender division of labor in rural Pennsylvania takes a step towards establishing a more complex framework than the previously accepted New England model. It helps us better to understand the different roles of men and women in North American craft production and the impact of migration and industrialization on them. Moreover, it suggests the need for more comparative work on other aspects of domestic textile manufacture such as the availability of raw materials, the extent of local markets and the consumption of locally made cloth relative to imported fabrics. As these pieces are put into place the industrialization puzzle will emerge in all its complexity.

ENDNOTES

I would like to thank James T. Lemon, Grant McCracken, Thiery Ruddel, Lucy Simler, Laurel Thatchter Ulrich and anonymous reviewers for helpful comments on earlier drafts of this paper. Funding for some of the research was provided by the Philadelphia Center for Early American Studies, the William F. Sullivan Research Fellowship, Museum of American Textile History, and the Arthur H. Cole grant-in-aid for research in Economoic History.

1.   For an overview of the literature on the British textile industry see Stanley Chapman "Industrialization and Production: a Bibliographic Survey," Beverly Lemire and Adrienne Hood, eds., "Surveying Textile History: Perspectives for New Research," special issue of *Material History Bulletin* 31 (Spring 1990): 15–21.

2.   For a review of the American scholarship on the topic see Gail Fowler Mohanty, "From Craft To Industry: Textile Production in the United States," Lemire and Hood, eds., "Surveying Textile History," pp. 23–31.

3.   William R. Bagnall, *The Textile Industries of the United States, Including Sketches and Notices of Cotton, Woolen, Silk, and Linen Manufacture in the Colonial Period, 1639–1810* (Boston, 1893); Perry Walton, *The Story of Textiles: A Bird's Eye View of the History of the Beginning and the Growth of the Industry by Which Mankind is Clothed* (Boston, 1912); Arthur Harrison Cole, *The American Wool Manufacture* (1925, reprint, New York, 1969).

4.   Rolla Milton Tryon, *Household Manufactures in the United States, 1640–1860* (Chicago, 1917); Victor S. Clark, *History of Manufactures in the United States, 1607–1860* v. 1 (1929, reprint, New York, 1949).

5.   Alice Morse Earle, *Home Life In Colonial Days* (1898, reprint, Stockbridge, Mass, 1974); Elizabeth Cynthia Barney Buel, *The Tale of the Spinning Wheel* (Litchfield, Conn., 1903); Carl Holliday, *Woman's Life in Colonial Days* (1922, reprint, New York, 1964); Edith Abbott, *Women in Industry, A Study in American Economic History* (1909, reprint, New York, 1916).

6.   Thomas Dublin, *Women at Work: The Transformation of Work and Community in*

Lowell, Massachusetts, 1826–1860 (New York, 1979); Elizabeth Hitz, "A Technical and Business Revolution: American Woolens to 1832" (Ph.D. diss., New York University, 1978); David J. Jeremy, Transatlantic Industrial Revolution: The Diffusion of Textile Technologies Between Britain and America, 1790–1830s (North Andover and Cambridge, Mass., 1981); Gail Fowler Mohanty, "Experimentation in Textile Technology, 1788–1790, and its Impact on Handloom Weaving and Weavers in Rhode Island," Technology and Culture 29 (1988): 1–31; Mohanty, "Putting up with Putting-Out: Power-Loom Diffusion and Outwork for Rhode Island Mills, 1821–1829," Journal of the Early Republic 9 (June 1989): 191–216; Philip Scranton, Proprietary Capitalism: the Textile Manufacture at Philadelphia, 1800–1885 (Cambridge, 1983); Scranton, "Varieties of Paternalism: Industrial Structures and the Social Relations of Production in American Textiles," American Quarterly 36 (1984): 235–257; Cynthia J. Shelton, The Mills of Manayunk: Industrialization and Social Conflict in the Philadelphia Region, 1787–1837 (Baltimore, 1986); Barbara Tucker, Samuel Slater and the Origins of the American Textile Industry, 1790–1860 (Ithaca, 1984); Anthony F. C. Wallace, Rockdale, the Growth of an American Village in the Early Industrial Revolution (New York, 1972).

7. Joan M. Jensen, Loosening the Bonds: Mid-Atlantic Farm Women, 1750–1850 (New Haven, 1986); James A. Henretta, "The War for Independence and American Economic Development," in Ronald Hoffman, John J. McCusker, and Russell R. Menard, eds., The Economy of Early America, the Revolutionary Period, 1763–1790 (Charlottesville, 1988); Allan Kulikoff, "The Transition to Capitalism in Rural America," William and Mary Quarterly 3rd series, v. 66 (January, 1989): 120–144.

8. The only recent study that focuses on the colonial period is Adrienne D. Hood, "Organization and Extent of Textile Manufacture in Eighteenth-Century Rural Pennsylvania: A Case Study of Chester County," (Ph.D. diss., University of California, San Diego, 1988).

9. Laurel Thatcher Ulrich, "Martha Ballard and Her Girls: Women's Work in Eighteenth-Century Maine," in Stephen Innes, ed., Work and Labor in Early America (Chapel Hill, 1988), p. 90, says that in the late eighteenth century in the Kennebec Valley over 60% of households had wheels and over 25% had looms.

10. Ibid., in 1730, in York County Maine, 40 percent of inventoried households had spinning wheels, but only 3 percent had looms. D. T. Ruddel suggests that a similar shift in the gender of weavers occurred in late eighteenth-century Quebec, "Domestic Textile Production in colonial Quebec, 1608–1840," Material History Bulletin 31 (Spring 1990): 44–45.

11. Jean B. Russo, "Self-sufficiency and Local Exchange: Free Craftsmen in the Rural Chesapeake Economy," Lois Green Carr, Phillip D. Morgan, and Jean B. Russo, eds., Colonial Chesapeake Society (Chapel Hill, 1988), pp. 392–93.

12. Ibid., 402.

13. Lemon, The Best Poor Man's Country, pp. 13 and 47. Lemon, "The Agricultural Practices of National Groups in Eighteenth Century Southeastern Pennsylvania," Geographical Review v. 56 (1966): 468, Table 1.

14. Ethnicity is difficult to assess with accuracy because there was a tendency to Anglicize names and very few sources specifically identify a person's ethnic origins. However, based on genealogical information Table 1 was derived from categorizing 69 probated loom owners by last name.

15. For discussions of English and Welsh woolen production see: Peter J. Bowden, The Wool Trade in Tudor and Stuart England (London, 1962); E. Lipson, The History of the Woollen and Worsted Industries (London, 1965); J. de L. Mann, The Cloth Industry in the

THE GENDER DIVISION OF LABOR   555

West of England from 1640–1880 (Oxford, 1971); Alan Rogers, "Rural Industries and Social Structure: The Framework Knitting Industry of South Nottinghamshire 1660–1840," *Textile History* v. 12 (1981): 7–26; and J. Geraint Jenkins, *The Welsh Woollen Industry* (Cardiff, 1969).

16. For details on the Irish linen manufacture see Conrad Gill, *The Rise of the Irish Linen Industry* (1925, Reprint, Oxford, 1964), pp. 31–60; and Alex J. Warden, *The Linen Trade, Ancient and Modern* (1864, reprint, London, 1967), pp. 388–420. Information on German linen production can be found in Eckart Schremmer, "The Textile Industry in South Germany, 1750 to 1850," *Textile History* v. 7 (1976): 60–89.

17. An analysis of 115 inventories of loom owners in Chester County shows that 80 percent (91) had crops and/or farming implements as well. The inventories are in the probate records at Chester County Archives, West Chester, Pennsylvania (hereafter CCA). For a more detailed analysis of the bi-occupationalism in Chester County see Paul G. E. Clemens and Lucy Simler, "Rural Labor and the Farm Household in Chester County, Pennsylvania, 1750–1820," in Stephen Innes, ed., *Work and Labor*, pp. 121–23.

18. I expected to find differences among the ethnic groups, especially in terms of the types of cloth they wove. However, despite detailed attempts to discern these, I was unable to find clearly defined variations. This could be because the surviving evidence is heavily weighted towards the English-speaking population and it is not always easy to distinguish among the groups of which this was comprised. Wherever possible I will try to indicate if there were noticeable differences.

19. For evidence that spinning was women's work in Europe see Gill, *Irish Linen Industry*, p. 38; Gay L. Gullickson, *Spinners and Weavers of Auffay, Rural Industry and the Sexual Division of Labor in a French Village, 1750–1850* (Cambridge, 1986), pp. 59 and 69; and Schremmer, "The Textile Industry in South Germany," p. 61.

20. Based on data from a sampling of 825 Chester County inventories (hereafter inventory data base). These numbers are probably low and do not account for property given away during the decedent's lifetime or that many women's estates were not inventoried.

21. Chester County Wills and Inventories, CCA (hereafter CCWI) #1545, Hugh Boyd, West Nottingham Township, filed Sept. 19, 1754. For other examples of men leaving spinning equipment to their wives, see the following files: CCWI #562, Michael Blunston, d. 1763; CCWI #1652, John Holland, d. 1757; CCWI #2877, William Mason, d. 1774; CCWI #4251, Daniel Solberger, d. 1792.

22. CCWI #2844. both his daughters, Isabel and Elizabeth were given their spinning wheels.

23. CCWI #2822.

24. CCWI #4387.

25. See Robert Power file CCWI #1417 and James Guthery, file CCWI #2808.

26. Elizabeth England, Petition, Quarter Sessions, August 25, 1772, CCA.

27. For a discussion of female apprenticeship in England at the time see K. D. M. Snell, *Annals of the Labouring Poor: Social Change and Agrarian England 1660–1900* (Cambridge, 1985), pp. 270–319.

28. For example, CCWI #51 shows that the two spinning wheels were located in the kitchen, which would have facilitated the incorporation of spinning with women's other tasks.

29. Lucy Simler, "She Came to Work/She Went to Work, The Development of a Female Rural Proletariat in Southeastern Pennsylvania, 1760–1820," (unpublished paper for meeting, "Women and the Transition to Capitalism in Rural America, 1760–1940," April 1989), pp. 16–22 describes in detail how women spinners worked for wages.

30. *American Weekly Mercury*, Apr. 9–16, 1730. For other ads selling black women who could spin see *ibid.*, Oct. 9–26, 1721; *Pennsylvania Gazette*, May 10, 1733; *American Weekly Mercury*, Jan. 11–18, 1736/7; *Pennsylvania Gazette*, Apr. 12, 1764; *ibid.*, Nov. 6, 1776.

31. *American Weekly Mercury*, Apr. 20–27, 1738; *Pennsylvania Gazette*, Feb. 2, 1744; *ibid.*, July 27, 1774.

32. Sharon V. Salinger, *"To Serve Well and Faithfully," Labor and Indentured Servants in Pennsylvania, 1682–1800* (Cambridge, 1987), pp. 137–52 and Lucy Simler, "The Landless Worker: An Index of Economic and Social Change in Chester County, Pennsylvania, 1750–1820," *The Pennsylvania Magazine of History and Biography* CXIV (April 1990): 172–73.

33. George Brinton Account Book, 1781–1800, Thornbury Township, Chester County, Pennsylvania. Box E-G, Family File. Chester County Historical Society, West Chester, Pennsylvania (hereafter CCHS).

34. CCWI #117, Robert Power vendue list shows that women bought fiber to spin. Elizabeth Williams bought tow and linen cloth from weaver Joseph Eldridge as well as Indian corn and buckwheat in the 1780s and 90s and paid him in part in cash and in part by spinning tow and yarn for bedticks; Joseph Eldridge, Account Books, 1788–1795, man. #3786, CCHS. In 1803, "widow grace" paid a portion of her account with fuller, Calvin Cooper by spinning, Calvin Cooper Account Book, 1791–1802, W. Bradford B.H., v.1, CCHS.

35. Simler, "She Came to Work," p. 19.

36. In 1765 weavers comprised 17.6% of all craftsmen who were taxed; 20.2% in 1781; and 13.8% in 1799. They comprised 1.3%, 1.9%, and 2.9%, respectively of the entire taxable population. These numbers are based on a tabulation of all taxable artisans in the townships of Darby, East Fallowfield, Goshen, East Nottingham, Pikeland, Thornbury, and Tredyffrin for 1765 and 1781; Darby was separated from the county by a boundary change in 1789 so is not included in the 1799 analysis (hereafter tax list data base). For a detailed breakdown of all artisans in the sampling see Hood, "Organization and Extent of Textile Manufacture," pp. 38–9.

37. Genealogical information is from J. Smith Futhey and Gilbert Cope, *History of Chester County Pennsylvania, With Genealogical and Biographical Sketches* (Philadelphia, 1881), p. 530. Other data for the following discussion of Joseph Eldridge can be found in CCWI #4344; and Joseph Eldridge, Account Books, 1788–1795, man. #3786, 3787, and 3788, CCH.

38. For details of the preceding generations of weavers from whom Eldridge was descended see Hood, "Organization and Extent of Textile Manufacture," pp. 140–43.

39. Futhey and Cope, *History of Chester County*, p. 530.

40. Lucy Simler, "The Landless Worker:" p. 176 says that artisans who lived as cottagers or inmates of a landholder paid rent by working at their trade. If they did field work it was for wages (though it was not required) and as long as they gave priority to the landlord's weaving, a weaver could weave for others if time permitted.

THE GENDER DIVISION OF LABOR   557

41. CCWI #4344.

42. Joseph Eldridge, Account Book, 1788–1795, man. #3786, CCHS.

43. Lucy Simler, "Tenancy in Colonial Pennsylvania: The Case of Chester County," *William and Mary Quarterly* 3rd series, v. 43, 4 (October 1986): 548, describes freemen as single, nonlandowning individuals, "usually an artisan, farmer, or laborer living in the household of another." These men were subject to a poll tax since they owned no property and after 1758, "freemen living with their parents and helping them on the farm or at their trade also appear on the lists, being no longer exempt from taxation by either law or custom."

44. This is what happened with Yarnall's predecessor, James Alcorn, who worked for Eldridge in 1794. After Eldridge settled accounts with Alcorn for his year's work, he hired Yarnall with a similar agreement. Both Alcorn and Yarnall were single and trained as weavers. It appears that Yarnall worked for Eldridge for several years because in the tax assessment of 1798 for Goshen, Yarnall was taxed as a weaver and freeman living with Eldridge.

45. Eldridge's great uncles, Samuel Garrett Jr. and Thomas Garrett, had indentured servants to help them with their work, especially needed since none of the former's children appears to have followed their father's trade and Thomas died without offspring. CCWI #1031 (Samuel Garrett) and CCWI #1097 (Thomas Garrett).

46. The evidence is in the form of indentures, court petitions and depositions, and will and inventory notations, see for example: James Wiley, Petition, Quarter Sessions, Aug. 31, 1731, Bound Volume of Servants and Apprentices, CCA; Petition of Divers Inhabitants of Newtown to Court of General Quarter Sessions, Chester Co., PA, May, 1741, CCA; CCWI #727, Thomas Garret of Darby (d. 1748); CCWI #1669, William Lewis of Newtown (d. 1757); Deposition of Samuel Oakes, Court of Quarter Sessions, May 1774, CCA; Indenture of Apprenticeship Between Abishai Ottey and James Baker, May 7, 1788, ms 28062, CCHS.

47. For more detailed analyses of the system of apprenticeship in North America see: Jean-Pierre Hardy et David-Thiery Ruddel, *Les Apprentis Artisans à Québec, 1660–1815* (Montreal, 1977); Marcus Wilson Jernegan, *Laboring and Dependent Classes in Colonial America* (New York, 1931); Richard B. Morris, *Government and Labor in Early America* (New York, 1965, first published 1946); Ian M. G. Quimby, *Apprenticeship in Colonial Philadelphia*, (New York and London, 1985); W. J. Rorabaugh, *The Craft Apprentice, from Franklin to the Machine Age in America* (New York and Oxford, 1986); Salinger, "To Serve Well and Faithfully," pp. 6–8; Mary M. Schweitzer, *Custom and Contract: Household, Government, and the Economy in Colonial Pennsylvania* (New York, 1987), pp. 34–41.

48. According to Robert Malcolmson, *Life and Labour in England, 1700–1780* (London, 1981), p. 64, after male children were trained they "continued to work in the family shop until, on the death of the father or at the time of their marriage, they set up their own households in which, as a rule, weaving was their principal means of support. Some parents may have helped their children purchase a loom." In eighteenth-century England, only a small percentage of children were apprenticed to masters outside their own families and it was common for sons of craft workers (e.g. weavers) to be taught a trade by their fathers, older brothers or another relative. It was also the case in eighteenth-century French Canada. Hardy and Ruddel, *Les Apprentis Artisans*, p. 92.

49. Rorabaugh, *Craft apprentice*, p. 83.

50. Although a few loom owners had slaves (3 out of 115), they were rare and generally not used as an alternative labor force among these artisans. A survey of the 115 Chester

County loom owners shows that 13 owned servants, the peak periods being the mid decades of the eighteenth century, declining sharply after the 1760s (1710–29 = 7.8%; 1730–49 = 15.4%; 1750–69 = 46.1%; 1770–89 = 30.7%; 1790–1800 = 0%). According to Salinger, "To Serve Well and Faithfully," pp. 137–152, this follows the pattern within the artisan population in Philadelphia. John J. McCusker and Russell R. Menard, The Economy of British America, 1607–1789 (Chapel Hill and London, 1985), pp. 202–03 give a good synthesis of the periods of immigration to Pennsylvania.

51.   The American Weekly Mercury and Pennsylvania Gazette are full of ads throughout the eighteenth century for boat loads of servants for sale who were weavers and for runaway servants who were weavers. There are too many to enumerate fully, but see for examples of the former, American Weekly Mercury, Oct. 31–Nov. 7, 1728; Pennsylvania Gazette, July 9, 1741; Pennsylvania Gazette, Aug. 14, 1755. For examples of the latter see American Weekly Mercury, Apr. 4–11, 1728; Pennsylvania Gazette, July 8, 1742; Pennsylvania Gazette, Sept. 20, 1764; Pennsylvania Gazette, Apr. 19, 1775.

52.   It is extremely difficult to determine the ethnicity of bound labor. Two things allow us to have some indication of this: ads for runaway servants usually mention their country of birth and arriving ships advertised servants for sale and designated the port from which they embarked. Runaway ads must be used with caution as it is possible that one group had a greater propensity for running away than others. However, many of the shiploads of servants during the 1720s to 1750s originate from England and Ireland, which seems to correlate with the ethnicity of runaway servants (though Germans could have gone through these ports as well). Given that there was a large influx of Germans to Pennsylvania at this time it is surprising not to see more indication of weavers from this group. Were there no German weaver servants or were they less likely to run away? These questions are unanswerable at the present. In general, there seem to be no major discernable ethnic differences in cloth production, a conclusion similar to that of others who have worked on this region, see Simler "The Landless Worker," p. 186.

53.   See Simler, "The Landless Worker," for a good discussion of the transition to wage labor.

54.   Ibid., p. 176 shows that some contract weavers had their own looms which they moved around with them.

55.   Based on the tax list data base, in 1765 there were 28 propertied weavers and 27 without; in 1781 there were 36 with and 97 without; in 1799 there were 54 with and 129 without.

56.   Sharon V. Salinger, "Artisans, Journeymen, and the Transformation of Labor in Late Eighteenth-Century Philadelphia," William and Mary Quarterly 3rd series, v. 40 (1983): 62–84, argues that in Philadelphia by the last decades of the eighteenth century there was a transformation within the artisan population from a labor system which was heavily dependent on servants and slaves to one of free wage laborers. This change produced job insecurity and widened the gap between masters and workers. While late eighteenth-century, Chester County landowning artisans may have moved more toward becoming employers and away from being practicing craftsmen, they continued to rely on the same type of labor (contractual and live-in) as they had throughout the eighteenth century.

57.   This is similar to the situation in Yorkshire, England a century earlier as described in John Smail, "Manufacturer or Artisan? The Relationship Between Economic and Cultural Change in the Early Stages of the Eighteenth-Century Industrialization," Journal of Social History v. 25, #4 (1992): 803, where there was little social difference between master weavers and journeymen as they all shared the same artisanal culture.

58.   I would like to thank Lucy Simler for bringing this case to my attention. The

THE GENDER DIVISION OF LABOR   559

information on Benjamin Simcock is from a Deposition from Simcock, May 29, 1788 and an Order of Removal, April 16, 1788, Court of Quarter Sessions, CCA.

59. CCWI #241, John Lea's inventory shows he died in January 1727 leaving three looms, one of them a broad loom, and a great deal of miscellaneous weaving equipment.

60. In addition to the 115 loom owners, the analysis is based on the tax list data base.

61. For those taxed as weavers in the tax list data base, 26.2% had property while 30.8% were identified as inmates, 16.3% as freemen and 19.1% as renters. It is difficult to know for certain whether the nonlandholders worked full time at weaving, but the designation and taxing of an occupation suggests that it occupied the majority of a person's time. See Hood, "Organization and Extent of Textile manufacture," Chapter I for a discussion of the landholding categories of eighteenth-century Chester County residents.

62. See for example, CCWI #1958, William Downard, d. 1761 (at about age 70) who was called a "yeoman" in his bond of administration, but in 1736 when he was about 45 years old he was called "weaver," Pennsylvania Archives, series 1, v. 1, p. 512; CCWI #2834; John Taggart, d. 1774 in Vincent Township, was called "yeoman" on his inventory, but in 1765 he was taxed as a weaver living in Uwchlan township; CCWI #5283 William Mann, d. 1806 in Sadsbury called himself a "farmer" in his will, but in 1799, he was taxed as a "weaver" in the adjacent township of East Fallowfield.

63. Out of 56 people taxed as weavers in the tax list data base, only 14 or 25% were taxed on property holdings while 42 or 75% were inmates, freemen, and nonlandholders. Clearly, those property holders identified as weavers were still devoting large amounts of time to their trade. Moreover, weavers owned an average of 80.5 acres of land and if one eliminates the two men who had very large holdings (500 and 315 acres) the others owned an average of 25 acres, well under the average eighteenth-century Chester County holding of 125 acres as estimated by Lemon, Best Poor Man's Country, p. 89. See Kulikoff, "Transition to Capitalism," p. 141 for a discussion of the meaning of the term "yeoman." Smail, "Manufacturer or Artisan," p. 797–98 argues that status for late seventeenth-century West Riding clothiers came not from cloth production but from attaining yeoman status by having enough money to rent or own land in addition to the income earned from artisanal work.

64. Clemens and Simler, "Rural Labor," p. 140. For a detailed discussion of the inmate system see Simler, "The Landless Worker," pp. 175–177.

65. Ibid., pp. 15–28; and Jensen, Loosening the Bonds, pp. 43–45; Clemens and Simler, "Rural Labor," p. 135.

66. CCWI #697, James Shortledge (d. 1739) had two looms listed as "Goods in the house." Jack Michel, "'In a Manner and Fashion Suitable to Their Degree'," p. 46 says that in many houses the hall was the room used for a variety of purposes and it would have been here that weaving might have been done.

67. The action of pulling the beater forward to ensure that each weft thread is properly in place can be very noisy; weaving produces a lot of dust or lint (especially when working with bast fibers); and linen, tow and hemp often have to be kept damp to weave, thereby making a space separate from the daily household activities desirable.

68. CCWI #5448, James Clark (d. 1808) had a loom in the "spring house."

69. Dimensions for other weavers' shops were specified in the West Caln tax assessment for 1799 as: 16 x 20, 18 x 18, 10 x 15, and 14 x 12 feet, CCA.

70. Based on information contained in the inventories of loom owners and people whose

560   journal of social history   spring 1994

shops appeared on tax lists. The average size of land holding for 12 people identified with weaving shops was 287 acres, compared with the 125 acre average for the population as a whole according to Lucy Simler, "Tenancy in Pennsylvania," p. 551.

71. For example, weaving shops turn up in 1717, CCWI #65; 1756, CCWI #2362; 1770, CCWI #2564; 1772, CCWI #2720; 1773, CCWI #2771; 1774, CCWI #2819; and 1792, CCWI #6401.

72. The women with weaving equipment were: Mary Hutton, d. 1736 (CCWI #553); Martha Hobson, d. 1776 (CCWI #2975); Mary Smith, d. 1743 (CCWI #442). Hanna Shortledge (no probate) and Rebecca Davis, d. 1772 (CCWI #2720), were identified through bequests made in their husbands' wills.

73. Martha Hobson was the only one who specifically mentioned her loom, willing it to her grandson, Francis Hobson.

74. Gullickson, *Spinners and Weavers of Auffay*, pp. 104–05, finds that in the region of France she examined, women were not recorded formally as weavers until 1808. Although she has little proof, she feels that women probably wove on the equipment of a male relative on an informal basis prior to that time. Smail, "Manufacturer or Artisan," p. 802, thinks this was also the case in early eighteenth-century West Riding woolen cloth production.

75. Several ads in the *Pennsylvania Gazette* suggest that when a weaver died his widow hired someone to continue the business. See for example, *Pennsylvania Gazette*, Sept. 16–23, 1736 where a widow placed the following ad: "a Hand is wanting in the business of Weaving Hair-Cloth. The proper Loom and all other Utensils belonging to that Business are ready, and a Piece in the Loom half done, by which one not before used to that Sort of weaving may have an Insight of the Method of Working." In this case it is clear that the widow did not know how to do the weaving.

76. When John Pennick, weaver, of Concord township died in 1717, his widow sold the loom to Joseph Townsin, CCWI #47. An ad in the August 13, 1741 issue of the *Pennsylvania Gazette*, shows that a widow was selling six looms and everything that went with them including several servant weavers.

77. Gervase Markham, *The English Housewife*, Michael R. Best, ed. (Kingston and Montreal, 1986), p. 152.

78. Alice Clark, *Working Life of Women in the Seventeenth Century* (1919, reprint, London, 1982), pp. 103–04, outlines the various British regulations prohibiting women from weaving. That these regulations were effective is corroborated by the research of Lorna Wetherill using seventeenth- and early eighteenth-century probate data in "A Possession of One's Own: Women and Consumer Behavior in England, 1660–1740," *Journal of British Studies* 25 (April 1986): 145 and 148. John Rule, "The Frontier of Skill: Artisan Defences in the Eighteenth Century," essay delivered at the conference "The Social World of Britain and America, 1600–1820: A Comparison from the Perspective of Social History," Williamsburg, September 5–7, 1985, p. 11, says that there was a concerted effort to keep women out of skilled crafts and that the weavers' union was successful in doing so until 1825.

79. Gullickson, *The Spinners and Weavers of Auffay*, p. 73–74 describes women spinning and men weaving in Auffay, France; see Linda Stone-Ferrier, "Spun Virtue, the Lacework of Folly, and the World Wound Upside-Down: Seventeenth-Century Dutch Depictions of Female Handwork," in Annette B. Weiner and Jane Schneider, eds., *Cloth and the Human Experience* (Washington, 1989), pp. 215–242, for a discussion of how strongly entrenched the gender divisions of textile production were in Holland. It should be noted that there were exceptions to this as discussed in Maxine Berg, "Women's Work, Mechanisation

THE GENDER DIVISION OF LABOR   561

and the Early Phases of Industrialisation in England," in Patrick Joyce, ed., *The Historical Meanings of Work* (Cambridge, 1987), p. 80, but the stringency of the laws excluding women from cloth making loosened and tightened according to the demand for labor.

80. Smail, "Manufacturer or Artisan?" p. 803.

81. Malcolmson, *Life and Labor in England*, pp. 35 and 38; and Ann Kussmaul, *Servants in Husbandry in Early Modern England* (Cambridge, 1981), pp. 22–23.

82. Hood, "Organization and Extent of Textile Manufacture," pp. 37–41.

83. The Chester County numbers are from the Inventory Data Base and break down as follows: 1715 = 6 wheels to 1 loom; 1734 = 7 to 1; 1754 = 6 to 1; 1773 = 8 to 1; 1792 = 7 to 1. The Essex County numbers come from a sampling of Essex County Inventories that included the first fifty inventories for each of the above periods from the Essex County Court House, Salem, Massachusetts, and break down as follows: 1715 = 2 to 1; 1734 = 8 to 1; 1754 = 2 to 1; 1773 = 3 to 1; 1792 = 2 to 1.

84. *Ibid.*, the percentage of decedent households with looms in Chester County: 1715 = 5.9; 1734 = 6.7; 1754 = 9.4; 1773 = 7.9; 1792 = 9.9; in Essex County: 1715 = 14; 1734 = 4; 1754 = 30; 1773 = 20; 1792 = 22.

85. Daniel Vickers, "Working the Fields in a Developing Economy: Essex County, Massachusetts , 1630–1675," in Innes, ed., *Work and Labor*, argues that although early immigrants brought servants to Massachusetts, this system collapsed as soon as the first servants dispersed and was not replaced by a system of wage labor.

86. Duane E. Ball, "Dynamics of Population and Wealth in Eighteenth-Century Chester County, Pennsylvania," *Journal of Interdisciplinary Studies* v. 6 (1976): 630. Ball, "The Process of Settlement in Eighteenth-Century Chester County, Pennsylvania," (Ph.D. dissertation, University of Pennsylvania, 1973), p. 70, notes that according to the 1790 census, for every 1,000 women there were: in Massachusetts, 960 men; in Pennsylvania, 1,057 men; and in Chester County, 1,077 men.

87. For example see Gullickson, *Spinners and Weavers of Auffay*; Shelton, *The Mills of Manayunk*; Gail Barbara Fowler, "Rhode Island Handloom Weavers and the Effects of Technological Change, 1780–1840" (Ph.D. dissertation, University of Pennsylvania, 1984).

4
¿Proto-Industria Colonial?

Manuel Miño Grijalva

HACE YA APROXIMADAMENTE veinte años que emergió el concepto *proto-industrialización* en el marco de la historia económica y social contemporánea para caracterizar y redefinir la etapa previa a la revolución industrial en Europa. Desde entonces, la discusión ha tomado cuerpo y los argumentos a favor o en contra han proliferado extendiéndose incluso en regiones fuera del contexto europeo. Retomar esta discusión para el caso novohispano y latinoamericano en general puede parecer a primera vista inútil, sin embargo, tengo la impresión de que el análisis del sector industrial en el caso colonial ha permanecido aislado y superficialmente desechado del proceso general cuando, por una parte, existen muchos problemas que en una perspectiva más amplia ayudan a comprender su dinámica y, por otra, ha sido restringido a la expresión más acabada del trabajo manufacturero como fue el obraje colonial, dejando de lado la producción doméstica, posiblemente la más extensa y dinámica, particularmente durante el periodo de transición (1530-1570), en la segunda parte del siglo XVIII y principios del siglo XIX.

Este breve artículo intenta centrar la discusión en el problema anterior, acogiendo en líneas generales la caracterización hecha para el caso europeo y contrastándola con las evidencias empíricas existentes en especial para Nueva España cuyos rasgos se observan en distintos lugares de latinoamérica. De la extensa literatura generada relativa a Europa, sólo haré mención de los estudios que señalan los puntos medulares de la discusión. No pretendo tampoco alcanzar un nivel analítico complejo, pues nuestras propias evidencias, a pesar de ser importantes, son menores en relación al caso europeo, no sólo por la abismal diferencia en cuanto al propio proceso, sino particularmente por la escasez de investigaciones en torno al problema. Por lo mismo, creo que en este punto radica la importancia del concepto de *proto-industrialización*, porque más allá de su validez implica una aproximación que metodológicamente es de gran relevancia y puede generar nuevas investigaciones que reorienten radicalmente la discusión.

Dos aspectos parecen caracterizar la tesis de la proto-industrialización: uno de tipo económico y otro más ligado al problema social. Para el primero es una etapa, una fase, *the first phase* del desarrollo industrial que se produjo en diversas partes del mundo europeo entre fines del siglo XVII y la revolución industrial, con la manufactura textil como sector clave de este proceso. Los trabajadores del campo dividían su tiempo entre la agricultura y la industria, y su producto no estaba destinado al consumo local, sino básicamente al mercado mundial. Los productores manufactureros vivían en regiones en donde sus ingresos agrícolas eran más bajos, hecho determinante para que los campesinos volvieran su mirada al trabajo industrial, en busca de un complemento. El nexo que unía al productor con el mercado fue el comerciante que viajaba por los pueblos, ubicados en las regiones caracterizadas por la industria doméstica, comprando los efectos manufacturados. En esta vasta red, los pueblos no cumplían el papel de centros productivos industriales, sino más bien eran lugares en donde los productores vendían sus efectos y se abastecían de materia prima y alimentos que ellos no producían. Estos alimentos tenían su origen en las regiones caracterizadas por una agricultura comercial.[1] En otras palabras, la proto-industria y su concepto está ligado a la producción dispersa rural, cuya dinámica se caracterizó por la interdependencia entre agricultura e industria, sugeri-

[1] CLARKSON, 1985, p. 51.

da por Mendels en su clásico ensayo.[2] Estos elementos configuran la tesis fundamental: antes de que la inversión de capital manufacturero llegara a ser dominante, fue sustancial y determinante la industrialización a través de la multiplicación de unidades domésticas de producción que disponían de un modesto capital y se ubicaban en las regiones rurales alrededor de centros mercantiles. Este proceso, sin embargo, parece persistir hasta bien entrada la economía urbano-industrial en el siglo XIX.[3] De esta manera, industria rural, mercado externo y la simbiosis entre la industria rural y el desarrollo de una agricultura comercial constituyen el marco de la proto-industrialización.

Los factores que contribuyeron al desarrollo proto-industrial europeo fueron básicamente la lentitud del ciclo coyuntural agrícola, las tendencias de crecimiento demográfico y, en consecuencia, el creciente desempleo en las zonas rurales y las crisis agrícolas del siglo XVII y de principios del XVIII. Fueron determinantes también en esta fase expansiva, el incremento en la demanda doméstica, así como una demanda externa en franca expansión.[4] Este movimiento no fue homogéneo; sin embargo, a pesar de la disparidad que puede encontrarse regionalmente, parece existir lo que Medick ha llamado una "base estructural común", que encontró en la economía familiar y la organización capitalista del comercio (trabajo a domicilio y comercialización de la producción) su expresión típica y más generalizada. De esta forma, una numerosa clase de subempleados campesinos o trabajadores rurales pobres constituyeron la brecha por donde penetró la producción industrial en el campo y pudo mantenerse gracias a un trabajo barato, cuyos costos de reproducción fueron absorbidos por la organización doméstica y su acceso a la tierra,[5] que cubrieron buena parte del trabajo impago. Así el comerciante pudo con éxito *evadir la presión* de los gremios urbanos y trasladar la producción al campo, dado que; por otra parte, el potencial productivo de las

[2] MENDELS, 1972.
[3] COLEMAN, 1983, pp. 436-437.
[4] KRIEDTE, MEDICK y SCHLUMBOHM, 1986, pp. 43-44.
[5] Véase ELEY, 1984, pp. 522-523.

ciudades no era ya suficiente para abastecer la demanda.[6]

En el sector agrario, el proceso de diferenciación y polarización ante el creciente ''individualismo agrario'' creaba profundas fisuras en el mundo rural, pues parcelaciones, cercados y distribución de tierras determinaban que un número cada vez mayor de familias buscaran una ocupación secundaria, como lo hicieron aquellas que poseían granjas que no rendían lo suficiente para cubrir sus necesidades. De esta forma el campesino se encontró frente a dos alternativas: a) asegurar los ingresos mediante una explotación más intensiva de la tierra, aunque dada la progresiva disminución del tamaño de ésta, llegó un momento en que el rendimiento total no podía ser incrementado y b) compensar el déficit de los ingresos a través de ocupaciones secundarias, no agrícolas, con lo cual se solucionaba también el problema del desempleo estacional. Así, la industria doméstica se convertía en la única solución posible y la agricultura de subsistencia en la base agraria de la proto-industrialización.[7]

Finalmente estaba el problema del mercado. La proto-industrialización estuvo estrechamente ligada a la formación de mercados, cuyas condiciones se fueron alterando en principio, porque la población crecía y se incrementaba la demanda del consumo de textiles, mientras se abría el mercado ultramarino,[8] con lo cual los mercados interregionales e internacionales se articulaban a la formación de un sistema mundial dominado por las metrópolis europeas, caracterizadas por un mayor desarrollo capitalista.[9] Así, la proto-industrialización ''se desarrollaba entre dos mundos: el limitado mundo de la aldea y el mundo sin fronteras del comercio; entre la economía agraria y el capitalismo comercial. El sector agrario aportó mano de obra, habilidades comerciales y empresariales, capital, productos y contribuciones al mercado. El capital mercantil abrió camino a la producción manufacturera rural hacia los mercados internacionales, de cuya capacidad de expansión dependía este sec-

[6] Kriedte, Medick y Schlumbohm, 1986, pp. 19, 20 y 41.
[7] Kriedte, Medick y Schlumbohm, 1986, pp. 33 y 47.
[8] Clarkson, 1985, p. 17.
[9] Kriedte, Medick y Schlumbohm, 1985, p. 22.

tor para poder emprender la fase de la proto-industrialización [...] La particular simbiosis del capital mercantil y la
sociedad campesina, marca, por tanto, una de las fases más
importantes del camino hacia el capital industrial".[10]

La discusión generada por el nuevo modelo ha seguido
varios cauces determinados por sus propios elementos, que
son ahora objeto de una atención sistemática, desde la propia perspectiva teórica que anima a sus proponentes y la eti-
mología del prefijo *proto*, hasta problemas como la dinámica
de la unidad familiar, la división del trabajo y el comporta-
miento de los campesinos proto-industriales. Coleman ad-
vierte que el propio término parece vago y confuso, pues el
prefijo, derivado del griego, sólo parece indicar situaciones
o hechos distintos a los que define la proto-industrialización,
pues su acepción original alude a temprano, original, primero en el tiempo, primitivo y, aunque es menos común, también se refiere a primero en rango o importancia, principal,
jefe. Por otra parte, en torno al movimiento general, según
Coleman no hay duda de que entre 1380 y 1750 existen ya
amplias evidencias de una industrial textil que sigue los li-
neamientos propuestos por Mendels y Kriedte, Medick y
Schlumbohm, aunque en circunstancias demográficas distintas. Coleman, por otra parte, hace hincapié en que las regiones en donde se produjo la proto-industrialización no
fueron únicamente las ásperas o estériles y, en general, la
explicación del desarrollo de la industria rural y su distribución en el campo incluyó también otras causas básicas en la
comprensión del proceso y que operaron de manera simultánea o en diferentes momentos: los patrones hereditarios, la
facilidad en los asentamientos, la energía hidráulica, la dis-
ponibilidad de materia prima, el tipo de agricultura, el tamaño de las propiedades, la densidad de la población local,
etc. Se necesitaría evidencia también de que la proto-
industrialización haya seguido, como rasgo distintivo, la vía
matrimonio temprano-crecimiento de la población.[11] Las
críticas se han centrado también en torno a las evidencias

[10] KRIEDTE, MEDICK y SCHLUMBOHM, 1986, pp. 63-64.
[11] COLEMAN, 1983, pp. 440-448.

empíricas que sustentan la geografía de la proto-industria. Ésta no fue lineal, en el sentido de que las regiones de agricultura comercial no experimentaron un proceso proto-industrial, ya que existen zonas de industria rural ubicadas en zonas fértiles.[12] Las evidencias muestran también que existe el consenso de que el trabajo campesino fue más barato que el urbano dadas la competencia y presión que ejercían los empleadores sobre los salarios en los pueblos y, que en el caso del sector artesanal, las restricciones que imponían los gremios servían para controlar los salarios y mantener alto el costo del trabajo, lo cual determinó que la producción industrial empleara trabajadores que periódicamente podían estar desempleados; sin embargo, estas circunstancias no determinaron que el trabajo rural fuera más barato en todas las regiones,[13] ni que los pequeños productores fueran todos iguales: unos ejercieron el comercio durante los ciclos de desempleo y otros se dedicaban todo el tiempo a la producción artesanal y reaccionaron de manera diferente en relación con el mercader capitalista. La crítica no ha dejado de señalar el hecho de que no existen evidencias sólidas y por tanto una relación directa entre el cambio de las condiciones materiales y las prácticas sociales, sexualidad y conducta dentro y fuera de la familia proto-industrial.[14]

Así, las limitaciones impuestas al modelo advierten sobre su validez, sobre todo cuando se trata de aplicarlo de manera mecánica, subsumiendo en él diversas estructuras e implicaciones regionales en ''una supuesta universalidad del cambio''[15] o cuando se llega a la exageración de afirmar que la industria rural condujo a la industria moderna. Todo lo contrario, estudios de caso muestran cómo las actividades proto-industriales en una región pueden retardar, incluso bloquear el desarrollo industrial.[16] Tampoco hay que descuidar el hecho de que este concepto, y el intenso proceso que implica, está enfocado especialmente a los textiles, res-

[12] GULLICKSON, 1983, pp. 831-850; CLARKSON, 1985, p. 53.
[13] CLARKSON, 1985, p. 20.
[14] Véase ELEY, 1984, p. 525.
[15] ELEY, 1984, p. 527.
[16] SCHREMMER, 1981, p. 670.

tricción que omite otras ramas industriales.[17]

Sin embargo, las objeciones y las implicaciones sobre la validez del modelo muestran, de todas formas, no sólo que en líneas generales el proceso históricamente es válido y tradicionalmente reconocido, y que, aparte de cualquier discusión, las réplicas y contrarréplicas sólo muestran los vacíos y lagunas por llenar, pues los mismos proponentes se preguntan si en realidad es lícito aplicar el término todas las veces que aparece un oficio en la zona rural; así como la necesidad de revalorar el papel de las ciudades y matizar suficientemente la vinculación entre industria doméstica rural y economía urbana dada su complementariedad, más que el desplazamiento de la producción manufacturera de ésta hacia aquella. Finalmente, los resultados de las investigaciones parecen sugerir que sería más fructífero no atenerse a un modelo único de proto-industrialización, sino distinguir desde la manufactura con un escaso nivel de desarrollo de la división del trabajo hasta aquellas producciones que se habían liberado por completo de la economía agraria y se mostraban con un alto nivel de división del trabajo.[18]

En síntesis, el éxito de la discusión europea parece depender más de una permanente redefinición de elementos a través de análisis regionales que puedan afinar el modelo, pues ese amplio movimiento que se produce inmediatamente antes de la revolución industrial parece incuestionable. Para regiones extraeuropeas, como es el caso del sur asiático, ha sido constatado y caracterizado por Perlin como un crecimiento secular en el uso y explotación de grandes cantidades de trabajo disperso, basado en el uso de tecnologías simples y adecuado a los requerimientos de la expansión comercial.[19]

En este marco de discusión, ¿cuál sería la virtud de acoger el concepto de proto-industria para el caso novohispano y latinoamericano en general, cuando los efectos de la revolución industrial sólo se consolidaron en las últimas décadas del siglo XIX? ¿Podría hablarse de una primera fas en el

[17] CLARKSON, 1985, p. 19.
[18] KRIEDTE, MEDICK y SCHLUMBOHM, 1986, pp. 300-301.
[19] PERLIN, 1983, p. 50. Un primer acercamiento al caso latinoamericano puede verse en MIÑO GRIJALVA, 1987.

MANUEL MIÑO GRIJALVA

camino hacia la industrialización cuando ésta en la actuali-
dad muestra rasgos de una débil y dependiente estructura?
O de una manera más general bajo la perspectiva de Kriedte, Medick y Schlumbohm, como una etapa de la transición
hacia el capitalismo. ¿Puede ésto tener validez cuando las
dimensiones del proceso no tienen comparación por los vo-
lúmenes de producción o la propia extensión de los mercados? Sin embargo, a pesar de las limitaciones a favor del término está el hecho de que la industria colonial, básicamente
la textil, ha permanecido obscurecida y relegada principal-
mente al obraje, dejando de lado el amplio sector de tejedores indígenas y tejedores urbanos que aparecen en los pueblos o en las zonas rurales. ¿Pero este hecho es suficiente
para hablar de proto-industria colonial? En principio su uti-
lidad radica en que nos ayudaría a definir mejor diversas
expresiones industriales que aparecen desarticuladas en el
contexto de la economía colonial. Más allá del modelo ''clásico'' o ''único'', los rasgos que se observan en muchos de
los parajes europeos y los diversos elementos que sirven para
definir la proto-industria están presentes en el caso novohispano y latinoamericano con variantes regionales y diversas
proporciones especialmente durante el siglo XVIII.

En principio, el propio prefijo *proto* se adecua mejor eti-
mológicamente al caso colonial en una acepción flexible de
primero (como forma inicial), incluso como *primitivo* y *original*,
y habla de formas y técnicas de trabajo combinadas entre la
aportación europea y la sobrevivencia de las indígenas, formas que en diversos espacios y coyunturas tuvieron manifes-
taciones de amplia magnitud, aunque contra esta asevera-
ción atente la falta de una cuantificación. Por otra parte, el
concepto de proto-industria tiene la virtud de subsumir en
su proceso diversas formas de organización y subsana, en lo
posible, la discusión entre la dependencia del tejedor al comerciante (trabajo a domicilio o *putting-out system*) y su independencia de éste (*Kaufsystem* o *cottage*), porque fuera de la
intervención del comerciante, la producción textil adscrita al
concepto de proto-industria es una producción para el mercado y que en el caso latinoamericano, bajo diversas formas
de organización estuvo presente desde los albores del siste-

ma económico colonial. Además, en términos del rigor conceptual, "la base estructural común" de la que habla Medick es en este caso la determinante, es decir, es un trabajo doméstico con la familia como unidad básica de producción y se produce para el mercado. Estos dos rasgos deslindan desde el principio la organización manufacturera del obraje como forma distinta de organización, aunque ambas presentan elementos característicos de la proto-industria, dada la presencia del comerciante que interviene directamente en la organización y funcionamiento de las unidades productivas y porque su producción está destinada a un amplio mercado consumidor. Incluso los gremios de Oaxaca y Tlaxcala reconocen esta injerencia de una manera acentuada en el siglo XVIII, aunque no sea un trabajo doméstico. Pero más allá del problema conceptual, la evolución histórica del sector textil y los diversos componentes de la organización productiva muestran la validez del modelo —con sus límites y en sus justas proporciones— para una época sin caracterización, pues desde el primer siglo colonial, particularmente hasta 1570, las comunidades indígenas entregaron grandes cantidades de tejidos y ropa como tributo a los encomenderos, momentos durante los cuales la relación población-tributo no había llegado a sus límites más bajos y la monetización del tributo no se había generalizado.[20] Esta extensa producción tuvo como base el trabajo doméstico indígena, con la familia como unidad productiva básica y con una tecnología simple y ancestral, aunque en varios casos se reconocen formas concentradas de trabajo, como se dio en el caso de Pánuco o Yucatán.[21]

Esta forma ampliada de producción que se extendió a lo largo del espacio colonial tuvo como referente principal la encomienda y la compulsión, y su organización productiva estuvo en función de la relación asimétrica impuesta por el estado colonial, fuera de las normas de reciprocidad que caracterizaron las relaciones prehispánicas y, por supuesto, lejos de la relación salarial. Es una etapa de dramática explo-

[20] Por ejemplo, MIRANDA, 1980; GONZÁLEZ DE COSÍO, 1952.
[21] ZAVALA, 1985, II, p. 273; QUEZADA, 1986, p. 23.

tación del grupo indígena, pues no sólo el trabajo era más barato, sino que quedaba totalmente impago; su dominio territorial se veía presionado por la naciente propiedad agraria colonial, y los propios miembros de la comunidad atravesaban por una crisis que no se detendrá sino hasta mediados del siglo XVII. La caída de la población indígena repercutirá de manera acentuada en la producción que abastecía buena parte del mercado colonial.[22]

Entre 1570 y 1620 el panorama del trabajo textil parece reorientarse. La comunidad indígena, *reducida* o *congregada* en pueblos o en permanente lucha por conseguir el *status* de tal, se encontró nuevamente impulsada a realizar una producción para el mercado a través de corregidores y alcaldes mayores: el repartimiento será el nuevo eje articulador de la producción y circulación de la mercancía textil en el caso del algodón, particularmente en el sur de Nueva España. Ésta es la época de expansión del *repartimiento*, que llega a constituir una forma nueva de reorganizar el comercio dadas las circunstancias que planteaba la crisis. En este movimiento los comerciantes siguieron un doble mecanismo: por una parte los grandes comerciantes de México, Puebla y Veracruz enviaban a sus correspondientes apostados en provincia dinero y productos de consumo indígena (como vino y cera) a precios altos —en relación a su valor real— para ser vendidos entre las comunidades. A cambio, el comerciante obtiene el producto local que, a su vez, remite a los centros mercantiles. Las mantas y los tejidos ocuparon un lugar importante en estas transacciones, hasta el punto de que en 1594 se expidió una nueva cédula que prohibía el *repartimiento de mantas*, cuyo abuso llegó a ser la causa inmediata de una

---

[22] En Oaxaca, sin embargo, existió un importante sector de trabajo femenino ligado directamente al mercado. Los indígenas de esta región compraban por 1580 algodón en Veracruz y Yucatán, los manufacturaban y vendían telas y mantas en el centro del país. MORENO TOSCANO, 1968, p. 87. En el caso peruano, las *Ordenanzas de Indios* del oidor Cuenca de 1566 revelan también que para entonces ya existía un sector textil independiente al ordenamiento estatal, pues mencionan que a las indias les "suelen dar los mercaderes [6 tomines] cuando les dan a hacer ropa". En ASSADOURIAN, 1987, p. 403.

resistencia violenta por parte del indígena. Si bien el comerciante es el eje del funcionamiento de este sistema, la intermediación del alcalde mayor como parte del estado colonial
y como agente mercantil rompe la figura clásica del trabajo
a domicilio, al menos su estructura formal, aunque se readecua de manera *informal*, con la compulsión como mecanismo
articulador, pues de todas formas es el comerciante el desti-
natario de la producción.[23] Durante este tiempo y de manera simultánea, el gremio se fortalece en el interior de los centros manufactureros más importantes como la ciudad de
México o Puebla, con base en el trabajo de la lana que se
expande también a través del obraje colonial como un proceso propio, que a la inversa del europeo, reconoció un amplio
sector de trabajo concentrado. Las características que distin-
guen al obraje colonial: división del trabajo (cooperación
compleja), concentración de fuerza de trabajo, un nivel tecnológico superior al indígena trasladado de la Península,
disposición de un capital de alguna importancia y un amplio
mercado consumidor ubicado fuera de las regiones productoras, confieren jerarquía a la producción manufacturera de
Nueva España y Perú. Sin embargo ¿se puede considerar al
obraje como una expresión proto-industrial? De hecho, fue
una forma de producción con un alto nivel de división del
trabajo y un funcionamiento semiautónomo de la propiedad
agraria en Nueva España, perfectamente articulado a ella en
el caso del espacio andino. Este tipo de organización tuvo
una vinculación relativa con la comunidad indígena, en el
primer caso, adscrita sólo al hilado, como sucedió en varios
casos de obrajes de Tlaxcala, Tacuba, México o Querétaro
en distintos momentos. Y en el segundo repercutió sensible-
mente en la vida de la comunidad. Es un *tipo* de producción
proto-industrial, distinto y sin referencias en el caso europeo. Sin embargo, el obraje no fue el embrión de la fábrica
y, por lo tanto, su evolución no condujo a la industria *moderna*, pero ciertamente constituye una etapa previa y clave del

[23] PASTOR, 1985, pp. 208-211. Para el caso de Yucatán, véanse,
QUESADA, 1986 y GARCÍA BERNAL, 1972, pp. 250 y 254-259; GARCÍA
BERNAL, 1979, pp. 128-135. Un ejemplo para Michoacán puede encon-
trarse en LEMOINE, 1960, pp. 201.

proceso industrial andino y novohispano, pues su producción alcanzó un amplio radio de comercialización. En el caso novohispano los tejidos de Puebla llegaron a consumirse
en el virreinato del Perú y los de Quito cruzaron el espacio
peruano hasta Chile, Tucumán, el Alto Perú y Buenos
Aires, con un dinamismo poco usual.

Por otra parte, el problema de la concentración del trabajo, visto comparativamente, presenta diferencias importantes. Según Kriedte, Medick y Schlumbohm, en el caso de la
Europa occidental se produce por los obstáculos que presen-
taba la cada vez más extensa red de campesinos y trabajadores proto-industriales hacia un eficiente control de la calidad
de los efectos manufacturados, mientras que la concentración de trabajadores obrajeros tiene como base fundamental
la dinámica y los niveles demográficos decrecientes, así como la especialización de un trabajo desconocido en el mundo indígena, pues la manufactura de la lana no formó parte
de la economía familiar sino hasta después de la conquista
y el lino prácticamente fue desconocido hasta finales del periodo colonial.[24]

Entre la organización manufacturera del obraje y la forma doméstica de producción, las formas gremiales sólo tuvieron en la práctica una relativa capacidad de presión en
los lugares donde ésta se dio. En Nueva España, la ciudad
de México y Puebla fueron los sitios más importantes. En
el área andina se desconoce por completo el papel que juga-
ron los gremios, diferencia que puede sugerir una mayor
fuerza de los centros urbanos novohispanos y un dominio total del mundo agrario-manufacturero en el segundo caso,
hecho que será determinante al finalizar el periodo colonial
para definir la estructura espacial de la producción textil.
Este proceso se revelará con mayor fuerza en el siglo XVIII
en Nueva España cuando los centros urbanos, particularmente de Puebla, México, Tlaxcala, Querétaro y Guadalajara se conviertan en lugares de atracción que absorverán al
trabajador del campo que salía de sus regiones para acogerse

[24] Sobre el lino y cáñamo en Nueva España, véase SERRERA CONTRE-
RAS, 1974.

a la sombra de la ciudad, particularmente en tiempos de crisis (al menos en la región de Puebla-Tlaxcala). En la región andina, en cambio, en Socorro en Colombia, Cuenca en la real audiencia de Quito, Cuzco en Perú y Charcas en el Alto Perú o Córdova, el hilador y el tejedor compartirán, en líneas generales, el trabajo de la agricultura con el de la industria. Pero este movimiento es sustancialmente diferente del que se dio durante el siglo XVI.

En el siglo XVIII, en especial durante la segunda mitad, tejedores domésticos independientes, criollos, mestizos e indígenas, se multiplican por diversas regiones del espacio colonial con una estrecha vinculación al mercado y una dependencia directa o indirecta del capital comercial.[25] Este movimiento expansivo supera las formas gremial y obrajera y adquiere gran dinamismo a lo largo del espacio colonial en niveles y proporciones que responden claramente a un incremento en la demanda de tejidos, sobre todo de algodón, y que desborda claramente la producción de autoconsumo. Por otra parte, sin comparar los niveles que alcanzó esta producción, los elementos analizados en el caso europeo resultan sugerentes en el caso americano, en especial dos de los ejes en torno a los que se produjo esta multiplicación: el trabajo doméstico urbano o rural y la presencia del sector mercantil, sin dejar de observar también sustanciales diferencias, que a la postre confieren especificidad al caso novohispano.

En este sentido, varios factores explican la expansión del trabajo doméstico y a domicilio que se produce en el espacio colonial novohispano en el siglo XVIII, pero particularmente después de 1750, fecha que para el caso textil no es arbitraria. En otros trabajos expuse los factores del cambio de manera más detallada, por lo que aquí sólo daré una corta referencia. Durante este tiempo las siembras de algodón se

[25] Además de las iniciales observaciones realizadas por Potash y Bazant en 1959 y 1964, respectivamente, ahora contamos con evidencias más amplias y concretas sobre este sector y su relación con el capital comercial. Por ejemplo, GONZÁLEZ ANGULO y SANDOVAL ZARAUZ, 1980; GONZÁLEZ ANGULO, 1983; MIÑO GRIJALVA, 1983, 1984 y 1987; THOMSON, 1986; SALVUCCI, 1987, TUTINO, 1985.

expanden por el sur de Nueva España, impulsadas por la legalización del repartimiento y el impulso de la corona, que veía una posibilidad de abastecer las fábricas catalanas. Este movimiento significó el fortalecimiento de una red bien estructurada por los comerciantes, que fueron los principales beneficiarios del monopolio que ejercieron sobre la materia prima, lo cual repercutió en un control directo de los agentes mercantiles sobre hiladores y tejedores, aunque ciertamente regiones importantes conocieron independencia y movilidad. Este hecho se vio complementado, durante las últimas décadas del siglo XVIII, por la expansión y multiplicación de giros mercantiles en el espacio novohispano y una acentuada tendencia al alza de los niveles de la producción minera, a pesar de los altibajos que se observan en su dinámica. Por otra parte, la expansión de los mercados y el crecimiento de la población en general constituyen dos factores clave del desarrollo textil de esta época. El primero estuvo relacionado con la ampliación de las provincias del norte y la ocupación de áreas antes vacías; en este sentido, los propios reales de minas fueron un mercado consumidor importante. El segundo, en cambio, a pesar de crisis y epidemias que afectaron particularmente a la población indígena, está estrechamente vinculado con un proceso de crecimiento especialmente del sector no indígena, aunque en ciertas coyunturas más que en otras. Sin embargo, las variantes regionales de la agricultura y las crisis agrarias van a configurar procesos migratorios distintos: la región de Puebla-Tlaxcala experimentará los efectos más agudos de las crisis que provocará una migración acentuada hacia México o de pueblos menores hacia Puebla,[26] en cambio, Querétaro, el Bajío y Gua-

---

[26] En esta región la inestabilidad de la población parece clara y su ritmo, a pesar de rasgos de crecimiento, sufre graves alteraciones que, como en el caso de Cholula, son definitivas. Una idea bastante clara de este proceso se encuentra en VOLLMER, 1973, pp. 47-49; CALVO, 1973, pp. 79-80; MALVIDO, 1973, p. 83; MORIN, 1973, GARAVAGLIA y GROSSO, 1987, p. 224. En todo este movimiento la ciudad de México cumplirá el papel de centro de atracción de la población. MORENO TOSCANO, 1973; MORENO TOSCANO y AGUIRRE, 1974, pp. 36-37; DAVIS, 1972, pp. 502-503; BOYER y DAVIS, 1973, pp. 41-42.

najuato se caracterizarán por un claro crecimiento demográfico y una estabilidad mayor con escasa movilidad de su población.[27] Hacia el occidente, Guadalajara, otro centro textil importante, crece con una numerosa población de inmigrantes.[28] Expulsión y permanencia, de todas formas, no cambiarán el hecho de que la industria textil se ubique, por una parte, a la sombra de los centros urbanos y, por otra, que muchos pueblos indígenas continúen produciendo tanto para sí mismos como para el mercado. Este doble movimiento determinó que en el caso de la industria urbana, el hilador o tejedor se desvinculara de su entorno agrario. Es entonces cuando la agricultura de subsistencia deja de ser la base agraria que absorbe parte de los costos. En el segundo caso, el tejedor rural, como sucedió en Tepeaca,[29] Acatzingo, Villa Alta, Toluca y otras zonas hacia el sur, continúa vinculado a la agricultura como actividad principal. Sin embargo, el tejido no fue para el campesino o agricultor pobre la única alternativa. En otras partes, hay evidencia de que durante el tiempo de paro estacional se dedicó también a la arriería como un recurso complementario.[30]

Lamentablemente, hasta ahora no es posible cuantificar las dimensiones de la producción doméstica, pero los testimonios sobre la importancia que adquirió esta industria son claros, sobre todo debido a la interrupción del comercio transatlántico. Pero al contrario de la europea, esta indus-

[27] BORAH y COOK, 1975; MORENO TOSCANO, 1972; MORIN, 1983, p. 9 y 1979, pp. 72-83. Para una apreciación numérica de la población textil de Querétaro, véase WU, 1984, p. 295.

[28] VAN YOUNG, 1981, p. 35 y 1988, pp. 147-148.

[29] La simbiosis agricultura industria en los pueblos indígenas puede ser ejemplificada por Tepeaca, sobre la cual se decía en 1792 que en esta "ciudad hay mucha cantidad de obrajes y en ellos muchos indios que sirven y tienen tierras que cultiban" CALVO, 1973, p. 13. Sin embargo, el observador de la época confunde talleres domésticos con obrajes.

[30] El subdelegado de Taxco decía en 1792 que "la arriería es el recurso de toda gente pobre, y las utilidades que resultan de esta ocupación son imponderables. A este ejercicio se dedican no sólo los que por profesión la ejercitan, sino todo labrador, fuese indio o español, pues pasando el tiempo de la labranza, que son cuatro meses, ocupaban el resto del año en conducir sus frutos a los mercados". En SERRERA, 1977, pp. 265-266.

tria se vio golpeada y reducida por los efectos del comercio exterior y la propia expansión de la industrialización capitalista, que terminará por integrar a sus esferas de influencia el extenso mercado colonial.

Así, todo el amplio movimiento que se observa en las regiones registradas por los censos de tejedores de 1781, 1793 y 1801 configuró centros textiles con características particulares definidas por su relación con el sector mercantil, por la simbiosis agricultura-industria y por el papel que cumplió el estado colonial y la propia condición étnica. Sin embargo, a pesar de las diferencias que pudieran encontrarse, llegaron a configurarse rasgos semejantes que prevalecieron en el trabajo doméstico de la época: el tejido fue ocasional, determinado por los ciclos de la producción agrícola, y por la mayor o menor disposición de la materia prima. Hubo casos en que el tejedor combinó también el trabajo en las minas con el textil. Por otra parte, el comerciante era el eje articulador entre capital y trabajo y actuaba como *habilitador*, *aviador* o *fiador* de la lana o algodón y el tejedor se reservaba la propiedad de los instrumentos de producción. En el caso de los centros algodoneros y textiles del sur de Nueva España, cuando el *repartimiento de mantas* renace con fuerza, la comunidad fue articulada por los alcaldes mayores. Éstos eran los encargados de repartir la materia prima para su hilado y tejido y, en un paso posterior, extraer la producción hacia los centros mercantiles a nombre de los comerciantes aviadores.[31] En otros casos el algodón salía hacia los centros urbanos, en donde los grandes comerciantes lo redistribuían hacia los pueblos con destino a sus *correspondientes*, que cumplían con la función de vender o habilitar a hiladores y tejedores.

En este movimiento hay que destacar, como se hizo respecto al siglo XVI, el carácter compulsivo de la organización textil del sur de Nueva España, que estuvo respaldado por el poder del estado colonial, y diferenciarlo del carácter abierto (aparentemente) de las relaciones entre tejedores y

---

[31] Borchart de Moreno ilustra perfectamente este caso. Véase BOR-CHART DE MORENO, 1977.

comerciantes de los pueblos y ciudades de Puebla, Texcoco, Tlaxcala, León, Zamora, etc. También es necesario distinguir de esta red de articulaciones el trabajo doméstico independiente en pueblos y lugares donde el tejedor indígena contribuía directamente al mercado, sin la intermediación del comerciante, como sucedió en Tepeaca[32] o Tlapa, cuyas ferias y mercados cumplían un papel fundamental. Este último pueblo puede ilustrar algo que pudo ocurrir en muchos otros. Aquí, la producción textil de la comunidad se vendía directamente a los comerciantes locales y forasteros que llegaban en ocasión de las ferias. En el propio mercado de Tlapa los indígenas vendían o intercambiaban sus tejidos y conseguían el algodón en greña. En general, según Dehoeve, era "impresionante ver cómo circulaban los productos textiles de una provincia a otra en el siglo XVIII. Así los mixtecos de la sierra vendían mantas y huipiles a las mujeres del norte de Tlapa. Sin embargo éstas compraban también huipiles de lana de Texcoco y faldas hechas en Puebla. Los hombres llevaban [ropa] de algodón tejida en Puebla. Mientras tanto, parte de las mantas y huipiles, junto con las medias, calcetas y rebozos se comercializaban en otras partes de Nueva España''. Transacciones en las que en la mayoría de los casos intervenía el dinero.[33]

No hay duda que en general la participación de la comunidad indígena en la producción textil para el mercado fue en muchos casos determinante. Este mercado no competía con la producción extranjera, a la que estuvo más sujeta la producción del tejedor urbano. Este hecho le proporcionó especificidad, dado que, además, su funcionamiento mostró rasgos que la diferenciaron del caso europeo. La diferencia

[32] En Tepeaca, el grupo indígena traficaba constantemente con lana en los pueblos cercanos a la cabecera y otros más distantes, mientras que hacia el sur los indios "serranos", mixtecos y del Valle de Oaxaca comerciaban con algodón. La contribución de los tejedores domésticos se realizaba con tratos directos con los comerciantes. "Es ropa de lana, para vestuario de Yndios que ellos mismos trabajan y comercian con los españoles para conduzirlos a otros territorios". En GARAVAGLIA y GROSSO, 1987, pp. 235 y 239.

[33] DEHOVE, 1988, pp. 90-91.

fundamental se encuentra en que el componente del sistema no es en sí mismo el tejedor individual que actúa en el marco de "un creciente individualismo agrario", sino a la sombra de la comunidad como ente corporativo y más bien frente a un crecimiento y expansión constante de la propiedad agraria privada española, al menos en el centro de Nueva España. Por otra parte, en el caso del tejedor urbano, la base agraria de subsistencia al parecer fue inexistente. De esta forma, el trabajo textil en su conjunto es un trabajo complementario entre la producción del campo y la ciudad, separado quizás por los usos y costumbres de la población. Otra diferencia importante es que desde principios del periodo colonial el trabajo doméstico y el trabajo *informal* a domicilio se producen, al contrario de lo que sucedía en Europa, en el sector del algodón, mientras que el de la lana queda adscrito básicamente al obraje manufacturero y al gremio urbano. Ciertamente el trabajo del algodón en el primer siglo colonial también fue compartido por artesanos tejedores, particularmente en Puebla. Por otra parte, la producción local fue muy sensible a las variaciones del comercio exterior, aunque en términos de su comercialización alcanzó no sólo a abastecer al mercado local, sino también al interregional, pero la producción no tuvo como destino el mercado internacional. En cuanto al salario, no fue sólo el dinero y coexistió con los pagos en especie, aunque con un valor referente al mercado. Otra característica diferente importante es que en las zonas de trabajo compulsivo la organización del trabajo tuvo a la mujer indígena como eje en torno al cual giró la producción, mientras que en las zonas urbanas fue el hombre y la familia la unidad básica de producción. Finalmente es necesario mencionar que el componente tecnológico reconoció tradiciones distintas. En general, al finalizar el periodo colonial buena parte de la producción textil se dio en torno a los pueblos y ciudades, pero como en el caso de Europa occidental, éstos también fueron centros en donde los tejedores e hiladores vendían sus efectos, y se abastecían de materia prima y de alimentos que ellos no producían. En el caso del tejedor urbano, parece haber estado articulado precariamente al mundo económico y socialmente fue catalogado como "gente infeliz y miserable", ubicada en los barrios marginales de los centros textiles, en los "suburbios" como decían los administradores de alcabalas. Era, en buenas cuentas, un trabajo realizado por la "plebe".[34]

No quisiera dejar de anotar un problema en nuestro análisis que me parece importante: la constitución de la unidad familiar como eje del trabajo proto-industrial, para las regiones de *compulsión y repartimiento*. En éstas, al contrario de lo que sucedía en el modelo clásico, no es la familia completa, "toda la casa", la que interviene en el proceso productivo, sino sólo *parte* de la casa, con la mujer como centro del movimiento. Este hecho fractura el modelo, aunque desde el principio se había visto afectado al intervenir el estado colonial como ordenador del trabajo, primero como parte del tributo y luego como repartimiento. Por ahora no se pueden saber los alcances ni repercusiones de este problema, pero creo que es necesario señalarlo.

En conclusión, se puede percibir en la dinámica del trabajo textil colonial un acentuado nivel de patrones hereditarios en torno a la comunidad indígena, que tiende a perderse en el caso del tejedor urbano. Se percibe una clara localización espacial de los centros y regiones dedicados a labores industriales cerca de las zonas productoras de materia prima o ligadas económicamente a ellas, como fue el caso de la región de Puebla, Tlaxcala, Villa Alta y otros pueblos de la jurisdicción, o la misma Guadalajara en el siglo XVIII. Además, en el caso de la lana, si bien se reconoce una continua expansión de las fronteras de la crianza de ganado lanar desde el Bajío hacia el norte, existen multitud de haciendas y

---

[34] Los casos de San Luis Potosí o Celaya pueden ilustrar este hecho. "Esta gente aplicada a la industria apenas le quedaba después de sus fatigas, un triste jornal con que subsistir. Difícilmente pueden pagar los dos o tres o cuatro reales mensuales en que está pensionado cada telar. Y finalmente, que con atención a que en temporadas no trabajan por falta de avío, interrumpen sus obras o se ausentan por varios accidentes." También: "Ahora —decía el administrador de Celaya— habiendo yo pasado a reconocer personalmente los parajes en que están los telares, me he llenado de compasión al ver dentro de una estrecha pieza... de adobe, hombres casi desnudos, sin más aperos que su telar donde están trabajando". Miño Grijalva, 1984, pp. 274-275.

ranchos al interior del reino —como los complejos jesuitas, por ejemplo— que inducen a pensar en la importancia de la producción lanera. En el caso colonial se puede hablar de que la producción textil se produjo precisamente en las regiones caracterizadas por una agricultura comercial, como es el caso del Bajío, Jalisco y la región de Puebla y Tlaxcala, a pesar de coyunturas críticas y epidemias que repercutieron en el ritmo de la población, particularmente de la indígena. En este sentido la presión sobre los recursos pudo disminuir en unos casos e incrementarse en otros, producida por el crecimiento natural de la población y, sobre todo, por la extensión de la propiedad agraria sobre la tierra de los pueblos. Así, el problema de la densidad de población como factor importante para el desarrollo de la industria textil se reduce y se vuelve secundario, como en el caso del factor matrimonio temprano-crecimiento de la población, acerca del cual, como piensa Thomas Gerst, todo indica que en el caso novohispano la edad en que las parejas contraían matrimonio siempre fue muy temprana.[35] Sin embargo, esta diferencia en relación al caso europeo no termina por anular el propio proceso colonial, como tampoco el hecho de que buena parte de la producción industrial se haya ubicado alrededor de las ciudades más importantes. Todo lo contrario, creo que estas diferencias proporcionan rasgos específicos al caso novohispano. Entre estos límites se ubica también el problema del mercado interno colonial, destino de la producción de tejedores y obrajes americanos; por ello, me parece que lo importante no es la extensión de los mercados, sino la constatación del hecho de que hubo un sector textil mercantilizado y un amplio mercado consumidor, complementado por una extensa red de unidades domésticas vinculadas al proceso de producción, que finalmente constituye esa "base estructural común" que caracterizó a la protoindustria. Por ello no encuentro obstáculos para hablar de proto-industria colonial, aunque ciertamente *éstos se vuelven insuperables* si pensamos en aplicar el término *proto-industrialización*, como un proceso secular de crecimiento que desem-

[35] En WOBESER, 1989.

bocó en la siguiente etapa: la industrialización.

REFERENCIAS

ASSADOURIAN, Carlos Sempat

    1987   "Señores étnicos y los corregidores de indios en la conformación del sistema colonial", en *Anuario de Estudios Americanos*, XLIV, pp. 325-410.

BAZANT, Jan

    1964   "Evolución de la industria textil poblana (1544-1845)", en *Historia Mexicana*, XIV:1 (53), (ago.-sept.), pp. 131-143.

BORAH, Woodrow y Sherburne F. COOK

    1975   "El centro urbano como foco para la emigración en la Nueva España", en Jorge E. HARDOY y Richard P. SHAEDEL (comps.): *Las ciudades de América Latina y sus áreas de influencia a través de la Historia.* Buenos Aires, Ediciones Siap, pp. 113-132.

BORCHART DE MORENO, Christiana Renate

    1977   "Los miembros del Consulado de la ciudad de México en la época de Carlos III", en *Jarbuch für Geschichte von Staat, Wirtschaft und Gesellschaft Lateinamerikas* (14), pp. 134-160.

BOYER, Richard E. y Keith DAVIS

    1973   *Urbanization in 19th-Century Latin America, Statistics and Sources.* University of California, Los Angeles University Press.

CALVO, Thomas

    1973   *Acatzingo. Demografía de una parroquia mexicana.* México, Instituto Nacional de Antropología e Historia.

CLARKSON, L. A.

    1985   *Proto-Industrialization: The First Phase of Industrialization?* Macmillan, Hong Kong, Economic History Society, Macmillan.

COLEMAN, Donald Cuthbest

    1983   "Proto-Industralization: A Concept too Many", en *Economic History Review*, XXXVI:3 (ago.), pp. 435-448.

814   MANUEL MIÑO GRIJALVA

Davis, Keith A.

    1972   "Tendencias demográficas urbanas durante el siglo
            XIX", en *Historia Mexicana*, XXI:3(83) (ene.-mar.),
            pp. 481-524.

Dehove, Daniele

    1988   "El pueblo de indios y el mercado: Tlapa en el siglo
            XVIII", en Arij Ouweneel y Cristina Torales Pache-
            co (comp.), *Empresarios indios y estado. Perfil de la econo-
            mía mexicana (Siglo XVIII)*. Amsterdam, Centro de Es-
            tudios y Documentación Latinoamericanos, «Latin
            American Studies, 45», pp. 86-102.

Eley, Geoff

    1984   "The social history of industrialization: 'proto-
            Industry' and the origins of capitalism", en *Economy
            and Society*, 13:4, pp. 519-539.

Garavaglia, Juan Carlos y Juan Carlos Grosso

    1987   "El abasto de una villa novohispana: mercancías y flu-
            jos mercantiles en Tepeaca (1780-1820)", *Anuario del
            Instituto de Estudios Históricos y Sociales* (2), pp. 217-253.

García Bernal, Manuela Cristina

    1972   "La visita de Fray Luis de Cifuentes, Obispo de Yu-
            catán", en *Anuario de Estudios Americanos*, XXIX, pp.
            229-260.

    1979   "El gobernador de Yucatán Rodrigo Flores de Alda-
            na", en *Homenaje al Dr. Muro Orejón*. Sevilla, Facultad
            de Filosofía y Letras, Universidad de Sevilla, pp. 123-
            153.

González Angulo Aguirre, Jorge

    1983   *Artesanado y ciudad a finales del siglo xviii*. México, Secre-
            taría de Educación Pública-Fondo de Cultura Econó-
            mica.

González Angulo, Jorge y Roberto Sandoval Zarauz

    1980   "Los trabajadores industriales en Nueva España,
            1750-1810", en Enrique Florescano (coord.), *La cla-
            se obrera en la historia de México. De la colonia al Imperio*.
            México, Siglo Veintiuno Editores, pp. 173-238.

González de Cosío, Francisco

    1952   *El libro de las tasaciones de pueblos de la Nueva España. Siglo xvi.* México, Archivo General de la Nación.

GULLICKSON, Gay L.

1983   "Agriculture and Cottage Industry: Redefining the Causes of Proto-Industrialization", en *The Journal of Economic History,* XLIII:4 (dic.), pp. 831-850.

KRIEDTE, Peter, Hans MEDICK y Jürgen SCHLUMBOHM

1986   *Industrializacion antes de la industrialization.* Barcelona, Editorial Crítica.

LEMOINE, Ernesto

1960   "Relación de agravios de los naturales de la Provincia de los motines de Colima contra su Alcalde Mayor y Juez Congregador (1603-1604)" Introducción y notas por E. L., en *Boletín del Archivo General de la Nación,* 2ª Serie, I:2, pp. 201-212.

MALVIDO, Elsa

1973   "Factores de despoblación y de reposición de la población de Cholula (1641-1810), en *Historia Mexicana,* XXIII:1(89) (jul.-sept.), pp. 52-110.

MENDELS, Franklin

1972   "Proto-Industrialization: The First Phase of the Industrialization Process", en *Journal of Economic History,* XXXII, pp. 241-261.

MIÑO GRIJALVA, Manuel

1983   "Espacio económico e industria textil: los trabajadores de Nueva España, 1780-1810", en *Historia Mexicana,* XXXII:4(128), pp. 524-553.

1984   "Obrajes y tejedores de Nueva España, 1750-1810", tesis doctoral, El Colegio de México.

1987   "Capital comercial y trabajo textil: tendencias generales de la protoindustria colonial Latinoamericana", en *Revista Latinoamericana de Historia Económica y Social* (9), pp. 59-79.

MIRANDA, José

1980   *El tributo indígena en la Nueva España durante el siglo XVI.* México, El Colegio de México.

MORENO TOSCANO, Alejandra

1968   *Geografía económica de México. Siglo XVI.* México, El Colegio de México.

816   MANUEL MIÑO GRIJALVA

1972   "Economía regional y urbanización: tres ejemplos de
       relaciones entre ciudades y regiones en Nueva España
       a finales del siglo XVIII", en *Urbanización y proceso social
       en América*. Lima, Instituto de Estudios Peruanos.

MORENO TOSCANO, Alejandra y Carlos AGUIRRE

1974   "Migraciones hacia la ciudad de México durante el siglo
       XIX: perspectivas de investigación", en *Investigaciones so-
       bre la historia de la ciudad de México*. I, México, Instituto
       Nacional de Antropología e Historia.

MORIN, Claude

1973   *Santa Inés Zacatelco, 1646-1812. Contribución a la demogra-
       fía histórica del México colonial*. México, Instituto Nacio-
       nal de Antropología e Historia.

1979   *Michoacán en la Nueva España del siglo XVIII. Crecimiento
       y desigualdad en una economía regional*. México, Fondo de
       Cultura Económica.

1983   "Proceso demográfico, movimiento migratorio y mez-
       clas raciales en el estado de Guanajuato y su contorno
       en la época colonial", en *Relaciones. Estudios de Historia
       y Sociedad*, IV:16, pp. 6-18.

PASTOR, Rodolfo

1985   "El repartimiento de mercancías y los alcaldes mayo-
       res novohispanos. Un sistema de explotación. De sus
       orígenes a la crisis de 1810", en Woodrow BORAH
       (Coord.), *El Gobierno Provincial en la Nueva España,
       1570-1787*. México, Universidad Nacional Autónoma
       de México, pp. 201-236.

PERLIN, F.

1983   "Proto-Industrialization and Pre-Colonial South Asia",
       en *Past and Present* (98), (feb.), pp. 30-95.

POTASH, Robert

1959   *El Banco de Avío de México. El fomento de la industria,
       1821-1846*. México, Fondo de Cultura Económica.

QUEZADA, Sergio

1986   "Producción del tributo y mercado colonial. El caso
       de Yucatán. Una provincia novohispana, 1550-
       1580", Ponencia presentada en el VII Simposio Inter-
       nacional de Historia Económica, Lima, CLACSO/IEP.

Salvucci, Richard

    1987   *Textiles and Capitalism. A Economic History of the Mexican Obrajes, 1539-1840*. Princeton, Princeton University Press.

Serrera Contreras, Ramón María

    1974   *Cultivo y manufactura de lino y cáñamo en Nueva España, 1777-1800*. Sevilla, Escuela de Estudios Hispanoamericanos.

    1977   *Guadalajara ganadera. Estudio regional novohispano, 1760-1805*. Sevilla, Escuela de Estudios Hispanoamericanos.

Schremmer, Eckhart

    1981   "Proto-Industrialization: A Step Towards Industrialization?", en *Journal of European Economic History*, x, pp. 653-670.

Thomson, Guy

    1986   "The Cotton Textile Industry in Puebla during the Eighteenth and Early Nineteenth Centuries", en Nils Jacobsen y Hans-Jüngen Puhle (comps.) *The Economies of Mexico and Peru during Late Colonial Period, 1760-1810*. Berlin, Colloqium Verlag, «Bibliotheca Ibero-Americana 34», pp. 169-202.

Tutino, John

    1985   "Guerra, comercio colonial y textiles mexicanos: El Bajío 1585-1810", en *Historias* (11), (oct. dic.), pp. 15-46.

Van Young, Eric

    1981   *Haciendas and Market in Eighteenth-Century Mexico: The Rural Economy of the Guadalajara Region, 1675-1820*. Berkeley, University of California Press.

    1988   "Island in the Storm: Quiet Cities and Violent Countryside in the Mexican Independence Era", en *Past and Present* (118), (feb.), pp. 130-152.

Vollmer, Günter

    1973   "La evolución cuantitativa de la población indígena en la región de Puebla (1570-1810)", en *Historia Mexicana*, xxiii:1(89), (jul.-sept.), pp. 43-51.

Wobeser, Gisela von

    1989   "Sobre Thomas Gerst: Die wirstchaftliche Entwick-

818   MANUEL MIÑO GRIJALVA

                    lung Mexikas und das Problem des Proto-Industriali-
                    sierung am Ausgangder Kolorualzeit'' en *Historia Me-*
                    xicana, XL.:2 (154) (oct.-dic.).

Wu, Celia

        1984   ''The Population of the City of Querétaro in 1791'',
                    en *Journal of Latin American Studies*, (16), (nov.), pp.
                    277-307.

ZAVALA, Silvio

        1985   *El servicio personal de los indios en Nueva España, 1521-*
                    1575. México, El Colegio de México-El Colegio
                    Nacional.

5

Reconsidering Textile Production in Late Colonial Brazil: New Evidence from Minas Gerais

Douglas C. Libby

Scholars have long recognized that the final quarter of the eighteenth century in Brazil witnessed an agricultural renaissance in which traditional exports expanded and new tropical products began to find their way overseas (Prado Júnior 1967; Novais 1979; Arruda 1980, 1986; Alden 1984). In recent years, more attention has been paid to the diversified productive activities supplying an increasingly consolidated domestic market during this period (Brown 1986; Barickman 1991; Fragoso 1992). Although most of those activities were agricultural, artisan trades also flourished and domestic industry appears to have been growing, particularly the cottage textile industry. My examination of an unexplored and unusual primary source has revealed grounds for assuming that cloth and thread were being made throughout much of late colonial Brazil. The primary evidence also suggests that this cottage industry resembled the incipient stages of so-called European proto-industrialization to a remarkable degree, although important differences cannot be ignored. Nor does the regionalized nature of the source allow for generalizing about the colony as a whole. This research is thus a preliminary investigation that calls for further research. It nevertheless points out the potential importance of domestic industry within the overall Brazilian colonial economy and stimulates awareness of its complexities.

Homespuns, particularly cotton homespun fabrics, were fairly common throughout Brazil in the colonial period (Holanda 1957). Several varieties of cotton were native to the colony, and long before the arrival of the Portuguese, indigenous tribes were spinning and weaving cotton (Branner 1885). By the 1770s, colonial officials began to complain that local cloth production was threatening to make Brazil independent of Portuguese manufacture (Carvalho 1916, 8–10). As part of a strategy aimed at protecting home industry, the crown issued a decree known as the *alvará* (judicial writ) of 1785, which prohibited colonial production of all but the coarsest plain cotton textiles.[1]

Some historians have held up the alvará as yet another example of draconian mercantile policies that stifled colonial development (Prado Júnior 1967, 261; Lima 1961, 167). But the more accepted interpretation now is that it represented an overreaction to a nonexistent problem, in view of the fact that the decree resulted in the seizure of no more than 13 looms used in weaving the prohibited categories of cloth (Novais 1979, 272–74; Maxwell 1973, 107). Thus one could conclude that textile production was marginal in Brazil and that the alvará amounted to much ado about nothing.

Such a conclusion leaves a number of questions unanswered, however, and ignores the fact that in Minas Gerais at least, textile production later burgeoned into what I have described elsewhere as a peculiar form of proto-industrialization (Libby 1991).[2] What were the dimensions of this cottage industry in Brazil during the 1780s? Was it adversely affected by the alvará, and who were the so-called marginal producers engaged in spinning and weaving? Is it possible to estimate levels of production and productivity? How might distribution have been organized, and how did textiles fit into the overall scheme of subsistence production if this peasant-oriented categorization is fully adequate? These questions are very difficult to answer, given the present state of scholarship and the sources available. Yet certain observations made by foreign travelers clearly indicate that domestic textile production was relatively common throughout Brazil in the late eighteenth and early nineteenth centuries, even though historians have largely chosen to ignore them up to now. Moreover, these indications suggest that the alvará had little or no effect on production of thread and cloth largely because the final product usually consisted of coarse cottons used for slaves' clothing and for sacking, products specifically exempted from the prohibitions. Rather, the sources point to the opening of Brazilian ports to foreign trade in 1808 and a resulting flood of British factory-made textiles as the decisive factors undermining the domestic industry in regions where transportation costs did not overburden the final price of imports.

Although foreign travelers largely entered Brazil after 1808, their observations often reflected recent history. In 1810, for example, Henry Koster stated that coarse homespun cottons were still common in the interior of the Northeast and had only recently been displaced by British textiles in the urban and coastal markets of the region (Koster 1966, 30–

1. For a transcription of the *alvará*, see Carvalho (1916, 10–11). A companion decree spelled out heavy penalties for smuggling textiles into Portugal. Contraband of British origin represented a real threat to Portuguese manufactures.
2. *Proto-industrialization* is defined here as any manifestation of widespread domestic manufacture potentially oriented toward commodity production.

31, 66–67). About the same time, English merchant John Luccock mentioned that spinning and weaving were important female activities in the city of Rio de Janeiro and its environs (Luccock 1820, 115). Later in the same decade, German naturalists Johann Baptist von Spix and Carl Friedrich Philipp von Martius noted locally produced coarse cotton goods in São Paulo, Goiás, Bahia, Sergipe, and Maranhão (Spix and Martius 1976, 1:106, 1:125, 2:101, 2:150, 2:259, 2:261). French naturalist Auguste de Saint-Hilaire also mentioned homespuns in São Paulo and Goiás (Saint-Hilaire 1976, 186; 1975, 23, 27). Until the 1860s, all travelers in Minas Gerais commented on the flourishing cottage textile industry in the province, where this activity survived the pressures of foreign imports and even consolidated along proto-industrial lines.[3] To that extent, Minas represented an exception. Nevertheless, these early-nineteenth-century observations strongly suggest that domestic textile production may have been widespread throughout much of Brazil during the preceding decades. Thus evidence relating to spinning and weaving in Minas in 1786 may shed light on the state of production in the rest of the colony.

The *Inventário dos Teares Existentes na Capitania de Minas Gerais*

A few looms were actually sequestered as a result of the alvará. Most were located in the city of Rio de Janeiro and were used in fabricating luxury textiles that included gold or silver thread or both (Novais 1979, 272–73). Notwithstanding the limited scope of these seizures, they indicate that attempts were made to comply with the dictates of the alvará. It therefore seems likely that these efforts should have generated some kind of official documentation relating to domestic textile production, aside from the well-known high-level bureaucratic laments about its diffusion (Carvalho 1916, 8–12; see also Novais 1979; Maxwell 1973). Attempts surely were made to quantify and qualify that production, possibly a thorough canvassing of looms throughout Brazil. Given that a fair amount is already known about the cottage textile industry in nineteenth-century Minas Gerais, it would be particularly gratifying to come across sources relating to other regions of eighteenth-century Brazil. Thus far, unfortunately, that has not happened. What has recently become available to researchers is a set of loom inventories entitled "Inventário dos Teares Existentes na Capitania de Minas Gerais," elaborated in 1786, which covers roughly half of the captaincy.[4]

On 1 August 1786, the governor of Minas Gerais posted a circular

3. For a discussion of the nineteenth-century cottage textile industry in Minas and its similarities to European proto-industrialization, see Libby (1991).
4. Inventário dos Teares Existentes na Capitania de Minas Gerais, 1786, Arquivo Público Mineiro, Seção Colonial, microfilm of the manuscript (the Arquivo possesses a microfilm copy of the original, which belongs to the Arquivo Histórico Ultramarino in Lisbon).

soliciting certain information from the commanders of the colonial militia headquartered in each of the captaincy's 8 *vilas*. The commanders reproduced the circular, which was then forwarded to the chief officers in all of the districts of the vilas. A copy of that circular has yet to be located, but the responses that eventually found their way to Lisbon make it clear that the information sought related to efforts to execute the alvará of 1785 by canvassing existing looms.

Given the difficulties inherent in administering so vast a territory, it is no surprise that the responses varied considerably in the quality and quantity of information furnished. Generally speaking, they came in the form of nominal lists, that is, lists of names identifying the owners of the looms, sometimes in detailed fashion but usually mentioning only sex and marital status and perhaps racial origins. In the few instances where an individual owned more than one loom, the fact was duly noted. Weavers were also identified in terms of their racial origin and the nature of their relationship to the loom owner. Often 2 or more inhabitants of a household were listed as being "occupied with the loom." Diverse combinations of relatives, slaves, and unrelated dependents of the owners were listed as weavers, although most were almost certainly engaged in spinning rather than weaving. Most responses indicated the type of textiles being produced, and the lists were evidently accompanied by a fair quantity of cloth samples. Annual production of the looms was reported in more than two-thirds of the cases. All but 4 percent included information about the destination of textiles produced, the basic distinction being those made for use at home versus those woven for sale. Regular provision of this information seems to suggest that the original circular must have solicited it, perhaps implying that the overriding preoccupation of the colonial administration was the growing commercialization of Brazilian textiles. The Minas inventory turned up few looms producing for the market, however. Thus although the circular must have insisted on information regarding the income generated by the sale of textiles, such entries were uncommon.

The Inventário dos Teares Existentes na Capitania de Minas Gerais is incomplete in canvassing of the captaincy. It includes nominal list responses from 4 of the 8 vilas established at the time, and not all the districts in each vila were represented. Responses from the vilas of São João and Vila Nova da Rainha appear to have been quite complete, but those from Sabará and Minas Novas partial. The districts of Sabará and Vila Nova da Rainha fanned out to the north and the west, and thus most of the area covered fell outside the central mining district. The territory of Minas Novas included the vast and sparsely populated northern reaches of the captaincy. São João served as the administrative center of the southern region of Minas. Thus the Inventário included a few urban centers, but most of the districts canvassed were rural. Little of the more

Latin American Research Review

heavily populated mining district was included, and the same is true of the more agriculturally oriented west. The sparsely populated north-western and southeastern regions were not covered. Because reliable censuses are not available, it is difficult to say what proportion of the population lived in the districts canvassed, but roughly half would seem a reasonable guess. No local censuses have turned up that correspond to the nominal lists of the Inventário, precluding the possibility of determining the percentage of households that possessed looms in at least some of the districts. Despite such limitations, the data provided by the Inventário allow for a detailed examination of a colonial cottage industry.

Textile Production in Minas in 1786

The Inventário consists of a total of 63 district responses to the circular. Fifty-nine took (at least partially) the form of nominal lists that account for 1,242 households and 1,248 looms. Although more than 63 districts made up the 4 vilas canvassed, the overall coverage was fairly extensive.

Even the responses that do not list separate households attest to the fact that spinning and weaving were common activities in the captaincy. One official from the north of Minas noted a single household in which 3 daughters, their mother, and 2 female slaves produced, on request from outsiders, fine cotton tablecloths. He continued, "the rest of the looms in this district belong to people so poor (who weave a few yards for their own use and that of their families) that, given that the weaving takes up little of their time, it does not seem necessary to mention each one separately."[5] Another response from the north claimed, "With respect to weaving manufactures, there are none in this district, although it is true that those who have their own cotton weave or seek out others to weave plain cotton cloth for them, and there are those who occasionally sell a few lengths—all plain cotton—but none are doing so at the moment. . . ."[6] Truncated as these responses may be, they hint at some of the main characteristics of the cottage textile industry in Minas toward the end of the eighteenth century: the workforce was predominantly female; the cloth woven was largely used within the households; spinning and weaving may have been intermittent or seasonal activities; and commercialization was at best irregular.

The nominal list responses begin by denominating the loom owner, generally the male head of household, although women accounted for one-quarter of all owners. In 38 percent of the cases, no mention was made of the marital status or racial traits of the owners; in another 23

5. "Senhor Capitam Mor em observancia da ordem do Ilmo. e Exmo. Senhor General do primeio de Agosto . . . ," 1786.
6. "Senhor Capitam Mor Jozé de Oliveira Lemos Devo Resposta as ordens de v. m.," 1786.

TABLE 1   Owners and Looms in Minas Gerais, 1786

	Number of Owners	%	Looms Owned	%
Men	932	75	936	75
Women	310	25	312	25
Totals	1,242	100	1,248	100

Source: Inventário dos Teares Existentes na Capitania de Minas Gerais, 1786, Arquivo Público Mineiro, Seção Colonial, 1786, manuscript, microfilm.

percent, they were designated merely as married men or women. The 37 other combinations of sex, civil status, and reported race render detailed analysis of owners extremely complex and not particularly meaningful. Suffice it to say that while everyone from white married males to single black mothers owned looms, the former probably constituted the largest single group of owners. A breakdown of ownership by sex is provided in table 1.

What stands out in table 1 is the extreme rarity of households owning more than 1 loom, only 5 in number: 1 with 3 looms and 4 with 2 looms. The implication seems to be that Minas textile production was in its infancy in 1786. This hypothesis will be considered in examining production figures.

Weavers or groups of weavers were identified for 1,120 households. The wording of the responses shows that the workforce was engaged in both spinning and weaving. Moreover, spinning, which took up most of the time of household work groups, must be understood in the broadest possible sense here. The looms "occupied" many more workers in preparing thread (which often included separating out seeds and carding raw cotton as well as actual spinning) than in weaving per se. The Inventário reveals no fewer than 42 categories of weavers and groups of weavers in which the predominant criterion for classification is relationship to the owner (racial classification is statistically insignificant). Such listings of weavers as "his [her] daughters," "she and her sisters" or "some female slaves [escravas]" discouraged any attempt to quantify the actual workforce. But classification of weavers and weaving groups according to their relationship to loom owners (including slaves as property) and by gender allows for a fairly detailed look at textile workers. Table 2 considers all weavers as groups, including groups of one person, to arrive at a classification that highlights the family and household orientation of textile production in late-eighteenth-century Minas Gerais.

Table 2 suggests the overwhelming predominance of women workers in this incipient cottage textile industry. Because in 20 of the cases classified as "others" the workers are known to have been women, the proportion of exclusively female work groups totals 96.1 percent—and

Latin American Research Review

T A B L E 2 *Textile Workers Groups in Minas Gerais according to Relationship to Loom Owner, 1786*

Workers in Relationship to Loom Owners	Number of Households	Percentage of Households
Female loom owners	118	10.5
Wives	247	22.1
Daughters	283	25.3
Wives, mothers, and daughters	106	9.5
Female slaves	156	13.9
Other female household members[a]	30	2.7
Female household members and female slaves	115	10.3
Total female groups	1,055	94.3
Male loom owners	34	3.1
Sons	2	0.1
Male slaves	4	0.3
Other male household members[a]	2	0.1
Male household members and male slaves	1	0.1
Total male groups	43	3.7
Husband and wife groups	1	0.1
Others[b]	21	1.9
Total of all groups	1,120	100.0

Source: Inventário dos Teares Existentes na Capitania de Minas Gerais, 1786, Arquivo Público Mineiro, Seção Colonial, 1786, manuscript, microfilm.

[a] These categories include relatives such as sisters, nieces, cousins, and in-laws as well as nonrelated household members such as godchildren, legal wards, and *agregados* (attached dependents).
[b] Twenty of the cases in this category involved unidentified women, some from other households, and one case of children (*crianças*) whose sex was not specified.

that is probably an underestimate. The listings that register male owners as weavers are couched in ambiguous language, and most, if not all, of the looms were likely worked by female household members (hypothetically increasing the share of female work groups to 99.2 percent). The individuals listed as owners were not necessarily doing the actual weaving themselves. The military officers charged with elaborating the district inventories may have considered it unnecessary to stipulate that only female household members were involved in cloth and thread production because that was clearly the norm.

Excerpts from some of the responses demonstrate just how common that norm was. Most of the unidentified women mentioned were registered in a single district response that stated laconically, "The persons who occupy themselves on [the looms] are only women, both free and slave and of all colors."[7] A second response noted that one loom was inactive because the owner "no longer has a wife, nor has he any daughters."[8] Another officer reported, "There are also many small farmers who have their looms for weaving threads spun by their wives, daughters, and children who are unfit for work in the fields."[9] Another official observed:

the product of this manufacture is neither traded nor commercialized, nor are male slaves involved in it; those occupied in it are women unable to work in mining or in the fields.

It can be said that this loom industry was inspired by God for the salvation of the miserable poor. The utility of these textiles is that they employ those idle hands of the women, a great number of whom live in these [areas of] Minas and who every day multiply; they have no other legitimate occupation and the few lengths they weave contribute to the upkeep of their households, all of which are in debt to merchants and the royal treasury owing to the diminished incomes that are now the rule here.[10]

These excerpts bring up several aspects of textile production during the period under examination. At this point, what stands out are two interconnected and somewhat pejorative concepts. In the first place, weaving and spinning were relegated to the diminished status of "women's work." Second, that status derived from the supposition that women were unfit for "proper work" in agriculture or mining.[11] In the absence of cottage industries, women were viewed as idle hands that might become socially and morally disruptive. The result was an implied disassociation of men's work from women's work, in other words, a rigid gender division of labor. Table 2 corroborates this interpretation. One husband and wife team represented the single sexually mixed work group listed in the entire Inventário. In the 9 other instances in which men indisputably participated in spinning and weaving activities, the work groups were exclusively masculine. There was no intermingling of the sexes in the workplace. The origins of this sexual division of labor are difficult to pinpoint, but they may well have arisen in an ongoing gender struggle

7. "Lista dos Tiares q. ha neste destrito da Itabira de mato dentro do tro. da villa Nova da Rainha assignada e tirada pello comde. Manoel da costa Rocha aos 27 de obro. de 1786," 1786.
8. "Lista dos Teares e Fábricas de Algodão, q. se achão neste Destro. da Logoinha, Gramiães e Sta Anna, de que he Capitam Bento Jozé de Macedo Ferreira," 1786.
9. "Na forma da Ordem de Va. Exa. do premro. de Agosto do prezente anno; ponho na sua prezença 19 relaçoens dos Comdes. deste Termo . . . ," 1786.
10. "Em virtude da Ordem do Illmo. e Exmo. Sr. Luis da Cunha e Menezes Governador, e Capm. General desta Capitania ao meu Capm. Mor Senhor Manoel Jose Pena do pro. de Agosto do prezente anno, a mim destribuida pelo mesmo Sr respectiva aos terssumes dos teares que ha no meu destrito," 1786.
11. These militia officials were clearly exaggerating. Many of the nominal lists explicitly state that women, free as well as slave, spun and wove and also worked in the fields and cared for livestock, aside from carrying out housework. It is true that no mention of female participation in mining was found, which seems to imply that men were anxious to limit the occupational range of women's work.

related to the transition from a more freewheeling society based on mining to a more sedentary one based on agriculture and domestic industry.

The contrast with the European experience of cottage textile industry could not be more stark. By definition, domestic industry in the proto-industrial vein in every stage was a full-fledged family enterprise in which husband, wife, and those children fit for work all participated (compare Medick 1981; Schlumbohm 1983; Gullickson 1991; Vardi 1993, 130–39). Whether this bias against male entry into textile production was a broad characteristic of Brazilian society or merely a *mineiro* quirk remains to be seen. I have argued elsewhere that male lack of interest in the domestic textile industry at least partially thwarted any potential evolution toward the factory system during the nineteenth century (Libby 1993). This combination of bias and lack of interest was evidently present at the inception of the industry.

The innocuousness of the alvará, at least regarding Minas Gerais, becomes clear when the responses related to the types of cloth produced are examined. Almost 95 percent of valid cases alluded to plain white cottons, most of which were probably of the coarse variety, although with some variation in the delicacy of the weave. The second-most-frequent category (another 3 percent of reported cloth types) was a mixture of plain whites with patterned cottons, which may have involved the use of other colors or simply the embossing of white on white. At any rate, nothing indicates that this particular textile variety constituted a violation of the prohibitions. The remaining 2.3 percent of the reported textiles were also mixtures: mostly interweavings of coarse cotton and coarse wool in which the wool yarn served merely as decoration but also some fustians (a mixture of cotton and linen). This type of fabric would have violated the alvará, but because none of the responses raised a red flag, the purpose of the linen may also have been decorative. The absence of pure wools and linens is conspicuous and, given the predominance of white cottons, may have rendered the mixtures pardonable. Ultimately, this relative lack of variety probably reflects the infant state of the cottage industry in Minas and may have distinguished it from other regions of Brazil.

Annual production was reported for slightly more than two-thirds of the households. Quantities registered were undoubtedly estimates because the practice of rounding becomes apparent when household production is arranged in ascending order of magnitude. Table 3 summarizes the available data.

The clearest indication of the incipiency of the Minas cottage textile industry in 1786 is that it was dominated by small-scale producers. Households that produced up to 50 *varas* (55 meters) per year accounted for nearly three-quarters of all cases and just under half of total production. As will be shown, nearly all small-scale production of cloth was

TABLE 3 Annual Textile Production of Households in Minas Gerais, 1786

Annual Household Production in Varas[a]	Number of Households	%	Total Production in Varas	%
Up to 20	196	23.3	3,146	8.0
From 21 to 30	182	21.7	5,127	13.0
From 31 to 40	136	16.2	5,263	13.4
From 41 to 50	114	13.6	5,578	14.2
From 51 to 60	71	8.5	4,156	10.6
From 61 to 70	32	3.8	2,169	5.5
From 71 to 80	35	4.2	2,776	7.0
From 81 to 100	27	3.2	2,652	6.7
From 101 to 200	38	4.5	5,811	14.8
From 201 to 500	9	1.0	2,690	6.8
Totals	840	100.0	39,368	100.0

Source: Inventário dos Teares Existentes na Capitania de Minas Gerais, Arquivo Público Mineiro, Seção Colonial, 1786, manuscript, microfilm.

[a] One vara equals 1.1 meters

used by the households themselves. At this stage, then, the industry remained largely at subsistence level, even in most households producing more than 50 varas a year. The implication is that looms were not being used at full capacity, leaving considerable potential for growth. Some of the district responses contain observations corroborating the idea that weaving (along with spinning) were carried out on a part-time basis, either seasonally or throughout the year as allowed by the press of other housekeeping and farming duties. The latter situation is illustrated by two entries from the district of São Domingos in the north:

Ignacio Alvares dos Santos, a married man, has a loom on which a *crioula* [a female slave native to Brazil] weaves plain cloth for use in his house and for those who bring their own thread. The charge is 30 *reis* for each vara, but this is not continuous work for the slave is occupied in other services, including fieldwork, nor is thread always available. . . . Alexandre da Cunha Braga, a married man, has a loom on which his daughters weave plain cloth for his house. Because he has no other people [meaning no slaves], most of their time is taken up in farming for their own subsistence.[12]

An official from Paraupeba, a district attached to the vila of Sabará, began his closing remarks in the following fashion: "I declare that, at present, the [female] weavers and spinners are not occupied during the whole year, but rather the work is carried out during a few months of the year. That is partly because of the scarcity of cotton, which is not abundantly produced in this district because of the cold that damages the

12. "Lista dos Tiarez que a de panos de Algudão nesta ma. Comandancia do Arrayal de São Domingos é a Seguinte," 1786.

plants; some supplies are obtained from areas where it is produced in abundance."[13]

From Cocais, a district under the jurisdiction of Vila Nova da Rainha, another official reported about the 15 looms in that district, "Most of the time, all these looms do not operate, so that if 2 or 3 of them were to work continuously throughout an entire year, they would produce as much, or more, than those listed as operating during this past year."[14]

The reporting official from São Miguel do Piracicaba, also attached to Vila Nova da Rainha, noted scrupulously the number of months of the year during which each loom was used. The periods ranged from 1.5 months to a full 12, yielding an average of 4.5 months. This official made no mention of the quantities produced.[15] For the district of Brumado da Paraupeba, the number of months of loom operation as well as the annual production of each loom are available. The range was smaller, from 1 to 5 months, while annual production varied from 20 to 80 varas, averaging almost 16 varas per month.[16] That figure does not represent full capacity, however, because the meticulous official went on to note that the women were also occupied with housekeeping and fieldwork. Given that the median annual household production calculated from table 3 was 40 varas, the average figure from Brumado da Paraupeba would indicate that the typical mineiro loom operated roughly 2.5 months out of the year.

These work patterns parallel those found for the early stages of European proto-industrialization and underscore the intimate relationship between domestic textile production and subsistence farming (Kriedte 1981; Vardi 1993, 130). Household production figures have not been available to scholars dealing with incipient proto-industrialization in Europe, making comparison difficult. As in Europe, the potential for growth by increasing the allocation of labor time to spinning and weaving is clear.

As table 3 demonstrates, at least some households were already weaving at capacity or close to it in 1786. The most extreme case was registered in the northern district of Santo Antonio da Itacambira, where

13. "Em virtude da Ordem do Illmo. e Exmo. Sr Luis da Cunha Menezes Governador, e Capm General desta Capitania ao meu Capm Mor Sr Manoel José Pena do pro de Agosto do prezente anno, a mim destribuida pelo mesmo Sr respectiva aos tesumes dos teares que ha no meu destrito," 1786.

14. "Relação dos Tiares de teçer Aldodão que ha no Destrito de Cocaes com declaração das pessoas a quem pertencem, suas Gerarchias, situaçoens, possibilidades, utilidades que tirão dos ditos teçumes, sahidas que lhes dão, e para onde," 1786.

15. "Em observancia da ordem do Illmo. e Exmo. Senhor Governador e Capm General, datada do 1° do Corrente e dado V M de 12 do mesmo sobre averiguação do numero de tiares, qualidade de pessoas que os ocupam, que fazendas perduzam, e sua sayda. Respondo o seguinte ao dipois de ha exacto conhecimento da materia," 1786.

16. "Rellação dos teares que ha no Destrito do Brumado da Paraupeba debaixo de que he Capm João Marques da Eyra sedo a ordem do Illmo. e Exmo. Sr Gnal expedida ao pro de Agosto de 1786," 1786.

"Manoel de Oliveira has a loom that produces satined and plain cloths; throughout the year, from 400 to 500 varas of these will be sold, and this workshop occupies 4 [male] slaves full time."[17] Oliveira must have had a large slave force to be able to dedicate 4 males to full-time textile production, although cloth sales might have supported the entire household. No mention was made of the income derived from the trade. This case is unique as the only example of an all-male slave work group. Two other households in Santo Antonio da Itacambira produced a total of 350 varas for sale, in addition to an undisclosed quantity for home consumption. Ten female slaves were engaged in production, including spinners and weavers, although it was considered only part-time work.

When examining the most productive households, no clear correlations emerge among magnitude of production, consumption, destination, and workforce composition. Of the 33 cases in which 150 or more varas were produced annually, in 13 at least part of the cloth was woven to be sold. Slaves were clearly involved in 4 of the work groups, while another 7 were made up of free women. In the 2 remaining cases, the male owners were listed as the weavers, but in ambiguous language. Twenty of these households were producing exclusively for domestic consumption. In 11 cases, spinning and weaving were partially or wholly turned over to slaves; in the remaining 9, the workers were free women. Yet slavery almost certainly pervaded all these cases. In the first place, most of the domestically consumed textiles were used to clothe large numbers of slaves, the only plausible explanation for such elevated levels of internal consumption. Second, even where the work groups were composed of free women, slave domestic help must have freed the labor time allocated to textiles.

For just over two-thirds of all cases (67.2 percent), information is available on annual production and work-group composition, allowing for crude comparisons of productivity levels. Slave participation in work groups tended to increase production. The 25.6 percent of all work groups in which slaves were engaged accounted for 33.5 percent of total annual production. The average annual production of the work groups in which slaves participated amounted to 60.9 varas, while the corresponding figure for free groups was 41.7 varas. But the difference cannot be presumed to signify that slave labor was somehow inherently more productive. Most of the free work groups must have belonged to non-slaveholding households at a time when lack of ownership of chattel amounted to a declaration of poverty. Indeed, many of the district responses commented on the destitute state of the households listed. As one official noted

17. "Snr Capam M Jozé de Olivra Lemos Recebi a de a mce de 20 de 7bro e juntamte a copia da carta de Ilmo. e Exmo. Sr Gnal de pro de Agosto de 1786 . . . Itacambira 15 de 8bro de 1786," 1786.

dramatically, "the time spent in harvesting, spinning, and weaving is of great utility to them, for they would otherwise succumb to nudity, such is the measure of poverty into which this district has fallen."[18] The lower productivity of the free work groups reflected the fact that subsistence needs demanded labor time and held production levels down to meeting immediate requirements. If surplus production had become readily marketable, those circumstances could change and textiles might have played a larger role in overall household survival strategies.

Twenty-seven of the work groups were identified as exclusively masculine, although most involved the dubious designation of male owners as weavers. The annual average production of the male groups was 75.9 varas, substantially higher than the overall average of 46.6 varas. But the inclusion of Manoel de Oliveira's exceptionally productive male slave group heavily weighted the average. Exclusion of that group brings the average down to 59.6 varas, very close to the average for all work groups that included slaves. This finding suggests that the supposed male owner-weavers in fact used slaves in spinning and weaving.

It is also possible to compare production levels among male and female loom owners, although no clear pattern emerges. Of the 840 cases for which annual production figures are available, in 186 (22.1 percent) the looms were listed as belonging to women. They produced 20.9 percent of total output. The women's looms produced an annual average of 44.2 varas and the men's 47.6. Both figures approximate the overall average, and thus it appears that the gender of loom owners had little influence on productive levels.

All but 4.2 percent of the responses to the Inventário indicated whether household textile activities involved any sort of commercial transactions. In 83.7 percent of the cases, they did not, again underscoring the subsistence nature of the Minas cottage textile industry in 1786. Commercial relations were carried out in a total of 194 households. According to the responses, only 11 households produced cloth exclusively for sale. Some 81 households produced both for domestic consumption and for the market. Another 53 households produced for internal consumption and wove thread provided by outsiders at a fixed rate per vara. Forty-six households specialized in weaving at a fixed rate thread spun by their customers. In the remaining 3 cases, cloth was produced for the market and outsiders' thread was woven. Thus pure commercial production prevailed in less than a third (30.9 percent) of this reduced group, and these exclusively market-oriented households represented a mere 5.1 percent of total households. Cases in which market orientation was coupled

18. "Rellação dos Teares que ha no Destrito do Brumado da Paraupeba debaixo de q. he Capam João Marques da Eyra sedo a ordem do Illmo. e Exmo. Sr Gnal expedida ao pro de Agosto de 1786," 1786.

with domestic consumption represented 11.2 percent of all households. While these percentages are not particularly impressive, they indicate that commercialization was already a viable option for households willing to allocate substantial labor time to textile production. If marketed textiles were making a reasonable contribution to household income, the fact can hardly have been lost on neighbors looking for ways to increase their own incomes.

Annual production figures are available for 58 of these market-oriented households. Annual production averaged 95.8 varas, slightly more than double the overall average. What is remarkable is that slave participation in partially or fully commercialized production was low. Work groups that included slaves apparently represented only 13.4 percent of the total, although a few of the groups were labeled as having male owner-weavers, which may have obscured some degree of slave participation.[19] Relatively significant, if predictable, differences show up when turning to the average annual production figures for the various categories of commercialization. For the small set of households producing cloth for the market using their own thread, annual production averaged 312.5 varas. That figure is based on a sample of only 4 households and includes Manoel de Oliveira's male slaves. It therefore is probably exaggerated yet still indicative of the effect of full-scale market orientation on production levels. Among households where looms were dedicated to weaving thread brought in by customers, annual production averaged 104.8 varas. The corresponding figure for households producing for domestic consumption and weaving outsiders' thread was 78.8 varas. Finally, producers making cloth from their own thread whose output was divided between domestic consumption and sale averaged 62.5 varas a year. The database here is tiny, and little may be gleaned from these simple calculations except that the commercial potential of the Mineiro cottage industry was already evident in 1786. Inventories have yet to be found for other regions of Brazil that would allow comparison of degrees of commercialization. Later inventories would indicate the extent of commercial inroads in the industry.

Cloth sales and the weaving of outsiders' threads at a fixed rate were not the only market relations engendered by the cottage textile industry. Most responses to the Inventário make no mention of the origin of the cotton used in the industry, and one can reasonably suppose that the bulk of this raw material was grown and harvested on the land of the producers themselves. When the cloth was used domestically, the cottage industry remained entirely within the closed circuit of subsistence pro-

---

19. It should be noted that these percentages related to slave participation in the work groups are based on a larger sample of 164 households, including ones for which no production figures are given.

Latin American Research Review

duction. But soil types and climatic conditions varied considerably in the regions under examination, and cotton did not grow well in all the districts inventoried. Textile production in some areas must have depended partially or wholly on interregional trade in raw cotton. In some cases, cotton brought in by traders augmented local supplies, but other areas depended entirely on trade. An official in Rio Pardo in the northern vila of Minas Novas commented, "what little is woven is made with cotton from elsewhere because of the unfavorable weather here. . . ."[20] In the urban center of Vila Nova da Rainha, some households depended wholly on buying cotton, while others supplemented their home-grown supplies with purchases.[21] The same was true in the districts that composed the seat of Sabará, probably the largest city in Minas Gerais at the time.[22] Dependence on trade was not merely an urban phenomenon, however. As shown, the trade in cotton also supplemented the cottage industry in rural Paraupeba. Other rural districts such as Morro Vermelho (Vila Nova da Rainha) and Pedra Branca (Sabará) also supplemented local supplies with raw cotton shipped in from other areas.[23] The trade could cover considerable distances and supply a varied market, as evident in the following response of the official stationed at Antônio Dias Abaixo (a district of Vila Nova da Rainha): "Of those listed above, all have looms totaling 25, and they also plant their own cotton, although the product is so sparse as to hardly bear mentioning. Because cotton does not grow well here, the inhabitants cover their nakedness by buying the cottons that come from Cuyethe, and many of those who have no looms buy the cotton that they spin, having the threads woven by others, although the results amount to little more than clothing for themselves. . . ."[24]

Cuyethe lies far to the northeast of Antônio Dias Abaixo, and thus this observation suggests that the trade in raw cotton was already developed in 1786 and capable of meeting demands over long distances. Equally significant is the reference to an apparently large segment of the population engaged in spinning, a segment that thus far appeared only indirectly as those who paid to have their thread woven. The implications here are clear. Certain regions were already specializing in cotton cultivation to meet the demands of a widespread domestic textile industry, and

20. "Snr Capam Mor Jozé de Oliveira Lemos Emcluzo Remeto a V m a lista . . . Rio pardo de 9bro o Pro de 1786," 1786.
21. "Lista dos Tiares que ha no destrito de Villa Nova da Raynha," 1786.
22. "Lista das pessoas q tem Teares no Distrito da Igreja grande da Va Real de N Snra da Conceição do Sabará; em cumprimento da Orde do Illmo. e Exmo. Snr Genal desta Capitania," 1786; and "Rellação dos Tiares q ha no destrito do Arral Velho tro da Va do Sabará da onde ha Capam Domingos Pereira da Oliveyra com expreção de seus donos suas moradas, qualide das pessoas q se ocupão no do Exercicio," 1786.
23. "Lista das pessoas q tem Theares neste Destrito de Morro Vermelho," 1786. "Rellasam dos Tiares de Destrito de Pedra Branca de q he Commde o Alfes Jozé Rois Guerra," 1786.
24. "Relação dos Teares que se acham neste Destrito de Antonio Dias abaixo," 1786.

in doing so, they tapped into and expanded existing trade and transportation networks. At the same time, the industry was considerably broader than it would appear from examining only loom inventories, given that many households specialized in spinning. Would it be too much to suggest that the elements for a proto-industrial takeoff were solidly in place by 1786?

The income generated by textile activities could be calculated for only 57 of the households listed in the Inventário. This meager sample may or may not be representative of the range of incomes earned by households involved in the various aspects of market relations. To make matters worse, little work has been done to date on prices in eighteenth-century Minas, rendering meaningful comparisons difficult. Overall income averaged 5,405 reis. Among male loom owners, the average stood at 8,214 reis, while female owners earned an average of 3,210 reis for their efforts at spinning and weaving. The highest earners were the few households that used their own thread to produce cloth for sale on the market, averaging 24,720 reis a year. These 5 cases generated 40 percent of the total income registered in the Inventário. Virtually all the rest were households that wove outsiders' thread, although many also produced cloth for domestic consumption. Annual income for this group averaged 3,548 reis. Slaves were conspicuously absent from all but 6 of the work groups in the sample. The average yearly income from textiles for households using slaves in production came to 21,233 reis, as compared with 3,542 reis for households with work groups made up of free individuals.

Although it is not easy to put these averages into meaningful perspective, indications are that textiles may have been making a fairly significant contribution to overall household income. Alida Metcalf has calculated the average income from crops of peasants and planters for the year 1798 in the town of Santana de Parnaíba, in the captaincy of São Paulo. Crops generated an annual average income of 2,080 reis for peasants and 110,890 reis for planters with slave holdings producing cash crops like sugar and cotton. For 1775, Metcalf found that the average value of agricultural production of peasant households varied from roughly 7,500 reis for nuclear families to about 1,000 reis for households headed by unmarried women. She also pointed out that during the eighteenth century, a mature adult male slave cost between 100,000 and 150,000 reis.[25] According to a recent article by Laird Bergad, the average probate evaluation (theoretically based on fair market value) of adult male slaves between 15 and 40 years of age in the Mariana region of Minas Gerais during the 1780s was slightly more than 102,000 reis (Bergad 1994, 517).

25. See Metcalf (1992, xvi, 80–81, 134–36). The author also notes that spinning and weaving were part of the survival strategy of Paulista peasant families in the late eighteenth century (1992, 143–47).

Given that few Mineiro households concentrated solely on textile production, the average income generated by spinning and weaving compares
well to peasant incomes and agricultural production values in São Paulo
for the same period. Although few were likely to become wealthy in the
domestic textile industry, it apparently could provide significant supplemental income to households. That potential would have been the key to
a deepening of market relations and further spread of the industry.

Conclusions

While the data from late-eighteenth-century Minas Gerais do not
necessarily reflect the state of textile production in the rest of Brazil,
when coupled with observations made by foreign travelers, they at least
suggest that in some regions, cottage industry may have been a good deal
more significant than previously imagined. Indirectly, the Inventário demonstrates the considerable dimensions of the domestic textile industry.
Because production seems to have been entirely manual, each loom and
corresponding weaver were maintained by a much larger contingent of
spinners who were probably also engaged in separating seeds from raw
cotton and carding it. These auxiliary spinners frequently came from
households unconnected to those where the looms operated. How many
additional households were thus involved in cottage industry is uncertain, but the Minas data point to the potential multiplier effect inherent in
this labor-intensive industry.[26] Given indications that Maranhão was already shipping cloth to Pará in the final decades of the eighteenth century (Dias 1971) and that the typical dress in the northeastern interior
was homespuns (prior to regular trade with Britain), can it not be presumed that the scale of cottage textile industry in those regions may have
actually surpassed that of Minas? If so, peasants from the Northeast may
also have supplied coastal sugar zones with textiles for clothing slaves.
Similarly, why did spinning and weaving survive in the city of Rio and
the surrounding countryside (surely the region most profoundly affected
by the opening of ports to foreign trade) if not because these activities had
previously been widespread? This line of thinking is all conjecture, but as
informed conjecture, it begs for further study.

The evidence marshaled thus far consistently demonstrates that
the alvará had little or no effect on the cottage textile industry in Minas
simply because it did not target the cloth most commonly produced. As
to the question of the source of labor for the industry—the marginal
producers of economic history dominated by the logic of mercantilism—
the Minas data are intriguing and suggestive. At present, it remains un-

26. Data from the 1830s reveal 24 spinners for each weaver. If the same ratio held true for
the 1780s, the looms listed in the Inventário may have been generating employment for
some 31,000 people. See Libby (1988, 201).

known whether the feminine composition of the labor force in the domestic textile industry was a strictly Mineiro phenomenon or not. The implication is that the female population, free and slave, constituted an underutilized segment of the workforce that could be allocated to textile production as subsistence needs dictated or as market opportunities arose. This notion of women as a relatively untapped source of labor or a segment of the labor force more likely to be engaged in meeting immediate needs envisions a certain flexibility of female workers and does not equate with marginality. In the context of export recuperation and economic diversification marked by import substitution and consolidation of the domestic market, it seems logical that women would play an increasingly important role in overall economic development. It might be posited that herein lies an explanation for the distinction between the family-oriented cottage industry of proto-industrial Europe and the gender-biased orientation of the Brazilian variety of domestic industry. In the European case, textile production represented initial entry into the export trade for most regions, thus requiring a major, if gradual, reallocation of labor factors. In Brazil, the export economy already commanded a large share of the labor force, leaving to residual and flexible (but not marginal) labor the chance to take advantage of opportunities that arose in the domestic economy.

The Minas data on production demonstrate no clear trends, nor can they simply be transposed to other regions of Brazil. They strongly suggest that the industry was in its infancy and that a great deal of potential productive capacity remained untapped. The fact that most looms were operated during only part of the year underscores the similarity of the Mineiro domestic textile industry and the earliest stages of European proto-industry, in which the distaff and loom were taken up on a seasonal basis governed by the agricultural calendar (Vardi 1993, 130). One district official reported, "the women and female slaves are occupied on the looms during the rainy period,"[27] suggesting that a certain seasonality also permeated textile production in Minas. But in households where production was clearly geared toward the market, the seasons no longer counted. If a market orientation was more prevalent in certain other regions of Brazil, then seasonality probably did not apply and productivity was substantially higher. Once again, further investigation is needed.

Given that colonial administrators were particularly concerned with possible commercialization of domestically produced textiles, it is curious that the Inventário offers no information as to how output was distributed on the market, except in the cases involving the weaving of thread

27. "Rellação dos Teares que ha no Destrito do Brumado da Paraupeba debaixo de q he Capam João Marques da Eyra sedo a ordem do Illmo. e Exmo. Sr Gnal expedida ao pro de Agosto de 1786," 1786.

prepared in independent households. In fact, merchants (except those dealing in raw cotton) were conspicuously absent from the district responses. The reasons for this absence cannot be ascertained at present. If and when additional inventories are uncovered in the archival mazes of Lisbon and Rio de Janeiro, some light may be shed on merchant participation in the Brazilian domestic textile industry.

In occupying the "idle hands" of women and eliminating the need to purchase textiles on the market, domestic production fit neatly into the scheme of subsistence farming. But the presence of slaves in many Mineiro households and the proportionately more frequent participation of slave spinners and weavers in households producing strictly for domestic consumption suggest that labels such as "subsistence production" or "peasant strategies of survival" do not do justice to the complexities of the phenomena under examination here. As has been argued, households producing large quantities of cloth for domestic production must have possessed numerous slaves, and as such they were certainly not engaged in mere subsistence production. In Minas at least, domestic production must have represented considerable savings over buying imported textiles in every kind of household. Participation in the industry was socially varied and far from restricted to peasant households. This aspect also distinguishes the Mineiro cottage textile industry from the European phenomenon. Given the ubiquity of slavery in late-eighteenth-century Brazil, the same would doubtless hold true for other regions where domestic textile production flourished.

Overall, the Inventário allows for a rather detailed, although frustratingly synchronic, glimpse into an incipient domestic textile industry. In many ways, that industry bears a striking resemblance to the early stages of what has been labeled "textile proto-industrialization in prefactory Europe," although certain features differentiate it from the European experience. The regionalized nature of the documentary source makes it difficult to generalize about textile production in all of late colonial Brazil, but the findings can serve as a basis for wider investigation. A great deal remains to be done. More inventories must be uncovered and analyzed, and if possible, the colonywide canvassing process should be reconstructed. Beyond that, however, in order for researchers to understand the evolution of the industry up to the arrival of the Portuguese court in Rio in 1808 and the subsequent opening of Brazilian ports to foreign trade, other sources will have to be tapped. Because little administrative documentation dealing with cloth production has been located aside from inventories, different types of sources will have to be examined. Probate records would be the logical choice, although access can be a problem in Brazil, and investigating them is a time-consuming process. It is to be hoped that these challenges can be met.

BIBLIOGRAPHY

ALDEN, DAURIL
1984   "Late Colonial Brazil, 1750–1808." In *The Cambridge History of Latin America*, edited by Leslie Bethell, 2:601–60. Cambridge: Cambridge University Press.

ARRUDA, JOSE JOBSON DE ANDRADE
1980   *O Brasil no comércio colonial.* São Paulo: Atica.
1986   "A produção econômica." In *O Império Luso-Brasileiro, 1750–1822*, coordinated by Maria Beatriz Nizza da Silva, 85–153. Lisbon: Estampa.

BARICKMAN, B. J.
1991   "The Slave Economy of Nineteenth-Century Bahia Export Agriculture and Local Market in the Recôncavo, 1780–1860." Ph.D diss., University of Illinois, Urbana-Champaign.

BERGAD, LAIRD W.
1994   "Depois do boom: Aspectos demográficos e econômicos da escravidão em Mariana, 1750–1808." *Estudos Econômicos* 24, no. 3:495–525.

BRANNER, JOHN C.
1885   . *Cotton in the Empire of Brazil: The Antiquity, Methods, and Extent of Its Cultivation, Together with Statistics of Exportation and Home Consumption.* Miscellaneous Special Report no. 8. Washington, D.C.: U.S. Department of Agriculture.

BROWN, LARISSA V.
1986   "Internal Commerce in a Colonial Economy: Rio de Janeiro and Its Hinterland, 1790–1822." Ph.D. diss., University of Virginia.

CARVALHO, DANIEL DE
1916   *Notícias históricas sobre o algodão em Minas.* Rio de Janeiro: Typographia do Jornal do Comércio.

DIAS, MANUEL NUNES
1971   *A companhia geral do Grão-Pará e Maranhão (1755–1778).* 2 vols. Pará. Imprensa Oficial.

FRAGOSO, JOÃO LUIS RIBEIRO
1992   *Homens de grossa aventura: Acumulação e hierarquia na praça mercantil do Rio de Janeiro (1790–1830).* Rio de Janeiro: Arquivo Nacional.

GULLICKSON, GAY L.
1991   "Love and Power in the Proto-Industrial Family." In *Markets and Manufacture in Early Industrial Europe*, edited by Maxime Berg, 205–26. London: Routledge.

HOLANDA, SERGIO BUARQUE DE
1957   *Caminhos e fronteiras.* Rio de Janeiro: José Olympio

KOSTER, HENRY
1966   *Travels in Brazil.* Carbondale and Edwardsville, Ill.: Southern Illinois University Press.

KRIEDTE, PETER
1981   "The Origins, the Agrarian Context, and the Conditions in the World Market." In KRIEDTE, MEDICK, AND SCHLUMBOHM 1981, 12–37.

KRIEDTE, PETER, HANS MEDICK, AND JÜRGEN SCHLUMBOHM
1981   *Industrialization before Industrialization* Cambridge and Paris: Cambridge University Press and Editions de la Maison des Sciences de l'Homme

LIBBY, DOUGLAS C.
1988   *Transformação e trabalho em uma economia escravista Minas Gerais no século XIX* São Paulo: Brasiliense.
1991   "Proto-Industrialization in a Slave Society The Case of Minas Gerais." *Journal of Latin American Studies* 23, pt. 1:1–36.
1993   "Sociedade e cultura escravistas como obstáculos ao desenvolvimento Notas sobre o Brasil oitocentista." *Estudos Econômicos* 23, no. 3:445–76

LIMA, HEITOR FERREIRA
1961   *Formação industrial do Brasil: Período colonial.* Rio de Janeiro: Fundo de Cultura.

LUCCOCK, JOHN
1820   *Notes on Rio de Janeiro and the Southern Parts of Brazil: Taken during a Residence of Ten Years in That Country from 1808 to 1818.* London: Samuel Leigh.

Latin American Research Review

MAXWELL, KENNETH
1973   *Conflicts and Conspiracies: Brazil and Portugal, 1750–1808.* Cambridge: Cambridge University Press.
MEDICK, HANS
1981   "Households and Family in Agrarian Societies and in the Proto-Industrial System: An Approach to the Problem." In KRIEDTE, MEDICK, AND SCHLUMBOHM 1981, 38–73.
METCALF, ALIDA C.
1992   *Family and Frontier in Colonial Brazil: Santana de Parnaíba, 1580–1822.* Berkeley and Los Angeles: University of California Press.
NOVAIS, FERNANDO A.
1979   *Portugal e o Brasil na crise do antigo sistema colonial (1777–1808).* São Paulo: Hucitec.
PRADO JUNIOR, CAIO
1967   *Formação do Brasil contemporâneo (colônia).* São Paulo: Brasiliense.
SAINT-HILAIRE, AUGUSTE DE
1975   *Viagem a Província de Goiás.* São Paulo and Belo Horizonte: Editora da Universidade de São Paulo and Itatiaia.
1976   *Viagem a Província de São Paulo.* São Paulo and Belo Horizonte: Editora da Universidade de São Paulo and Itatiaia.
SCHLUMBOHM, JÜRGEN
1983   "Seasonal Fluctuations and Social Division of Labour: Rural Linen Production in the Osnabrük and Bielefeld Regions and the Urban Woolen Industry in the Niederlausitz." In *Manufacture in Town and Country before the Factory,* edited by Maxime Berg, Pat Hudson, and Michael Sonenscher, 92–123. Cambridge: Cambridge University Press.
SPIX, JOHANN BAPTIST VON, AND CARL FRIEDRICH PHILIPP VON MARTIUS
1976   *Viagem pelo Brasil.* 2 vols. São Paulo: Edições Melhoramentos.
VARDI, LIANA
1993   *The Land and the Loom: Peasants and Profit in Northern France, 1680–1800.* Durham, N.C.: Duke University Press.

108

6
La production textile dans
la Chine traditionnelle

K. Chao

Cette étude analyse les rapports entre l'industrie domestique et les manufactures * artisanales pendant la période préindustrielle. On construira d'abord un modèle théorique pour montrer les éléments qui sous-tendent le choix des modes d'organisation de la production dans une économie pré-moderne. Sur cette base analytique, on verra mieux le contraste qui oppose, dans l'histoire de la Chine, les modèles de développement de l'industrie de la soie et de l'industrie du coton.

Le choix des formes de production : un modèle explicatif

On peut construire un modèle théorique indiquant comment chaque unité domestique, dans une économie préindustrielle, ordonne ses ressources si aucune contrainte institutionnelle n'entrave son libre choix. Pour simplifier, supposons que tous les intrants *(inputs)* soient homogènes, que toutes les activités productives soient connues, que les marchés de produits et de facteurs de production soient compétitifs et que la terre et le capital puissent s'échanger librement. Un individu privé de capital ou de terre a le choix entre les possibilités suivantes : travailler comme salarié dans un latifundium, louer une terre cultivable, travailler à plein temps dans une manufacture, ou enfin prendre une parcelle en location tout en assurant à domicile et à temps partiel une production complémentaire non agricole. De même, un individu disposant d'un capital ou d'un bienfonds important a le choix entre exploiter un latifundium avec des ouvriers salariés, mettre sa propriété en location, entretenir une manufacture avec des ouvriers à plein temps ou disperser son capital dans une industrie rurale à domicile et à temps partiel. Entre ces deux extrêmes, il y a encore le cas de l'individu qui possède, en plus de sa propre force de travail, un capital

* Par « manufacture », on entendra ici des établissements d'industrie où un nombre important d'ouvriers-artisans à plein temps sont réunis sous un seul toit. Il ne s'agit pas encore du système de la fabrique, ni encore d'usines, dont la création n'est pas le sujet de cet article. Il s'agit de la juxtaposition sous un même toit d'un grand nombre de travailleurs utilisant une technologie artisanale (NdT).

LES FORMES PROTOINDUSTRIELLES

médiocre ou une petite propriété. Cet individu peut choisir d'exploiter directement une terre en s'engageant exclusivement dans la petite production agricole, ou d'être fermier-exploitant et de compléter son activité agricole par une production subsidiaire, ou enfin il peut avoir un atelier familial.

Si l'on utilise la lettre L *(labor)* pour désigner les intrants de travail, et la lettre K pour le capital dans les diverses formes d'organisation de la production présentées ci-dessus, on peut décrire les fonctions de production comme suit :

$F_1 (L_1, K)$ pour les latifundia à ouvriers salariés
$F_2 (L_2, K)$ pour l'exploitation indirecte de la terre
$F_3 (L_3, K)$ pour la production des industries rurales à domicile
$F_4 (L_4, K)$ pour les manufactures concentrées.

Si tous ceux qui disposent de ressources essaient de maximiser leur revenu en l'absence de contraintes institutionnelles, les conditions d'équilibre sont, au premier ordre,

$$\frac{\partial F_1}{\partial L_1} = \frac{\partial F_2}{\partial L_2} = \frac{\partial F_3}{\partial L_3} = \frac{\partial F_4}{\partial L_4} = W$$

où W est le taux de salaire d'équilibre. De plus,

$$\frac{\partial F_1}{\partial K_1} \quad \frac{\partial F_2}{\partial K_2} \quad \frac{\partial F_3}{\partial K_3} \quad \frac{\partial F_4}{\partial K_4} = r$$

où r est le taux d'équilibre des bénéfices du capital.

Ces résultats sont les conclusions classiques des économistes marginalistes. Leur signification est directe et parfaitement claire. L'individu privé de capital et de terre consacrera ses efforts à une production donnée jusqu'à ce que le produit marginal de son travail égale le revenu qu'il aurait pu gagner dans n'importe quelle autre forme de production. De même, le propriétaire de capital (ou de terre) assignera ses ressources à une forme de production donnée jusqu'à ce que le produit marginal de son capital (ou de sa terre) égale ce qu'il aurait pu gagner en employant ses ressources ailleurs. Le faire-valoir direct et les ateliers familiaux sont tout simplement des cas où les propriétaires possèdent les deux ressources eux-mêmes (travail et capital) et n'ont donc pas besoin d'acquérir des ressources complémentaires sur le marché des facteurs de production. Cependant les conditions d'équilibre établies ci-dessus leur sont également appliquées, car les prix de marché de ces ressources sont les coûts d'opportunité des ressources qu'ils ont fournies eux-mêmes.

Dans une telle économie, différentes formes d'organisation de la production se côtoient et se substituent les unes aux autres, jusqu'à ce qu'un équilibre global soit atteint. Des complications et des contraintes nouvelles peuvent cependant modifier cet équilibre. Une contrainte importante et bien connue est le caractère saisonnier de la production agricole qui laisse dans l'oisiveté des quantités assez considérables de ressources de main-d'œuvre pendant la morte-saison. Ce travail non utilisé ne peut être réaffecté à F_4. Il doit être absorbé par F_3. Il n'est pas étonnant que chaque pays ait connu, dans l'ère préindustrielle, une longue expérience historique d'industrie rurale complémentaire d'un type ou d'un autre.

Autre élément décisif de complication : les frais de transaction qui, dans une définition large, englobent tous les frais et tous les désagréments, en termes monétaires ou psychiques, qui surviennent entre le moment où une marchandise est produite et celui où elle est consommée par l'usager. Ainsi les frais de transaction sont nuls si l'on consomme ce que l'on produit soi-même. L'économie des frais de transaction justifie le développement de l'autoconsommation dans les sociétés d'autrefois. A vrai dire, l'économie dite « naturelle », ou « de subsistance », n'est qu'un cas extrême où les frais de transaction sont prohibitivement élevés. Historiquement, l'autoconsommation privée a reculé à mesure que ces frais — surtout le prix du transport et de la commercialisation — baissaient. Si les frais de transaction deviennent minimes, même les familles rurales peuvent écouler les produits de leur industrie subsidiaire dans les marchés éloignés. Comme on le montrera plus loin, ce sont là les cas où la faible compétence des paysans en matière de commercialisation est compensée par l'existence de marchands professionnels bien organisés.

Les économies d'échelle apportent encore un autre élément de complication. Pour beaucoup de produits, elles favorisent indiscutablement les manufactures aux dépens de l'industrie domestique. Les manufactures peuvent pratiquer la division du travail, utiliser des techniques et un équipement plus efficaces, et former leurs employés à un travail plus qualifié. A moins que les avantages d'échelle ne soient compensés par une dépense élevée pour le transport, la production familiale tend à abandonner la partie. Il y a souvent une division du travail entre les manufactures et l'industrie domestique, celle-ci se spécialisant dans les produits demandant un équipement simple et une faible qualification. Les manufactures sont habituellement plus dynamiques, ayant la possibilité de générer des technologies nouvelles. La fonction de production F_4 tend à se déplacer vers le haut. C'est dans ce secteur que l'industrialisation et la mécanisation se manifesteront d'abord.

A l'inverse, si dans la production d'une certaine marchandise les manufactures ne bénéficient pas d'économies d'échelles et sont techniquement obligées d'utiliser le même genre d'équipement que celui de l'industrie domestique ordinaire, elles sont alors menacées d'extinction. De même pour les latifundia utilisant la main-d'œuvre salariée. Avec la croissance démographique, la rareté relative des facteurs de production tend à se modifier. Quand la population a augmenté au point où le produit marginal du travail s'abaisse au-dessous du niveau de subsistance, ce niveau constitue un plancher de salaire pour les latifundia autant que pour les manufactures. Ces unités de production doivent cesser d'embaucher au moment où le produit marginal du travail égale le salaire de subsistance. Les conditions de premier ordre deviennent alors :

$$\frac{\partial F_1}{\partial L_1} = \frac{\partial F_4}{\partial L_4} = Ws$$

où Ws représente le salaire de subsistance. Les travailleurs excédentaires seront

LES FORMES PROTOINDUSTRIELLES

recueillis par leurs familles qui seront obligées de les absorber. Par conséquent

$$\frac{\partial F_2}{\partial L_2} = \frac{\partial F_3}{\partial L^3} < Ws$$

ce qui veut dire que les produits marginaux de la main-d'œuvre dans les exploitations agricoles familiales en faire-valoir direct, dans les ateliers d'artisanat familial, dans les fermes en location, et dans la production artisanale à temps partiel, seront considérablement en dessous du coût de subsistance. En conséquence, les produits marginaux du capital (ou de la terre) dans les différentes formes de production commenceront à diverger :

$$\frac{\partial F_1}{\partial K_1} = \frac{\partial F_4}{\partial K_4} < \frac{\partial F_2}{\partial K_2} = \frac{\partial F_3}{\partial K_3}$$

Autrement dit, les propriétaires de capital (ou de terre) gagneront moins à exploiter des latifundia ou à diriger des manufactures qu'à louer leurs terres à des fermiers ou à disperser leur capital dans des industries à domicile. Il faut s'attendre alors à voir disparaître les latifundia et les manufactures concentrées, car l'investissement du capital y est moins rentable.

Notons bien que le marchand-fabricant qui distribue le travail à domicile n'engage pas des ouvriers pour un salaire donné. Le contrat entre le travailleur à domicile et celui qui passe les commandes est ici un accord de vente dans lequel le second spécifie le prix de vente de la matière première qu'il fournit et le prix du produit fini qu'il reçoit. La différence entre ces deux prix est le salaire du ménage par unité de produit fini. Contrairement au salaire des ouvriers à plein temps, cette différence de prix n'est pas limitée par le coût de subsistance, donc le donneur d'ordres, en réduisant les revenus des travailleurs à domicile, peut obtenir un taux de profit pour son capital comparable à celui qui lui reviendrait ailleurs. Dans un certain sens, la famille ne possède qu'une créance résiduelle sur la vente de la marchandise : elle recevra un certain revenu inférieur au niveau de subsistance dans la mesure où elle maintient sur place la main-d'œuvre excédentaire. Le donneur d'ordres ressemble au propriétaire foncier qui maximise son revenu en louant sa terre à un locataire donné pour une rente égale à celle qu'il pourrait obtenir en disposant de son fonds ailleurs. Il n'a à subir aucune perte du fait de l'emploi d'une main-d'œuvre excédentaire.

Ce qui est le plus fâcheux, c'est que l'existence d'un grand nombre de travailleurs superflus tend à étouffer l'organisation de la production la plus dynamique, la plus favorable à l'innovation technologique au sein du monde préindustriel. L'existence de main-d'œuvre en excédent peut aussi contrarier l'importation de technologies étrangères avancées. Par conséquent, le surpeuplement d'un pays retardera inévitablement son industrialisation.

La diversité des structures de production dans l'histoire de la Chine

La théorie des choix des formes de production exposée plus haut est remarquablement confirmée par l'expérience historique de la Chine. Contrairement aux pays européens, la Chine a connu pendant deux millénaires un système centralisé qui imposait un minimum de restrictions institutionnelles et légales à la vie économique, et laissait à la population une complète liberté de choix. Les marchés de produits et de facteurs de production restèrent la plupart du temps assez concurrentiels. Par conséquent, le pays connut une juxtaposition des diverses structures de production.

Pendant près de deux millénaires, un individu pouvait vendre sa force de travail sur le marché du travail libre ou se vendre, ou vendre les membres de sa famille, au marché d'esclaves. Un esclave pouvait très souvent mettre fin à sa servitude en se rachetant. On pouvait acquérir de la terre en propriété par achat ou par d'autres moyens, et la mettre en location ou l'exploiter à sa guise [1]. Les détenteurs de capitaux pouvaient les investir de diverses manières. Dans la production agricole, les latifundia utilisant des travailleurs libres, des esclaves ou des ouvriers de statut intermédiaire, coexistèrent depuis 200 av. J.-C. avec le fermage et le faire-valoir direct. La large circulation du capital entre le secteur urbain et le secteur rural est un fait bien connu, même sous la dynastie des Han antérieurs (206 av. J.-C.-2 apr. J.-C.), quand de riches hommes d'affaires achetaient des biens à la campagne. Pendant presque toute l'histoire de la Chine, les paysans étaient engagés activement dans la production non agricole, à temps partiel, pour leur propre consommation, et, plus tard, pour le marché [2]. Il y avait de nombreux ateliers appartenant à des artisans individuels, des manufactures privées et des entreprises d'État. Malheureusement, la plupart des documents qui nous restent signalent seulement l'existence de ces institutions productives sans nous donner des détails sur leur fonctionnement.

Parmi les différentes structures de production, nous avons relativement plus d'informations sur les fabriques d'État grâce aux documents officiels. D'une manière générale, ces établissements jouèrent un rôle décisif dans l'économie nationale avant le xve siècle. Puis leur importance déclina. Pendant toute la dynastie des Han (206 av. J.-C.-220 apr. J.-C.), le gouvernement central et les autorités locales contrôlaient un grand nombre d'entreprises dans le textile, la métallurgie, les mines et la construction navale, en plus de quelques entreprises de travaux publics [3]. Le nombre et la dimension des entreprises d'État augmentèrent d'une manière considérable sous la dynastie des Tang (618-907). Il y avait quatre administrations *(jian)* : chacune d'elles était partagée en plusieurs bureaux *(shu)* ; et chaque bureau, à son tour, contrôlait un grand nombre de fabriques ou d'entreprises. Par exemple, sous le Bureau du Tissage et de la Teinturerie, il y avait 25 grandes manufactures qui produisaient différentes sortes de tissus de soie. Dans deux des quatre administrations des industries d'État, il y avait à un certain moment jusqu'à 34 850 travailleurs. On pense que ce secteur connut son apogée au temps des Song (960-1279). Les documents officiels indiquent qu'un des hôtels des monnaies employait 300 personnes, qu'une grande mine de cuivre occupait 100 000 ouvriers et 800 chambres sur le site, avec une production annuelle de 3 millions de *catties* [4] de cuivre, que la manufacture de soieries au Sichuan était équipée de 154 métiers actionnés par 340 travailleurs, qu'une imprimerie d'État comptait 204 employés et qu'un moulin à papier employait 1 200 travailleurs [5].

Jusqu'à la dynastie des Song, les manufactures d'État recrutaient leur personnel à plusieurs sources, notamment dans le marché libre du travail. Le code

LES FORMES PROTOINDUSTRIELLES

civil du régime des Tang stipulait de façon précise que les travailleurs des fabriques d'État n'étaient pas des esclaves et qu'ils jouissaient de tous leurs droits civiques[6]. Le gouvernement offrait des salaires élevés (8 000 sapèques* par mois, plus la nourriture) et les payait d'avance. Il y avait pourtant pénurie de travailleurs[7]. Dans un autre décret, le gouvernement des Tang interdit aux établissements publics de recruter des travailleurs en recourant à des « mesures coercitives », ou de leur payer moins que le « taux de salaire du marché *(shijia)* »[8]. Le contrat de travail était désigné par le mot *hegu*, ce qui veut dire que l'emploi était établi par accord mutuel. Le même système de recrutement continua sous la dynastie des Song[9].

Ce fut pendant la dynastie des Yuan (1279-1368) que les souverains mongols fixèrent le statut professionnel des artisans en même temps que leur domicile sous le régime de l'enregistrement des familles. Les travailleurs furent conscrits pour servir dans les entreprises publiques avec des salaires médiocres. Le gouvernement des Ming (1368-1644) qui succéda à la dynastie des Yuan, hérita du même système d'enregistrement des ménages pendant quelque temps, puis relâcha le contrôle du marché du travail.

Un coup d'œil sur la liste des entreprises publiques indique que la plupart de ces établissements étaient spécialisés dans la fabrication du matériel de guerre et d'intendance. D'autres furent créés pour la manufacture de produits de consommation de premier choix, principalement pour les membres de la Cour ou de la famille impériale. Très souvent la capacité des entreprises publiques était supérieure à la demande de l'État, et on leur permettait de vendre sur les marchés civils. A cause de leur qualité supérieure, les produits des manufactures d'État étaient bien reçus par les consommateurs privés. Par exemple, les porcelaines produites dans les fours publics pendant la dynastie Song et à d'autres époques étaient toujours prisées par les collectionneurs. Finalement, il y avait des entreprises publiques fabriquant des marchandises exclusivement pour le marché. Il s'agissait en fait de monopoles d'État.

L'histoire des petites et grandes manufactures privées est tout aussi longue, sinon plus encore que celle des établissements publics. Sous les premiers Han (vers 200 av. J.-C.) beaucoup de familles devinrent célèbres dans tout le pays par leur réussite dans les mines de fer et la fonderie. Quelques-unes avaient plus de mille ouvriers[10]. En fait ces entreprises devinrent si grandes et si puissantes qu'elles déclenchèrent une controverse parmi les lettrés et les grands fonctionnaires du gouvernement Han qui se demandaient si l'État devait garder le monopole de la production du sel et du fer. Dès lors, dans toute l'histoire de la Chine, les mines relevèrent alternativement du monopole de l'État ou de la production privée. La plupart du temps elles relevèrent d'entreprises privées, avec privilège de l'État, surtout dans le cas de métaux monétaires tels que le cuivre et l'argent. Par exemple, dans les mines de cuivre du Jiangxi, il y avait plus de 100 000 mineurs dans les années 1140, employés par un nombre inconnu d'entreprises minières sous franchise de l'État. En travaillant jour et nuit, on pouvait extraire plusieurs douzaines de millions de *catties* de cuivre et de plomb. La production était ensuite rachetée par l'État au taux de 250 sapèques par *catty*[11].

L'industrie de la porcelaine et du papier sont les deux autres domaines pour

* Un millième de tael (NdT).

lesquels les manufactures sont fréquemment mentionnées[12]. Ces produits étaient renommés et on les trouvait dans tout le pays, comme en témoigne le fait qu'on les appelait soit par le nom de leurs lieux de production, soit par leurs propres marques.

Jusqu'au XIIIᵉ siècle, les travailleurs étaient vraiment libres, en ceci qu'ils pouvaient chercher du travail loin de leur domicile, voyager librement, quitter leur emploi, et négocier leurs salaires avec leurs maîtres[13]. En fait, beaucoup de travailleurs habitaient la campagne et se déplaçaient quotidiennement vers leurs lieux de travail. Ils pouvaient probablement changer aussi de profession. C'est sous la dynastie des Yuan et au début de celle des Ming que le système d'enregistrement imposa des restrictions sur le domicile et la classification professionnelle des artisans. Ils étaient des spécialistes à plein temps dans les régions urbaines. En 1421, le troisième empereur de la dynastie des Ming décida de déplacer sa capitale de Nanjing (Nankin) à Beijing (Pékin), accompagné de 27 000 familles d'artisans. La population totale de Nanjing en fut réduite de moitié[14]. Selon les archives officielles, le nombre total d'artisans enregistrés sous la dynastie des Ming atteint le chiffre de 300 000[15].

Dans certains cas il y avait effectivement une division du travail entre les entreprises privées et les entreprises publiques. Les premières fabriquaient pour la consommation de masse, tandis que les secondes se spécialisaient dans les produits de luxe ou ceux qui exigeaient une technicité ou un outillage plus avancés. De fait, de nombreux progrès technologiques dans l'histoire de la Chine furent introduits dans les entreprises publiques. Mais la division du travail entre les deux secteurs se brouilla avec le temps du fait du transfert technologique effectué par les travailleurs qui quittaient les entreprises publiques pour entrer dans le secteur privé. Pour la plupart des industries, les manufactures privées et les manufactures d'État produisaient des marchandises identiques. Les entreprises d'État avaient vu le jour parce que les produits du secteur privé étaient jugés insuffisants ou moins fiables. Bien entendu ces entreprises publiques eurent tendance à décliner ou à disparaître dès que le secteur privé fut devenu capable de fournir des quantités suffisantes à l'État. Le déclin des entreprises publiques commença après le XVᵉ siècle. Incapable d'employer à temps plein la totalité des 300 000 artisans enregistrés dans les manufactures publiques, le gouvernement des Ming leur demanda de travailler pendant deux mois par an, ou une année de temps à autre[16]. Pendant le reste du temps, les artisans pouvaient travailler dans leurs propres ateliers ou dans des établissements privés. Devant l'augmentation des fournitures du secteur privé, le gouvernement Ming décida finalement de transformer le système de production publique en un système d'approvisionnement.

Tandis que les écrivains chinois considéraient pour acquise l'extension des manufactures privées en Chine, dont ils ne se préoccupaient pas de faire des descriptions détaillées, les observateurs étrangers étaient vivement impressionnés par ces manufactures. Le meilleur exemple est fourni par ce que Marco Polo rapporte de son long voyage en Chine vers 1292 sur l'ancienne capitale des Song du Sud, Hangzhou. Il remarqua que pour chacun des douze secteurs de production les plus importants, il y avait à peu près 1 000 manufactures artisanales, chacune employant dix, quinze, vingt, ou même quarante travailleurs. Ces manufactures étaient en propriété privée, et héréditaires[17].

LES FORMES PROTOINDUSTRIELLES

La soie

Parmi les diverses industries chinoises, c'est la production textile qui nous livre les informations les plus abondantes. Nous pouvons prendre ce secteur comme exemple pour montrer comment les variations dans la rareté des facteurs de production exercent des effets sur le choix des structures. La production des textile par les familles paysannes comme activité secondaire a été, en Chine, une pratique générale pendant plus de 2 000 ans. Le caractère saisonnier des travaux agricoles laissait une quantité considérable de temps libre à la population rurale, et la fabrication des textiles semble avoir été adaptée à une production à temps partiel. Le tissage et la filature exigeaient une dextérité minimale et peu de capital. En outre, la demande familiale était continue, de sorte que les ménages pouvaient toujours produire au moins pour leur propre consommation. Enfin, pendant la plus grande partie de l'histoire de la Chine, le gouvernement exigea des impôts en nature, versés par les familles sous la forme de produits textiles.

Jusqu'au XIIᵉ siècle, les familles rurales ne fabriquaient que de la soie ou une toile de ramie car la fibre de coton n'était pas encore disponible en Chine même. Les soieries étaient aussi produites dans les villes par des ateliers familiaux, des manufactures privées et des établissements publics. Mais il y avait une division du travail entre ces divers organismes : les familles paysannes fournissaient de la soie grège et de simples tissus produits sur des métiers primitifs. Les ateliers urbains moulinaient la soie par des procédés plus raffinés et produisaient des étoffes de meilleure qualité aux dessins chatoyants. Les grandes manufactures fournissaient des étoffes encore plus complexes, comme les brocarts tissés sur des métiers à la tire. Les familles rurales autant que les ateliers urbains dépendaient de la main-d'œuvre familiale, tandis qu'au contraire les manufactures employaient des tisserands spécialisés et des dessinateurs professionnels salariés.

Bien qu'il y eût plusieurs manufactures publiques sous la dynastie Han, les documents nous disent peu de choses sur leur fonctionnement. Parmi ces unités de production, la plus connue était la fabrique de brocarts du Sichuan : ses beaux tissus étaient estimés dans tous le pays. Du VIIᵉ au IXᵉ siècle, il y eut vingt-cinq manufactures d'État dans la capitale Chang'an des Tang. L'une d'elles, appelée Lingjin fang, est réputée avoir employé 640 ouvriers divisés en quatre catégories[18].

Les indications sur les manufactures privées avant le XIIIᵉ siècle sont plutôt maigres. Un certain Pi-i, vers la fin du Vᵉ siècle, fut poursuivi pour avoir possédé plus de dix métiers à la tire pour la manufacture de brocarts[19]. Comme chaque métier à la tire devait être actionné par au moins trois personnes, il devait y avoir près de trente travailleurs dans cet établissement, beaucoup plus que dans les ateliers familiaux ordinaires. Un autre exemple fréquemment cité est celui de He Mingyuan de Dingzhou, sous la dynastie des Tang. Il possédait 500 métiers à la tire pour la manufacture du satin[20]. Plus intéressantes sont les archives officielles découvertes en Chine par une équipe d'archéologues japonais dans la province du Xinjiang. Elles apportent des informations sur les activités commerciales et l'administration de cette région frontière au VIIIᵉ siècle. Quelques pages de documents énumèrent les produits textiles traités sur le marché local avec leurs prix[21]. On y trouve du pongé de Zizhou, dans le Sichuan, du satin du Henan et du satin de Buzhout, dans le Shanxi. Ces produits devaient provenir du secteur privé puisque aucune des localités mentionnées n'avait de manufacture publique. Le fait que les soieries portent le nom de leur lieu d'origine indique que ces produits n'étaient pas confinés aux marchés locaux et qu'un grand commerce existait entre cette région périphérique et les provinces de l'intérieur.

En l'absence de données qualitatives, il est difficile de déterminer l'importance relative du secteur privé et du secteur public dans la manufacture avant le XIVe siècle. Mais on sait que sous les Ming et les Qing la production privée l'emportait. A partir du XIVe siècle les gouvernements Ming et Qing n'entretinrent que les grandes tissanderies de Nanjing, Suzhou et Hangzhou, trois nouveaux centres de production de la soie. Ces trois manufactures, selon les archives officielles, atteignirent leur taille maximum dans les années 1740, avec une capacité combinée de 1 863 métiers, 5 512 travailleurs ordinaires, et 1 550 techniciens spécialisés[22].

Pour les manufactures privées, la première description détaillée nous en est fournie sous les Yuan par un lettré qui visita une petite filature de soie à Hangshou vers 1360 et y engagea la conversation avec quelques travailleurs[23]. Le narrateur nous donne des détails sur le nombre des métiers dans la fabrique, sur le nombre des ouvriers, sur le salaire de base et les horaires de travail. Il paraît que les travailleurs acceptaient cet emploi volontairement et se trouvaient satisfaits malgré les mauvaises conditions de travail. Plus tard, d'autres rapports nous décrivent l'énorme marché du travail de la soie dans la vallée du bas Yangzi. Dans la ville de Suzhou seulement, par exemple, la gazette locale nous renseigne :

> Sous le règne Wanli (1573-1620) de la dynastie des Ming... de nombreuses personnes à Suzhou gagnaient leur vie en tissant les étoffes de soie. Le quartier nord-est de la ville était plein de zhihu (ateliers de tissage)... Chaque travailleur spécialisé avait ses employeurs attitrés et recevait son salaire à la journée... Ceux qui n'avaient pas d'employeur attitré se rendaient chaque matin à quelques ponts (qui servaient de bourses de travail) en y attendant l'emploi, les tisserands de satin se tenant debout sur le Pont du Temple de Kuanghua, et les fileurs sur rouets attendant dans la rue Lienhsifang... les travailleurs s'y attroupaient par dizaines et par centaines...[24].

On estime le nombre total d'ateliers de tissage dans la ville à plus de 10 000 au XVIIe siècle[25]. Dans la ville de Nanjing, autre centre de l'industrie de la soie, il y avait plus de 30 000 métiers, ce qui nécessitait 60 000 à 90 000 travailleurs[26].

Les ateliers de tissage étaient au départ des entreprises familiales employant quelques salariés. Mais plusieurs s'étaient développés en de grandes fabriques. Une nouvelle du romancier Feng Menglong, sous les Ming, raconte comment, au milieu du XVIe siècle, la famille Shi, de la commune de Shengze, avait réussi à étendre son atelier d'un métier à pongé à une unité de production comptant 40 métiers. Toujours au XVIe siècle, une autre histoire connue se situe chez la famille Pan de Suzhou qui, à partir d'un atelier, créa une manufacture valant un million de taels d'argent[27]. Ce sont là des histoires typiques de l'époque. Au XVIIe siècle, pendant une courte période, le gouvernement Mandchou essaya de

LES FORMES PROTOINDUSTRIELLES

mettre un frein à l'extension des manufactures privées en imposant un plafond de 100 métiers par entreprise. Mais en raison de l'opposition vigoureuse des ateliers, le décret fut bientôt révoqué et plusieurs unités atteignirent jusqu'à 500 ou 600 métiers chacune [28].

Le développement de l'industrie de la soie entraîna un boom des entreprises de teinturerie et de moulinage. A cause des économies d'échelle considérables dans ces deux secteurs, leurs entreprises étaient toujours très grandes. Li Wei, gouverneur général du Zhejiang, rapporte dans son mémoire de 1730 que dans le quartier de la Porte Chang de Suzhou, il y avait 450 établissements de moulinage employant au moins 10 900 travailleurs [29]. Un autre rapport officiel de Cao Shibin, en 1601, indique que l'imposition d'une taxe sur les métiers provoqua la fermeture de nombreux ateliers de tissage, ce qui jeta bientôt des milliers de teinturiers au chômage [30].

Les ateliers urbains ne se sont pas développés aux dépens de l'industrie domestique rurale ; celle-ci prospérait aussi, comme en témoigne la croissance des bourgs ruraux de la vallée du bas Yangzi où les négociants se rassemblaient pour ramasser les produits des tisserands des campagnes. Un bon exemple est fourni par la gazette *(gazetteer)* du district de Wujiang de la préfecture de Suzhou, à propos de l'histoire d'un bourg de ce district appelé Shengze :

> La ville de Shengze est située à environ 60 li au sud-est de la capitale du district. Ce n'était qu'un petit village de 50 ou 60 familles pendant les premières années de la dynastie Ming. Le nombre d'habitants doubla avant même le règne de Jiaqing (1522-1566) et le village fut promu au rang de shi (bourg) à cause de son grand marché de soieries. La population actuelle est cent fois plus grande et la quantité de tissus de soie qu'on y traite a plus que décuplé. Tous les jours, de grands négociants convergent vers la ville avec des chariots remplis de pièces d'argent. Quand le marché s'ouvre chaque jour à midi, les jetées sont embouteillées de bateaux et les rues encombrées par la foule. C'est l'endroit le plus prospère parmi les bourgs de la préfecture.

Les soieries du bas Yangzi, produites soit dans les ateliers urbains, soit par les ménages paysans, étaient écoulées dans toutes les provinces du pays et dans quelques marchés d'outre-mer. Les négociants en soie les plus influents n'étaient pas les hommes d'affaires locaux mais les groupes de commerçants du Shanxi, d'Anhui, et de Fujian.

A partir du début du XIXe siècle, la soie chinoise fut mortellement menacée par l'intrusion des soieries étrangères et des cotonnades tissées avec des fils de haut titrage. Ces grandes manufactures furent les premières à disparaître devant la concurrence aiguë. L'industrie fut bientôt laissée à la fabrication paysanne et aux petits ateliers familiaux, et au système du travail à façon connu sous le nom de *shangfeng*, ou « comptoirs ». Le système de distribution du travail à domicile existait probablement depuis longtemps, mais il n'est pas souvent mentionné avant le XIXe siècle. La subordonnation des petits ateliers aux grands comptoirs de marchands-fabricants est résumée par Liu Gunyi dans son Mémoire de 1896 :

> En général les marchands-fabricants eux-mêmes achètent le fil de soie pour la chaîne et la trame, et le distribuent aux ateliers pour les faire tisser. Ces entre-

prises sont appelées des comptoirs ; par rapport à ces comptoirs, les ateliers sont comme des locataires par rapport à leurs propriétaires[11].

Une enquête conduite en 1899 montre que dans la ville de Suzhou il y avait plus de 100 grands comptoirs de plus de 100 000 taels de capital chacun, plus de 500 comptoirs moyens avec à peu près 10 000 taels de capital chacun, en même temps que 600 petits comptoirs avec un investissement de 2 000 à 3 000 taels[32]. L'intensité de la concurrence augmentant, même le travail à façon éprouva de la peine à survivre ; de sorte que le nombre total de comptoirs à Suzhou était brutalement tombé à 57 vers 1910. Ces comptoirs donnaient alors de l'ouvrage à près de 1 000 ateliers qui employaient en tout 3 000 à 4 000 tisserands ; le nombre total de métiers tomba à 1 524[33].

Comparée à la situation antérieure, la taille moyenne des ateliers au xixe siècle était plus réduite ; la plupart d'entre eux possédaient 5 ou 6 métiers, les plus petits n'en avaient que 2 ou 3 ; même les plus grands n'avaient guère plus de 20 métiers[34]. D'après les indications données ci-dessus, il semble que la capacité moyenne des ateliers de Suzhou ait décliné jusqu'à 1,5 métier par atelier au début du xxe siècle. Il semble que seules les petites unités de production aient pu survivre. Ces unités de production avaient elles-mêmes peu de capitaux. Non seulement les comptoirs leur fournissaient le capital de roulement et la matière première, mais dans de nombreux cas ils leur louaient aussi les métiers et le reste de l'outillage. Leur capacité de survie dérivait du fait qu'elles s'appuyaient pour la plupart sur le travail familial et n'étaient donc pas soumises à la contrainte du coût de la main-d'œuvre. Afin de nourrir leurs membres excédentaires, ces familles tendaient à porter au maximum le chiffre d'affaires brut plutôt que le profit net. Mieux valait gagner un sou de plus que ne rien gagner du tout. Pour elles, la force de travail familiale était une ressource donnée et fixe, non une variable ; on l'exploitait donc comme telle.

L'industrie cotonnière

Malgré plusieurs ressemblances techniques, le développement de l'industrie du coton offre un contraste marqué avec celui de la soie. Le coton fut introduit en Chine comme culture commerciale à la fin du xiie siècle, mais la filature et le tissage ne se répandirent pas avant le xve siècle, c'est-à-dire le milieu de la dynastie des Ming. Ce fut aussi la période où la croissance démographique dépassa si largement celle des surfaces cultivées que la présence d'une main-d'œuvre excédentaire était devenue une constante dans les provinces peuplées. Aussi, deux changements importants se produisirent-ils dans l'organisation de la production.

Premièrement, les latifundia, jadis majoritaires, cédèrent maintenant la place au fermage. Libres de la contrainte du salaire minimum, les familles de tenanciers pouvaient mobiliser la force de travail excédentaire. Cette transformation du mode de production agricole est attestée d'une manière assez frappante par un auteur de l'époque des Ming. Le *Manuel d'agriculture de Shen*, rédigé dans les années 1630, nous donne d'abord un rapport détaillé sur le coût annuel des salaires agricoles. Ensuite il démontre qu'après avoir déduit tous les

LES FORMES PROTOINDUSTRIELLES

frais du produit potentiel brut, le revenu net pour le propriétaire n'était guère plus élevé que s'il mettait sa propriété en location. De plus, le propriétaire d'une exploitation ayant recours à une main-d'œuvre salariée devait consacrer tout son temps à coordonner et à surveiller les travaux sans aucune rémunération, tandis que le propriétaire bailleur pouvait recevoir le même revenu net sans aucun effort. Shen conclut que c'est la raison pour laquelle tous les propriétaires des villages de sa région étaient passés du faire-valoir direct à la location de leurs terres, et prédit que les propriétaires de son propre village ne sauraient tarder à prendre des mesures semblables.

Par ailleurs, la production du coton fut introduite à un moment où la main-d'œuvre excédentaire dans les régions rurales était en hausse. Les entrepreneurs chinois n'eurent donc pas la possibilité d'introduire la manufacture dans le coton. Ainsi l'industrie du coton ne suivit pas la même voie que celle de la soie. Les cotonnades étaient produites exclusivement par l'industrie domestique, surtout rurale, comme production complémentaire. A vrai dire, les deux développements se renforcèrent mutuellement. Le remplacement des latifundia par des tenures familiales augmenta le volume de la force de travail excédentaire que le secteur agricole pouvait accueillir. Cette pression incita plus que jamais les familles rurales à trouver des activités complémentaires adaptées. C'est pourquoi la part des productions d'appoint dans l'activité des familles rurales s'accrut d'une manière importante dans les derniers siècles de l'histoire de la Chine.

La filature et le tissage du coton s'adaptent très bien à la production rurale à temps partiel. Ces activités exigent très peu de capital ; la dextérité requise est assez faible, si bien qu'une main-d'œuvre marginale peut s'en charger ; le procédé de fabrication n'est pas si complexe qu'il nécessite le travail en équipe ; ce n'est pas non plus un processus continu, donc les membres de la famille peuvent travailler à leurs moments perdus et interrompre ce travail à tout instant. Il n'est pas surprenant de voir que le tissage et la filature du coton intéressaient davantage les familles rurales que beaucoup d'autres activités productives.

Comme les fabriques de coton devaient utiliser le même équipement et les mêmes techniques que les familles, sans aucune économie d'échelle, elles ne pouvaient faire concurrence à ces dernières que sur la base du prix de revient. Les fabriques ne pouvaient guère survivre. Par conséquent, les familles rurales produisant des cotonnades avec leur force de travail excédentaire étaient prêtes à vendre leur produit à n'importe quel prix, pourvu que la recette ne fût pas nulle ou négative.

La plupart des familles rurales qui produisaient des cotonnades en avaient cultivé la matière première. C'est ce qu'observe Mitchell, représentant britannique à Canton dans les années 1850 :

> Quand la récolte est rentrée tous ceux qui vivent à la ferme, jeunes et vieux, se mettent à carder, à filer, et à tisser ce coton ; et c'est de cette étoffe domestique, un tissu lourd et inusable, adapté au traitement qu'il devra supporter durant deux ou trois ans, qu'ils s'habillent, tandis qu'ils portent l'excédent à la ville la plus proche, où le marchand l'achète pour l'usage de la population des villes et des habitants des bateaux sur les rivières.
>
> De tous les pays du monde, c'est peut-être une caractéristique unique à la Chine qu'on peut trouver un métier à tisser dans chaque ménage. Les habitants

de tous les autres pays s'arrêtent à ce point, envoyant le fil au tisserand professionnel qui le transformera en étoffe. Il revint au frugal Chinois de porter la
chose à la perfection. Car non seulement il carde et file son coton, mais il le tisse
lui-même avec l'aide de sa femme et de sa fille [35].

Bien que la description de Mitchell soit fondée sur les observations faites au
Guangdong et au Fujian, elle vaut pour toute la Chine en général, sauf pour les
provinces extérieures.

Dans certaines régions, les conditions climatiques étaient favorables à la
culture du coton, mais non à la fabrication du textile. Les paysans de ces
régions trouvaient dans le coton une culture rentable, mais ne pouvaient
consommer son produit sur place. Ils devaient le vendre à d'autres régions.
Même à l'intérieur d'un district donné, la qualité de la terre variait d'un village
à un autre, si bien que les ménages des villages déficitaires pouvaient avoir à
s'approvisionner en matière première dans les villages produisant un excédent
de coton. La commercialisation du coton était encore plus nécessaire là où un
grand nombre de familles citadines étaient engagées dans la filature et le tissage.
Quand c'était possible, les familles tendaient à considérer la filature et le tissage
comme un processus de production intégré. C'est pourquoi la plus grande
partie du fil de coton était destinée à l'auto-consommation. Mais on trouve
encore des documents historiques concernant la mise en vente du fil de coton,
bien qu'à une échelle plutôt limitée.

Au contraire du fil, le marché des cotonnades était extrêmement actif et
étendu. Le plus grand marché d'étoffes de coton dans l'histoire de la Chine
était dans la région de Songjiang, à 30 km au sud-ouest de Shanghai, dont on
dit qu'il fournissait tout le pays [36]. La densité démographique était si élevée dans
cette région que la somme rassemblée des petites quantités d'excédents de
chaque famille pouvait facilement créer une offre énorme sur le marché. Autrement dit, si chaque famille réussissait à produire dix pièces par an pour le
marché, un million de ménages pouvait fournir 10 millions de pièces aux
régions qui n'en produisaient pas assez.

La localisation de ces marchés indique bien ce qu'était l'organisation de la
production des cotonnades. Même à Songjiang, les marchés d'étoffes étaient
situés non pas dans les villes du comté *(xian)* ou de la préfecture *(fu)*, mais dans
les petits bourgs ruraux. Ainsi, Fengjing : 54 li au sud-ouest de la ville de
Songjiang ; Zhujing : 36 li au sud-est de la ville de Songjiang ; Zhujiajiao : à
l'extérieur de la ville de Quingpu ; Qianjiaqiaozhen : à l'extérieur de la ville de
Fengxian ; Tinglin : à l'extérieur de la ville de Fengxian. Ces marchés se trouvaient près des foyers de l'industrie rurale domestique. Autrement dit, c'était
les centres de ramassage les plus commodes.

On sait que les débouchés des étoffes produites de manière artisanale s'éten-
daient au-delà des frontières de la Chine, bien que les données statistiques ne
soient pas disponibles pour la période la plus lointaine. Des documents japonais
indiquent que les produits textiles de Songjiang avaient été importés au Japon
d'un bout à l'autre de l'ère Tokugawa (1603-1867). L'exportation de cotonnades vers les pays européens et vers l'Amérique du Nord et du Sud remonte au
moins à 1730. Les étoffes commercialisées sur le marché mondial s'appelaient
les nankins, un produit de Songjiang. Quelques statistiques, bien qu'approxi-

LES FORMES PROTOINDUSTRIELLES

matives, ont été rassemblées par H. B. Morse : les exportations augmentent assez remarquablement jusqu'à la fin du XVIIIe siècle, pour s'effondrer par la suite, le flot annuel de 1,7 million de pièces atteint en 1805 se réduisant à un filet de 31 000 pièces de cotonnades en 1833 [37].

Pour compléter notre connaissance du développement de la production du coton dans la Chine traditionnelle, il faut encore souligner le rôle fondamental joué par les négociants en cotonnades. Ce sont eux qui permirent à un système d'industrie domestique de gagner un marché s'étendant à l'ensemble du pays. On sait que l'inconvénient le plus grave de l'industrie dispersée est la difficulté de commercialisation. Travaillant à temps partiel, le paysan-tisserand était peu capable de vendre ses surplus au-delà du marché local. Il pouvait essayer de porter de temps à autre ses produits vers les villes ou les bourgs avoisinants. Mais même cet effort, coûteux par le temps qu'il occupait, ne lui permettait d'étendre son rayon de vente que de quelques douzaines de kilomètres. La présence de marchands résolvait ce problème pour les tisserands des campagnes.

Sur le marché des cotonnades à Songjiang, les sources ne manquent pas : l'exposé qui suit est basé en grande partie sur ce que nous avons appris sur la situation de cette région. En général, les négociants en étoffes étaient divisés en deux catégories. A la première catégorie appartenaient les marchands itinérants qui venaient acheter périodiquement des étoffes à Songjiang pour les porter ensuite vers des régions déficitaires. C'est ce groupe de négociants qui avait créé le marché national pour les produits de la région. Afin de financer leurs achats en quantité et leur transport sur de longues distances, ils disposaient habituellement d'un capital important. Selon un observateur, les capitaux d'acquisition dépensés par les marchands itinérants pendant chaque voyage variaient de plusieurs dizaines à plusieurs centaines de milliers de taels d'argent [38].

Du fait que les dialectes, les coutumes commerciales et les préférences des consommateurs variaient suivant les régions du pays, les négociants itinérants avaient formé plusieurs groupements *(bang)* concentrant leurs activités de vente dans une ou dans plusieurs régions données. On a ainsi le groupe du Shanxi, de l'Anhui, du Fujian, et du Guangdong. Le sort de chaque groupe était naturellement lié à la conjoncture commerciale dans la région qui servait de débouché principal. On a ainsi remarqué, par exemple, que le groupe du Shanxi, qui commerçait principalement avec les marchés de la Chine du Nord, avait régressé au XVIIe siècle à cause de l'expansion des activités de la filature et du tissage dans les provinces septentrionales. La position dominante du groupe du Shanxi à Songjiang fut bientôt reprise par le groupe des négociants du sud-ouest qui concentraient leurs activités commerciales dans le sud [39].

Les correspondants locaux des marchands itinérants formaient la deuxième catégorie de négociants. Celle-ci à son tour se divisait en sous-classes : ou bien les marchands utilisaient leurs propres capitaux pour rassembler dans les magasins locaux les produits des tisserands ruraux dispersés pour les revendre au détail aux citadins, ou, en gros, aux marchands itinérants ; ou bien il s'agissait d'agents qui disposaient de très peu de capitaux personnels et qui n'avaient parfois même pas de bureaux ou de magasins. Leur fonction principale était de jouer le rôle d'agents collecteurs pour le compte des négociants itinérants. Cependant, la démarcation entre les deux sous-classes n'était pas toujours très précise et les termes qui les désignaient étaient souvent interchangés.

Le commerce local des cotonnades connut une évolution. Certains marchands avaient amassé suffisamment de capitaux et s'étaient assez instruits sur les conditions de commercialisation dans d'autres régions et sur les techniques de vente pour devenir des négociants itinérants eux-mêmes. Les marchands d'étoffe qui avaient le mieux réussi commencèrent à organiser des grands systèmes de distribution avec des magasins à succursales multiples situés à la fois aux points d'achat et aux points de vente.

Ce qui est intéressant, c'est l'absence de manufactures de coton. On ne peut l'attribuer à l'absence d'un marché. A vrai dire, étant donné les dimensions de la Chine, le marché des étoffes de Songjiang avant le XIXᵉ siècle est à peine moins étendu que celui du commerce mondial des textiles britanniques dans la période qui suit immédiatement la révolution industrielle. Ce n'est pas non plus le manque de capitaux qui empêche la formation de manufactures. Nous avons déjà remarqué les quantités appréciables de capitaux que les négociants en étoffes contrôlaient sous les dynasties des Ming et des Qing. On sait que quelques marchands d'étoffes avaient investi leurs capitaux dans des grands établissements de teinturerie, des moulinages, et dans la manufacture dispersée. Néanmoins, personne n'avait créé d'établissements de filature ou de tissage. Il est également difficile de prétendre que l'esprit d'entreprise faisait défaut, car le succès des manufactures de soie devait inciter à suivre leur exemple. La seule conclusion plausible est donc la moindre rentabilité des manufactures de coton.

C'est vers la fin du XIXᵉ siècle que les choses changent, avec l'ouverture, en 1883, de la première manufacture de coton installée par Chen Bojian à Fuzhou, avec un total de 1 000 métiers à bras. Cinq ans plus tard, le gouvernement ouvre une autre unité dans la même ville, sous l'ordre du gouverneur général Bian Baidi [40]. En 1896-1897, la mission Blackburn note l'existence d'une autre manufacture de travail à la main située à Wanxian, dans le Sichuan, et employant 80 ouvriers pour 50 métiers à bras [41]. Ces trois manufactures utilisent des métiers à bras mais du fil mécanique [42]. A vrai dire, elles n'ont pas précédé l'industrie moderne, mais formaient plutôt des succursales des fabriques modernes installées ailleurs. Dès lors qu'il était facile de s'approvisionner à un prix modique en fil mécanique importé, la marge de profit du tissage sur des métiers à bras s'était élevée au-dessus du coût de subsistance. Il était donc possible d'employer à plein temps des tisserands professionnels. Ceci explique aussi pourquoi il y avait des manufactures de tissage à la main, mais non de filature à la main.

Les manufactures artisanales de ce type se multiplient ensuite dans les grandes villes de Chine : on compte trois établissements de tissage manuel à Chongqing en 1905, et deux unités semblables s'ouvrent à Pékin la même année [43]. Un rapport officiel du Bureau des Douanes maritimes mentionne 13 manufactures de tissage à bras dans la ville de Guangzhou (Canton) en 1910, toutes trois récemment ouvertes [44]. Peng Zeyi a assemblé les données statistiques sur les manufactures de tissage mises en route entre 1899 et 1913 [45]. Le nombre des métiers est connu pour quelques-unes de ces unités ; pour d'autres on n'a que le nombre des travailleurs ; pour d'autres encore nous avons à la fois le nombre des métiers et celui des travailleurs. Sur la base de ces dernières données on peut déduire qu'il y avait à peu près deux travailleurs pour chaque

LES FORMES PROTOINDUSTRIELLES

métier. En appliquant cette proportion aux données fournies par Peng, on obtient le tableau suivant :

Années	Nombre de manufactures ouvertes dans l'année	Nombre de métiers à bras mis en service dans l'année
1899	1	15
1900	2	656
1904	6	381
1905	3	45
1906	6	780
1907	7	197
1908	7	540
1909	19	1 545
1910	19	886
1911	14	837
1912	43	2 102
1913	14	779

Ces données sont sans doute incomplètes, les sources portant généralement sur les grandes unités et négligeant les petits ateliers : si le nombre des métiers paraît refléter assez correctement la réalité, celui des manufactures semble être considérablement sous-évalué. Néanmoins, les données témoignent pour une institution nouvelle, à son premier stade de développement. Pendant les premières années de l'époque républicaine, le ministère de l'Agriculture et du Commerce du gouvernement de Pékin publie deux séries de statistiques pour 1912 et 1923 respectivement, montrant la répartition par province des fabriques de tissage à bras du coton. Ces données, vraisemblablement assemblées d'après les dossiers locaux d'enregistrement, sont présentées dans le tableau 1, en annexe.

Selon les enquêtes industrielles conduites par D. K. Lieu, en 1933, il y avait alors 2 281 manufactures et 27 431 métiers à bras [46]. Étant donné la méthode plus systématique et l'étendue plus ample de cette enquête, les résultats de D. K. Lieu semblent être plus dignes de foi. Mais l'industrie du tissage à la main atteint son apogée dans les années 1920 et commence à décliner au début des années 1930. Les conclusions de l'enquête ne représentent donc pas la situation de ces manufactures à leur apogée. D'après les sources dispersées nous pouvons réunir des indications pour montrer le nombre des manufactures de tissage manuel dans les villes principales pendant leur période de développement maximum : plus de 5 000 au total, soit plus de deux fois le nombre obtenu par le recensement de D. K. Lieu. Or des manufactures de tissage ont dû exister dans d'autres villes et bourgades.

Si on les compare à l'industrie rurale domestique et aux usines modernes de coton, les manufactures de tissage artisanal formaient le secteur le plus faible de toute l'industrie cotonnière. Sans énergie électrique et sans outillage moderne, leur productivité était naturellement inférieure à celle des usines modernes. D'autre part, du point de vue des coûts de la main-d'œuvre, elles n'avaient pas la flexibilité caractéristique du système de production familial. C'est pourquoi, tandis que le secteur moderne se développa graduellement dans les années 1930,

K. CHAO   EN CHINE

Localité	Année	Nombre approximatif des manufactures de tissage à bras
Shanghai	1925	1 500
Guangzhou (canton)	1929	300
Beijing (Pékin)	1924	100
Nanjing (Nankin)	1928	350
Huaining	1926	190
Shenyang	1927	300
Fuzhou	1929	270
Chengdu	1920s	730
Chongqing	1920s	235
Wuhu	1920s	240
Tianjin	1924	530
Xinmin	1926	300

les manufactures de tissage manuel furent les premières à être éliminées, laissant l'industrie domestique poursuivre sa résistance tenace. En face des cotonnades importées et de la production croissante des usines modernes en Chine, l'industrie familiale trouva encore le moyen de fournir plus de 60 % de la consommation nationale au milieu des années 1930 [47].

Karl Marx a été l'un des premiers économistes qui ait reconnu la nature de la production textile du coton dans la Chine traditionnelle. Frappé par le rapport Mitchell, cité plus haut, Marx écrivit un article en 1859 au sujet du commerce avec la Chine, qu'il conclut ainsi : « Nous avons trouvé que l'obstacle principal à une expansion subite du commerce d'importation en Chine, est la structure économique de la société chinoise, fondée sur la combinaison d'une petite agriculture avec l'industrie domestique [48]. » Plus tard, il réalise que la même combinaison créait un obstacle sérieux à l'industrialisation de la Chine. Cette observation entrant en contradiction complète avec sa théorie générale, il dut créer le soi-disant « mode de production asiatique », à côté de son modèle général de développement économique, pour rendre compte du phénomène. Le troisième volume du *Capital* nous propose ceci :

> Les relations de l'Angleterre avec les Indes et la Chine nous fournissent un exemple frappant de la résistance que des modes de production précapitalistes fortement organisés peuvent opposer à l'action dissolvante du commerce. La large base du mode de production était constituée par l'union de la petite agriculture et de l'industrie domestique à laquelle il faut ajouter, comme aux Indes, par exemple, l'institution de la propriété commune du sol sur laquelle reposaient les communes rurales hindoues, et qui, au demeurant, était également la forme primitive en Chine. Aux Indes, les Anglais employèrent à la fois leur puissance politique et leur pouvoir économique, comme gouvernants et propriétaires fonciers, pour désagréger ces petites communautés économiques... Pourtant les Anglais ne réussirent que graduellement dans leur œuvre de destruction, et cela encore moins en Chine, où ils ne disposaient pas directement du pouvoir politique. Dans ce pays, l'alliance de l'agriculture et de la manufacture permet, grâce à l'économie des frais de temps, d'opposer la résistance la plus opiniâtre aux produits de la grande industrie anglaise... [49].

LES FORMES PROTOINDUSTRIELLES

Ce que Marx n'avait pas vu, cependant, c'est que le système de production familiale en Chine résista aux manufactures autant qu'aux fabriques modernes. A vrai dire, ce système pouvait résister à n'importe quelle institution rivale dans le même secteur de production. Marx ne s'est pas rendu compte que la capacité de résistance du système de production familial reposait, en dernière analyse, sur le surpeuplement plutôt que sur quelque mystérieux « mode de production asiatique ». Dans toute économie, asiatique ou européenne, tant que la main-d'œuvre est rare, le coût du travail dans l'industrie familiale n'est pas inférieur à ce qu'il est dans les autres formes de production. Les manufactures artisanales pouvaient se développer et frayer ainsi un chemin à l'industrialisation. Après l'apparition des usines modernes, ces dernières devaient remplacer tôt ou tard l'industrie domestique dont la faible productivité ne pouvait être compensée par le coût modique de la main-d'œuvre s'il n'y avait pas surpeuplement. L'incapacité de Marx à voir cette relation causale est compréhensible, car il n'admit jamais le concept de surpeuplement.

* La traduction de cet essai est de Kay Hawkins et de Franklin Mendels. Ce dernier remercie son collègue Ka-che Yip pour ses conseils et renseignements.
Nous avons utilisé la transcription Pinyin pour les noms de lieux et de personnes, avec une traduction française entre parenthèses lorsque celle-ci est courante (NdT).

NOTES

1. Kang Chao, « Tenure Systems in Traditional China », à paraître dans *Economic Development and Cultural Change.*

2. Mark Elvin, *The Pattern of the Chinese Past*, Stanford, Stanford Univ. Press, 1973, p. 167.

3. Bai Shouyi et Wang Youzhuan, « Sur les rapports entre les industries artisanales publiques de Chin-Han à la fin des Ming et le système féodal », *Lishi yanjiu* (Études historiques), 1954, n° 5, pp. 63-98.

4. Une *catty (jin)* = 604,5 grammes (NdT).

5. Ge Zhangji, « Une étude préliminaire des relations d'emploi pendant la dynastie Song », *Lishi yanjiu*, n° 2, p. 32.

6. Bai Shouzi et Wang Youzhuan, *op. cit.*, p. 93.

7. Département d'histoire, Université populaire, *Quelques problèmes concernant les relations économiques féodales en Chine*, Pékin, San Lien, 1958, p. 201.

8. *Ibid.*

K. CHAO   EN CHINE

9. GE Zhangji, *op. cit.*, p. 32.

10. *Traité du sel et du fer.*

11. *Sung hui yao gao* (Section d'argent et d'alimentation), t. 34, année 1142.

12. GE Zhangji, *op. cit.*, pp. 35-43.

13. *Op. cit.*, pp. 26-27.

14. CHEN Jishi, *Une étude sur l'industrie artisanale publique pendant la dynastie des Ming*, Wuhan, Presses populaires Hubei, 1958, p. 87.

15. *Op. cit.*, p. 74.

16. *Op. cit.*, p. 71.

17. Cf. la traduction chinoise par LI Ji, *Les Voyages de Marco Polo*, t. II, chap. 76.

18. BAI Shonyi et WANG Yüzhuan, p. 73.

19. WANG Fang zhong, « L'industrie artisanale privée sous la dynastie des Song », *Lishi yanjiu*, 1959, n° 2, p. 43.

20. *Ibid.*

21. Kang CHAO, « A Study of the Prices of Textile Products shown in the Ta-ku Document », *Youth Monthly*, 1978, n° 4, p. 23.

22. *Ta-Ching Hui-Tien*, t. 1190.

23. XU Yigui, *Shi feng gao*, t. 1, « Une conversation avec des tisserands ».

24. *Suzhou fuzhi*, t. 16.

25. *Yuanhe Xianzhi*, t. 16.

26. *Jiangning fuzhi*, t. 15.

27. SHEN Defu, *Wanli yehubian*, t. 28.

28. *Jiangming fuzhi*, t. 7.

29. Mark ELVIN, *op. cit.*, p. 280.

30. *Op. cit.*, p. 278.

31. *Op. cit.*, p. 283.

32. SHI Minzhong, *Le Développement de l'industrie de la soie sous la dynastie des Ching*, Paipei, Presses commerciales, 1968, p. 79.

33. *Op. cit.*, p. 78.

34. *Ibid.*

35. *Correspondence Relative to the Earl of Elgin's Special Missions to China and Japan, 1857-1859*, Londres, 1859, p. 244.

36. YE Mengzhu, *Yueshi bian*, t. 7, section 5.

37. H. B. MORSE, *The Chronicles of the East India Company Trading to China, 1635-1834*, Oxford, 1926, t. 1, p. 224.

38. YE Mengzhu, *op. cit.*

39. *Ibid.*

40. PENG Zeyi (sous la direction de), *Zhongguo jindai shougongye shi ziliao*, Pékin, 1957, t. 2, pp. 25 et 258.

41. *Report of the Mission to China of the Blackburn Chamber of Commerce, 1896-1897*, Blackburn, 1891, p. 256.

42. Bank of China, *Chungking Cotton Textile Industry*, Chungking, 1935, p. 3.

43. PENG Zeyi, t. 3, p. 104.

44. Chinese Maritime Customs, *Trade Reports*, II, p. 111.

45. PENG Zeyi, t. 2, pp. 367-376.

LES FORMES PROTOINDUSTRIELLES

46. Kang CHAO, *The Development of Cotton Textile Production in China*, Cambridge (Mass.), 1977.

47. *Op. cit.*, p. 236.

48. Karl MARX, « Trade with China », *New York Daily Tribune*, 3, déc. 1859.

49. Karl MARX, *Œuvres*, t. 2 : *Économie*, Maximilien RUBEL éd., Paris, Gallimard, Bibliothèque de la Pléiade, 1968, pp. 1101-1102 (NdT).

ANNEXE

TABLEAU 1. — Manufactures de tissage à bras
du coton, par province, 1912-1913

	1912		1913	
	Manufactures	*Employés*	*Manufactures*	*Employés*
Hopei	–	–	118	2 788
Liaoning	1	30	41	522
Jilin	–	–	30	405
Jiangsu	44	869	45	938
Jiangxi	–	–	178	3 938
Zhejiang	3	122	102	4 209
Fujian	–	–	60	1 959
Hebei	38	448	12	297
Hunan	17	258	61	1 561
Shandong	4	38	63	1 666
Henan	8	66	3	45
Shanxi	–	–	1	8
Shaanxi	–	–	10	219
Gansu	–	–	8	322
Xinjiang	–	–	17	182
Sichuan	–	–	176	7 221
Guangdong	–	–	49	628
TOTAL	115	1 831	974	26 008

Source : Peng Zeyi, t. 2, p. 433.

7

Textiles and Trade in Tokugawa Japan

William B. Hauser

INTRODUCTION

Any discussion of the textile trade in Tokugawa Japan (1600-1867) requires that the socio-economic and political context first be outlined. Japan was a state divided into many separated political jurisdictions, with around one-quarter of the country controlled directly by the Tokugawa Shogunate and the other three-quarters under the local control of around 265 local barons or daimyo. While each of these local power-holders was subordinated to the shogun and required to spend half his time in attendance on the shogun at the Tokugawa capital of Edo (modern Tokyo), within his own domain he was an autonomous ruler. Each daimyo owed fealty to the Tokugawa, but they paid no taxes and were left alone so long as they were not abusing the residents of their domains. Tokugawa power was centered in the Kantô plain around Edo but included direct control of the major cities of Edo, Kyoto, Osaka, and Nagasaki as well as the foreign trade conducted out of Nagasaki with Dutch and Chinese merchants.

Major features of the Tokugawa era were domestic peace, following a century of warfare in the battles for unification before 1615; the political integration of the country through the system of alternate attendance required of the daimyo; urbanization; and economic growth together with greatly expanded demands for consumer goods. As a consequence of urbanization and the withdrawal of most samurai from the villages into the cities, the agrarian model of society with a clear separation between warrior-bureaucrats and aristocrats at the top of society and farmers, artisans and merchants supplying their needs broke down. Over the course of the Tokugawa era, increased commercial agriculture and by-employment activities by farmers blurred the distinctions between handicraft industries and trade, on the one hand, and farming, on the other. This had a major impact on the textile trade in the eighteenth and nineteenth centuries.[1]

While largely secluded from the outside world, Tokugawa society was by no means static and unchanging. Between 1600 and 1867 the economy became increasingly monetized and commercialized, farming

Textiles and Trade: Japan

shifted from subsistence to market oriented cropping patterns, and new systems of production and distribution developed. In the seventeenth century Kyoto and Osaka were the primary foci of commercial activity. The Kinki region surrounding the imperial capital of Kyoto and Osaka had long been the center of the Japanese economy and of handicraft industrial production. While Kyoto was the center of silk textile production, Osaka became a center for the cotton trade. When cotton cultivation and processing expanded in the sixteenth century, the Kinki region was of major importance.

THE COTTON TRADE

By the early seventeenth century cotton had replaced linen as the staple fiber for Japanese commoner clothing. Cotton became a major commercial crop in the Osaka region and Osaka and nearby market towns developed as cotton processing centers. By the end of the seventeenth century merchant and artisan guilds developed to focus the marketing and processing of seed cotton into cloth on the city of Osaka. Protective trade associations or kabunakama were designed to regularize business procedures and trade routes and control access to the cotton trade. On the one hand guilds assured consistent quality and prices for cotton goods; helped define roles in the collecting, processing, and distribution of seed and ginned cotton, cotton yarn, and cotton cloth; and brought order to a complex system of economic relationships. On the other hand, once established the guilds limited innovation, restricted access, and monopolized various aspects of the processing and marketing of cotton and cotton textiles. In the 1660s and 1670s the Osaka city magistrates authorized guilds for cotton buying, shipping, processing and sales. The guilds helped stabilize the cotton trade, assisted government control of commerce, and helped preserve the separation between cotton cultivators and those who processed and marketed their crops. In a context in which handicraft industry and trade were seen as potential contaminants of the purity of self-sufficient agricultural villages, the kabunakama in the cotton trade were important for preserving the separation of commerce and agriculture. They also assured that regular supplies of cotton would be available for the urban residents of Osaka and, to a lesser extent, Edo.

As cotton cultivation became increasingly common as a cash crop in Kinki area villages, cotton processing also increased. Initially villagers processed enough cotton to provide cloth for household consumption. But

-114-

Textiles and Trade: Japan

from the 1730s on, cotton cultivating villages increased the volume of processed goods they produced.
This was especially true for cotton ginning and the
dominant position of Osaka cotton ginners was challenged. Local cloth production increased as well and
this threatened the position of the Osaka cotton
weavers. The Osaka guilds of seed and ginned cotton
dealers, processors and shippers declined in influence
and appealed to the city government for protection. In
1772 the Osaka city government ordered all those competing with the Osaka cotton guilds to join them and
abide by their regulations. The city government
stepped in to reinforce the position of the Osaka cotton guilds. In doing so, the city government demanded
new monetary contributions from the guild members, and
these licensing fees strengthened ties between the
cotton merchants and the city administration.[2]

Similar actions were taken to defend the interests
of the guilds of cotton cloth merchants. During the
1770s and 1780s, they too formed revised trade associations in association with the Osaka city government.
Included were the Osaka cotton cloth wholesalers
nakama (momen ton'ya nakama) and the Osaka cotton
cloth dealers nakama (nanakumi momen'ya nakama). The
cloth wholesalers purchased cotton cloth and sold it
to the cloth dealers for storage and distribution.
While a licensed monopoly the wholesalers guild offered to admit any newcomers who could afford its li-
cense fees and wished to enter the trade. The cotton
dealers guild included merchants who warehoused and
shipped cotton cloth to Edo and other areas of Japan
as well as local retailers. Each of its seven member
groups had long histories, with the Edo shippers association dating back to 1616.

The reinforced kabunakama served several purposes.
First, they enhanced the cotton merchants access to
the juridical power of the city administration to protect them from outside competition. Second, they intensified the pressures on guild members to adhere to
established business practices and limited the ability
of guild members to innovate. Third, they provided a
new source of revenues--through licensing fees--to the
city government. Finally, they helped insure the
stability of the cotton trade and the supply of cotton
goods to the city. Severe penalties including threats
of fines or expulsion from the trade helped keep members in line and retarded changes in the operation of
the Osaka cotton trade. While prior to the 1770s
guilds had defined spheres of activity and regulated
the Osaka cotton trade, by the 1770s more formal me-

Textiles and Trade: Japan

chanisms with closer ties to government power were required. Reorganized kabunakama protected the interests
of the Osaka cotton merchants. Direct sales by rural
cotton producers, new marketing and distribution
strategies by rural jobbers and transport merchants,
and increased rural processing of cotton collectively
weakened the dominant position of the Osaka guild merchants in the cotton trade. Kabunakama formation in
the 1770s and 1780s served to reassert Osaka merchant
controls and limit the expansion of rural processing
and trade.[3]

Village processors and merchants were not the only
sources of competition for the Osaka cotton merchants.
Local daimyo also worked to augment their incomes from
the cotton trade. In 1785, Wakayama domain tried to
established a ginned cotton buying office in Osaka to
improve access to supplies for its domain sponsored
reeled yarn industry. The domain tried to evade the
Osaka guild system and buy directly from ginned cotton
shippers in Osaka. The Osaka guild merchants protested
to the city government that this violated their
monopoly rights and Wakayama domain was forced to follow established market procedures. The city government
protected the cotton merchants' interests against an
encroachment by Wakayama domain.[4]

A more serious domain challenge came in 1821. Himeji
domain established a domain monopoly for marketing its
bleached cotton cloth and omitted the Osaka cotton
cloth merchants. Until 1821, all Himeji cloth exports
passed through the Osaka cloth merchants and the new
domain monopoly abruptly altered the marketing system.
The new monopoly increased domain revenues from cotton
exports. By shipping cloth directly to the higher
priced Edo market, all profits went directly into the
domain treasury and the Osaka merchants were excluded.
The impact of this and other challenges to the Osaka
cotton merchants was dramatic. White cotton cloth imports to Osaka declined from 8 million tan (12 yard
bolt of cloth suitable for one garment) in 1810 to an
average of 3 million tan between 1832 and 1841. At the
same time the price of cloth increased in Osaka by 50
per cent, even though cloth production in Himeji and
elsewhere increased. The dominant position of the
Osaka cloth merchants in the Kinki cotton trade was
shattered.[5]

Rural competition and challenges to the dominant
position of the Osaka cotton merchants continued from
the mid-eighteenth century. For example, northeast of
the city of Sakai near the modern city of Yao were

·116·

Textiles and Trade: Japan

three groups of rural cotton cloth traders. All were
formally organized by the 1750s, had established business regulations and attempted to limit outside competition. Yet their regulations illustrate the problems
they faced in controlling the rural cotton cloth
trade. Admonitions against roadside sales and under-
the-counter transactions suggest both were common.
Members competed for cloth supplies as evident from
the effort to discourage such practices. One member of
the Yao cotton cloth traders guild was Wataya
Kichibei, whose shop Watakichi was a large-scale
trader of cotton cloth, ginned cotton, cotton yarn,
and other dry goods from the 1750s into the twentieth
century. In 1759, for example, Watakichi sold 21,428
bolts of white and striped cotton cloth, 1720 spools
of cotton yarn, and 273 kan (8.72 lbs.) of ginned cotton. Originally a seed cotton dealer, in the 1750s
Watakichi became a major cloth wholesaler. Sales fluctuated from year to year with 52,178 bolts sold in
1826, 33,676 bolts sold in 1852, a high of 79,275
bolts sold in 1864 and only 35,297 in 1868. Documents
which survive indicate that Watakichi sold directly to
merchants from Omi and did not go through the Osaka
cloth traders guilds on route. While Watakichi was one
of the larger rural cloth merchants, he was not unique
in his independence from the Osaka cotton guilds. It
was this kind of competition in the 1760s and 1770s
that encouraged the Osaka merchants to reorganize
their guilds and request additional monopoly rights
from the Osaka city government. As Watakichi illustrates, it was difficult to control competition
outside of the city of Osaka.[6]

A major transition point in the Osaka cotton trade
occurred in 1823 when 1007 cotton cultivating villages
in Settsu and Kawachi, provinces near the city of
Osaka, complained to the Osaka city magistrate that
the Osaka cotton wholesalers guild was restraining
trade. The guild was accused of disrupting shipments
through Osaka, Sumiyoshi, Sakai, and Nada and con-
fiscating goods until it received its normal commission. This limited the market for village cotton and
enabled the Osaka guild to unilaterally determine the
price of seed cotton. The Osaka guild defended itself
and claimed only to be exercising its long established
rights in the cotton trade. Yet, with 1007 villages
claiming hardship for over 10,000 households of cotton
cultivators, the Osaka city magistrate was faced with
a difficult decision. At issue was continued government support for the kabunakama in the Osaka cotton
trade. The suit challenged the commercial policies of
the Tokugawa Shogunate.

Textiles and Trade: Japan

In its decision, the government did not deny the
monopoly rights of the Osaka cotton wholesalers guild,
but it sanctioned free trade outside of the city of
Osaka. This set a precedent which reduced the willing-
ness of the Shogunate to interfere in the Kinki cotton
trade. The decision abrogated the responsibility of
the city government to protect the Osaka cotton guilds
from outside competition. While the decision focused
on seed cotton sales, its impact was far greater. Important legal barriers to structural change in the
Kinki cotton trade disappeared as a result of the 1823
dispute. Thereafter, unrestricted rural trade would
further undermine the position of the Osaka cotton
merchants.[7]

THE SILK AND LINEN TRADES
Similar changes are evident in the silk and hemp
trades during the Tokugawa era. New cropping patterns,
weaving and spinning technology transfers to new
regions, and the expansion of rural cloth processing
and trade as by-employments challenged the position of
established textile production and marketing systems.
The Kyoto Nishijin silk textile industry is one example of this process. Kyoto developed as a center of
silk textile production in the Heian era (794-1185).
The Nishijin district of the city became the center of
silk weaving in the late fifteenth century. By the
mid-sixteen century the weavers guild received both
shogunal and imperial protection as the source of
luxury silks for upper class samurai and court consumption. From the 1590s demand for silk increased
among both samurai and wealthy commoners and Nishijin
weavers flourished. By 1706 there were over 2,000
households of guild weavers in Kyoto.[8]

Guilds were important both to restrict access to the
weaving trade and assure access to imported yarns from
China. In 1655 the yarn importing guild (Ito wappu)
was abolished and fierce competition for reduced supplies of yarn developed in Kyoto. Increased demand and
reduced supplies resulted in rapid yarn price increases which the city government attempted to regulate. From the late seventeenth century the Shogunate
encouraged domestic production of silk yarn in northern Japan and the Kantô region. This helped supply the
demands of the Nishijin weavers and eventually replaced imported Chinese yarns. At the time of the
great Nishijin fire of 1730, around 7,000 looms were
in operation in Kyoto. The fire destroyed over 3,000
looms and severely affected the Nishijin weaving industry.

-118-

Textiles and Trade: Japan

As domestic sericulture expanded so did provincial
silk spinning and weaving. Tangô, Kiryû, Nagahama,
Isezaki, Hachioji, Gifu and other areas competed with
the Nishijin silk industry. In the 1730s the superior
looms and weaving technology of the Nishijin weavers
spread to regional production centers. The 1730 fire
accelerated this diffusion as many weavers were displaced from Nishijin and welcomed invitations to
migrate elsewhere. Once rural silk production increased much of the cloth was shipped to Kyoto for
further processing and sale. The Nishijin weavers
quickly challenged this invasion of their primary
market.[9]

In 1744 the Nishijin weavers petitioned the Kyoto
city magistrates for protection from imports of
provincial textiles. Constraints on silk imports attempted to restrict competition in Kyoto, but the city
government was powerless to control rural production.
A limit of 36,000 tan (12 yd. bolt) of cloth from
Tangô and 9,000 tan from Kiryû illustrates the scale
of rural imports. To reinforce their position the
Nishijin weavers in 1745 formed a kabunakama of
takabata (tall loom) weavers, designed to stifle competition from both provincial weavers and outsiders in
the city of Kyoto as well as control the actions of
guild members. Even while this kabunakama was forming
new weavers proliferated in and outside of Kyoto. Efforts to strengthen the weavers guilds in the 1750s
and 1760s illustrate the severity of the competition.
A major fire in 1788 sent more Nishijin weavers to the
provinces as many apprentices left their masters and
became independent. In 1800, a further reorganization
of the kabunakama also failed to stifle outside competition.[10]

In 1816, the weavers guild attempted to stop weavers
from leaving Kyoto and relocating in the provinces.
Despite this and other actions, competition continued
to undermine the position of Nishijin. Kyoto weavers
still produced the finest silk textiles, but rural
competition was a serious threat to the Nishijin silk
industry. In 1833, 1836 and 1837 bad weather
devastated the rice crops and caused severe famine
throughout Japan. The market for silk textiles collapsed and many weavers left the craft. In the provinces, where weaving was usually a by-employment
rather than a full-time occupation, the recovery of
the weaving industry was more rapid after the famine
ended in 1838 and competition for silk yarn intensified. Silks from Tangô, Nagahama, and Kiryû

Textiles and Trade: Japan

flooded the Kyoto market and destroyed the remnants of
the Nishijin monopoly. The elimination of all guilds
by the Shogunate in 1841 furthered the destruction of
the Kyoto silk industry. The 2219 houses of <u>takabata</u>
weavers were reduced to 1201 households by 1852; 456
of these weavers were new entrants to the craft.
Rural competition had eliminated the dominant position
of the Nishijin weavers. While the imported Jacquard
loom would help restore the industry in the late nineteenth century, silk textile production had spread to
regions far from the control of the Nishijin weavers
and outside the jurisdiction of the Kyoto city government or the Tokugawa Shogunate.[11]

As centers of rural silk weaving proliferated, among
the most important were Tangô, Nagahama, and Kiryû.
Let us briefly examine each of them. While the Kiryû
area had a long history of textile production, it was
not nationally important until the mid-Edo period.
Most weaving was concentrated in the Kiryû Shinmachi
area or in the 54 villages which comprised Kiryû
domain, now included in Gunma and Tochigi Prefectures
north of modern Tokyo. Because of poor farm land, silk
and paper production were important sources of supplementary income. By the late Tokugawa era, Kiryû was
the second most important area for silk production
after Nishijin. Sales of Kiryû silk to Edo and Kyoto
date from the 1680s and 1690s. By 1718, seventeen
transport merchants were shipping silk from Kiryû and
in 1722 the Mitsui house opened an Echigoya branch
shop in Kiryû to purchase local textiles. By 1738 local weavers used high quality production technology
brought from Kyoto. Kiryû produced both silk twill
cloth and silk yarns. Kiryû silk competed effectively
with Nishijin as both shared common technology and
used similar yarns. Located close to major areas of
silk yarn production and two days from Edo by land or
water, Kiryû could compete with Nishijin in major urban markets. Because the area was divided administra-
tively into many separate jurisdictions under Tokugawa
bannermen (<u>hatamoto</u>) control, no single authority
could regulate the by-employment activities of local
farmers. This facilitated the rapid expansion of silk
weaving in the area.

In 1731 the market days for Kiryû silk were changed
to help Kiryû Shinmachi develop as a major silk market
in competition with Omama, the dominant market in the
area. The town grew substantially, especially after
the 1738 introduction of <u>takabata</u> looms from Kyoto.
Better looms increased output and weaving quality and
by 1744 Kyoto weavers were complaining about the com-

-120-

Textiles and Trade: Japan

petition from Kiryû. Until the 1770s most Kiryû silk
was white cloth, but thereafter dyers appeared in
Kiryû and dyeing increased. Water wheels improved yarn
quality and figured textile production increased after
1786. This made Kiryû silk more comparable to Nishijin
silk and made Kiryû the focal point of the Kantô silk
industry. In the nineteenth century, Kiryû faced
regional competition from Ashikaga and other Kantô
textile centers . Efforts to control competition in
the Kiryû region are evident in 1781, 1797, 1835,
1838, and 1846. Just as Nishijin lost its monopoly to
Kiryû, Kiryû Shinmachi lost its position as the primary Kantô silk market after 1832 when a rival market
opened in Ashikaga where traders could evade the controls of the Kiryû textile guilds.[12]

Tangô silk crepe (chirimen) was another major source
of competition for the Nishijin weavers. The Kaya valley in Miyazu domain was a silk production region until the seventeenth century when the local daimyo
relocated weavers to the castle town of Miyazu. In
1722, new weaving technology came to the region from
Nishijin and silk crepe production developed as an important by-employment industry. The closeness of Tangô
to Kyoto made access to new weaving technology easier
than in Kiryû, as local merchants regularly travelled
to the imperial capital. Domain authorization of silk
crepe production after 1722 resulted in a rapid increase in the number of looms. The Kaya valley had 205
looms in 1764-71, 423 in 1775, 503 in 1803, and 496 in
1829. By 1803, 956 looms existed outside the castle
town of Miyazu with most weaving concentrated in the
Kaya valley. Weavers in Miyazu domain prospered after
the transfer of silk crepe weaving technology from
Kyoto to Tangô. Nearby Mineyama domain also saw expanded weaving.

All Tangô silk crepe was shipped to Kyoto for dyeing
and sale. A marketing and distribution system controlled by Kyoto guild merchants dominated trade and used
advanced payments to weavers to monopolize access to
Tangô silk. Kyoto was also a major source of yarn for
Tangô weavers. In 1769 Kyoto yarn dealers suspended
provincial yarn sales to protect Nishijin weavers from
excessive rural competition. This policy failed as
rural yarn dealers stepped in to supply the demand and
silk crepe production continued to increase. Competition in the Tangô silk trade developed between Miyazu
castle town merchants and Kyoto merchants, with the
former supported by the domain government, and also
between rural and castle town cloth and yarn traders.
The rural weavers asserted their independence whenever

Textiles and Trade: Japan

possible. In 1820 a slump in the silk crepe weaving industry resulted in an effort by weavers from Miyazu, Mineyama, and Kumihama domains to collectively organize an independent organization to represent their interests in the textile trade. At each level of production and distribution, Kyoto merchants, Tangô castle town merchants, and provincial weavers asserted their own interests in the silk trade. This became particularly intense in the 1820s, just when the Kinki cotton trade experienced aggressive efforts by rural merchants and producers to assert their independence from Osaka guild controls.[13]

Nagahama silk crepe (chirimen) was another source of competition for Nishijin silks. The area around modern Nagahama city in Shiga Prefecture was an important sericulture and weaving center during the second half of the Tokugawa era. Nagahama silk production emerged between 1738 and 1752 as a form of by-employment activity in this part of Hikone domain. The local product was known as Hama or Nagahama chirimen and was largely marketed in Kyoto. In the 1750s the Nishijin weavers objected to imports of Hama chirimen and the city magistrate supported their objections and banned Hama chirimen from Kyoto. Hikone merchants turned to the domain government for support. Discovering that domain tax goods could be freely sold in Kyoto, the domain office arranged to sell the cloth through the domain office in the city. Merchants were appointed to inspect the cloth for quality and serve as sales agents for Hikone cloth. In 1763 the Kyoto magistrate approved the direct marketing of Hikone cloth and production of Hama chirimen increased. By 1797 the volume of cloth shipped to Kyoto was 8,000 to 13,000 rolls per year. In 1799 the domain ordered that all yarn, cotton wadding, and cloth produced in the domain as well as all chirimen be designated as official tax goods and sent to the Kyoto domain office. This created a domain products monopoly in Hikone. Regulations for chirimen production and sales were revised in 1815 to increase domain profits from the trade. In 1829 Hikone opened a domain products sales office in Edo in order to avoid paying commissions to Osaka merchants for transporting and marketing domain goods. In 1857 a domain products office was opened in Nagahama to certify the quality of Nagahama silk and reinforce the dominant position of the domain government in the silk trade. Hikone domain used its export controls over Nagahama chirimen as an important source of supplementary income and opened domain products sales offices to compete directly with guild merchants in Kyoto, Osaka, and Edo.[14] Other examples of the chang-

-122-

ing nature of the textile trade in the Kantô region
can be seen in the production and marketing of Gunma
silk yarns and Maoka cotton cloth. Both prospered in
the early nineteenth century in competition with textile products from other regions of the country.[15]
   The history of Nara bleached linen (Nara zarashi)
provides an analogy to the Nishijin silk weaving industry. The Nara area, the dominant source of this
luxury fabric in the seventeenth and early eighteenth
century, developed a highly specialized and tightly
organized system of production and distribution. By
the mid-eighteenth century the system was breaking
down due to both increased independence by rural merchants and artisans and also to competition from other
regions of the country. Like Nishijin silks, Nara
zarashi was dependent on yarn supplies from other
regions as local production was insufficient to meet
the demand from weavers. The Yamato region provided
only 10 to 20 percent of the necessary linen yarns and
80 to 90 percent came from other areas of the country.
Increased linen production in Echigo, Omi, Nôto, and
Satsuma competed with Nara zarashi after 1737 and production declined from 230,000 bolts (2 tan) in the
1730s to 150,000 bolts in the 1750s, and only around
100,000 bolts in the 1830s. Domain sponsored linen
weaving in hemp cultivating domains enabled lower cost
production and faced the Nara weavers with serious
competition which undermined their dominant position.[16]

CONCLUSIONS
   What generalizations can be drawn from the above
discussions of the textile trade in Tokugawa Japan?
First, urbanization increased the demand for textiles
and stimulated production. Second, the importation of
cotton cultivation in the sixteenth century and its
wide diffusion throughout Japan resulted in cotton
displacing linen as the staple fabric for clothing in
the seventeenth century. Third, In the seventeenth
century, both the Tokugawa Shogunate and the regional
daimyo tried to concentrate textile production in
cities and towns and separate handicraft production
from farming. Fourth, urban merchants established an
elaborate network of guilds to regulate the production, marketing, and distribution of silk, cotton, and
linen cloth and the raw materials required to produce
them. Fifth, the Shogunate as the national government
and the domain governments in the provinces assisted
the creation of urban merchant monopolies. The timing
of guild formation differed from one area to another,
with Osaka and Kyoto taking the lead in the seven-

Textiles and Trade: Japan

teenth century, but guilds of textile merchants and
artisans are found throughout the primary textile production regions by the mid-eighteenth century. Many of
these guilds were reinforced with additional legal
rights in the late-eighteenth century, a symptom of
the increased competition from rural traders and producers.

Sixth, a major feature of the textile trade was the
diffusion of cotton, silk, and linen processing technology and trade away from the cities and into the
provinces. This is especially evident in the Kinki
region around Osaka and Kyoto and the Kantô region
around Edo.[17] Provincial merchants competed with those
from the central cities and rural merchants and
artisans competed with those based in urban areas.
This was true in the silk, cotton, and linen trades.
Seventh, a further source of competition was domain
monopolies which by-passed the systems of marketing
and distribution controlled by Osaka, Kyoto, and Edo
merchants. The result of this and other sources of
competition was the decline of urban guild dominance
and of Kinki regional dominance of the textile trades
in the late-eighteenth and early nineteenth centuries.
Eighth, a major constraint which limited the effectiveness of urban merchant guilds was the lack of
uniform national authority. The Tokugawa Shogunate
controlled Edo, Osaka, and Kyoto and around 25 percent
of Japan's farm land. The rest was divided among 265
daimyo domains, court nobles, and Tokugawa bannermen.
No single authority could impose its will beyond the
limits of its own jurisdiction. The provinces of
Settsu and Kawachi surrounding Osaka and much of the
Kantô region surrounding Edo were divided among many
separate administrative jurisdictions. The authority
of city magistrates was limited beyond the city borders, and thus they had limited capacity to intervene
on behalf of urban guilds faced with rural competitors. Finally, the economic and social changes experienced by Tokugawa society resulted in many farm
households turning to cash crops and by-employments as
sources of supplementary income. Textile production
and trade were two major areas of involvement. Villages engaged in sericulture turned to yarn production. Those located nearby often turned to weaving.
Cotton growing villages learned to gin and then spin
their seed cotton harvests and others turned to weaving, not just to clothe their families, but to sell
for cash. Income from non-farming activities became a
major source of farm household income throughout
Tokugawa Japan. The distinctions between merchants,
artisans, and farmers blurred as did many of the dis-

-124-

Textiles and Trade: Japan

tinctions between urban and rural patterns of production and consumption. Tokugawa Japan was a time of transition. The textile trades provide a good illustration of some major features of economic and social change.[18]

NOTES

1. For a general discussion of Tokugawa commercial history see William B. Hauser, 1974. Economic Institutional Change in Tokugawa Japan: Osaka and the Kinai Cotton Trade. London: Cambridge University Press, pp. 7-58.

2. Hauser, Economic Institutional Change, pp. 59-73.

3. Hauser, Economic Institutional Change, pp. 73-80.

4. Hauser, Economic Institutional Change, pp. 83-84.

5. Hauser, Economic Institutional Change, pp.103-106.

6. Hauser, Economic Institutional Change, pp. 148-151.

7. Hauser, Economic Institutional Change, pp. 97-100, 160-165.

8. Gotô Yasushi, 1960. "Nishijin ori." In Chihôshi Kenkyûkai ed., Nihon sangyôshi taikei, Vol. 6, Kinki chihôhen, Tokyo: Tokyo Daigaku Shuppankai, pp.32-36.

9. Gotô, "Nishijin-ori," pp. 36-38.

10. Gotô, "Nishijin-ori," pp. 38-40. Sawada Akira, 1967. Edo jidai ni okeru kabunakama kumiai seidô, tokuni Nishijin oriya nakama no kenkyû, Kyoto: Daigakudô Shôten, pp. 88-93, 107-114.

11. Gotô, "Nishijin-ori," pp. 41-44.

12. Ichikawa Kôsei, 1959. "Kiryû no orimono," In Chihôshi kenkyûkai ed., Nihon sangyôshi taikei, Vol.4, Kantô chihôhen, Tokyo: Tokyo Daigaku Shuppankai, pp. 287-307.

13. Ikeda Hiromasa, 1960. "Tangô chirimen," in Chihôshi Kenkyûkai ed. Nihon sangyôshi taikei, Vol. 6, Kinki chohôhen, Tokyo: Tokyo Daigaku Shuppankai, pp. 70-85.

14. Egashira Tsuneharu, 1960. "Hama chirimen," In

Textiles and Trade: Japan

Chihôshi kenkyûkai, ed. Nihon sangyôshi taikei, Vol.6, Kinki chihôhen, Tokyo: Tokyo Daigaku Shuppankai, pp. 58-69.

15. Yamada Takemaro and Inoue Sadayuki, 1959. "Gunma no ki-ito," In Chihôshi kenkyûkai, ed. Nihon sangyôshi taikei, Vol. 4, Kantô chihôhen, Tokyo: Tokyo Daigaku Shuppankai, pp. 257-286; Aoki Kôji, 1959. "Maoka momen," ibid., pp. 248-256.

16. Kimura Hiroshi, 1960. "Nara zarashi," In Chihôshi kenkyûkai, ed., Nihon sangyôshi taikei, Vol.6., Kinki chihôhen, Tokyo: Tokyo Daigaku Shuppankai, pp. 90-103.

17. On this issue see William B. Hauser, 1974. "The Diffusion of Cotton Processing and Trade in the Kinai Region in Tokugawa Japan," Journal of Asian Studies, 33, 4: 633-649.

18. Addendum: Throughout the text I have used "linen" and "hemp" alternatively to refer to the Japanese word asa. Asa usually refers to hemp or ramie, and includes all plant-derived fibers except cotton. Western style linen is made from flax which was not grown in Japan until modern times.

8

Textile Producers and Production in Late Seventeenth-Century Coromandel

Joseph J. Brennig

I
The Industry

It is widely accepted that regional studies of industry in seventeenth and eighteenth century India are essential for the development of a pre-colonial economic history. To date such regional studies have concentrated on trade rather than industry.[1] This may be due to the large size of the geographic units chosen for study. Studies of the Malabar Coast, Coromandel, Bengal or Gujarat offer geographic and economic coherence as well as follow divisions within the important Dutch and English factory records, yet these regions are too diverse and extensive for the close examination of the abundant records available in the late seventeenth century. In an attempt to get closer to the information on industry, always partial and scattered, this study considers only a portion of the Coromandel Coast, the Godavari and Krishna deltas of northern Coromandel. European factory records for northern Coromandel in the late seventeenth century are abundant. Moreover, they contain useful references to industry, particularly the Dutch records. In this period the Dutch were seeking ways to gain control over their suppliers, the brokers, and therefore took time to study something of the relationship of the broker to the weaver.

This article is adapted from Chapters 7 and 8 of my dissertation, *The Textile Trade of Seventeenth Century Northern Coromandel: A Study of a Pre-Modern Asian Export Industry*, (Unpublished Ph.D. Dissertation, University of Wisconsin, Madison, 1975). I would like to acknowledge with appreciation the assistance of Dr. Sanjay Subrahmanyam of the Delhi School of Economics.

[1] An important exception is Vijaya Ramaswamy's *Textiles and Weavers in Medieval South India*, New Delhi, 1985.

334 / Joseph J. Brennig

The late seventeenth century is a significant period in northern Coromandel's economic history. After supplying relatively stable markets in Southeast Asia for centuries, northern Coromandel in this period found a new market for its calicos in Europe. European demand, explored by mid-century, exploded by the late 1670s. In the continuing search for the first stirrings of change in industrial organisation, or for explanations for why change did not occur, the weaving industry of northern Coromandel offers a useful ground for detailed examination. What signs of change, if any, can be seen in an industry adjusting to new demand?

Textiles of Northern Coromandel

The broadest categories of Coromandel textiles were patterned and plain. Some of the former, such as checked rumalls (handkerchiefs), were produced in the loom; most were patterned by the application of dyes after weaving. These were the famous chintz (from the vernacular 'chitta,' or spotted cloth) on which designs were applied in a complex process of painting using the techniques of mordant and resist dyeing.[2] Painted cloth was probably produced in greater quantity by block printing. Northern Coromandel chintz was in demand in the luxury markets of both India and Persia and later in the seventeenth century in Europe. It was probably the staple for the region's trade with the markets of Southeast Asia. Important though chintz is in the history of Indian textiles, the quantity produced was small,[3] involving relatively few weavers. Since the production of small quantities of chintz had little effect on a weaver's overall output, this part of the Coromandel's textile industry, important though it was for the textile industry of Europe in subsequent periods, is of less concern here than the plain varieties of Coromandel cloth.

There were two types of plain cloth produced in northern Coromandel, muslins and calicos. Muslins were of a finer quality than calicos. Their open weave made them of value for turban cloths and veiling, whence the Portuguese term *bethilles* (literally, 'veiling'), by which they were known among the European exporters of the region. Especially, valued were the Warangal bethilles, produced in the Deccan town of Warangal about eighty miles north of Hyderabad. Although the Dutch and English exported muslins, they held an even more important place in the trade of local exporters who sold their cloth in Persian Gulf markets.

Calicos varied in length and quality. Thus the common and coarse calico, the guinee or longcloth, was 35 yards long. The finer salempores and

---

[2] For details seen John Irwin and Katharine B. Brett, *Origins of Chintz*, London, 1970, p. 1; and J. Irwin, 'Indian Textile Trade in the Seventeenth Century: II. Coromandel Coast,' *Journal of Indian Textile Industry*, II, 1956, 40f.

[3] The intrepid French merchant Tavernier who visited northern Coromandel in the 1660s reported that only three bales of chintz might be collected from the painters of northern Coromandel in a season. Jean B. Tavernier, *Travels in India by Jean Baptiste Tavernier, Baronne of Aubonne*, trans. by V. Ball, 2nd edition, edited by W. Crooke, 2 vols., II, 4.

Textile producers and production in late seventeenth century Coromandel /335

parcalles were respectively 16 and 8 yards long. Widths varied but most were little more than a yard. All three of these varieties were produced in fine and ordinary grades. The coarsest calico, known as both dungaree and sail cloth, was produced in lengths of 12 yards and exported in large quantities. Whether it was used to manufacture sails in Europe is not known, for its name could be derived from its use in Asian shipping. Durable calicos of the finer sort found a great market in Europe where they were popular as household linens and draperies.

The attention given here to the weaving process is not intended to slight the importance of northern Coromandel's textile finishing industry. Cloth painting was the most complex part of the finishing industry, but while only a few of the salempores and parcalles were painted, most calicos were washed and bleached. In addition others weɪ dyed uniformly in the piece. Each of these processes involved considerable labor.

RAW COTTON AND THE BANJARA TRADE

A distinguishing feature of the export sector of northern Coromandel's textile industry was its dependence on imported supplies of raw cotton. Northern Coromandel's high humidity and frequent flooding in its lowlands made the region unsuited to cotton cultivation in appropriate quantities and qualities for an export industry. An eighteenth century observer of local agricultural practices stated that in the Godavari Delta, 'scarcely any cotton crop is gathered if the season is favorable for Paddy by the freshes rising in July or the rains, being seasonable which are both totally destructive to cotton.'[4] In the early nineteenth century, an East India Company report concluded that in northern Coromandel (Northern Circars) cotton was 'neither abundant in quantity nor good in quality.'[5] The cotton the reporter was referring to was probably Cocanadas, a reddish variety unsuited for export quality textiles.[6] North of the deltas in the hilly areas of the Sikakol region was found a coarse white cotton native to the red lateritic soils of the hill sides but its short staple also limited its use.[7]

Northern Coromandel's raw cotton had necessarily to come from outside the region. Then as in the later years the black soil districts of the central Deccan produced a high quality cotton in quantity, and it was this region which supplied the northern Coromandel weaving industry.[8] Bullocks carried

[4] Andhra Pradesh State Archives, Hyderabad, *Masulipatnam District Records*, 2794, 15 December 1789, p. 4.

[5] East India Company (English), *Reports and Documents connected with the Proceedings of the East India Company in regard to the Culture and Manufacture of Cotton-wool, Raw Silk and Indigo in India*, London, East India Company, 1836, p. 126.

[6] George Watt, *A Dictionary of the Economic Products of India*, 6 vols., London, 1890, IV, p. 101.

[7] D.F. Carmichael, *A Manual of the District of Vizagapatnam in the Presidency of Madras* (Madras Government Press, 1869), p. 140–41.

[8] Algemeen Rijksarchief, The Hague, *Koloniaal Archief* (hereafter *K.A.*). 1267, 18 April 1682, fol. 1067b.

the bulky and relatively low-valued raw cotton across the three hundred or more miles which separated the cotton growing region from the coast. This was accomplished by the nomadic Banjara community which escorted thousands of bullock loads of cotton from the Deccan to the coast every year.[9]

The Banjara migrations to the east coast represent an unusual instance of a major movement of commodities in response to developing export demand. Although export of cotton textiles from northern Coromandel dates from the sixteenth century, it did not assume large proportions until after 1630 with the expansion of Dutch trade in the region. The single reference to the transport of bulk goods early in the century does not refer to the migration of bullocks, but to river transport.[10] According to their own traditions, the Banjaras arrived in the Deccan as a part of Shah Jahan's invasion force in 1630.[11] If this evidence can be accepted, the Banjara bullock caravans arrived in the Deccan at the time that the demand for cotton in the weaving centers of northern Coromandel was growing.

A Banjara caravan usually contained about 10,000 bullocks and could rise to as many as 40,000.[12] With little overhead costs beyond the food required for subsistence, the Banjaras themselves added little to the cost of transport. Moreover, since their bullocks grazed as they moved, the cost of feeding them was negligible. At about two miles per day Banjara transport was leisurely, but then time was of little importance.[13] The Banjaras were more than transporters of cattle and transporters; they were also independent petty traders in their own right. Apparently they owned the cotton they brought from the Deccan. Records from the seventeenth century tell us little about the Banjaras, but their movements continued into the early nineteenth century when more details become available. From these sources we learn that when they sold their cotton, they purchased salt from the coastal salt pans for the return trip to the Deccan.[14] Since in the later seventeenth century salt production was an important government monopoly, it was probably their role in this official enterprise as much as any other reason which explains why the Kingdom of Golconda licensed the Banjaras, like

[9] *K.A.* 1262, 26 April 1682, fol. 1959. For a description of the Banjaras in seventeenth century Mughal India see Habib, *The Agrarian System in Mughal India (1556–1707)*, Bombay, 1963, p. 62.

[10] 'Anonymous Relations,' in W. Moreland ed., *Relations of Golconda in the Early Seventeenth Century*, Cambridge, 1931, p. 68. Moreland has mistranslated the word 'ballegats' as referring to the geographical region 'Balghat'. The 'ballegat' in this text was a round boat used in river and coastal transport in Coromandel and Deccan. See the original Dutch in Izaak Commelin, (comp.) *Begin ende Voortgangh van de Veerenigde Geoctroyeerd Oost Indische Compagnie*, 2 vols. (Amsterdam, 1646), II, XVII, 77.

[11] R.V. Russell, *The Tribes and Castes of the Central Provinces of India*, London: Government Press, 1916; II, 168–69.

[12] Habib, *The Agrarian System*, p. 62.

[13] *Ibid.*

[14] Andhra Pradesh State Archives, Hyderabad, *Godavari District Records*, 862, 5 October 1803, p. 311.

Textile producers and production in late seventeenth century Coromandel/337

the European Companies, to transport commodities toll free.[15] The annual migrations of the Banjara merchants between the Deccan and the coast, a development which occurred as a direct result of the expansion of textile exports, was a significant contribution to the rhythm of commercial and social life of the regions through which they passed. The indirect effects of this migration makes the opening of the Banjara trade a particularly pervasive consequence of the growth of northern Coromandel's èxports.

We should distinguish between the role of the Banjaras in trade in northern, Mughal India and their position in trade between the Deccan and northern Coromandel. Although notable in North India, especially when food scarcities in isolated regions required the movement of grains or when the Mughal Army required supplies, their movements did not have such a key relationship to an industry. In contrast to their occasional and irregular importance elsewhere, in the Deccan cotton trade they were an established part, not only of the textile industry as conceived in its wider sense, but also of the general exchange economy of northern Coromandel and the Deccan.[16]

The amount of cotton carried by the Banjaras into the Deccan can only be estimated by inference from information from a later period. According to a letter from the Commercial Resident of the East India Company stationed in the East Godavari Delta in the early nineteenth century, the amount of raw cotton sold at Hinghaun Ghaut, an important Deccan market for the Banjara trade, 'used to amount to 5,000 candies'.[17] The date being referred to here is not specified, but presumably it was in the late eighteenth century. Since in all probability the cotton trade in the eighteenth century was substantially below the peak years of the seventeenth century, the quantity of raw cotton sold in Highaun Ghaut a century and a half earlier would have been somewhere in excess of 5,000 candies or above 2,500,000 lbs. With a carrying capacity of between 240 to 260 lbs. per bullock, between 10,000 and 15,000 bullocks would be needed to supply the required amount, a number well within Banjara caravan capacities.[18]

Conternporary records do not describe Banjara trade routes and markets, but some information may be inferred from later records and indirect references. Of natural concern to the Banjaras were adequate fodder and water for their bullocks, supplies of which probably dictated their choice of routes across the eastern Deccan. A likely choice was the valley of the Godavari river, which not only extended from the cotton tracts in the Deccan to the heavily populated and industrialised Godavari delta, but also provided relatively assured supplies of both water and fodder. Their point of arrival was probably in the vicinity of Rajamundry, the easternmost market in the lowlands that the Dutch describe as a centre for the cotton

[15] *K.A.*, 1262, 1682, fol. 1950.
[16] *Godavari District Records*, 862, p. 311.
[17] *Ibid.*, 832, 1 February 1819, p. 105.
[18] For the capacity of a Banjara bullock, see *K.A.* 1262, 26 April 1682, fol. 1950b. The Dutch refer to the bullock load as a *cansam*, a term whose origins I have not been able to trace.

338 / Joseph J. Brennig

trade.[19] From Rajamundry the Banjaras probably moved south and east through what is today West Godavari district and into the Krishna delta.

The eastern bank of the Godavari was heavily populated with weavers. The Dutch factors in Draksharama refer to the villages of Dulla and Vemagiri as being particularly important sources of cloth.[20] More significantly the factors identified the village of Teeparu (Tiparoe) in what is today Tanku Taluk of West Godavari District as being a 'great marketplace of cotton.'[21] Since the source of this observation appears to have been the Draksharama factory on the other side of the Godavari in the East Godavari Delta, Teeparu was probably an important market for raw cotton for both banks of the Godavari.

Elsewhere cotton was probably sold in markets to the south in the Krishna delta.[22] Masulipatnam, significantly, was not among these. A Dutch source explicitly states that raw cotton could not be obtained in Masulipatnam, and buyers have to travel some distance inland.[23] The source offers no explanation for this, but I would suggest that it probably reflects the absence of weaving in or immediately around Masulipatnam. The high cost of rice in Masulipatnam would probably have acted as a disincentive for weaver settlement there.[24]

Dutch records contain information which indicates that the price of cotton rose steadily during the period in which demand for textiles was growing.

The price rise recorded in Table 1 is significant. If cloth prices did not increase correspondingly, the weaver would have found his margins shrinking through this period. The Banjaras however could only have profited by the growing value of the goods they carried.

INDUSTRIAL LOCATION

The available evidence for the distribution of weaver households in northern Coromandel falls into a discernible pattern, but while this pattern can be described, it remains difficult to explain. In the early 1680s the Dutch Governor of Coromandel, Laurens Pits, ordered the Dutch factors of northern Coromandel to count the weaving households in the villages supplying their respective factories. The Dutch records contain responses of varying comprehensiveness from Masulipatnam, Palikollu, Draksharama and Nagulawancha. The factors of the Draksharama factory gave the greatest detail, including not only the number of households but the total number of looms in each village.

[19] K.A. 1267, 18 April 1962, fol. 1067b.
[20] Ibid.
[21] K.A. 1464 R/Sd, 'Uittreksels uit brieven . . . ,' fol. 3.
[22] K.A. 1262, 1682. fol. 1972.
[23] Ibid., 20 April 1682, fol. 1950b.
[24] See Brennig, The Textile Trade, pp. 205–11.

Textile producers and production in late seventeenth century Coromandel / 339

Table 1

Cotton Prices in Northern Coromandel, 1660–80

Year	lbs/pagoda
1660	40
1668	40
1669	38
1670	38
1671	38
1672	32
1673	26
1674	25
1675	24.5
1676	22
1677	26
1678	26–20
1679	24–20
1680	24–22

Source: K.A. 4464 R/Sd, 'Uittreksels uit brieven . . .,'
fol. 8.

Table 2

Weaving Villages Supplying Draksharama

Village	Households	Looms
Chollangi (Tsalfengy)	350	400
Peddapuram	400	500
Pithapuram and Samalkota	600	800
Thuni	600	800
Ponara and Oupara	500	600
Peddada	170	200
Pandalapake	40	50
Kesavaram	60	80
Dulla	400	500
Mandapeta	180	200
Veerarallipalem	180	200
Angara	80	100
Amalapuram	900	1200
Nagaram	900	1200
Andrangi (Angringy)	500	600
Draksharama	100	100
Total	5960	7530

Source: K.A. 1262, 31 September 1682, fol. 602.

340 / JOSEPH J. BRENNIG

All of the villages in Table 2 were located within the eastern Godavari delta, which is to say on the north-eastern side of the Godavari delta. As given, the list cannot be said to be a comprehensive count of the productive capacity of this one region. Weaving villages that supplied other factories are not listed. Nevertheless, the list probably gives a fair idea of the size of the weaving industry in this part of northern Coromandel and usefully permits us to set a lower limit for the size of one section of the textile industry in northern Coromandel. The figures are evidently rounded approximations. The number of looms always exceeds the number of households, but the proportion varies enough to indicate it was probably based on concrete information and not a simply uniform rule of thumb applied throughout. The Dutch factors in Palikollu, located in the western Godavari delta, supplied a list of source villages unfortunately lacking the detail from Draksharama.[25] The Palikollu list contains eighteen villages, seven of which were located across the. Godavari river in the eastern delta. Four of the eighteen are mentioned in the Draksharama list, including the two large weaving villages of Nagaram and Amalapuram. The remaining three (Tatipaka, Mummidivaram and Baduralanka) are not to be found in the Draksharama list and serve as an indication of the partial character of the latter. We can assume that other villages, perhaps also omitted, supplied the English factory at Madapollem a short distance from Palikollu.

The Nagulawancha list turns out to have a different character from the others. Rather than a survey of villages supplying the Nagulawancha factory, it is a document best described as an 'itinerary'. It consists of a list of villages lying along a route between the Dutch factory of Palikollu and the factory at Nagulawancha, and against many of the villages is a short description of what might be found there of use to the Dutch. A summary of the contents of this 'itinerary' is contained in an appendix.

Unless the factors in Nagulawancha misunderstood Governor Pits's instructions, presumably they took this itinerary from their diary as a sufficient response. If less complete than the lists of Draksharama and Palikollu, the Nagulawancha itinerary is nonetheless interesting. The first section of the itinerary bears the heading 'under Palikollu' and contains the names of twenty-three villages. Most lacked weavers. The itinerary marks the boundary of the region under the Masulipatnam factory at village number 24. It is not clear whether the next fifty-eight villages all fall within this group or whether some should be listed as in the region 'belonging' to Nagulawancha. But the overall pattern emerging in this itinerary is maintained: weaving communities are scattered and generally smaller than those of the eastern Godavari delta.

In sum the lists prepared in the several Dutch factories of northern Coromandel show considerable variation in the distribution of the textile industry over the entire region. The eastern Godavari delta held the greatest

---

[25] *K.A.*, 1262, fols. 615b–618.

Textile producers and production in late seventeenth century Coromandel/341

number of weaver households. A number of villages had large concentrations of weavers. Their size could entitle them to be described as industrial centers. In the Krishna delta, however, there were fewer weavers and these were grouped in smaller concentrations.

Two factors were probably responsible for this variation. First, the weavers of eastern Godavari produced calicos, a relatively coarse fabric exported in large quantities. The Krishna delta weavers for the most part produced finer grades of cloth, the traditional export grades sent to markets in the Malay Archipelago. The second factor may have been assured supply of food stuffs. Over the course of the seventeenth century, Dutch and English records refer to periodic famines in northern Coromandel, most of which seem to have affected the area around Masulipatnam. Our information is incomplete, but any differentiation in reliability of food supply would have encouraged weavers to settle in greater numbers where supplies were most consistent.

DOMESTIC AND EXPORT SECTORS

The Nagulawancha itinerary includes the interesting comment against the village of Gollapudi (number 44) that its weavers were producing only for local consumption. This is a clear reference to a distinction maintained at the time between the domestic and export markets. We know from numerous sources that Coromandel's export markets in Asia were highly particularistic and that Coromandel weavers and merchants knew precisely what was necessary. This was true of the patterned goods industry of northern Coromandel.

If the production of Gollapudi weavers was of no interest to the Dutch, its quality must have been coarser than that of even ordinary calicos. Such cloth must have been a staple for domestic consumption. We have no information on the quantity produced of this local cloth or of its price, but we do have information on the price of the ordinary calicos of eastern Godavari. It is possible to show that this calico was produced at a cost the northern Coromandel consumer could afford. Thus, the weaver of ordinary guinees sold his production to a local merchant for 16 fanams per piece.[26] This merchant's selling price is unrecorded, but we can assume that it did not greatly exceed this amount in petty local markets. As for demand, the labourer, who probably wore no more than a breech-clout while in the fields, might possess one longer garment, reaching from his waist to his knees, for wear on other occasions.[27] Translating such customs of dress into an annual consumption of cloth expressed in yards cannot be done on the basis of seventeenth century sources. But today the poorest labouring classes of contemporary India consume about eight yards of cloth per capita

[26] *K.A.* 1267, 21 April 1682, fol. 2053.
[27] 'Anonymous Relation,' in Moreland, *Relations*, p. 77.

342 / JOSEPH J. BRENNIG

per year.[28] At this level of consumption, a labourer in seventeenth century Coromandel had to spend 3.6 fanams annually to purchase sufficient cloth for his personal clothing; or, given a wage of about six fanams per month, about five per cent of his gross income.[29] While the percentage of clothing expenditures of his net income after taxation must have been higher, these figures suggest that export quality calicos were within reach of many potential consumers. An industry dependent on local markets had little need for standardised output. The buyer had only to examine the cloth and pay the producer a negotiated price depending on its particular size and quality. In an export trade, however, middleman costs made the rejection of unsatisfactory qualities a serious problem; moreover, the more complex the enterprise and the greater capital invested, the more predictability is sought. Given the highly particularistic markets of Southeast Asia, the long established trade in patterned cloth was undoubtedly standardised before the arrival of the Europeans in Coromandel. The more important question is whether standardisation existed in the trade in calicos, an industry which developed from a domestic trade and expanded into exports with the expansion of demand in Europe.

Standardisation of cloth by quality was based on the division of the warp (or more accurately the loom's reed) into equal linear measures. A given width of cloth was divided into so many threads, the measure in Coromandel being the *punjam* (Tamil and Telugu, 'group' or 'collection') of 120 threads.[30] Each variety of cloth contained, for a given quality, a set number of *punjams*. Thus, the Dutch factor Havart observed that the Dutch factory in Masulipatnam received guinees with 17 *punjams*.[31] The English in Madras at one time received longcloth (calico) with 16 *punjams*, but in 1675 sought to have the quality increased to 18 *punjams*.[32] Parcalles and salempores purchased by the Dutch normally contained 18 and 19 *punjams*.[33] By the late seventeenth century, and perhaps no later than mid-century, calico producers were manufacturing cloth according to established standards of quality. Although the spread of standardisation in the calico industry may have been one significant result of the growth of Dutch and English exports, the evidence does not suggest that the industry adopted European conceptions or techniques of standardisation. It is reasonable to conclude from the use of

[28] Government of India (Ministry of Commerce), *Report of the Planning Sub-group of Cotton Textiles*, New Delhi, Government of India, 1966, p. 26.

[29] For documentation of these figures see notes 51 to 55 below.

[30] D. Havart, *De Op-en Ondergang van Coromandel*, 3 vols., Amsterdam, 1698, III, p. 42. The definition of *punjam* may have changed over time, for in the nineteenth century it contained 120 threads in Tamil areas of Coromandel, but only 60 threads in Telugu areas. See Madras (Presidency), *Manual of the Administration of the Presidency of Madras*, 3 vols. (Madras: Government Press, 1885–93), III, 707.

[31] *De Op-en Ondergang*, III, 42.

[32] Records of Fort St. George, *Diary and Consultation Book, 1672–1678*, 18 September 1675, p. 73.

[33] *De Op-en Ondergang*, III, 42.

Textile producers and production in late seventeenth century Coromandel / 343

a local term, the *punjam*, that the calico weavers adopted conceptions of standardisation existing among weavers already involved in producing for an export market.

INDUSTRIAL CAPACITY AND THE EXPORT TRADE

According to the list of villages in Table 2, the East Godavari Delta contained a minimum of 7,500 looms. How much cloth could these looms produce if fully employed? The technology of the throw-shuttle loom, the type probably employed in the northern Coromandel textile industry, probably has not changed over the last few centuries.[34] Data on the output of such looms are available from modern studies. But it is also possible to calculate the output of Coromandel looms in the seventeenth century from contemporary sources.

In 1680 the head weavers of three villages of the northern portion of the East Godavari Delta (in the vicinity of Tuni) informed an inquiring Dutch merchant of the number of weaver households in their villages and the output to be expected from each village. I have summarised this information in Table 3.

Table 3

Textile Production in Three Villages
(per year)

Villages	Weaver Households	Total Production* (Yards)	Output/Household (Yards)
Tuni	5–600	1,090,000	1,816–2,180
Ponara	350	577,000	1,648
Oupare	150	226,000	1,506

Source: *K.A.* 1262, 3 April 1682, fol. 1910b–1911.
Notes: * The varieties listed include ordinary guinees, salempores parcalles and bethilles. The high figure for Tuni was probably due to the large number of loosely bethilles (40,000) in its proposed output.

The figures in the table permit us to estimate that an average weaver household in these villages could produce as much as 1,600 yards of cloth per year. Since a weaver could not work during the monsoon rains, the working year was something less than the calendar year. Using a modern estimate of the handloom weaver's working year (276 days), and taking into account the slightly more than one loom per weaver household, a household producing 1,600 yards per year produced 1,379 yards on a single loom.[35] According to

[34] For the best survey of technological innovation in this period see Irfan Habib, 'The Technology and Economy of Mughal India,' *Indian Economic and Social History Review*, XVI, (1980).

[35] For the figure for the weaver's working year, see Government of India, Planning Commission, Programme Evaluation Organisation, *Study of Handloom Development Programme*, Delhi, Government of India, 1969, pp. 41–43. This total of 1,379 yards per year or about five yards per day falls within the range of the feasible output for the throw-shuttle loom producing coarse varieties of cloth; Government of India, The Fact-Finding Committee (Handloom and Mills), *Report*, p. 294.

this calculation then, the annual productive capacity of the 7,500 looms of the East Godavari Delta had was 9,653,000.

In 1682 the Dutch factories of Palikollu and Draksharama together exported 3,800,000 yards; the English factory at Madapollem exported 2,100,000 yards,[16] or together, a total of 5,900,000 yards of cloth in 1682, 59 per cent of the capacity of the 7,000 looms of the East Godavari Delta. But in fact the actual capacity from which these factories drew their supplies was larger, for it would properly include the industry in the West Godavari Delta. Hence, we can conclude that the European Companies' trade employed considerably less than 50 per cent of the industrial capacity of the Godavari delta.

That a large part of the capacity of the Godavari Delta's industry was idle in the 1680s seems improbable. If large numbers of weavers were available to produce the goods for the English and the Dutch, how is one to explain the complaints of local merchants in 1682 that large European orders made delivery in the usual time increasingly difficult?[17] Demand was apparently straining northern Coromandel's industrial capacity. But if northern Coromandel's textile industry was working at near capacity in this period, who, apart from the Dutch and English, were in the market purchasing cloth? There were smaller exporters—the Asians, Portuguese, Armenians, and Europeans trading on their own account—but their share of the region's exports was relatively small at this time.[18] Another source of demand may have been the markets of the Deccan and Mughal North India. But most probably the bulk of the remaining capacity not used by the Europeans was employed to meet domestic demand within northern Coromandel.

From the foregoing it is possible to reach certain tentative generalisations about the textile industry of late seventeenth century northern Coromandel. In the first place the industry was unevenly distributed over the northern Coromandel region. Location seems at least in part to have reflected specialisation, with calico or plain cloth producers being concentrated in the rich eastern Godavari region and the finer cloth and patterned cloth producers located primarily in the west Godavari-Krishna delta region. The former produced the bulk of Coromandel's output in terms of yardage while the latter produced its higher valued cloth long established in the traditional overseas markets of the region in Asia.

Because of its size and concentration, the calico industry is of particular interest. It is probable that these ordinary, plain cloths were first produced for a domestic market. The development, an entirely new and expanding market for this class of cloth in Europe undoubtedly caused an expansion of existing industrial capacity, although no evidence for this exists in the available records. The one new element which probably reflects this

[16] Brennig, *The Textile Trade*, Appendix A, pp. 286–89.
[17] Records of Fort St. George, *The Masulipatnam Consultation Book of 1682–1683.*, 30 October 1682, p. 13.
[18] Brennig, *The Textile Trade*; this is the argument in Chapter I.

Textile producers and production in late seventeenth century Coromandel / 345

expansion is the introduction of the Banjara trade. The Banjara trade in Deccan cotton to northern Coromandel is a unique example of a regular long-distance overland trade in a bulk commodity supporting an industry in the pre-colonial period. The importance of the Banjara contribution to the overall economy of the coastal region did not go unrecognised. The rulers of Golconda freed them from the usual taxes levied on internal trade, just as they had for the Europeans.

Whatever the imperfections in the statistics available in the Dutch records. it is probably safe to say that the industry of the Godavari delta was capable of producing at least twice the cloth which the Dutch and English companies exported in 1682. Assuming little idle capacity, the output over and above that exported was consumed by smaller overseas markets, a market further in the interior (an overland trade), and, most importantly, a local domestic market. In contrast to other parts of the textile industry, therefore, our argument here is that the calico industry was an integral part of a local domestic economy and, despite the importance of the export sector, continued to be dependent on domestic demand.

II
The Weaver

The Weaver held a central position in the complex inter-relationships between groups involved in the textile export industry. Despite his importance, however, the Europeans, having little direct contact with weavers, took little notice of his situation. What information exists has to be gleaned from isolated and passing references. The picture which emerges must necessarily be partial or incomplete in important respects, but since as yet no attempt has been made to examine the weaver in a pre-colonial setting, this picture represents an advance over our present position.

The weaver's relationship with the merchant did not change significantly as far as can be determined. This was so despite efforts by the Europeans to increase the local merchant's bargaining position with the weavers. Since the influence of merchant capital on the processes of production is of considerable interest in a comparative perspective of pre-modern economies, the reasons for the success of the weavers of Coromandel in resisting the consequences of dependence on merchant capital needs to be explored.

Social Organisation

Like other occupation groups of Coromandel, the weavers were organised into a number of castes. The caste was the first level of community organisation. The weaver castes present in northern Coromandel in the seventeenth century were similar to those present in the region in recent times. This a Dutch document records that in the village of Golepallem there were 'Saliwaars,' 'Kykelwaars' and 'Deerewaars'.[39] In modern transcription these

[39] *K.A.* 1401, (1692), fols. 1134–1142.

346/JOSEPH J. BRENNIG

were the Salis, Kaikolans and Devangas (also known as Deras).[40] Among the weavers in both Golepallem and Gondawaron, its neighbor, there were none who did not belong to one or the other of these major weaver castes. There is no evidence of low or outcaste weavers.

Weavers may have also been organised by type of cloth in which a particular group of weavers specialised. For example, the Dutch describe the Kaikolan weavers of northern Coromandel as weavers of ordinary calicos.[41] In Madras, the English report weavers who distinguished themselves as 'moree weavers' and 'kaingulong weavers'. Each of these groups maintained their own account books, implying a degree of corporate structure.[42] But apart from Thurston's observation that the Sali caste weavers were sub-divided into Padma Salis (Lotus Salis) and Pattu Salis (Silk Salis), the latter group specialising in the weaving of silk and fine cotton cloth,[43] ethnographers have given little support to a supposition that weavers defined their social organisation according to the type or quality of cloth they produced. But such specialisation may have been more common in the seventeenth century, and among groups traditionally associated with exports, than in recent years. Certainly in northern Coromandel there seems to have been a broad distinction between weavers of fine and weavers of coarse cloth, a distinction reflected in the specialised trade of certain textile merchants.

European records tell us in various places that weavers were highly mobile.[44] Demand for labour in the industry was therefore frequently met through migration. The labour force might also have expanded through entrance of new recruits, for example, from the ranks of agricultural labour. Some may have been previously unemployed weavers. It is also possible that the weaving labour force was expanded by the entrance of members of non-weaving castes. Such entrance of low caste labour into the weaving caste is evident in surveys conducted in the nineteenth century when Malas and Madigas, important untouchable castes of the Andhra region, are prominent as participants in the textile industry. No evidence tells us when these castes entered the textile labour force. For a low caste non-weaver to enter into the weaving labour force he would have to learn the technique of weaving. Assuming that weaving techniques were not common knowledge, who would teach the low caste labour seeking to become a weaver?[45] It is possible that as demand for export quality textiles increased, caste weavers ceased to produce coarser domestic fabrics to produce for export, opening

[40] Thurston, *Castes and Tribes of Southern India*, 6 vols (Madras, 1909), vol. VI, III, pp. 31ff; and vol. II, pp. 144ff.

[41] K.A. 1401, (16992), fol. 1203.

[42] W. Foster ed., *The English Factories in India, 1618–1669*, (hereafter *EFI*) 13 vols., Oxford, 1906–27, vol. 7, 1651–54, 4 April 1654, p. 258.

[43] *Castes and Tribes*, VI, p. 187.

[44] E.g., *EFI*, 1622–23, 26 July 1622, p. 105.

[45] According to the *Report of the Fact-Finding Committee* (Handloom and Mills), p. 64, the entrance of low status non-weaving castes into the handloom industry was a nineteenth century phenomenon.

Textile producers and production in late seventeenth century Coromandel/347

opportunities at the bottom of the weaving hierarchy for non-weaver caste labour.

Within each weaver village there were probably several weaver castes. For each there were probably one or more weavers of status and wealth who held a position as caste headman, or head weaver.[46] Seventeenth century records point to the existance of such individuals, and we can assume they fulfilled similar functions to those described in greater detail in the nineteenth century. The most interesting weaving community leader in nineteenth century Coromandel was known as the *careedar*.[47]

In a letter from the Commercial Resident of the East India Company stationed in Ingeram in the Godavari delta in the early nineteenth century, the *careedar* is described as possessing the right to collect certain fees on each piece of cloth produced under his supervision. His right to this fee was granted by the weavers for what amounted to a form of insurance:

> In a village of Weavers there are among them weavers of more responsibility than others to whom the lower sort look up for subsistence, when they are out of Employ. These people are called Careedars; they receive the full price from the contractors or Company, they weave some cloths in their own houses, they also employ outdoor weavers from whom they deduct the same fee.

The *careedar* also provided services for the local merchant or the Company:

> They are the security between the labourer and the public contractors or company and act as overseers of the work in the village . . .[48]

If a weaver was wealthy, he contracted for his product directly with the merchant rather than through the *careedar*. Caste and possibly other forms of community organisation based on the weavers' output or on subdivisions within an industrial village gave the weaving community the appearance of a complex of social structures. While it would be simple to view these headmen as some sort of oppressors, they equally could have acted to buffer more vulnerable members of the community against consequences of participation in the marketplace.

INCOME

Most weavers of northern Coromandel were relatively poor, a condition they shared with handicraft weavers in pre-industrial Europe. But the rural

[46] *K.A.* 1294, 8 January 1684, fol. 1519b. Vijaya Ramaswamy has surveyed the organisation of weaving communities in her 'The Genesis and Historical Role of the Master Weavers in South Indian Textile Production,' *Journal of the Economic and Social History of the Orient*, XXVIII, pp. 294ff. But whereas she argues that 'master weavers' were merchants outside of the weaving community, the evidence here suggests that they were members of the weaving community itself.

[47] The term *careedar* may be a Persianised form of the Telugu '*Karji*', headman. For *Karji* see H.H. Wilson, *Glossary of Revenue and Judicial Terms*, London, 1855, p. 262.

[48] *Godavari District Records*, 832, October 1802, p. 423.

348 / JOSEPH J. BRENNIG

weavers of Coromandel occupied a different social position than the rural weavers of eighteenth century England. For the latter, weaving was an 'unskilled, casual occupation which provided a domestic by-trade for thousands of women and children,'[49] but for the Coromandel weaver it was a full-time occupation restricted to the male members of the household. The Coromandel weaver was closer to Europe's urban weaver, who also had little or no opportunity to earn a supplementary income during the weaving season. In Coromandel women did work, but they were occupied in various ancillary activities associated with weaving such as preparing the yarn for the warp; they did not sit before the loom and could not release the weaver for alternative labour.[50] A shift from weaving to agricultural work would thus not be a part of the rhythm of the normal work year, but occurred rather as a large scale and singular phenomenon when there was a serious decline in demand.

Wages for various types of labour can be identified only generally. Methwold reported that the master workman—a category which included weavers—considered three pence per day good wages.[51] This was equivalent to 1/2 a *fanam* per day or about one *pagoda* per month.[52] His assistant received about 1/3 *pagoda* per month. The lowest wage reported in the first half of the century was paid to workers in northern Coromandel's diamond mines: 1/4 a *pagoda* per month.[53]

More information exists for the later seventeenth century. Particularly useful are lists of servants employed by the Dutch in their factories and their wages. One other interesting reference to wages at the time is also worth noting. A servant in a mosque in Hyderabad during the later 'seventeenth century received 12 *pagodas* per year.[54] The Dutch paid a servant of similar duties precisely the same wages. This confirms that the Dutch paid according to prevailing scales. A porter in the Draksharama factory received 1/2 *pagoda* per month; a water carrier, 3/4 *pagoda*. Wages were similar in Palikollu and Masulipatnam but lower in Nagulawancha and Bimilipatnam.[55]

A single piece of ordinary guinee paid the weaver who produced it 3 1/2 *fanams* for his labour alone.[56] Since the output of a loom working at full capacity was 1,379 yards,[57] the equivalent of 36 pieces of guinees at 35 yards

[49] Duncan Bythell, *The Handloom Weavers: A Study in the English Cotton Industry During the Industrial Revolution*, Cambridge, 1969, p. 270.

[50] E.B. Havell, *Reports Submitted by E.B. Havell during the years 1855–1888 on the Arts and Industries of Certain Districts of Madras Presidency*, n.p., (1888?), p. 28; and Government of India, The Fact Finding Committee (Handloom and Mills), *Report*, p. 63.

[51] Moreland, *Relations*, p. 27.

[52] *Ibid.*, Appendix, p. 94.

[53] Tavernier, *Travels*, II, 46.

[54] G. Yazdani, 'Inscriptions of the Qutb Shahi Kings in Hyderabad City and Suburbs,' *Epigraphica Indo-Moslemica*, edited by G. Yazdani (Calcutta, 1921), p. 54.

[55] For the wage rates in all of the Dutch factories, see *K.A.* 1228, 7 October 1678, fols. 479ff.

[56] *K.A.* 1267, 18 April 1682, fol. 2066.

[57] See note 35 above.

Textile producers and production in late seventeenth century Coromandel / 349

each, the weaver earned an annual income of 126 *fanams* or about 10.5 *pagodas* (12 *fanams* = *pagoda*). When these wages are compared to wages paid to other workers in this period, we find that an ordinary weaver with a single loom earned as much as a porter employed in the Dutch factory at Draksharama, 3/4 *pagoda* per month. It thus appears that the weaver's earnings placed him among the general labouring population; they were not paid the wage of a skilled labourer. It is of incidental interest that the lowest status work, the sweeper, received a lower wage in the Dutch factories than other work. Although in terms of skill or difficulty it was little different from the water carrier or porter, its unclean character relegated it to a lower category of pay. Moreland's estimation that wages were stable through the mid-seventeenth century, appears to have held true to the end of the 1680s, e.g., a *pagoda* per month for a weaver with a single loom.[58] A weaver could increase his income by reducing the amount of yarn used per unit of cloth and thereby reducing his input cost and increasing his rate of production, but much of the increased profit would have gone to the middleman merchant who purchased his product. In the 1680s when export demand peaked, European factors repeatedly complained about cloth being below standard. This reflected increased seller leverage in the market and possibly resulted in a rise in weaver income.

RICH WEAVERS, POOR WEAVERS

The material condition of the weaver at its most basic level was reflected in his ability to meet costs of subsistence, for the sake of argument assumed here to be the cost of the staple of northern Coromandel, rice. For much of the century, discounting famine periods, rice in the Godavari delta cost about 400 lbs. per pagoda. Spent entirely on rice, a weaver's annual income of 12 pagodas could theoretically purchase 4,200 lbs. of rice, an amount well above the subsistence level of 2,500 lbs. per year for a household of six.[59]

But frequently the weaver was unable to buy rice at market rates. A local tax on grain (*guddem*), applied to a portion of the grain purchased by non-agrarian workers, increased the price by as much as 100 per cent.[60] If forced to buy all of his grain at this taxed rate, a weaver would not be able to purchase sufficient grain for household subsistence. Probably he could avoid much of the burden of this tax by buying untaxed grain. Nevertheless, taxes effectively prevented the weaver with a single loom from existing much, if at all, above the subsistence level.

With two looms, however, a weaver graduated out of subsistence. His potential income of 20 *pagodas* per year enabled him to meet his subsistence needs and retain a substantial surplus. Moreover, if a weaver held a position of *careedar*, earning a commission on the production of subordinate weavers,

[58] W.H. Moreland, *From Akbar to Aurangzeb*, London 1923, p. 178.
[59] For the local prices of rice and paddy, see Brennig, *Textile Export Trade*, pp. 204–07.
[60] *Ibid.*, p. 199.

his income would be further increased. A prosperous weaver might hoard his surplus in the form of jewellery. Early in the century observers noted that one of the special values of gold as a commodity was its convenience in hoarding for weavers who feared expropriation by local officials.[61] The degree to which this occurred cannot be measured, but the goldsmiths of the weaving village of Gollapallem may have been kept busy by a local demand for jewellery manufacture.[62] But not all the weaver's wealth over and above his subsistence needs was unproductively hoarded. The data of a census taken by the Dutch company in 1692 in the village of Gollapallem, of those supplying the Draksharama factory with cloth, indicates that many weavers had cattle, not the oxen used in field work but milk cattle.[63] The largest herd belonging to a weaver consisted of eight cows and sixteen calves, two buffaloes and two buffalo calves. Investment in cattle not only provided added income from the sale of milk and milk products and an important nutritional supplement for household members, but also provided for a natural growth of investment as the herd expanded.

As this census information should indicate, the weaving community of northern Coromandel was differentiated into rich and poor weavers. Weaver households with two looms had a clear advantage. According to the Gollapallem census, this amounted to 10 per cent of the village households. But this census also shows that even households with only one loom might possess livestock. Why this was so is unclear, but in any case the evidence shows that by the late seventeenth century weavers had begun to accumulate assets. This may represent a change which had accelerated over the course of the century. Those of superior means were probably better able to take advantage of increased opportunities created by the expansion of European trade. Moreover, the *guddem* tax, being a tax on subsistence, was highly regressive in character. Income above subsistence had a lower tax rate. Insofar as the tax system placed a special burden on the lesser weavers, they would be more likely to seek to become the clients of superior weavers. Whether the *careedar* form of patron-client relationship within the weaver community antedates the seventeenth century cannot be determined, but it seems likely that the poorer weaver's vulnerability and the growing strength of the wealthier weavers encouraged the spread of this form of organisation.

INDUSTRIAL ORGANISATION: COTTAGE INDUSTRY VS. THE PUTTING OUT SYSTEM

The relationship between merchant capital and manufacture in the pre-modern industrial production may be distinguished ideally and analytically into two types: the cottage industry and the putting out system. In a cottage industry the producer was characteristically independent of the merchant

[61] *EFI, 1624–29*, 18 July 1627, p. 181.
[62] Brennig, *Textile Export Trade*, p. 154.
[63] *K.A.* 1401, 1692, fols. 1134ff. The most prosperous weavers of Gollapallem, to judge from livestock holdings, were from five single loom households. To judge from their names they were probably related, perhaps brothers, which may explain their superior economic position.

Textile producers and production in late seventeenth century Coromandel/351

and merchant capital. The producer purchased his own raw materials from the market, manufactured a commodity within the confines of his own house, deciding unilaterally when, how much and what kind of goods to make, and then sold his finished products on the market himself. In the putting out system, however, the producer lacked this independence. A merchant generally owned the raw materials and 'put them out' to be worked into a finished or semi-finished product in a worker's home. When the work was finished, the merchant would take possession of it, paying the worker a wage for the work completed, and either sell it if finished, or put it out for further steps in the finishing process. The producer in the putting out system was simply selling his labour and was not in a position to exercise much leverage in the market place. Also the producer in this situation surrendered control over important decisions connected with the design, size and time of output to the merchant. With the putting out system, the merchant gained control over production through his capacity to control capital.

Opinions might vary on the position of the merchant and producer in the seventeenth century. Leaning heavily toward the view that the putting out system was well established is Irfan Habib, who has argued that 'the putting out system was widely in use; and that cash advances and the giving out of raw materials were established practices.'[64] Habib's perspective is broad in this article, and certainly he would be among the first to recognise the need to investigate the level of development and the institutionalisation of the putting out system in particular industries and regions. Raychaudhuri's estimation of the organisation of the Coromandel textile industry is more cautious, stating that a 'full-fledged putting-out system . . . had not emerged.'[65]

The evidence is in fact ambiguous. The weaver had considerable independence. It was the weaver and not the merchant who purchased yarn from the local market. A Dutch description of the yarn trade (in a description of the cotton market of Teeparu) states that the yarn was spun by 'Pariahs, spinsters and poor women'.[66] The spinners took their product to local markets for sale

to weavers, and not to merchants, for the weaving of cloth. Thus merchants themselves are not involved with either yarn or cotton, but only contract with the weavers for cloth according to musters, for which cash must frequently be furnished in advance.[67]

In some cases the merchant may have supplied the yarn.[68] But it is the sense of the passage quoted above that the absence of merchants in the yarn trade was usually the case.

---

[64] 'Potentialities of Capitalistic Development in the Economy of Mughal India,' *Journal of Economic History*, XXIX, March 1969, p. 68.

[65] T. Raychaudhuri, *Jan Company in Coromandel, 1605–1690*, (The Hague, 1962), p. 11.

[66] K.A. 1262, 26 April 1682, fol. 1950.

[67] K.A. 4464 R/Sd, Uittreksels uit brieven . . ,' fol. 3

[68] K.A. 1294, 26 April 1684, fol. 1523.

Evidence for some features of the putting out system does exist. Finishing of cloth following the weaving process was the responsibility of the merchant, not of the weaver. Thus the Dutch, very early in their experience in Masulipatnam, had a group of painters under their direct control decorating the cloth brought from local weavers. The responsibility of the merchant, whether local or exporter, to 'put out' finished cloth to painters continued until the end of the seventeenth century. The merchant was also responsible for the proper washing and dyeing of his cloth. Thus in addition to being the predominant form of industrial organisation in the process of weaving, putting out was the norm in all the steps used in the production of finished cloth.

But it is equally necessary to stress that the merchant did not have complete control over the weaving process. The Dutch reported that merchants kept weavers on a short leash, never giving them enough of an advance to encourage them to abscond.[69] Thus small amounts were distributed on a daily basis, an amount the Dutch interpreted as a 'daily wage' (*dagloon*). Merchants were therefore vulnerable. Moreover, the *careedar* or head weaver stood between the merchant and weaver. The mobility of the weaver and the protection or cover he gained from the organisation of his community made it difficult for the merchant to translate his control over capital into a control over production.

Weavers were known to respond vigorously when they perceived their interests to be threatened. In the 1660s a dispute between the weavers and local merchants or brokers developed. The weavers then sought to circumvent their brokers by opening direct negotiations with the Dutch for sale of their cloth. However, the Dutch declined to take advantage of this opportunity, recognising an advantage in dealing through brokers, for they supplied an important share of the capital needed to finance trade. In the 1680s there was a second, more revealing incident, this time involving the joint stock company the Dutch had established among the Draksharama brokers. The weavers supplying cloth to the Draksharama factory protested when they perceived this new organisation would reduce their ability to force the brokers to compete among themselves (indeed, the primary reason why the Dutch encouraged the company's formation). The weavers not only complained, they raised 1,000 *pagodas* as a gift for the local governor of the region and demanded that the new merchant organisation be ended.[70]

The picture which emerges suggests that rather than being subjected to an exploiting merchant class, the weavers of northern Coromandel possessed the capacity to resist merchant demands. The weaving community was highly differentiated, with some members capable of accumulating capital, and investing it in new production capacity. But in terms of the preconditions

[69] *K.A.* 1267, 21 April 1682, fol. 1059b.
[70] Raychaudhuri, *Jan Company*, pp. 147, 164. For a general discussion of these merchant organisations of Coromandel, see J.J. Brennig, 'Joint Stock Companies of Coromandel,' in B.B. Kling and M.N. Pearson, eds., *The Age of Partnership*, Honolulu, 1979.

Textile producers and production in late seventeenth century Coromandel/353

for the emergence of even a primitive industrial capitalism, the risks imposed on the merchant and his vulnerability to demands by the weaving community, suggests that even in this period of flourishing trade, the merchant capitalist was yet to gain control over production. Thus it is the weakness of the intermediary merchant community engaged in putting out the materials for the production of cloth rather than the particularly oppressed character of the producer which appears to have been blocking any reorganisation of the textile industry.

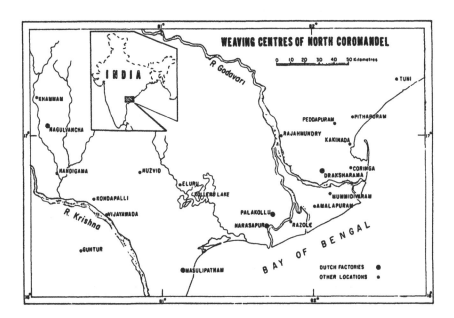

APPENDIX

Weaver Settlement in the Eastern Krishna Delta
Villages along a Route from Palikollu to Nagulawancha

Villages	Weaver Households	Remarks
	Palikollu Hinterland	
1 Pollapale	(Poelipilly)	0 ½ hour from Palikollu
2 ?	(Begapasseram ?)	0
3 ?	(Toleroe)	10 under Palikollu merchants
4 Dagguluru	(Dageloore)	0 no weavers and few farmers
5. Ballipadu	(Ballipadoe)	0 ,,
6 ?	(Sikkala)	0 ,,
7 Viravasavaram	(Wierwasseron)	40 site of abandoned Eng fac
8 Srungarvuksham	(Singawissam ?)	10 also 20 farmer households
9 Goraganamudi	(Goragoela moedi)	0 only farmers
10 ?	(Pennara)	0 ,,
11 Vissakoderu	(Wissakoeleroe)	0 ,,
12 Gunupudi	(Goenoepoedy)	60 under Palikollu merchants
13 Rayalam	(Begellam ?)	0 only farmers
14. Pedamiram	(Pennameram)	0 ,,
15 Bondada	(Bondara)	0 ,,
16. Doddanapudi	(Dodda Pondy)	15 under Palikollu merchants
17. Jakkaram	(D'zajkkawarron)	0 only farmers
18. Pedapulleru	(Pinnapoeleroe)	0 ,,
19. Sisali	(Tsintsaly)	20 under Palikollu merchants
20. Kalla	(Caala)	10 ,,
21. Kallakuru	(Caalakoeroe)	16 ,,
22 Elurupadu	(Eloer Padoe)	20 ,,
23. Kalidindi	(Calledıendı)	0 a large village
	Masulipatnam Hinterland	
24 ?	(Pararamondoery Peeta)	few farmers, under Masulipatnam, 50 revenue of 400 *pag*
25. Vemavarapadu	(Weemawarron)	0 some farmers and others
26 Bomminapadu	(Bammenimpadoe)	10
27 Korragunatapalem	(Coorangoentapalum)	50 under Masulipatnam merchants
28 Vadali	(Raddsly ?)	5
29 ?	(Baampalapalium)	5
30 Peyyeru	(Pereroe)	30
31. ?	(Saniwanpalium)	0 farmers sowing millets and paddy
32 Gudivada	(Goedewaera)	0 farmers only
33 Bethavolu	(Beetaoloe)	0 ,,
34 Bhushanagulla	(Boessaragoordla)	0 ,,
35. Ventrapragada	(Teentra Peggela)	20
36 Kalvapamula	(Khalapasol)	0 farmers only
37 Katur I	(Catoe oeroe)	5
38. Kulidalampadu	(Caendeloe)	0 farmers only
39. Kulavennu	(Coolaweennoe)	0 ,,
40 Kankipadu	(Kaanpipare)	0 a large village, a number of milk sellers, on the straight road from Masulipatnam to Nagulawancha
41 Poranki and Patamata	(Poaraenki and Patamatsa)	0
42. Beswada	(Bedzwara)	50 200 brahmins; 200 farmer and 50 Kometi households
43 Bhavampuram	(Bawanipolram)	0
44. Gollapudi	(Goollapondy)	— weavers producing only for local consumption
45. Ibrahimpatam	(Ibrahimpatnam)	0 a large village
46. Jupudi	(Sjoepoedy)	
47. (Trilochanapuram ?)	(Kuleesjapoeram)	
48. ?	(Doorna konda mettoe)	
49. Pantalla	(Pautala)	
50. Kanchikacherla	(Kantsiserla)	
51. Keesara	(Kiessera)	— a large village
52. Nandigama	(Nandigam)	0 weavers producing for local consumption
53. Senagapadu	(Sellagapadoe)	— ,,
54. Ponnavaram ?	(Ponnawaram)	— ,,
55. Penuganchiprolu	(Pennegentipoel)	50 150 brahmins, 100 Kometis, 4 moetjes and 300 farmer households.
56 Vatsarayi and Mushtikuntla	(Watswagoe and Molstigoenta)	
57. Nagulawancha	(Negelwance)	150

Source. *K.A.* 1267, 27 April, 1682, fol 1925 ff
Notes: Doddanapudi should have been placed between Kallakuru and Elurupadu, two villages in Bhimavaram Talum which fall on either side of it.

9

Weavers, Merchants and Company: The Handloom Industry in Southeastern India, 1750–1790

S. Arasaratnam

In the second half of the eighteenth century, major forces of change were unleashed on certain geographic regions of the Indian subcontinent as a result of the European contest for Indian trade and the assertion of political power that followed that contest. The maritime regions of southern India were among the earliest to feel the impact of these forces. The political revolutions of the years 1740 to 1780 had caused considerable economic and social disloca- tion in the entire Carnatic region and had left the English East India Company in a position of unquestioned political dominance, both in relation to its major European competitors, the French and the Dutch, and to the hinterland powers, the Nawab of the Carnatic and the Rajah of Tanjore. As the textile trade of southern India was the original *raison d'etre* of English entry into the region and the expansion of their interests there, it was this section of the economy and those elements of society connected with this industry that felt the full initial impact of English political power. The production process of the handloom industry, its marketing and export received the first concerted attention of English policy. Consequently, the first major economic and social changes, in response to the growth of English political power, were seen in these sectors and producing districts. As deliberate colonial policy the English sought to use their power to alter the conditions of production of handloom textiles and to transform existing relationships between producers and merchant middlemen. By the end of the century, the economic position of the weaver and of the traditional textile merchant had been completely transformed.

I have already discussed elsewhere the trend and direction of these changes in relation to merchant middlemen and to overall English aims.[1] I argued

*Most of the research for this article was undertaken when I was Smuts Visiting Fellow in Commonwealth Studies at the University of Cambridge in 1977. I am grateful to the University and to the Managers of the Smuts Memorial Fund for the facilities afforded to me during that period.

[1]S. Arasaratnam, "Trade and Political Dominion in South India, 1750-1790: Changing British-Indian Relationships," *Modern Asian Studies* 13, 1 (1971) pp. 19-46; S. Arasaratnam, "Indian Commercial Groups and European Traders 1600-1800: Changing Relationships in Southeastern India," *South Asia* (N.S.), Vol. I, No. 2 (1978), pp. 42-53.

258   S. ARASARATNAM

there that the traditional Indian merchant, who had been the link between the
producing weaver and the export market, had been gradually eliminated and
in his place had been substituted a group of Indian paid servants of the
Company and, in some cases, English entrepreneurs both servants of the
Company and English settler merchants. In this paper I propose to look at the
weaving village before and after these changes and to observe more closely the
implication of these changes to the position and status of the weaver. It will
be clear to students familiar with the primary sources of this period that I
have set myself a virtually impossible task. One would like to ask oneself a
number of questions on the status of the weaver before the intrusion of the
English and likewise to assess the exact conditions under which he was now
working for the Company. Many of these questions are answered by the
sources with a resounding silence. However, once English power entered the
weaving village, and once their officers had made direct contact with the
primary weaver, one comes across tantalizing, suggestive snippets of evidence
on the world of the weaving village. It is on the basis of this evidence, and in
the belief that half a loaf is better than none, that the following facts and
interpretations are offered to the student of India's economy and society in
the eighteenth century.

   The system that existed as at the middle of the eighteenth century, say
around 1750, under which European companies and Indian overseas exporters
procured textiles for their export markets, had evolved and had been standardized by over a century of operation. There is a good deal of evidence and an
abundant body of literature on the system as it operated on the port end, that
is, on the dealings between companies and their merchant suppliers.[2] Among
historians of these commercial relations, K.N. Chaudhuri has offered the most
detailed and incisive analysis of the marketing of textiles on a macro all-India
level, with random examples from individual regions. But he does not address
himself to the situation in the village and the economic relations operating

[2]The records of the three major Companies English, Dutch and French - have copious
references to the methods of textile supply. Of the literature on the subject, the more significant contributions are: T. Raychaudhuri, *Jan Company in Coromandel* (The Hague: Martinus Nijhoff 1962), pp. 144-148; T. Raychaudhuri, "European Commercial Activity and the
Organization of India's Commerce and Industrial Production 1500-1750" in B.N. Ganguli,
Readings in Indian Economic History (Bombay: Asia Publishing House, 1964), pp. 64-77;
S. Arasaratnam, "Aspects of the Role and Activities of South Indian Merchants" in *Proceed-
ings of the First International Conference of Tamil Studies* (Kuala Lumpur. International
Association of Tamil Research 1966), pp 582-96; A. Das Gupta, "The Merchants of Surat
c. 1700-1750" in E. Leach and S. Mukherjee, *Elites in South Asia* (Cambridge: Cambridge
Univ. Press, 1970), pp. 201-22; K.N. Chaudhuri, "The Structure of Indian Textile Industry
in the Seventeenth and Eighteenth Centuries," *The Indian Economic and Social History
Review*, XI, 203 (1974), pp. 127-82; S. Chaudhuri, *Trade and Commercial Organization in
Bengal 1650-1720* (Calcutta: K.L. Mukhopadhyaya, 1975), pp. 62-85; Joseph J. Brenning, "The
Chief Merchants and European Enclaves of Seventeenth Century Coromandel," *Modern Asian
Studies* XI, 3 (1977), pp. 321-40.

there.[3] By reading back from the evidence of the 1770s it is possible to provide some idea of the nature of the relationships between weavers, brokers and merchants as they existed before the extension of English power into these villages.

Some of our historians have attempted to characterize the relationship between merchants and weavers as a "putting out system."[4] There is here an obvious attempt to use the European concept of financing pre-capitalist industrial development to describe the Indian situation. Like some other attempts to use concepts in European experience to explain Asian phenomena, it obscures as much as it reveals. Admittedly there are many elements common to the putting out system of late medieval, early modern Europe and the financing by merchants of the weaving industry in India. Like the European system, it was in India a means by which exporters desirous of goods of quality, specification and regularity, could ensure their supply by providing the finances where they were lacking and where otherwise there was no likelihood of their procuring such goods. It enabled entrepreneurs to be involved in local manufactures and producers to have access to capital to be able to produe in scale. In India, as in Europe, the financier provided the weaver with an advance in money and sometimes raw materials. But while in Europe the goods produced belonged to the financier and the payment made to the producer consisted solely of the wages for his labour, in India the weaver appears to have retained his independence and his control over his produce, though his freedom to fix the price of his goods was not unrestricted. Often he only secured a money advance, not raw materials, had control over his tools and thus was master of the produced goods till they changed hands. There seems to have been a general agreement, though, that his creditor had first call on his goods as long as the money was unpaid.

Though there was this freedom to dispose of the final produce, the restricted nature of the access to the market and the near monopoly conditions in purchase of goods existing in many remote weaving villages made this freedom rather an empty one. Where there was a competitive market, however, such as in the coastal weaving villages, where middlemen suppliers to many

[3]K.N. Chaudhuri, "The Structure of Indian Textile Industry in the Seventeenth and Eighteenth Centuries," *IESHR* XI, 2-3 (1974), pp. 127-182.

[4]See, for example, T. Raychaudhuri, "Some Patterns of Economic Organization and Activity in Seventeenth Century India" in *Second International Conference of Economic History 1962* (The Hague: Mouton 1965), pp. 753-65, Irfan Habib, "Potentialities of Capitalist Development in the Economy of Mughal India," *The Journal of Economic History* XXIX, 1 (1969), pp. 66-68; Richard G. Fox, "Pariah Capitalism and Traditional Indian Merchants" in Milton Singer *ed*, *Entrepreneurship and Modernization of Occupational Cultures in South Asia* (Duke University 1973), pp. 24-27. K.N. Chaudhuri however refers to the distinction between the two methods and touches on it briefly. Chaudhuri, "The Structure of the Indian textile industry," *IESHR*, XI, 2-3 pp. 151, 156.

Companies sought their goods, this freedom over the final product was a real one. When the European demand for textiles exports expanded from the 1650s, and with the entry of the French into the market from the 1670s, the competition led to a significant improvement in the bargaining position of the weaver. The Companies were so alarmed at this cut-throat competition among their suppliers, and the resultant increase in prices, that they initiated a process of bringing their merchants into associations of a joint-stock character and of demarcating among them categories of goods and even areas of manufacture.[5] As in the case of the European "putter out" the Indian merchant financier also had no control over labour and over quality of the product, but, given the unsophisticated nature of much of the orders, this was no problem. It did later become a problem to the Companies, whose demands were getting more specialized and exact, both in quality and measurement, that the existing methods proved unsuitable. The Companies were looking for means, even before the expansion of political power into the interior, of establishing control over the production process in various ways. In general, therefore, the artisan did not lose his independence to the extent that the European artisan did. On the contrary, he treasured his independence and refused to end up as a wage labourer in the employ of the merchant financier.

This broad and general statement may appear too simplistic when we look closely at the complex relationships on the basis of the available evidence. There were four main weaving castes actively engaged in the profession of weaving in villages along the east Carnatic districts: *kaikolar*, *devanga*, *sale* and *seniyar*. Of these the first three were the most numerous and most prominent in the manufacture of textiles for export. The *kaikolar*, a Tamil-speaking caste, were the largest in number and were settled mainly in the middle districts of the Arcots, Salem, Coimbatore and Chingleput, with small concentrations in the southern districts of Tanjore, Trichinopoly, Madura and Tinnevely. They were also called *sengundar* (meaning "red dagger"), from a fable tracing their legendary origin from the deity Siva. The caste was subdivided into a number of clans and had a form of territorial government and judicial control. This control was centred on Kanchipuram where resided the Mahanattan (the territorial chief) whose authority *kaikolar*, at least in the Arcot, Salem and Chingleput districts, was recognized and acknowledged. This caste used the titular names of *Mudali* and *Nayanar*.[6] In the 1871 census, there were 273,823 *kaikolar* in the Madras Presidency, the second most

[5]J.J. Brennig, "Joint-Stock Companies of Coromandel" in B.B. Kling and M.N. Pearson, *The Age of Partnership. Europeans in Asia before Dominion* (Honolulu: The University Press of Hawaii, 1979), pp. 71-97.
[6]E. Thurston, *Castes and Tribes of South India* (Madras: Govt. Press 1909), Vol. III sv. *Kaikolar; Census of India*, 1901, Vol. XV, Madras, Pt. I, Glossary of castes in Madras, pp. 136-85.

numerous weaving caste was the *sale* with a total of 210, 928 persons.[7] The *sale* were the main Telugu weaving caste with a long tradition of activity in the weaving industry. They were mainly settled in the Telugu areas of the Carnatic, the districts of Vizagapatnam, Godavari and Kistna having the main concentrations. They were also found in smaller numbers in the southern Tamil districts of Tinnevely and Madura. In some areas they took the name of *saliyar* and *seniyar*. Under the former name, they had settled in the Malabar districts and there is every reason to believe that members of this caste migrated to coastal Ceylon (Sri Lanka) and were assimilated into Sinhalese society with the name *salagama*. The *devanga* are also a mainly Telugu caste, distributed over a wide area but with major concentrations in Vizagapatnam, Godavari, Salem, Coimbatore and Madura. They used the title *chetty* and by the end of the nineteenth century are known to have moved substantially out of weaving operations to other employment such as agriculture, carpentry and trade in cloth.[8]

The villages where weaving castes were heavily concentrated and lived as, in many ways, the dominant caste, were those where arose centres of manufacture for the export trade. It was the geography of these clusters of weaving villages that determined the ports of exit of the Coromandel trade. To the north the port of Vizagapatnam and a number of smaller ports such as Srikakulam, Jagannathpuram, Anakkanpalli and Bimlipatnam drew from the weaving centres to the interior. Just south of this group, in the large Godavari and Kistna districts, was located what may be described as one of the most productive and export-oriented cluster of weaving villages. The most favoured centres of production here were Tuni, Peddapuram and Rajamundry and the weavers of this entire area were mostly *devanga* and *sale*. The ports of outlet were numerous, the more significant among which were Kakinada, Yanam, Narsapore, Madapollam, Petapuli, Draksharama, Palikollu and the most ancient port of Masulipatnam. The English in the eighteenth century had factories in Vizagapatnam, Madapollam, Ganjam, Injiram and Masulipatnam. The Dutch, at the height of their power the largest exporters from the area, had a number of factories and purchasing agents: Bimlipatnam, Jagannathpuram, Srikakulam, Anakkanpalli, Kakinada, Narsapore, Petapuli and Draksharama. The French had a factory at Yanam. Southwards from Masulipatnam were the weaving districts of mid-Carnatic, another large area of production and export, most intensively competitive and again littered with ports of outlet for the goods. These markets had provided goods for centuries for the export trade of Indians and now, from the beginnings of the seventeenth

[7]*Report of the Census of the Madras Presidency* 1871 (Madras: Government Press, 1874), pp. 154-6.

[8]*Census of India 1901*, Vol. XV. Madras Pt. II (Madras: Government Press, 1902), pp. 395-60,

century, they were being increasingly relied upon by Europeans both for their home demands as well as for the inter-Asian trade. The area consisted of clusters of *kaikolar* and *devanga* weaving villages in the districts of Chingleput, North and South Arcot and Salem. The two major ports served by this region were Madras, the centre of English trade, and Pulicat, the seat of Dutch trade. South of Madras were the English port of Cuddalore (Fort St. David), the Dutch port of Sadraspatnam, the French at Pondicherry and the Danes at Tranquebar. The Indian port of Porto Novo was frequented by all-Indians and Europeans, and there were ports in the kingdom of Tanjore that drew their goods from South Arcot, Salem and Coimbatore and from some Tanjore weaving villages. In the far south, the significant concentrations of weaving villages were in Tinnevely and Madura whose goods were exported through the southern ports along the Madura Bay. This area largely fed the inter-Asian trade. The only Europeans who tapped it were the Dutch who made use of their exclusive presence in the inner Madura Bay.

In the weaving districts adjacent to the ports of export, it may be assumed that the rate of production increased substantially from mid seventeenth century. This increase was caused by the demand for the European market, a new element in the situation, and the aggressive pursuit of markets for Indian textiles in Asian trade, both by European competitors and by Indian sea faring merchants. The letters from the factories opened up by the officers of the Company in and near the areas of production constantly complain of a shortfall in the supply, of a difficulty in contracting for the required quantity of goods. This increased demand could only have been fulfilled by a number of weavers devoting more time to weaving tasks than to agriculture, their other main activity.

Before the Europeans came into the textile market, trade in textiles was erratic, seasonal and highly unpredictable. It shared this quality with other aspects of traditional Asian trade.[9] In such a demand situation, the weaver could work at leisure and weaving could be carried on side-by-side with cultivating the fields. This in itself contributed to keeping down the price of textiles. The increased and regular demand caused by the entry of Europeans into the market created more and steady work for the weavers, but by this very nature brought other problems in its train. The orders placed with him by merchants were more and regular and involved his devoting more hours of labour per day on his loom. In a number of villages near the big ports, the weaver found he had to work full time to satisfy the new demands. The entire family—men, women and children—became engaged in the various tasks related to weaving.

---

[9]The unpredictable and seasonal character of traditional Asian trade has been commented on by many historians. See W. van Lenr, *Indonesian Trade and Society* (The Hague-Banduug 1955), pp. 214-19, N. Steensgaard, *Carracks, Caravans and Companies* (Copenhagen, 1973), pp. 15-21, A. Das Gupta, *Indian Merchants and the Decline of Surat 1700-1750* (Wiesbaden: Franz Steiner Verlag, 1979), pp. 10-12.

The decision by the weaver to move away from agriculture and devote all his energies to weaving was, of course, a deliberate decision taken with an eye to the better returns from weaving that he was now getting. But it was to have long-term implications. Land-owning weaver families in the Arcot area were, it appears, either leasing their fields to other castes, or employing labour to work those fields. In either case, it meant that the weavers now needed enough cash on their hands to buy food grains and to pay their labourers and this cash had to be earned from the produce of their labour on the looms.[10] Weaver families were moving from what had been basically subsistence living to increased specialization and the use of money. This required the ability to provide a constant supply of cash from their earnings to purchase the daily needs of the family. Correspondingly, the increased activity on the looms required larger overhead expenses related to the maintenance of tools and the raw materials required for manufacture. All these needs required capital to be provided in advance of the returns that could be expected after production. The weaver had now to be, more than ever before, a man of credit or dependent heavily on available sources of credit.

The export market was of such a character that it restricted the weaver's freedom to take independent decisions. He could not anticipate the nature of the demand in all its details and produce for it. This was particularly true with regard to the European market, highly specialized in terms of quality, texture, prints and measurements. The types of weave and the specifications required could change from year to year. The initial outlay involved in cotton yarn, dyes and other requirements of the manufacture was such that the weaver could not decide to produce the goods independently so as to retain a measure of freedom as to their disposal. These initial capital costs, not to mention the numerous varieties and specialities involved, meant that the production had to be financed and the goods made to order on behalf of a merchant who guaranteed their purchase.[11]

The provision of credit was then a vital function in the weaver's employment. This function had also to be related to the marketability of his produce and therefore could not be performed by a professional moneylender. The *sawcar* had not made his entry into the weaving village in any marked manner in the seventeenth and eighteenth centuries. The provider of credit had also to ensure link between the weaver's produce and the outside world, to provide for it an outlet at rates which would cover the cost of raw material, the cost of living of the weaver and his family and the cost of the credit provided. There grew up a series of concentric circles of relationships with the weaver

[10]Humble petition of weavers of Chinnamanaikpollam and Naidapet, 20 August 1779, Madras Public Proceedings (hereafter, M.P.P.) 1779 India Office Records 240/48.
[11]This vital dependence by weavers on advances is discussed in detail with many examples in Chaudhuri, "The Structure of the Indian Textile Industry...," *IESHR*, XI, 2-3, pp. 150-5.

in the centre and the international markets on the periphery. A number of persons performed the vital linking roles between these two.

The textile merchant was one of these, performing seminal roles of providing credit and access to outside markets. Merchants were thus vital to the economy of a weaving village. They were generally settled in large numbers in villages whose dominant activity was weaving. In others they went in from outside and developed important contacts among weaving caste notables. The weavers felt more secure dealing with merchants settled in the village or in its vicinity. In the dominant weaving village of Arany, near Kanchipuram in the Chingleput district, the breakdown of castes and occupations of the inhabitants was as follows, according to a census taken by the Company's warehousekeeper in 1771:[12] Landowning weavers (*janmavar*) 90 households, weavers' labourers (also of weaver caste) 9 households, Tamil *pariahs* (cotton spinners) 38 households, Telugu *pariahs* (cotton spinners) 20 households, *valluvar* (cotton spinners) 10 households, *comatty* 19 households, *chetty* 21 households, *palli* and *ahamudaiyan* 15 households, unidentifiable 24 households. Thus *comatty* and *chetty* households, that is those living on mercantile occupations, made up 40, an unusually large proportion in the village total of 246 households, but an indicator of the opportunities for commerce in a weaving village. Whether he originated from outside the village or from within, it was the merchant financier who provided the funds to oil the wheels of the handloom industry. It is also significant that the activities of 90 loomowners was sufficient to maintain a total of 68 cotton spinners. It was possible that the village also produced cotton thread to be sold to other weaving villages.

Despite the key roles performed by the merchants as providers of credit and of access to a market, the extent of profit they realized does not appear to have been great. By all evidence, the merchant's profit from the whole transaction as a middleman between producer and exporter was about 4 to 5 per cent and no more.[13] This would appear to be a small profit margin for all the energies he exerted, the provision of credit and the risks of bad debts. There was some reason for this, however, as for many decades he was himself the exporter and had an interest in keeping the purchase price in India well down. When the Companies entered the market as exporters, they too saw to it that prices were pegged as low as possible. The low cost of Carnatic cloth made it very profitable to overseas traders. The first substantial increase in cost price occurs only in the 18th century as a result of the spiralling price of food grains and raw cotton.

It was not possible, however, for the merchant to enter into direct relation

[12]Diary of the Proceedings of a Journey through Weaving Villages in the Hon. Company's Jaghirs, Warren Hastings, Export Warehousekeeper, Minutes of Council, Fort St. George, 27 Dec. 1771, Madras Public Consultations (hereafter M.P.C.), 1771, 240/32.

[13]Minutes of Council, Fort St. George, 27 Sept. 1765, M.P.P. 1765, 240/23.

The Handloom Industry in Southeastern India 1750-1790   265

ship with the primary weaver in his search for goods for the market. The complex social structure of the weaving village prevented the emergence of such direct relationships. The merchant had to come to terms with the hierarchical structure of the weaving caste and to make some accommodation with those in authority and leadership in this caste. No detailed evidence is forthcoming on this social structure as the officers of the European Companies had no direct access to the weaving village—their records are our only source of evidence of the commercial relations of this period. It is only when the English attempted to bring these weavers directly under their control that the records begin to shed some light on these aspects. As noted above, it is by reading backwards from this evidence that the following picture is painted of the economic relations of a weaver village.

At the base of the structure is what may be called the primary weaver, whom the English records call the "cooly" weaver. He is the primary craftsman of the weaving industry. He sometimes owned his loom, sometimes not, and even if he did, he was probably indebted for it and was paying back in instalments to some *chetty* merchant or to a wealthier member of his caste. His entire family, including children, worked on the loom and on tasks associated with it. Above these weaver-craftsmen, and in some position of nebulous authority over them, were the head weavers, probably a hierarchy of persons knit together in a kin-group relationship, that had differentiated itself, similar to the internal differentiations among the *vellalar* or the *karaiyar*, on the basis of wealth and economic position.[14] This group had by now become hereditary. The head weavers appear to have exercised a paternal control over a particular group of weavers but had no economic control over the fruits of their labour. They generally looked after the interests of the weavers in their negotiations with merchants and, of course, got something in return from both the merchants and the weavers for their trouble. It does not appear that details of the negotiations such as specification of orders, prices agreed, delivery dates, penalty provisions, advances to weavers and so on were conducted through them, though it is possible that in some villages the head weavers had risen to fill such roles. Generally they were reluctant to get involved in these dealings, as was revealed when the English Company sought to persuade them to accept these functions.[15] Their role, then, seems to have been one of asserting their leadership in the community and a recognition of this by whoever sought to

[14]Over the years, such internal differentiations developed within a caste group. The *vellalar* are the best example of such marked internal differentiation. The *kondaikatti vellalar*, for example, had marked themselves out as an upper segment of that caste in the Chingleput area. The *karaiyar* had a less sharp distinction between *melongi* (i.e. those who aim high) and *kilongi* (those who aim low).

[15]Warren Hastings, Keeper of Export Warehouse to Governor of Fort St. George, 2 Dec. 1771. M.P.C. 1771, 240/32. Diary of the Proceedings of a journey through Weaving Villages in the Company's Jaghir, 27 Dec. 1771, M.P.C. 1771, 240/32.

enter into commercial dealings with the weavers. Thus merchants had to secure their general approval before they placed their orders in the village and the small commission allowed them was a means of keeping them on side, rather than a recognition of a concrete function they performed. The head weaver was there as the "big brother," intervening on behalf of an aggrieved weaver or interceding between a merchant and a recalcitrant weaver. His keeping an eye on things would also have had the general result of standardizing prices and ensuring that the prevailing terms were given to every weaver in respect of advances, penalties and other conditions.

Some of these functions were also performed by the *nattavar*, persons who were in more formal authority in south Indian village. *Nattavar* were the elected leaders of a village, whatever its caste composition was. In a predominantly weaver caste village, the *nattavar* were of the weaver caste. Though the office was elective, it tended to become hereditary and was held by families that owned more land and were in an undisputed position of authority over fellow caste members. They were thus drawn from the families that constituted the head weaver group. *Nattavar* were often also the rentiers of the village land tax and sometimes *polygars* of the village. In Tamil-speaking weaver villages, *nattavar* were called *Peria Desakaran* and among Telugu-speakers *Peddana Kaundoo*. Needless to say, in villages where weavers were not the dominant caste, *nattavar* were not of this caste and did not perform such functions in relation to the weaving industry.[16]

This rather delicate role of *nattavar* and the position held by head weavers were misunderstood by the English Company when it tried to effect changes to the system of marketing. It ascribed to them a role rather more active and more interventionist in the weaving industry than they actually performed. In the first stage of changes introduced into the Madras weaving villages in 1771, it treated the *nattavar* and head weavers as agents of the weavers and entered into contracts with them, made advances through them and made them securities for the weavers and responsible for the advances. For this they were allowed a commission of 5/8 per cent.[17] This was a failure and the Company soon realized its mistake, as these people had not been involved in the details of the negotiations between merchants and weavers but only kept an overall eye on things through their influence on the community.

More than the *nattavar* and the head weavers, the person who was really in the thick of the negotiations relating to marketing the weaver's produce was the broker. Every weaving village had a number of these brokers who were the intermediaries between merchants and weavers. In the weaving villages north of the Godavari river, the broker was known as *kopudarudu*, and occurs

---

[16]Warren Hastings, to Governor of Fort St. George, 2 Dec. 1771, M.P.C. 1771, 240/32.
[17]*Ibid.*

in the English records as *copdar*.[18] In the European perception he appears as a shady, though key figure, close to the weavers. Concrete evidence on his functions is hard to come by. He was the merchant's agent in negotiating the details of the orders with the weavers. He brought the merchant into the village, distributed his order among individual weavers, negotiated on the price and, most important of all, was responsible for the advances made by the merchant to the weaver. He was also responsible for the quality of the weave, and for sorting the cloth brought by the weaver in comparison with the samples that had been the basis of the order. For all this he received a commission from the merchant of 1 per cent.[19]

These tasks were of such a nature that the broker had to be someone closely connected to, and very knowledgeable of, the weaving industry. He was often a member of the weaving caste, though in some villages it appears that *chetty* textile merchants who had long been engaged in the business were also brokers. Generally, however, the brokers were persons of the village who had themselves been weavers and had gradually risen up the economic ladder. Some of them had continued the rise from village brokers to merchants and had gone outside the village to enter into dealings with the European Companies in the ports. Among the textile merchants of the two Companies, English and Dutch, are many with the suffix Mudaly, which was a title taken by leaders of the *kaikolar* weaving caste. Timanna, a prominent Madras merchant, and Pedda Venkatadri, his brother, belonged to a Telugu weaving caste. The broker did not always function as the merchant's agent but also bought cloth outright from the weavers and sold it to merchants outside, thus making a larger profit than his brokerage fee.[21] This was possible at a time of intense competition for textiles and in varieties of cloth that were interchangeable between Companies and was also in demand by private traders, Indian and European.

The English had a good deal of trouble with the *copdar* of North Coromandel and his counterpart broker of the southern villages. They had generally ignored him, not realizing his importance, and tended to rely on the visible power in the village, the head weaver and *nattuvar*. They found *copdar* offering intense resistance to the changes they introduced so that they were constrained to bring them back into the system in their former role and concede them a brokerage commission.[21]

There was among the weavers a territorial grouping of villages into an administrative unit that was recognized by them for a number of specific pur-

[18]Anthony Sadleir, Resident at Ingeram to Governor of Fort St. George, 21 Nov. 1774, M.P.C. 1774, 240/37.

[19]Report of the Export Warehouse Keeper, Minutes of Council, Fort St. George, 22 July 1776, M.P.P. 1776, 240/41.

[20]Anthony Sadleir to George Stratten, Chief of Vizagapatnam, 16 January 1775, M.P.C. 1775, 240/39.

[21]Minutes of Council, Fort St. George, 22 July 1776, M.P.P. 1776, 240/41.

poses. This territory is referred to in the English Company's records as a *paykat* or *paykit*[22] and we come across it mainly in the Chingleput and Arcot districts and in the northern Andhra districts.[23] A *paykat* had a central clearing house where cloth that was woven and ready for sale was brought for sorting and clearing of accounts with merchants or their agents. Some *paykats* were small, others large, consisting of several villages. Their formation has roots in past history and in weaver clan organization and rivalries. For example, a small weaving town of Chembaukam with 70 looms was a *paykat* of its own, while the Greater Arani *paykat* with its cluster of weaving villages had over 4,000 looms.[24]

When a merchant placed his orders with a weaver through the medium of a broker, an advance of cash was given to the weaver. This advance was made on the basis of an agreed price for the finished goods. The advance was crucial in many ways. It was a guarantee for the purchase of the goods ordered. More importantly, it provided the weaver with the money to buy thread and other essentials for the manufacturing process. And most important of all, it served to sustain him and his family for the period, sometimes of up to six months, that it took him to complete the order. The thread was the biggest single item. He had to purchase this at the best market price from another merchant in his village or in a neighbouring village. Sometimes the merchant who ordered the cloth would arrange to supply thread at an agreed price. The weaver always valued his independence to buy thread at the cheapest price as this maximized his earnings from the order. He always insisted on cash advances, and as high a proportion of the costs as he could negotiate, because cash in hand was what he needed above all else. There were a number of small items of expenditure and maintenance. His major problem was to apportion the money in hand judiciously between thread and other items for manufacture and the sustenance of the family. Here the prime expenditure was on food grains. The price of rice at any time was a major constituent in determining the price of cloth; the other main ingredient in the price was the price of cotton. If, for example, a sudden increase in the price of rice drove him to spend a large proportion of his advance on its purchase for his sustenance, he had less money to spend on cotton yarn and the other ingredients for his manufacture. He would then resort to cost-cutting measures such as using inferior cotton, reducing the measure of the cloth, and would ask for time to fulfil his order. These were the sorts of problems the merchants constantly had with the weavers which in turn created problems for the merchants with the Companies.

[22]Probably *payakattu* (Telugu).

[23]Warren Hastings to Governor of Fort St. George, 2 Dec. 1771, M.P.C. 1771, 240/32. Hastings compares the *paykat* to *aurung* in northern India saying: "It is synonymous with Hindustani word 'aurung' used in Bengal."

[24]Hastings to Governor of Fort St. George, 2 Dec. 1771, M.P.C. 1771, 240/32.

In such a situation, the merchant had a large say in determining the cost price of textiles. The major factors that went into the fixing of the price were the cost of raw cotton, cotton yarn, dyes and of food grain, particularly rice. This last item was an indicator to determine the cost of labour time that went into the manufacture. Through the eighteenth century, there was a tendency for the price of textiles of all varieties to increase, but little of this increase went to the weaver. Almost all the increase was taken up by the price of cotton and of rice. As an English Company Officer commented in 1768, labour wages in the handloom industry had been stationary for many years.[25]

The actual earnings of weavers in the period before English power expanded in the Carnatic is difficult to estimate. After that the picture becomes clearer. In a petition presented by the weavers of the Cuddalore *paleam* villages to the English Resident in 1779, they have outlined their work output and their earnings from it.[26] They calculate what they could earn from longcloth,[27] a staple cotton cloth popular in the Coromandel trade and valued in the European market. They say that a loom with two persons working could weave three pieces of 9 call. longcloth per month. The labour cost allowed for this cloth at no. 2 quality was 1 Pagoda 25 fanams 42 kasu.[28] This came to 34½ fanams or 3/4 Pagoda or 3 rupees each man per month.[29] It is possible that the weavers understated their monthly output but this under-statement if any could not have been substantial as the Company's officers had ways of checking on its accuracy. A later report of 1790 has a weaver completing 2 pieces of longcloth a month and earning over a Pagoda or 4 rupees monthly.[30] The wages of a Company sepoy at that time was Rs. 7 a month and of a peon Rs. 3.50. Company's servants had some fringe benefits while the weaver had to cope with other expenses.

The weaver's wage represented the earnings of the entire family. Weavers employed their wives ahd children in twining and untwining and running

[25]Chief of Cuddalore to Governor of Fort St. George, Minutes of Council, Fort St. George, 8 Nov. 1768, M.P.P. 1768, 240/27.

[26]Humble petition of weavers of Chinnamanaikpollam and Naidapet, 20 August 1779, M.P.P. 1779, 240/48.

[27]J. Irwin and P.R. Schwartz, *Studies in Indo-European Textile History* (Ahmedabad 1966), Appendix: A Glossary of Textile Terms, p. 67.

[28]During this period, the better varieties of cloth were sorted into five according to quality and the price was discounted in a descending order of quality from 1 to 5.

[29]A pagoda at this time was a very strong currency and was appreciating in value, while the fanam was depreciating. A Madras Star pagoda was worth 8 shillings or 4 rupees. The fanam varied in value depending on its weight. The standard heavy fanam seems to have been worth 24 to one Star pagoda. But here obviously the light fanam is referred to and its value appears to be 46 to a Star pagoda. The kasu (anglicised into "cash"), a copper coin, appears to have had the value of 80 to a fanam.

[30]Cited in H. Dodwell, "The Madras Weaver under the Company," *Proceedings of the Indian Historical Records Commission* 1922 (Calcutta 1922), pp. 41-47.

threads. They had expenses in the preparation of *kanji* to starch cloth, the cost of oil for lubricating the loom and in general maintenance of the loom.[31] There were taxes and other impositions. The loom tax varied from 3/4 to 2 Pagodas per year, levied by the Mughal Government.[32] This represented two months earnings. There were other authorized and unauthorized imposts by *amuldars* and regional authorities which were varied and uneven. Among these was a requirement to purchase paddy from the regional administrative authority and weavers complained that they did this at a premium of 25 per cent.[33] In some villages, there was a tax on the thread that was brought in for the weaver and on the cloth that was on the loom or taken out of the village.

These wage rates show that there had been no marked increase in wages from the seventeenth century for over a hundred year period. Estimates for the seventeenth century put artisan's wages at between 3 and 5 rupees a month.[34] The position had not changed in relation to weaver's earnings in the second half of the eighteenth century. On the other hand, the cost of food grains was always rising. Along the coast, rice sold throughout the seventeenth century at an average price of 65 pounds (avoirdupois) for a rupee.[35] By the early eighteenth century this had risen to 55 pounds for a rupee and by the middle of that century to 33 pounds per rupee. In the 1770s, in a good year, rice sold at 30 pounds per rupee.[36] If a weaver spent half his earnings on rice he could buy 60 pounds of rice per month for the family's consumption, giving him an average of two pounds per day.

The position was better for the weaver in other ways before the English Company acquired political power. When the three Companies, English, Dutch and French, were competing in the open market, making large orders from Coromandel, and these were supplemented by European private trade and Indian trade, the weavers had a greater flexibility and a larger freedom of operation. In such a competitive situation, they had a greater control over the disposal of their produce. The interchangeability of goods ordered by these various customers, who were aiming at broadly the same export markets, made it possible for weavers to play one against the other. They could time their contracts in such a way that they would engage with the Dutch Company's merchants in July and August and get advances from them at a time

---

[31]Humble petition of weavers . . . 20 August 1779, M.P.P. 1779, 240/48.

[32]Hastings to Governor of Fort St. George 2 Dec˙ 1771, M.P.C. 1771, 240/32.

[33]*Ibid.*

[34]W.H. Moreland, *From Akbar to Aurangzeb: A Study in Indian Economic History* (London: Macmillan, 1922, repr. 1972), pp. 194-95; Ishwar Prakash, "Organization of Industrial Production in Urban Centres in India during the 17th Century," B.N. Ganguli, *ed.*, *Readings in Indian Economic History* (Bombay: Asia Publishing House, 1964), p. 50.

[35]Moreland (*op. cit.*, p. 171) gives this as the governing price through most of Maritime India. It is confirmed by Dutch evidence for the second half of the seventeenth century.

[36]Minutes of Council, Fort St. George, 3 February 1775, M.P.C. 1775, 240/39.

when they were settling accounts with the English Company's merchants and get money from the English in February when they were settling with the Dutch.[37] If any cloth they made was rejected by the Companies, or "turned out" as the contemporary term was, they could sell it to English private merchants who were increasingly coming into the trade in the eighteenth century. This situation existed in many regions where the three Companies were in competition in the Chingleput and Arcot villages and in the upper Godavari districts. This free competition continued till about 1770 when weavers and village brokers did well out of it, to the discomfiture of the English Company's merchants and the Company itself. It appears that weavers would secure advances from the Company's merchants, take their orders and deliberately alter the measures and reduce the quality in the expectation of the cloth being rejected. The rejected cloth was promptly sold to European and Indian private traders and to rival Companies.[38] Thus weavers were profiting out of advances made by the English Company. The Carnatic wars that had raged intermittently from 1740 had interrupted trade and caused hardship to weavers. The peace of Paris (1763) that ended the war, besides reviving English trade, brought back the French and the Dutch who renewed their investments in the weaving villages.

This situation continued till the 1770s, when the English began to shut off weaving areas one by one from open competition. They claimed a prescriptive right to the labour of the weavers, using the political ascendancy they had gained in the Carnatic. They made interchangeability of the product difficult by varying specifications, chopping cloth on the loom with the Company's mark and imposing heavy penalties on rejected cloth. They made their merchants draw hard bargains with the weavers, imposed strict quality controls and closed all loopholes by which the weaver earned the extra *anna* on his labour. The justification offered for this restriction on the weavers' selling market was that the English were now providing protection to these weavers. To make this more plausible, they moved on to providing more tangible benefits in the progressive reduction of the loom tax in these villages which were producing exclusively for the English Company.[39] Admittedly, the freedom from arbitrary imposts under the Nawab's administration and later the reduct-

[37]Diary of the Proceedings of a journey through Weaving Villages in the Hon Company's Jaghirs. Warren Hastings, Minutes of Council, Fort St. George, 27 Dec. 1771, M.P.C. 1771, 240/32.

[38]Minutes of Council, Fort St. George, 8 November 1768, M.P.P. 1768, 240/27.

[39]Letters of protest from the officers of the French and the Dutch Companies were of no avail. See, for example, the letters exchanged between Law, Governor of Pondichery and the Fort St. George Government. Minutes of Council, Fort St. George, 26 May 1775, 12 July 1775, M.P.C. 1775, 240/39, 240/40; letters from Dutch chiefs of Palicol and Jagannathapuram to the Fort St. George Government. Minutes of Council, Fort St. George, 12 July 1775, 18 August 1775, 30 August 1775, M.P.C. 1775, 240/40.

tion of the loom tax were a boon to the weavers. Yet they preferred to retain their independence to deal with clients freely and resisted vigorously all attempts by the English to operate a closed shop of weavers and Company's agents.

To re-establish English trade on Coromandel and take full advantage of the newly acquired political power, they enacted a series of reforms in the manner of investment on textiles in the period 1771-1790. The reforms themselves have been discussed elsewhere.[40] Briefly the intention of these reforms was to eradicate the merchant middleman and bring the weaver into direct relationship with the Company with a view eventually to making him a wage labourer. The first spate of reforms were based on an improper understanding of the structure of the handloom industry of the Carnatic. The English officials used the term "cooly weaver," implying that he was working for someone and was not a free agent. In a rather simplistic view of the weaving industry, and in their enthusiasm to rush the new changes, they assumed that all they had to do was to do away with the merchant from outside and the broker from within the weaving village.[41] They would then have direct access to the weaver cut their costs and the benefits would be mutual. On the face of it, this was a desirable objective and the weaver should have stood to benefit from it. In fact, however, the English soon found the situation far more complex and among the most serious obstacles was the opposition of the weavers themselves.

In the first place, the weavers opposed the elimination of the merchant in the sale of their goods. Even though outside the weaver's society and himself benefiting from the weaver's labour, the merchant was considered as very much a friend and patron. Between weaver and merchant had grown a close nexus which the English found impossible to break. The merchant was the source of vital credit which he seems to have extended even beyond the needs of the manufacturing process. In times of drought and in particular crises such as sickness, robbery, fire, the merchant looked after the needs of the weaver's family.[42] In some villages the merchant was also the rentier and was able to exercise the authority of the *nattavar* and *amuldar* in his interest.[43] For the merchant, it was essential to keep the weaver employed on his behalf and

---

[40]S. Arasaratnam, "Trade and Political Dominion in South India 1750-1790. Changing British-Indian Relationships," *Modern Asian Studies*, 13, 1 (1979), pp. 29-35.

[41]For a statement of this view, see letter from Chief of Cuddalore to Fort St. George and the Council's resolution. Minutes of Council, Fort St. George, 23 Feb. 1768, M.P.C. 1768, 240/26.

[42]Report of a Sub-Committee to investigate the Investment in north Coromandel, Minutes of Council, Fort St. George, 26 Dec. 1775 M.P.P. 1776, 240/41.

[43]The land revenues were auctioned every three years and chetty merchants successful bid for the taxes of villages round Fort St. George and Fort St. David directly or by mortgage through *nattavar*. Minutes of Council, Fort St. George, 21 October 1766, M.P.C. 1766, 240/24.

ensure a continuous delivery of goods that would serve to wipe out some of the credit. Then more credit could be made available and thus the weaver kept in continuing dependence. Thus there was a continuing relationship and a permanent nexus between them.

The English tried to break this nexus and interpose paid servants in the form of *gumastahs* and *kanakapillais* as agents through whom they dealt with the weavers.[44] The servants so appointed were generally of the landowning *vellala* caste from outside the village, from the vicinity of Madras, or from the weavers' village itself. In the Andhra district, they were from the landowning *reddi* caste. Some were Brahmins who had influence in the area and may perhaps have been administrative officials under former indigenous rulers. There were also some of the previous merchants of the *chetty* caste who now found it profitable to take employment under the English. In some areas, there might already have been some traditional rivalry between the weaying caste and the landowning *vellalar* such as there was between the *kaikolar* and *kondakatti vellalar* of Chembaukam over the *mirasi* rights of the village.[45] In any case, there was not that paternal relationship as with the merchants and they were by no means the unending source of credit as were the merchants. On the contrary, they proved to be hard task masters, with all the arrogance of the Company's power behind them, storming the weaver's home with sepoys at the slightest conflict. There was always bound to be conflict over delivery dates, quality of goods, short measure and such issues. In all this these agents had the coercive power of the Company behind them to enforce unfavourable contracts entered into with the weavers.[46]

It was even more difficult to dispose of a more influential person, the broker, the *copdar* of Telugu villages, the man who was a part of weaver caste society. He was the man on the spot who reminded the weavers of what they missed out of free competition. The *copdar* was now no longer a weaver and was loathe to miss the small commission he enjoyed, his only sustenance. In the first flush of change introduced by the English, they ignored him altogether and wanted to eliminate him from the handloom trade altogether. They soon found that they could not do this.[47] He performed important professional

[44]The first place where this system was implemented was the *jaghir* villages near Cuddalore. Minutes of Council, Fort St. George, 23 Feb. 1768. M.C.C. 1768, 240/26. It was then extended to Chingleput and North Arcot. Minutes of Council, Fort St. George, 2 May 1771, M.P.C. 1771, 240/31.

[45]This dispute developed into a clash between the two castes in February 1775 and the Governor had to adjudicate. He found in favour of the *kondakattiv vellalar*. Minutes of Council, Fort St. George, 27 February 1775. M.P.C. 1775, 240/39.

[46]Minutes of Council, Fort St. George, 20 November 1772, M.P.C. 1772, 240/34. Minutes of Council, Fort St. George, 13 July, 1777, M.P.P. 1777, 240/43.

[47]Report of the Export Warehousekeeper. Minutes of Council, Fort St. George, 22 July 1776 M.P.P. 1776, 240/41.

functions. He kept control over quality in the interest of the financing merchant in whose absence he was responsible for sorting the cloth in comparison with the samples. This work was now being done by paid servants, who were not professionally qualified, and the Company found that the sorting of cloth, when accepted from the weaver, was done in a slipshod manner. The cloth was resorted again in the Madras warehouse and the large amount of rejected cloth was debited to the account of the weaver. He found this unacceptable and in violation of custom. Previously, when the goods were accepted by the broker, the weaver's responsibility was over, and after the goods left the village any loss was borne by the merchant. In 1776, weavers of Chingleput villages refused to work under this system. Consequently the broker was brought back as the Company's agent and he undertook to look after the Company's orders for a brokerage fee of 1½ per cent. [48]

The English found the weavers a very difficult people to impose upon with their rules and regulations. Among south Indian castes, they had great mobility. They could evacuate an entire village, move elsewhere and set up their looms for production in a short period. There is evidence of this happening not infrequently in the seventeenth and eighteenth centuries. Their extended kinship ties over a number of villages enabled them to take refuge in other villages for long periods. They appear to have been capable of collective action. In the seventeeth century, they were moving in large numbers into or near European settlements, to the English at Madras and Cuddalore, the Dutch at Pulicat and Nagapatnam and the French at Pondichery. New weaving townships were being established near these coastal settlements. From the 1760s such migratory movements, away from the reaches of English power, were happening in response to the changes introduced by the English. [49] As long as the English were present on the Carnatic coast as traders, generating demand in textiles and thus increasing productivity by their investment, weaving castes were attracted towards their settlements and were desirous of living under their protection. As soon as the English presence became political and they showed an inclination to use this political power in the interests of trade, the weavers vote with their feet, as it were, and migrate away from the reaches of this power to other European settlements or places in the interior. Some of them are even prepared to abandon weaving altogether rather than work under direct English control.

The changes introduced by the English provoked widespread reaction from the weavers over a number of scattered weaving districts. This reaction ranged from passive resistance to subtle undermining of the new system through channels of traditional authority, united action in laying down tools

[48]*Ibid.*, Minutes of Council, Fort St. George, 16 January 1775, M.P.C. 1775, 240/39.
[49]Minutes of Council, Fort St. George, 18 August 1775 M.P.C. 1775 240/40. Minutes of Council, Fort St. George, 20 February 1778, M.P.P· 1778, 240/45.

and abandoning the village and, in some rare instances, to violent revolts against Company's Indian servants in the village.[50] This weaver response of the period 1770-1780 is the first popular reaction to the imposition of British rule in the Carnatic. It is the response of an independent (as it strove to be) craft-based mode of production to a centralized, modernizing management control that was being applied from outside. The causes of the weavers' grievances and their methods of combating them show the constant pull between these two forces.

One of the causes of conflict was the hostility that existed from the outset between the weavers and the Company's Indian servants who were mostly external to the weaving village. These servants went into the viilage armed with the full authority of the Company and accompanied by visible means of coercion in the form of the Company's sepoys and peons. Where the servants —the *Gumastah* and *Kanakapillai*—were corruptly linked with their masters the English Company officers, to their mutual benefit, the oppression of the weaver was more intense. The servants went into the village to advance thread and money to the weavers. In both these, corruption was possible by over-valuing the thread to the detriment of the weaver and by fiddling exchange rates in making cash advances. Then there was abuse in sorting cloth delivered by the weavers which was done into five categories with prices allowed to weavers varying according to each category. All these abuses were possible on their own initiative and in league with senior officers of the Company. In the atmosphere of widespread corruption then prevalent, the collusion between Company's European and Indian servants extended into the weaving village the opportunities for such corruption.

In the welter of evidence on such corruption two examples may be singled out. In both these areas it is significant that weaver discontent took its most violent form. In the Vizagapatnam districts, we have evidence of one Venkatachalam, who, besides being the Company's *gumastah*, was also a personal servant of Anthony Sadleir, the Resident of Injiram. Venkatachalam was permanently stationed in the weaving districts, with Company's sepoys at his disposal. He appears to have terrorized weavers into signing contracts with the English, forcing advances on them so that they were in a perpetual state of indebtedness to the Company. Weavers were flogged into obedience and constantly subject to intimidation by the sepoys. They were forcibly prevented from dealing with merchants of the French and Dutch Companies, though the English had not as yet imposed such restrictions. These allegations of the weavers were found to be substantially true when they were inquired into by Walter Hamilton, the Resident of Madapollam.[51] Grievances of a similar

[50]The facts pertaining to these revolts are dealt with in S. Arasaratnam, "Trade and Political Dominion. . ." *Modern Asian Studies* 13, 1 (1979), pp. 33-36.

[51]Hamilton to Governor of Fort St. George, 30 Sept. 1775, Minutes of Council, Fort St. George 18, Oct. 1775, M.P.C. 1775, 240/40.

nature were found in the major weavers' disturbance in the Cuddalore district. Here allegations were made by the weavers against a *gumastah* called Mukunthan. He and others associated with him were accused of corruption in the advance of thread to the weavers and in the sale of paddy.[52] In both these cases the *gumastahs* were strongly defended by the English officers with whom they were closely associated.

Another source of difficulty in the relation between English Company and the weavers was the *nattavar* and head weavers and their real roles in the weaving industry. Their influence in the weaving village was clearly visible and it was deemed necessary to bring them in to support English investment. On first acquaintance with the system, the English assumed the head weaver to be like the master craftsman of medieval Europe who employed a number of journeymen who were the "cooly weavers." They thought it possible to use these head weavers in place of merchants and brokers as agents through whom to contract for the supply of cloth. In 1772, contracts were entered into with head weavers, who may or may not be *nattavar*, for the delivery of cloth on a commission basis. They were made responsible for the cash advance made in the village and for the delivery of goods to the required quality and specification.[53] The English soon realized that they had misunderstood the position of the head weaver. Head weavers had no control over the craft of weaving. They were social rather than economic leaders of the community. Each weaver was an individual economic unit working on his own and for his own profit. The contracts with head weavers produced arrears and bad debts with weavers for which the head weavers took no responsibility.[54] In a conflict of interests between weavers and Company, they were so obviously on the side of their fellow caste men.

When in response to this problem, head weavers were ignored and direct contracts were entered into with weavers, head weavers felt slighted and turned against the Company. Head weavers and *nattavar*, together with village brokers of the weaver caste, used their influence to disrupt English investment. They missed the perquisites they had enjoyed from the merchants and the informal authority they had enjoyed over the weavers which had now been usurped by Company's servants from outside the caste. Their hand was visible in the prolonged resistance of the weavers. They used their kinship connections with other villages to provide moral and material support to the strik-

[52]Resident of Pollam to Chief of Cuddalore, 14 April 1778, Minutes of Council, Fort St. George, 24 April 1778, M.P.C. 1778, 240/45.

[53]Warren Hastings to Governor of Fort. St. George, 2 Dec. 1771, M.P.C. 1771, 240/32.

[54]The Export Warehousekeeper reported that in the period 1772-4 in the Chingleput, North Arcot villages, weavers were in arrears to the amount of 40,480 Pagodas. *Nattavar* and head weavers who were securities for these arrears were men of little property and refused to be in any way responsible for these debts. Report of Export Warehousekeeper, 22 July 1776, M.P.C. 1776, 240/41.

ing weavers.[55] The determination of the English to break the power of the head weaver eventually succeeded in a number of villages.

From 1780, with the entry of English power into the weaving villages, the private English entrepreneur made his appearance in these villages, making direct investments there. The immediate cause of this was a serious shortage of capital faced by the Company after the Carnatic wars. The Company, having established a structure by which it dominated the handloom industry, was not in a position to take advantage of it because of shortage of capital. In the meanwhile, there was an expanding private trade of English merchants in textiles for the Southeast Asian and China markets. These English private traders had, up till that time, secured textiles through Indian merchants. Now they saw an opportunity to make direct purchases from the weavers, thus cutting middleman's costs. They went further and offered to provide the Company with its supplies of textiles for the European market. It was for them a means of remitting their profits to Europe. A number of individuals, some of them officers of the Company, set themselves up as agents for the supply of textiles. John Skardon, the Company's Resident in Cuddalore, offered in 1787 to participate in the Company's investment in that quarter.[56] He had for long managed the Company's trade there and had achieved a position of influence in the weaving villages. He was hoping to turn that to his advantage. John Fannin, an English private merchant on the north coast, wrote in 1780, offering to supply for the Company's European market and asking in return the lease of two villages in the hinterland of Ganjam for 12 years.[57] He was already engaged in supplying the private trade and was now proposing an ambitious project of founding weaving factories. Two others, Basil Cochrane and John Snow, were successful in being awarded contracts to supply the Company for its European market from the northern villages.[58]

Cochrane was a typical example of the aggressive new entrepreneur. When the Company advertised for tenders to provide cloth to its specifications in the ports of Injiram and Madapollam, he tendered and won the contract. He went into the hinterland villages and made individual contracts with weavers. To strengthen his position, he won his way into the favour of the zamindar of Peddapuram, Jagapathy Rauze. He persuaded the zamindar to issue an order to the weavers instructing them to enter into contracts with Cochrane

[55]Minutes of Council, Fort St. George, 7 April 1775, translated copy of letter from Mahanadu of Jaganadapuram to Mahanadu of Mandapettah (26 Feb. 1775), M.P.C. 1775, 240/39.

[56]Skardon to Governor of Fort St. George, 28 May 1787, M.P.C. 1787, 240/67.

[57]John Fannin to Chief of Ganjam, 30 June 1780. Minutes of Council Fort St. George, 19 July 1780, M.P.P. 1780, 240/51.

[58]Minutes of Council, Fort St. George, 24 Nov. 1786, M.P.C. 1786, 240/65.

on stipulated prices.[59] The Company's sepoys and peons were used to enforce this exclusive order in the weaving villages. The Board of Trade in Madras was not happy with this use of state power to create a monopoly on behalf of a private entrepreneur. It recommended that the use of the Company's sepoys and peons be stopped.[60] The procedure was no different from what the Company's Officers were doing elsewhere on behalf of the Company. Cochrane went ahead with his investment without the active support of the Company's power, though the knowledge of his influence with the zamindar was of advantage to him. Private capital and Company capital had entered the weaving village to displace the capital of Indian merchants who now lost the custom of the English Company and thus a major source of capital.

Despite its difficulties, the English Company had established a degree of control over the Carnatic handloom industry by 1780. The control was effective in producing results. Costs were cut down considerably, prices were reduced in real terms as they did not keep pace with the spiralling price of food grains. At every annual investment, prices were agreed anew with the weavers, taking into account the current price of cotton and rice. The English were thus able to determine the cost price of textiles more rigorously, leaving no room for the weavers to make extra profits. The fact that, in many villages, the weaver was allowed to weave only for the English made him little more than a wage labourer.

One by one, the ingredients of independent production enjoyed by the weavers were eliminated. They could not produce for any customer they chose. They had to accept part of their payment in cotton yarn. They were subject to a strict supervision of the process of manufacture by the Company's servants who were located in the village. They were subject to a stringent quality control by specialist professional sorters and any shortfall was debited to the weaver's account with the Company. This had, for the English, the great advantage of improving quality. They had now made certain that the quality of the thread used was appropriate to the type of textile ordered. They had ensured that the finished product exactly followed the samples provided. Strict penalties for defaulting on production dates made certain that the orders were delivered in time. Raw material such as cotton could now be procured at the cheapest market and a profit was made on its supply to the weavers. All these innovations were resisted by the weavers but eventually the English wore down their opposition.

A further stage in the exercise of control was the appointment in 1786 of a number of Superintendants of looms in the various districts. It was the duty

[59]Chief of Masulipatnam to Governor of Madras, 4 January 1787. Minutes of Council, Fort St. George, 16 Nov. 1787. M.P.C. 1787 241/3. Basil Cochrane to Chief of Masulipatnam, 15 Nov. 1787 *ibid.*
[60]Board of Trade to Governor of Madras, 26 Jan. 1788, M.P.P. 1788, 241/4.

The Handloom Industry in Southeastern India 1750-1790   279

of the Superintendants to keep lists of looms and weavers, to supervise them and attend to their welfare, to check on *gumastahs* and other agents to prevent their exploiting weavers. It was now possible to extend the area of control to the tools of manufacture, to see that looms were kept in good repair so that the quality of the product was not affected. An example of the operation of this control is seen in the Paleam villages of Cuddalore where the English Resident saw that the combs on a number of looms had wasted. He made the weavers exchange these for new combs, which he himself supplied and paid for, and deducted the cost from the payments made to weavers for their manufactured cloth. The weavers reacted violently to this interference with their business but the Resident stood firm and the weavers were forced to buy the new combs from him in instalments.[61] The loom tax was gradually abolished in all the Company's *jaghir* villages.[62] Weavers were not to be subject to military service or other personal services.[63]

The eighteenth century was a period of volatility and change in economic relations in the Indian subcontinent, particularly in respect of these sectors of society and economy that were subject to direct assault by European power. It is not possible to chart with accuracy the direction of these changes, not only because the evidence is scanty but also because it is difficult to establish the state of economic relations before the massive impact of European power. As forces of change were unleashed both from the sea coast and from the interior it is difficult to disentangle external factors from internal disintegration.

In the Carnatic, the handloom industry had expanded as far as it could by the beginning of the eighteenth century within the framework of the existing social and economic structure. Weaver craftsmen had increased their earnings and production for export had expanded. By the same token weavers were becoming more cash-oriented and their standard of living was tied more closely to the movement of prices in those commodities essential to their work and livelihood. They were thus becoming more heavily dependent on the earnings from their labour in a situation where they could not control the price of their manufactures.

In spite of the expanding investment in handloom produce, the producing weaver sturdily retained his independence. This expansion underlined the importance of credit and of persons who provided credit to the industry. Yet, the merchant, the provider of credit, did not extend his control over the process of production and through this over the weaver craftsmen. The social

[61]W.H. Torriano, Resident at the Pollams to James Daniell, Chief of Cuddalore, 3 Feb. 1778, Minutes of Council, Fort St. George, 10 Feb. 1778, M.P.P. 1778, 240/45.

[62]Abolished in Paleam villages 1776, Minutes of Council, Fort St. George, 22 July 1776, M.P.P. 1776, 240/41. Suspended in Chingleput and Arcot villages 1784, later abolished. Board of Trade to Governor, 6 Oct. 1786, M.P.P. 1786, 240/62.

[63]Board of Trade to Governor, 6 Oct. 1786, M.P.P. 1786, 240/62,

structure of the weaving village, and the forces of traditional influence and hierarchy in this structure, prevented the reduction of the independence of the weaver. There was a certain organic unity in the weaving village that the merchant could not penetrate. Nor did there arise, from within the weaving village, elements which were able to expropriate to themselves the means of production of the weaver. Thus, at the beginning of the period of English expansion, the weaver was still in control of the means of production. All that he lacked was capital and an independent access to the market. He was, in Max Weber's terms, a "price worker" not a "wage worker."

Weber, in his analysis of economic change, has these two extremes of pre-industrial craft production. The "price worker" produces freely for the market, stocks, and sells his products, and has command over raw material and tools. At the opposite extreme is the craftsmen in the service of an entre-preneur as a wage worker, not in possession of raw material and tools but only bringing to market his labour. Between these two extremes is the crafts-man who produces to order and sells to a merchant or to an entrepreneur who possesses the monopoly of his labour power.[64] Weavers of the Carnatic villages tend to fall in the more independent "price work" end of this spec-trum. Though they were reliant on the merchant for advances, they were able to sell their product in the most favourable market, bought their own raw materials and certainly owned their own tools. In these they were assisted by the brokers of their own caste. As the demand became specialized and the market (for the weaver) was consequently restricted, and more remote, his independence was curtailed and he found himself accepting terms that were tantamount to wage work. This wage work and price work existed side by side.

The drift of the changes introduced by the English Company was to make the weaver a wage worker. The chief weapon in this was to restrict the weaver's access to the market and to impose a monopoly over his labour. Another means to curtail his independence was to pay him partly in kind, by the supply of raw material. The imposition of supervisory control over the process of production was a further nail to his independence. In this way, the English were able to extend control over the manufacture, to control quality and, most important of all, to determine prices.

This ability to control prices proved invaluable at a time when the price of essential commodities in the Carnatic was rising steeply. The English were able to ensure that the price of textiles did not rise correspondingly and this added to the profitability of the textile trade of the Company as well as of English private traders. By the same token, the earnings of weavers may be said to have declined in real money terms. They were getting a lot more work

[64]Max Weber, *General Economic History*. Transl. by Frank H. Knight (New York, Collier Books, 1961), pp. 99-101.

but less rewards for it. This comes through from all available evidence of the period and from the desperate actions taken by the weavers in response to the changes.

As far as the development of the handloom industry is concerned, there is a historical inevitability to the changes of the period. The Company and the English private traders, as the chief buyers in the market, desired to exercise greater control of the manufacturing process, and to impose on it a more efficient management. This they did by introducing into the village a body of paid servants receiving instructions from them with coercive authority over weavers that none had before. They had virtual monopoly of the market, and had effectively exercised control over raw materials and began to extend this control over the weavers' tools. Under the Company weavers had virtually become wage workers on terms and conditions over which they had no control.

10

The Textile Industry in
Southeast Asia, 1400–1800

Kenneth R. Hall

Abstract

This study of Southeast Asia's regional and native textile trade highlights the transitional patterns of textile use in sixteenth and seventeenth century Banjarmasin, an important Borneo coast port-polity in that era's international pepper trade. Cloth was a multi-purpose commodity bearing rich indigenous legacy that served as the point of reference for revised political, economic, and cultural transactions. In the new order that was emerging, upstream and downstream regularized their interactions and shared in a common cultural bond that was defined by cloth. This was a locally meaningful response to the changing economic circumstances of the seventeenth century, and was only in part a reaction to an increasingly assertive European presence in the eastern Indonesian archipelago.

Textile production and use in Southeast Asia reflects the regional diversity of cultures. Yet there were commonalties. Practical demand for textiles involved a synthesis of traditional values and contemporary needs that defined the materials used, the techniques employed, and the patterns depicted. Over the centuries Southeast Asian textiles evolved in numerous forms ranging from the simple, with designs painted, dyed, pasted, or embroidered into bark cloth,[1]) to time consuming dye-resist cotton batiks and high quality woven silk that was market competitive to that of China.

It is incorrect to characterize Southeast Asia's textile industry as locally induced, but it is equally inappropriate to attribute its development exclusively to external stimuli. Southeast Asia's central position in the East-West maritime route made it a natural recipient of cotton textiles produced in India and silks from China, which were accepted in exchange for the region's pepper, spices, and jungle reserves.[2]) In some instances these textile imports temporarily displaced local output—because the imports were, or were perceived to be of

---

*) This study is an extensive re-write of a paper originally prepared for a panel on "Textile Industry and Trade in the Indian Ocean Basin" chaired by Robert van Niel at the Second International Conference of the World History Association in Honolulu, Hawaii 24-27 June 1993. Final research for this project was made possible by the financial support of the National Endowment for the Humanities and the assistance of the staff of the Koloniaal Archief section of the Algemeen Rijksarchief in The Hague during May and June 1993.

1) R. Maxwell, 1990: 36, plate 35. The Miao tribesmen of upland Laos are also well-known for their embroidery of bark cloth (see below).
2) K.R. Hall 1985, 1992.

higher quality than those crafted locally, and/or the imports were so inexpensive that it made economic sense for locals to buy the imported textiles rather than create their own. Buoyed by the opportunities and prosperity derived from international trade, Southeast Asian consumers, from kings to commoners, at one time or another gained access to cloth that had its origin beyond the region. But local cloth engendering was never totally displaced; it was common that this periodic preference for foreign cloth would induce local craftsmen to modify their technique, designs, or materials until local textiles once again achieved a competitive edge, either because of parochial economic downturns precipitated by transitions in the indigenous or international marketplace or because local craftsmen created a more desirable yield.

The fluctuations in Southeast Asia's textile industry run parallel to the region's early history. Recent studies of the Southeast Asian socio-economy by Anthony Reid focus on the critical transitions in Southeast Asia's material culture that are coincident to the fifteenth through seventeenth century era, when significant structural adjustments were taking place within the region.[3] In this period new states emerged that could effectively administer diverse populations; new cosmopolitan societies were unified under Islam, Theravada Buddhism, and Christianity, which became the dominant religions and overlay earlier Hindu-Buddhist and animistic traditions. Reid posits that enhanced external demand for Southeast Asia's pepper and spices was in no small part responsible for the age's cultural evolutions. The multiple internal stimuli of political development, religious conversions, and the first integrated marketing systems induced rapid urbanization and movement toward secularization.

Reid presents an encyclopedia of cultural details to project regional patterns. In doing so he comes to terms with the writings of J.C. van Leur, whose scholarship on early Southeast Asian trade argued against prevailing colonial era images of regional dependency and pre-European "colonization" by Indians and Chinese.[4] Van Leur characterized early external contact as being carried on by an autonomous and vagabond trading class largely isolated from local cultures and polities, and who occupied otherwise disconnected and self-contained port towns, as was permitted by the seasonal monsoons, small "peddling" ships, and limited availability of cash in that age. In contrast, during the early 1960s M.A.P. Meilink-Roelofsz presented a picture of sixteenth and seventeenth century trade at the time of the European arrival as a steady, organized, large bulk trade in foodstuffs and practical necessities that was carried by larger or smaller magnates under the protection of politically competitive harbor princes, sea

---

3) A. Reid, 1988; see also J. Kathirithamby-Wells and J. Villiers, eds., 1990.
4) J.C. van Leur, 1955.

ramblers, or trade barons.[5]) While van Leur projected the oriental bazaar, Meilink-Roelofsz posited the Venetian counting house. Reid finds himself drawn to the latter view, wherein there were internal movements of bulk rice from granary regions to cities and coasts, and where metals, cheap cottons, and earthenware pots all widely circulated in developing market systems. But while the spices, silks, porcelains, lacquerware, and dyewoods set off this "age of commerce," they did not drive it.

Integrated by the warm waters of the South China Sea and Java Sea, China, India, Japan, Persia, Arabia, and Europe were drawn into the region to the great port cities: Pegu, Ayutthya, Melaka, Aceh, Pasai, Banten, Japara, Gresik, Makassar, Brunei, and Manila, among others. Regionally a "polychrome" population was connected by an acquaintance with the "market Malay" and common interest in profit. Reid points to the cultural channels of the age wherein Arab, Persian, and Indian ideas and literary styles stimulated commonalties of local beliefs, legal systems, clothing, building styles, gongs, cockfights, kites, and shadow theaters. There was also seemingly continuous warfare that had critical ceremonial value. Intermixed with these were universalistic Islam, Theravada Buddhism, and Christianity. This golden age of regional development and integrations finally ended when the Europeans, who hungered for the region's luxuries, took key ports-of-trade by force.

As this era of evolution relates to textiles, Reid reports that in the pre-fifteenth century society the body was universally viewed to be the source of magical potency; in this traditional order upper torso nudity and tattoos bestowed status distinctions and separated man from the natural world of animals. By the sixteenth century, due to political and religious transitions as well as the widespread prosperity and ease of access to Indian and Chinese textiles, status was defined instead by one's clothing and other tangible decorations of the body. Social status was increasingly based on material wealth rather than physical prowess. State hierarchical regulations and pageantry incorporated all-important corporeal displays; what one wore or was allowed to wear defined one's social and political command.

In Reid's view, until the mid-seventeenth century Southeast Asians were equal to the competition of the European traders, due to Southeast Asia's critical role in the international spice trade. But in the mid-seventeenth century external demand for these spices diminished due to an international market glut

---

5) M.A.P. Meilink-Roelofsz, 1962. Needless to say, this view was consistent with the self-image of the newly independent and assertive Southeast Asian polities in that era, and also lay the groundwork for speculation that Southeast Asia's inability to continue as a major participant in the global trade was a direct consequence of European intervention.

and the Dutch East India Company (VOC) subsequently attempted to consolidate its control over Southeast Asia's spice exports by imposing a mercantile monopoly. Consequently, Southeast Asian upstream urban centers began to withdraw into relative isolation and thereby reversing the previous trends toward cosmopolitanism evolved in the dynamic fifteenth through mid-seventeenth century era. In common with "World Systems" theorists, Reid highlights the loss of the indigenous role in international trade, which he characterizes as "isolating, stagnating, and generally taking the vitality out of the Southeast Asian region."[6])

Reid places stress on the ultimate victory of Western power globally over local initiative and the subsequent dependency of the indigenous. This places him in direct opposition to a revisionist group of Southeast Asia scholars, who reject any possible period of dominance by an external entity prior to the nineteenth century. Those of the "Cornell School" in particular are reluctant to project their commentary beyond a single society to consider the existence of regional or global patterns, and search for a "localization" process that is ultimately controlled by an indigenous population, who over the long run are never submissive to forces external to the region, and are adept at reshaping the external into locally meaningful patterns.[7]) Reid, too, acknowledges a powerful indigenous base, but he postulates that circumstances radically changed when the Europeans and their "World System," which they willingly and capably imposed by force, made the region economically, politically, and, ultimately, culturally subordinate—initially in the Indonesian archipelago in the late seventeenth century and then region-wide in the nineteenth century.[8]) In common with both approaches, my task is to identify the body beneath the indigenous or foreign cloth as this may document the ebb and flow of Southeast Asia's textile manufacture and usage.

---

6) See I. Wallerstein, 1974, 1979; Wallerstein's writings are influenced by those of F. Braudel, 1974, 1976. Reid admittedly organized his *Age of Commerce* book consistent with Braudel's themes of analysis (A. Reid, 1988: xiv, xv).

7) The "Cornell School" view is restated in K. Taylor, 1992: 180-181. Cornell University/"Cornell School" scholarship was initially shaped by G. McT. Kahin, 1952. O.W. Wolters, 1992, introduces the concept of "localization" as the basis for comparative regional study of early societies; B. Anderson, 1990, reasserts the importance of "localized" study of individual cultures, and especially highlights how modern politics is often shaped by the indigenous historical tradition. Similar topical debate is introduced in D.D. Buck, 1994.

8) A. Reid, 1988: xv, 235. J. Kathirithamby-Wells, 1990, responds to Reid that there was an overall integrity and continuity within the Southeast Asian region, even in the critical seventeenth through nineteenth centuries, when the indigenous port-polities fell from their positions of eminence, and acquired a reduced but essential role at the lower levels of the new international commercial hierarchy. The authors in the *Port and Polity* book address region-wide and global patterns to substantiate the resiliency of autochthonous institutional traditions in the face of significant economic transitions within the Southeast Asian region.

Seventeenth Century Cloth Exchange in the Hikayat Banjar

Such a reference to the body beneath the cloth is a graphic allusion that I have found to be well-known to the people of the Southeast Asian region. Over the past several years I have conducted intermittent research on Banjarmasin, a trade center on the southern Borneo coast that became an important international source of pepper during the sixteenth and seventeenth century era that Reid considers so critical. Similar to other Malay states during that age, Banjarmasin produced a court chronicle that provides us with a window into the local setting. The authors of the most complete version of this stylized interpretive history, which reports the activities of the fifteenth through seventeenth century courts, are obsessed with the importance of proper dress among the local population. Dress was viewed by the chronicle authors as crucial to the success or the failure of the realm:

> ... everyone in the land ... had given up dressing in the [old] style. Young and old, male and female alike, dressed in the Javanese way. The king ... once said ... Let none of you [elite court dignitaries] dress like the Malays or the Hollanders or the Chinese or the Siamese or the Acehnese or the Makassarese or the Buginese [i.e., those with whom the local population traded]. Do not imitate any of them. You should not even follow [our] old customs of dress .... We have now set up a country of our own, following the ways and manners of Majapahit [Java]. Therefore we should all dress like the Javanese. According to the stories of olden times handed down by the elders, whenever the inhabitants of a country imitated the clothing of people from elsewhere, misery inevitably fell upon the country that had turned to foreign ways of dressing....⁹)

The *Hikayat* contains repeated reference to the dress of its characters, the court elite as well as subordinate commoners. A character's clothing was appropriate to his status. Further, cloth goods were prime commodities in gift-giving ceremonies that are a focal point of the *Hikayat* text.

There is common reference in archipelago sources to the double gifts (beyond food, which is widely used in gift exchanges) of cloth and metal (e.g., gold, silver, and iron). In these sources cloth bestows vitality, well-being, fertility, and connects the living to the spiritual or ancestral forces. Cloth also enhances the moral and legal obligations that bound partners to transactions. The *Hikayat Banjar* is thus representative of the Malay chronicle genre that depict the ceremonial function of cloth. The *Hikayat* reports the gradual conversion of Banjar to Islam during the fifteenth through seventeenth centuries. Frequent references to cloth, even in a rewriting of the chronicle that took place after Banjar's court had fully converted to Islam, demonstrates a value judgment on the local population's behalf. In making these textual revisions new values appropriate to a Muslim state were conveyed, yet there was a continuum of certain old values that provided the context for a legitimate transfer of power. Significantly, in the chronicle's account cloth exchanges were an integral part of the initial political transitions to Islamic rule, but once Islamic statecraft was established chronicle references to cloth exchanges ceased. Therein the chronicle provides documentation of a significant shift in court values.

In summary, cloth references in the *Hikayat Banjar* are of ten types:

1. *Curing disease.* Cloth was given as a reward to those who cured disease as well as to those among an audience who surrounded the ill person and in effect were participants (by being there) in the curing rituals.¹⁰)

---

9) J.J. Ras, 1968: 264-265.
10) *Ibid.*, 232-234, 438-439.

2. *Death rites*. At the death of a ruler "countless textiles of all kinds were handed out,"[11]) in addition to gold and silver coin gifts. There are two reasons implied. A redistribution of the wealth (cloth and metal) acquired by the deceased in life was taking place. First, the redistribution of such valuable commodities was a celebration of the dead monarch's successes in life; it conveyed symbolic honor on the deceased and also shared his success with the living, in theory leaving the living with items possessing stored magic. Second, the redistribution ushered the deceased into "the other," an existence beyond this life; it was a symbolic destruction (by redistribution) of the dead monarch's worldly possessions that allowed his clear break with the present material world.[12])

3. *Sanctifying icons*. Cloth gave power to statues or icons. Wooden, metal, or stone figures were powerless until ritually bestowed with perfumes and cloth.[13])

4. *Payments for services*. Cloth honored or paid craftsmen for services rendered, or was granted to others who performed services critical to the court. The honorific cloth presentation was stressed far more than was payment for services.[14])

5. *Tributary payments*. Cloth assumed an important role in tribute payments. Locally woven cloth made its way upward via local notables, who had collected cloth as part of their annual tribute (tax) collections that were due from their subject population, and who then passed a portion of the collected cloth on to the monarch. Fine (imported?) cloth moved downward as a reward for such tributary payments.[15]) The *Hikayat* text relates that when such exchanges took place all "would now live in peace, without killing each other any more, thanks to the effectiveness of . . . [the monarch's] rule."

6. *Decorating the royal compound*. Cloth decorated the royal palace, it covered ceilings and carpeted floors, and thereby set the stage, so to speak, for the status-bestowing ceremonies of the royal court.[16])

7. *Ceremonial display*. Cloth was the focal point of ceremonial events, an elaborate reference to the clothing and dress of participants is made in the *Hikayat*. Saturday audiences receive extensive attention, and were important displays of the clothing and dress that proclaimed the status and rank of those in attendance.[17])

---

11) *Ibid.*, 232-234.
12) On the importance of items endowed with power see S. Errington, 1989.
13) J. Ras, 1968: 240-241.
14) *Loc. cit.*
15) *Ibid.*, 242-243.
16) *Ibid.*, 234-235.
17) *Ibid.*, 248-249.

8. *D'plomatic exchanges.* Cloth was the basis of diplomatic exchanges. Royal envoys to China and Java received cloth gifts as reward for their services,[18]) but ceremonial cloth exchanges between the Chinese (Ming) and Java (Majapahit) monarchs and the Banjarmasin river basin monarchs' envoys were the dramatic climax in the *Hikayat*'s account of the diplomatic missions.

9. *Local mythology.* Cloth redefined and "localized" external myth. The *Hikayat* incorporated the widely-referenced legend of the marriage of the *naga* princess of the sea realm to the local ruler of the land. Locally this myth symbolized the unification of the land and the sea in a period in which the Banjarmasin river basin population was shifting its prime urban center. The myth was used to legitimate the transition from one culturally recognized political center to another. What is important beyond the use of this myth at this crucial juncture in local history is the Banjar chronicle's retelling of the myth, which focused on the clothing the *naga* princess wore. Since numerous earlier references to the myth in other Southeast Asian societies never place similar focus on the clothing/cloth of the characters,[19]) this version of the folk legend well demonstrates the seventeenth century cultural importance of cloth locally in Banjarmasin society, and in Southeast Asia more generally.

10. *Initiating historical change.* This enhanced value of cloth is also conveyed in the account of Banjarmasin's conversion to Islam. Cloth was the critical ingredient to the initiation and legitimation of Banjar's Islamic court. In the report of the Banjar transition the general story line is consistent with the conversion plots related among the various earlier Malay chronicles, which begin with the thirteenth century *Hikayat Raja Pasai.*[20]) But in the Banjar account the retelling again highlights elaborate reference to the dress of those involved, and proudly proclaims that a substantial quantity of traditionally valued cloth gifts were bestowed on all participants. Thereafter, though, the chronicle account shifts its tone. References to cloth exchanges and gifts abruptly cease after the ritual investiture of the new court. Instead the activities of the Islamic court are reported with three new topics that dominate the Hikayat account: law, the efficient organization of the state, and legitimate royal succession.

A partial rewrite of earlier versions of the chronicle was then undertaken to modify some pre-Islamic episodes and descriptions to accent these three themes. For instance, in a revised death bed scene a ruler leaves behind "kingly commands" (*perentah kerajaan*) as his fondest accomplishment,[21]) in contrast to the

---

18) *Ibid.,* 254ff.
19) *Ibid.,* 274-277. K.R. Hall, 1985: 50, 147.
20) A.H. Hill, 1960; K.R. Hall, 1977.
21) Ras, 1968, "Recension I," 3.2. Ras' "Recension I" is a composite of several surviving

same incident in the previous chronicle text in which emphasis was on the ruler's terminal pride in his accumulated tangible possessions.[22]) Accounts of the pre-Islamic state that stressed the apparel of state elite rather than their duties[23]) were rewritten to elaborate on the successful fulfillment of their administrative duties with no such concern for their proper attire.[24]) Interestingly, though, in the revised chronicle Islamic rulers still reiterated the traditional warning that to dress in foreign manner would cause the state to fail.[25]) But in this revised text to simply clothe in foreign manner would cause the government to fail, as opposed to earlier textual concerns voiced by monarchs that if foreign garments prevailed then local status distinctions would no longer be honored, and local society (not local government) would falter.

Other thirteenth through seventeenth century archipelago chronicle literature documents similar patterns of intensive cloth exchange. For example, the author of the *Nagarakertagama* Javanese chronicle poem that honors the fourteenth century Majapahit court, stipulates that parochial elite periodically provided ceremonial fabric and food gifts (local commodities) to the monarch and received metal (money) and personal merit (status) in return.[26]) The *Sejarah Melayu*, which "documents" the fifteenth and sixteenth century Melaka court and was the model for most of the subsequent Malay chronicle literature, provides even more elaborate reference to attire distinctions and redistributions of cloth. This selection from the Melaka chronicle addresses the central role of cloth in royal installation ceremonies:

> ... Robes of honor were brought in. If it was a Bendahara [the executive officer of the king] (who was being installed) five trays were used for the robes of honor: the jacket was laid on one, the headkerchief on another, the scarf on another, the waistband on another and the sarong on another. In the case of a prince or a minister or a royal warrior, there were four trays, the waistband being omitted. For a herald, courtier, or war-chief there were three trays only—one for the sarong, one for the jacket and the third for the headkerchief together with the scarf. Some were entitled to two trays only, one for the sarong and the other for the jacket and the headkerchief. In some cases all the articles of raiment were put on one tray, while in others there was no tray at all and the sarong, jacket, and headkerchief were just heaped together and borne on the raised and upturned hands of the bondservant who carried them. When they reached the man who was being installed, he folded his arms around them and took them outside ...

---

texts of the "written" *Hikayat*, in contrast to the earlier "Recension II," which is considered to be the written version of a previous local oral tradition.

22) Leiden Codex Or. 6664 ("Recension II"), 8aff.; this text is summarized with commentary in A.A. Cense, 1928.

23) J.J. Ras, 1968: 248-249.

24) *Ibid.*, 460-461.

25) *Ibid.*, 442-443.

26) Th.G.Th. Pigeaud, 1960-1963: 31.2, 32.1.4, 33.1.3.

where he put them on. He then came in again and was invested with frontlet and arm-
lets. The procedure was the same in regard to robes of honor for envoys, each envoy
being treated according to his rank . . . .[27])

In contrast to these later references, a different type of gift exchange takes
place in the Telaga Batu inscription from the seventh century Srivijaya realm,
one of the first written records of Malay history.[28]) Here the literary focus is on
a curse and magic that brings prosperity (or failure). But the inscription, which
is written on a ceremonial stone that is guarded by the seven-headed *naga* of
Buddhist tradition, and which reports an oath of allegiance to the monarch that
was sworn via the consumption of water that was poured over the inscription
and its oath, warns that those who did not honor their ruler "will be killed by
the curse of [this] imprecation . . . you will be punished with your children, your
wives, your prosperity, your clans, and your friends." But, "if you are submissive to me and do no harm [against me], an immaculate *tantra-mala* will be
my recompense [to you]. You will not be swallowed with your children and
wives . . . eternal peace will be the fruit produced by the curse which is drunk
by you."[29])

While the later focus of the Malay chronicles was on the material "this
worldly," the Telaga Batu inscription is concerned with the magical "other
worldly." The response to the gift of loyalty by his subjects was the monarch's
reciprocity of a life beyond this world (a return beyond this world) that is never
an option in the *Hikayat* accounts.[30]) The implication of the Telaga Batu inscription is that reciprocity in this world would lose one unseen "fruit." The inscription seems to state that gifts returned materially reaped their own reward, and
were a matter of worldly reciprocity. This by extension is not different from the
act of buying or selling. That is, material gifts reciprocated by material gifts are
like market transactions, whereby one has something to show for one's efforts,
in contrast to special gifts that are not of this world and that are beyond repayment—of the *tantra-mala* sort.

In the later Malay chronicles there is no option of repayment in another
world, only of a material reciprocity in this world. This is reflected in the following account of a redistribution at the death of a Banjarmasin ruler:

---

27) C.C. Brown, 1952: 46-47.
28) K.R. Hall, 1985: 81-102.
29) This translation is from the transcription of the original text as published in J.G. de
Casparis, 1956: 15-46.
30) A discussion of the applicability of the anthropological concepts of "reciprocity" and
"redistribution" in early Southeast Asia is provided in P. Wheatley, 1975: 227-283. See also
Hall, 1992: 270-272.

> ... Countless textiles of all kinds were handed out by way of alms-giving, thousands of dinars (gold coins) and tens of thousands of reals (silver coins) were strewn in the streets. Everyone taking part in the ceremonies was pleased.[31])

Regular corporeal reward as acknowledgment of the stature of those who faithfully served the monarch is an important theme in these Malay chronicles. This was the case in the above citation from the *Sejarah Melayu* as well as in the following description of an investiture at the Banjar court:

> ... The king presented [this man of status] with ten men and ten women [as bondservants], four scores of fine batik clothes and four sets of clothes. Four accompanying elders each received three sets of clothes, another dignitary received two, and ten sea-captains one set each....[32])

This episode from the seventeenth century *Hikayat Banjar* text downplays the mythical aspects of royal authority and instead highlights the material symbols of royal power:

> ... When this whole organization of the state was established the king ... every Saturday received his dignitaries in the audience-hall where he was surrounded by his court-ladies.... and forty pages, all wearing a scarf adorned with gold and fringed with precious stones, and carrying his golden mat, his casket made of gold and encrusted with diamonds and opals, his boxes for betel and lime—these were made of gold and encrusted with emeralds and chyroysolites—, his tobacco box—a gold cock of state encrusted with luminous gems—and his pipe which was made of gold and had a bowl of carbuncle [all of these were magically endowed possessions of the monarch]. The king wore a purple *kain* [cloth wrap] which was embroidered with gold and studded with emeralds, a batik sash bearing a *garingsing* pattern [a diagonal batik pattern reserved exclusively for royalty] with the ornamentation of gold, and a kris with a wavy blade adorned with applied filigree edging.... He had two state sunshades, that is, fringed umbrellas embroidered with gold-thread, four state blowpipes adorned with a mesh of gold, state lances with applied golden ornamentation on the blades, four with sheaths of yellow brocade [*ikat*, or striped cloth of silk, gold, or silver thread inlays], four of red, four of white, four of green and four of black....[33])

Thus the thirteenth through seventeenth century Malay sources reflect movement to a material (market) culture in which cloth was central, but there is even earlier evidence of this transition. While the noted seventh century Malay inscription from Sumatra may stress reward beyond this world, there is no reason to conclude that a sense of the material was absent in Srivijaya. There are no epigraphic references to cloth exchanges, yet contemporary Arab records relate that at the death of the Srivijaya ruler the deceased monarch's wealth (represented by gold bars that were daily deposited in the local river) were redistributed to

---

31) J.J. Ras, 1968: 232-233.
32) *Ibid.*, 308-309.
33) *Ibid.*, 250-251; on the importance of royal symbols of authority in this era see S. Errington, 1989.

his loyal following in rank order. Local Buddhist statuary provides additional evidence of a developing material culture. In contrast to what we know from Arabic and Chinese sources to have been the indigenous bark cloth norm of that place and time,[34]) deceased monarchs, who were memorialized in stone as Bodhisattvas, are clothed in the garb appropriate to rulers of an "Indic" court: Indian-style long cotton skirts draped and folded in-front-of the body and held with clasps, belts, and sashes. But unlike the contemporary standard of Buddhist dress in India, which required cloth covering of a monk's top, Srivijaya's royalty are portrayed bare-chested, except for an abundance of jewelry and ornaments that displayed personal wealth in a manner totally inappropriate of one who was supposedly free from worldly attachments.[35])

Marcel Mauss' writing on *The Gift* provides a useful theoretical construct relative to these Malay sources. Mauss argued that there were three stages in the evolution of societies from "traditional" to "modern." In the first stage of "total prestation," familial gift-giving predominated. This was a gift-giving with little concern for repayment in kind: persons and things were fused (as opposed to a "law" of persons and a "law" of things). In contrast Mauss perceived a second stage in which there is a gift competition wherein society is characterized by obligatory giving, receiving, and reciprocity. Gifts are extensions of a giver's self and require return in this world or the next. To receive is to become dependent, to lose one's superiority, but to refuse to receive from a potential superior is a statement of one's own superiority and may require actions to support one's refusal. Expected reciprocity may be of this world, but there may also be a return beyond this world. The third stage is characterized by a society in which exchanges in this world are the only possibility, where one loses the potential to receive (or give) unseen fruit and all is reduced to marketplace-like transactions, which are not different from sale and purchase transactions that result in transfers of ordinary material goods. Personal bonds that were secured via earlier gift exchanges were replaced by impersonal calculated and calculatory redistributions, purchases, and sales.[36])

Indeed there is an indigenous perception of the Maussian stages of evolution as the *Hikayat Banjar* warns against the approaching material (market) culture. This movement towards a material (market) economy is associated with the development of commercial pepper growth as well as inappropriate dress. The

---

34) M. Gittinger, 1989: 237-238.

35) T.W. Rhys Davids and H. Oldenberg, 1965-1969; see below. For examples of Srivijaya statuary see C. Holt, 1967: 37; and Hall, 1985: 87. On the debate among scholars relative to association of past rulers with Indonesian iconography, especially the depiction of their facial images ("portrait sculpture"), see J. Fontein, 1990: 54-55.

36) M. Mauss, 1966: *passim*.

THE TEXTILE INDUSTRY IN SOUTHEAST ASIA, 1400-1800   99

Hikayat authors warn that when such actions became common the general population would no longer remain subordinate to the elite and the farmers and other non-aristocrats would go their own way:

> ... The rural people will become pretentious towards the townsfolk [i.e., the court elite] if pepper is grown for commercial purposes ... for the sale of money [i.e., a commercial economy].[37])

Thus strict social and economic controls were imposed:

> ... No one dressed like the Makassarese or Buginese [the principle maritime trade communities in the eastern archipelago]. No one was allowed to plant more than a few pepper trees per head, just enough for private consumption only. If more should be planted for the purpose of making money, this would bring misery over the country: prices would go up and much malice would result; instructions from above would not be executed because people would lack respect for the king ... the government would fall into disorder, because the people [would] follow foreign customs of dress.[38])

When in the seventeenth century commercial pepper growth expanded it seemed perfectly reasonable to the chronicle's authors that social stability ceased. This move toward market-based materialism and away from local tradition resulted in Banjarmasin's fall to the Dutch in the early 1700s. Just prior to its demise a member of the court elite warned:

> ... in the future ... this place Banjarmasin will go to ruin, for it is like a banana-tree in front of one's gate, too many people take an interest in it. Since this place lies near the sea it is an easy prey for an enemy.... [Some time later] the Hollanders came. Four ships anchored ... and bombarded the town. [Although various court members, including the ruler, asserted that they could defeat the Dutch, the monarch made the decision to move his court inland] ... there they blocked the river with a barrier ... and carried away the vegetation on the opposite bank. Then they started to raid the Hollanders, but these fled and dared not fight [from their new urban base the local population continued to successfully participate in the external trade, but with a renewed commitment to traditional values]....[39])

Southeast Asian Textile Consumptive Patterns: 1400-1800

While the Malay chronicle literature thus highlights the importance of cloth in the developing material culture, one may also come to terms with this transition by a study of local patterns of production. The complexity of local cloth production in the seventeenth century is conveyed in the *Hikayat Banjar*:

> ... forty maidens set to work on the yellow [cotton ceremonial cloth]: some of them did the picking, some did the rolling, some the bowing, some the pulling, some wound

---

37) J.J. Ras, 1968: 264-265.
38) *Ibid.*, 442-443.
39) *Ibid.*, 462-465; D.G.E. Hall, 1981: 563-564.

Map II. *Early Southeast Asian Centers of Trade.*

the fiber on spindles, some did the spinning, some wound the yarn on reels, some did the dyeing, some the combing and others did the weaving. . . .[40])

While earlier textile production did not involve this degree of specialization, there was no less labor implicit to local cloth manufacture.

Southeast Asians commonly wore high quality indigenous textiles made of inner tree and shrub fibers (bast) well into the sixteenth century. When he arrived in the Moluccas in 1521, Antonio Pigafetta described how the women of Tidore made cloth of beaten bark by soaking it in water until it was soft:

---

40) J.J. Ras, 1968: 274-275.

... They then beat it with bits of wood and thus make it as long and as fine as they wish. It becomes like a veil of raw silk and has certain threads within it which appear as if woven.[41])

Bark cloth of everyday use was plain or very simply decorated with dyed or painted geometric symbols, or stylized depictions of humans or animals. The cloth was made by boiling, soaking, and fermenting the bast, which was then beaten into cloth fiber with wooden or stone mallets. The bark cloth texture ranged from rough to a soft paper-like quality, and took two to nine days to produce, dependent upon the quality.[42]) What we know about bark cloth is largely derived from our study of current production; the Toraja populations of Sulawesi are conceded to make the bark cloth of the highest technical and artistic level, but there is also sophisticated production among surviving upland hunters and gathers.[43]) Among these tribal groups bark cloth is used in rites of age passage: birth, circumcision, tooth filing, tattooing, marriage, and death. Some scholars believe that the practice of tattooing was a symbolic complement to the minimal coverage afforded by bark cloth.[44]) Since bark cloth had to be removed lest it disintegrate in the rain,[45]) tattooing was a continuous means of protecting a man (or woman) from natural harm.

Bark cloth, as with other Southeast Asian textiles, is made exclusively by women, who clean and spin the threads and weave patterns. These "women's goods" are associated with fertility and life-giving properties—women alone can take beings (i.e., bearing children) through the passage between this world and "the other." Textiles, which are products of woman's creative powers, can likewise provide protective passage. Thus cloth is not just a useful object, but can transform. In producing bark cloth (as well as later cotton textiles) women provide structure to previously raw and natural materials, through the processing, weaving, and dyeing process. Metaphorically spinning thread is equivalent to bonding the parts of the soul and creating "the thread of life;" weaving cloth in turn creates life itself—it bestows protection and fertility on the wearer as well as the broader community.[46])

Often there are strong traditional prohibitions against cutting cloth. To do so would unleash life's powers in potentially harmful ways, and would minimally destroy the protective powers of the cloth. Cloth can only be cut by those endowed with sufficient powers to neutralize the cloth's potential danger: women,

41) J.A. Robertson, 1906: II, 89; discussed in B.W. Andaya, 1989: 29.
42) P.M. Taylor and L.U. Argon, 1991: 198.
43) The Miao/Hmong of upland Thailand and Laos, for example. See W.R. Geddes, 1976.
44) W. Warming and M. Gaworski, 1981: 56.
45) Antonio Pigafetta (1524), in J.A. Robertson, ibid.
46) M. Gittinger, 1979: 28-30; and S. Kooijman, 1963.

who are perceived to be inherently more spiritually empowered than men, and "men of prowess," local chiefs, kings, or others who have demonstrated their special linkage to "the other" due to their "feats of merit."[47]) In some societies the female act of weaving cotton or silk cloth received its complement in the process of dyeing, which was done by men in secret rituals where outsiders were forbidden.[48]) Earliest dyeing reproduced the symbolic colors of life itself: brown of the earth and blue of the heaven were placed on the white of the air. These metaphysical principles were expanded by symbolic forms such as plants, animals, pavilions, and mountains.

It is undoubtedly significant that references to bark cloth in Southeast Asian languages are always in an indigenous form, while those to cotton and silk derive from Sanskrit.[49]) This seems appropriate since the first widespread use of cotton textiles coincides with the rise of the initial Indic-style courts in the first centuries of the Christian era. Local populations made use of "powerful" and "magically endowed" Indian and Chinese textile imports, the control of which reinforced the quest for status among the early self-styled "Indic" monarchs.[50]) Srivijaya's seventh century statuary synthesis of Indic and traditional clothing styles is representative of other primary regional sculpture and icons; even more telling is the early temple architecture that conspicuously incorporated iconographic carvings of draped Indic and Chinese textiles, which must reflect actual usage.[51]) Consistent with Southeast Asia's other adaptations of Indic and Chinese cultures, primordial use of cloth stressed its magical properties. Stone, wood, or metal statues and temples or shrines were powerless until they were properly wrapped in cloth; this is still the case today in Bali and much of the eastern Indonesian archipelago.[52]) In Thailand, the Thai monarch has since the

---

47) R. Barnes, 1989: 17, 31-32.

48) M. Gittinger, 1979: 120, which cites two examples from Java, wherein men traditionally dyed the indigo blue color; in contrast see R. Barnes, 1989: 16, 31-32:

Whenever I asked whether a man, or even a small boy, might participate [in the dyeing of threads] I was told that this was not done. However, I was assured many times that there was no prohibition associated with dyeing. Men or boys were not strictly prohibited from participating; it was not "man's work . . ." (p. 31).

49) R. Maxwell, 1990: 155.

50) S.J. Tambiah, 1976.

51) H.W. Woodward, Jr., 1977. This reference is to a silk cloth that was carved on the wall of a ninth century temple in central Java. Documentation of cloth's early cultural importance is provided in contemporary Javanese inscriptions, in which one of the ritual gifts most frequently mentioned is cloth. See A.B. Jones, 1984: 33. On the dress of early Indonesian statuary in contrast to that of India compare J. Fontein, 1990: plates 35, 36, 39, 58, and 59.

52) In Banjarmasin, for example, royal power in the pre-Islamic court was initiated symbolically when statues were carved and then vested with cloth; only when the cloth was placed did the icons have power. Likewise, the king's audience hall had to be properly draped with rich textiles to legitimate the reciprocal gift exchanges that took place there on a weekly basis. J.J. Ras, 1968: 240-241, 262-263, 274-275.

origin of the Thai state personally changed the clothing of the Emerald Buddha, the most sacred of Thai icons, the symbolic source of Thai sovereignty as well as Thai well-being, at the three seasonal transitions in the Thai calendar.[53]) Temples and icons in India have never been similarly dependent on an appropriate cloth garb to vest them with power. Visibly, thus, Southeast Asians accommodated the Indian form, but gave it a Southeast Asian character. This initial synthesis was based on indigenous perceptions of physical prowess, which was enhanced by the possession and wearing of powerful and symbolic foreign cloth. But native cloth alone had the independent capacity to bestow good or bad fortune on the holder.

Southeast Asian textile weavers initially incorporated magical Indian religious symbols into their bark cloth production, and, by the sixteenth century, began to duplicate the more durable imported Indian cotton cloth.[54]) One important distinction, however, was that in Southeast Asia women continued to dominate not only cloth production but also its marketing.[55]) In India, by contrast, male dominance of the weaving industry evolved as the external market for South Asian cotton textiles increased. Women may have woven cotton textiles, but Indian men controlled its production and distribution.[56])

Barbara Watson Andaya documents the transitions in the textile market of Sumatra that mark this conversion to cotton textiles.[57]) By the twelfth century Sumatra ports were importing Chinese silk for court consumption. This lay the groundwork for Gujarati and south Indian merchants, who became dominant in the sixteenth century by trading their silk and cotton cloth for pepper.[58]) The

---

53) S.J. Tambiah, 1976: 97.

54) B. Solyom and G. Solyom, 1984: 3-8; M. Gittinger, 1979; and J. Boow, 1988: 21.

55) B.W. Andaya, 1989: 26-46.

56) T. Raychaudhuri and I. Habib, 1982: I (1200-1750), 77, 315. See also K.R. Hall, 1980: 114-116.

57) B.W. Andaya, 1989. Andaya's study is largely based on Dutch and English "company" sources.

58) On the emergence of the Gujarati merchants as the dominant agents in the international maritime trade in Southeast Asia during the sixteenth century see P.-Y. Manguin, 1993. Manguin makes the case that Gujarati (and Chinese) merchants successfully allied with the elite of new states to the detriment of local merchants. Foreign merchants could be more easily controlled than locally-based merchants who might have their own client networks (indeed, in Aceh the local merchant community briefly seized control of the state in the sixteenth century), and could guarantee access to the two products most desired locally: namely cloth and guns. Assertion of Gujarati merchant dominance in archipelago ports-of-trade during this era is challenged in a new study by S. Arasaratnam, 1994, which argues that south Indian merchants, not Gujaratis, were Sumartra's favored trading partners and that south Indian textiles, not those of Gujarat, were the mass market preference through the seventeenth century. This book revises previous views (e.g., Manguin) of the Indic role in the interactive Southeast Asian port-polity.

key in this transition to cotton textiles was the increase in international demand for Sumatra's pepper, which induced a market for imported textiles at the
lower levels of Sumatra society. In this first mass market, coarse cotton textiles
became the commodity of exchange demanded by the pepper growers of the Sumatra hinterland.[59])

Andaya probes why Indian textiles and seafarers gained this market dominance. One explanation is cultural. Sumatra's elite, who had recently converted
to Islam, favored traders from India who shared a common textual tradition.[60])
By their support of Islam, Sumatra's court elite were able to enter direct diplomatic dialogue with the Ottoman centers of power in the Middle East. Local
rulers derived enhanced stature through their regular exchanges with the other
leading Muslim courts that shared the Indian Ocean. They also secured military
advisors and guns with which to assert and protect their power in an age in
which regular armed competition among increasingly militarized Southeast
Asian states was the norm.[61])

There were also technical reasons for the Indic success. The spread of Islam
into India in the fourteenth century introduced carding bows and spinning
wheels, which made cotton production more efficient. With this new technology
Gujarati and Coromandel weavers were able to offer greater variety in pattern,
color, texture, and size, and the market value of their textiles was further
enhanced when in the seventeenth century the European trading companies
brought out dyers to teach Indian craftsmen how to produce certain new and
more permanent colors.[62])

In the seventeenth century when specie temporarily became scarce, due to
declines in the transmission of silver from American and Japanese sources and
the coincident unavailability of Chinese lead picis,[63]) cotton textiles took the
place of coinage in numerous Southeast Asian marketplaces.[64]) Textiles were
more durable and had greater variety of local use. That is, cloth had real mar-

---

59) The Chinese were by that time producing four grades of silk. The cheaper varieties
were used to secure Southeast Asian pepper. See E. Zen Sun, 1972: 79-108.
60) B.W. Andaya, 1989: 32; see also A. Reid, 1993c. Reid stresses the sharing of a common textual tradition; part of the local appeal of Islam was as the universalistic alternative
to Christianity and its assertive counter-reformation era Portuguese and Spanish advocates.
The proposition that the India-based merchants gained a market advantage because they were
Muslim is supported by the fact that Chinese merchants who regularly worked out of
Southeast Asian archipelago ports commonly converted to Islam (see below).
61) See also A. Reid, 1993b: 12-14; and P.-Y. Manguin, 1993.
62) Citing T. Raychaudhuri and I. Habib, 1982: I, 77-81, 269, 282.
63) A. Reid, 1990: 646-649. See also W.S. Atwell, 1986: 229.
64) B.W. Andaya, 1993: 104-105; see also L. Andaya, 1993: 33. By contrast, V. Lieberman, 1993: 234, documents increased use of coinage in Burmese market transactions in this
supposed age of "crisis."

ket value as well as symbolic ceremonial worth in a society in which those with wealth found their potential for return to be greater if they invested in service and status rather than long-term material investments—expenditures to acquire patronage and manpower were the basis of personal security and power.[65])

By the sixteenth century peasant women in Sumatra and elsewhere found it more profitable to cultivate pepper or other cash crops rather than weave.[66]) There was so much international competition for their products, and such an oversupply of imported textile available that local populations could even dictate their market preferences for colors and designs, which frequently changed from floral patterns to stripes and from one color to another. Sumatra's consumers were especially noted to demand novelty. The Minangkabau favored black and white bafta cotton cloth—black was for everyday wear and white was for burials; red was universally considered to offer protection; yellow and white were widely reserved for royalty;[67]) light blue was desired by Sumatrans, but Javanese considered it "common;" and green was prized among Malay Muslims because it was a color worn by the Prophet, and therefore only a few significant elite might wear it.

By the seventeenth century Chinese traders based in Southeast Asia's ports gained a market advantage on the Europeans, who only offered the corge, a pack of twenty cloth pieces. Chinese traders were willing to deal in smaller cloth lots and to regularly take smaller profit margins; they would also carry debt for several seasons.[68]) Also, Chinese were more sensitive to the importance of women in the indigenous market system, and thus used local women as their trade agents. In Sumatra, for example, seafaring merchants "bought" female bondservants, and resident Chinese merchants reinforced their local roots by adopting Islam and taking a local wife.[69]) In either case local women supervised cloth shops and assisted in the pepper buying trips into the hinterlands, where most of the transactions of exchange were negotiated with women producers. Chinese merchants were so successful as economic middlemen in Sumatra's pepper trade that Europeans began to regularly use the Chinese as their agents in the upstream trade. There, however, these Chinese commercial specialists encountered a good deal of competition from local traders in a rapidly evolving and hierarchical marketing system.[70])

---

65) J. Kathirithamby-Wells, 1993: 123-148.

66) B.W. Andaya, 1989: 33; L. Andaya, 1993: 33.

67) As stipulated in the *Sejarah Melayu*: "White was more strictly a royal privilege than yellow, white . . . was reserved for rulers while yellow . . . could be used by princes . . . (C.C. Brown, 1952: 44)."

68) B.W. Andaya. 1993: 104-109.

69) B.W. Andaya, 1989: 36. On bondage in early Southeast Asia see A. Reid, 1983.

70) B.W. Andaya, 1993: 103-104.

While the Sumatra market system placed the foreign-based businessman at a significant disadvantage, the foreign tradesman's problems were even more pronounced in meeting the demands of the courts. Because of the universal consumption of imported textiles, foreign traders were constantly under pressure to derive new cloth that the courts might use to distinguish themselves from commoners in their own dress as well as in their gifts to subordinates. The courts, which might otherwise have been hesitant to regulate commercial activities in their ports, thus imposed strict regulations wherein the courts had first choice among all cloth imports—not for the court's direct economic benefit, but to provide for its political, cultural, and social needs.[71])

In the late seventeenth century there was a transition in the Sumatra cloth market, which was mostly precipitated by the decay of the international pepper market, but was also a consequence of political upheaval within India that had a negative consequence to India's export of inexpensive textiles. There was a resulting overall rise in the market price of Indian textiles and a corresponding decline in the quality of India's less expensive exports.[72]) What is most significant about the seventeenth century commercial restructuring in Southeast Asia is that there was no local retreat from the marketplace. Due to the widespread penetration of the international market system into the upriver hinterlands, local societies had become culturally if not economically dependent upon foreign cloth. Instead of withdrawing into self-sufficiency there was energetic readjustment to maintain the recently evolved marketing networks. The incentive was local desire to sustain access to imported cotton textiles, which were by that time considered to be necessities of life.

---

71) There is a good deal of debate whether Southeast Asia's ports-of-trade were regulated: did Southeast Asia's monarchs directly participated in trade for profit; what were the nature of royal monopolies; were the ports-of-trade subject to the direct administration of indigenous bureaucrats, or were port marketplaces largely controlled by the local and foreign merchants under royal alliance? See J. Kathirithamby-Wells, 1990, 1993. B.W. Andaya, 1993, makes a strong case that when the Jambi port's market became overly regulated by Jambi's court elite in the eighteenth century (in alliance with the Dutch, who wished to equally salvage their fortune in the face of the diminished pepper trade) the upstream populations shifted their marketing alliances to other ports, especially to the less-regulated Palembang marketplace.

72) S. Arasaratnam, 1986: 272, 336-341; O. Prakash, 1985: 144; A. Das Gupta, 1979: 7-8; M.N. Pearson, 1976, 1991: 52-61, 96-100, 105-116. There is general agreement among these sources that the Indian weaving industry began to concentrate on the production of higher priced quality textiles in response to new political circumstances, namely the demise of Mughal authority, as well as new international marketing patterns. India's major producers began to deemphasize the manufacture of the less profitable quality low-priced cotton cloth for the import-export market. With the decline of international demand for pepper and spices, and new emphasis on the China market as the foundation of the international trade, there was no longer need to produce lower cost quality textiles to entice Southeast Asia's peasant producers.

Local consumers responded to these seventeenth century adjustments in the price and quality of the available Indian textiles by pursuing alternative fabrics and found them regionally. There was no significant decline in the Sumatra market system, but only a decline in local demand for high priced and poor quality Indian textiles. With limited potential to market their pepper at a price they considered commensurate to their labor input, and continuing high demand for cotton textiles, Sumatra's peasant producers shifted to cotton as their principal cash crop. Some of this cotton was consumed locally, as native producers began to weave their own cotton cloth, but there was also demand among the new regional weaving centers that emerged to supply reasonably priced quality textiles. Thai and Cambodian cloth initially helped to fill this void. Java's batik gained a significant market share in the late seventeenth and early eighteenth centuries, partially due to "Javanization" campaigns among a number of Malay courts, although there was some consumer reluctance due to local feeling that Java's batik cloth was too subdued and concern that Java's dyes were impermanent. Java's weavers responded to the new regional market opportunities by producing wider variety of textile designs:

> The trend in the late seventeenth century can clearly be seen in Java where local textile production was increasing. By the 1680s Javanese favored their own "painted cloth" over imported Coromandel textiles.[73]) In 1683 the cargoes of Javanese cloth arriving in Jambi and Palembang had become so great that there was a short-lived attempt by the Dutch to extend their monopoly of Indian fabrics to cover all cloth. The great attraction of Javanese imports was the price. Whereas the Dutch sold Indian piece goods for an average of 1-2 reals [of silver], those from Java could cost as little as .25 real each and were even said to be of superior quality and more durable than their Indian counterparts. In 1691 when a Dutch envoy visited Palembang he noted that most of the men "from the king to the lowest peddlers" were wearing Javanese and Madurese cloth. Though most were termed "*bobar tsjankring* [canting?]" he distinguished a number of styles. Two popular designs featured "blue flowers with tendrils" and "a purple background with sprinkles." Another smaller cloth was called simply *batik*, "rough blue flowers on a white ground" which was mostly worn by children, as was another Madurese type, white and thin, called *sampan*.[74])

Barbara Andaya argues that although some old centers such as Jambi and Aceh declined in this era, due to a complexity of circumstances that were only partially a consequence of new European initiatives, distinct states such as Palembang and Minangkabau took their place, and these vigorous courts and their

---

73) T. Raychaudhuri, 1962: 162.
74) B.W. Andaya, 1989: 40, drawing from V.O.C. 1498 Isaac van Tihije to Batavia 22 June 1691, fols. 60v-61v. On the transitions in textile design and production in Java during this era see P. Kitley, 1992: 5-10. Continuing complaints over the impermanence of Java's dyes were not resolved until the nineteenth century, when batik production was standardized (see below).

elite maintained their demand for the brightly colored, gold embroidered, and fine silk textiles typical of India.[75]) Andaya notes that among these elite price was never a factor, but a lack of quality merchandise was. Thus these courts, largely through the initiative of court women, avoided European economic monopolies by financing economic expeditions by land or sea to seek alternative textile supply sources, including India itself. When these efforts proved inadequate, they even resorted to weaving their own high quality cloth from raw silk thread they acquired from Thailand and China. They also developed their own ability to affect effective dyeing. The result was the high-quality Palembang gold and silk thread weaving tradition that continues today.[76]) Thus the Palembang and Minangkabau courts created their own alternatives by securing or producing quality textiles. Due to these successful initiatives eighteenth century court dress protocol changed, wherein the silk sarong displaced the Javanese style kain (wrapped cloth) as fashionable male dress.

This evidence concerning the western archipelago's cloth trade is inconsistent with Reid's characterization of a seventeenth century region-wide crisis. In Reid's view Southeast Asia's response to the collapse of the spice market, which was coincident to an imposed Western economic monopoly over Southeast Asia's external trade, was one of withdrawal into economic and cultural stasis. Barbara Andaya's research on Sumatra, as well as the noted studies by Lieberman on Burma and Dhjiravat na Pombejra on Thailand, refute the notion of withdrawal or monopoly in this early modern era, but instead point to new regional patterns of trade that were less dependent upon European trading partners to sustain the local economies or to stimulate their evolution to higher levels of social welfare.[77])

---

75) B.W. Andaya, 1993: 109-121; and *idem*, 1989: 41-45. Other examples of local response to new international market opportunities (wherein foreign cloth was the central commodity in foreign exchanges for local product) are provided in Burma, where the new Ava-based Burmese state encouraged local response to new Indian Ocean demand for teak, cotton, and tea (Lieberman, 1993: 226, 232), and the Ayutthaya-based Thai state, which exported deerskins, tin, sappanwood and elephants to secure Indian textiles from India, which "were considered to be essential imports by the Siamese court." D. Pombejra, 1993: 263-265.

76) M. Gittinger, 1979: 102; R. Maxwell, 1990: 380-381.

77) V. Lieberman, 1993, reports new Burmese trade partnerships in the Bay of Bengal as well as new overland routes to South China and east to Thailand, but perhaps even more important was the development of the internal marketing system, wherein the trade in textiles was an important variable. In the case of Thailand, Ayutthya based monarchs excluded their former trade partners the French, who were major players in the affairs of the Thai court until a 1688 "coup." In their place the new Thai court elite renewed a long-standing relationship with the Dutch (who held a royal monopoly in the trade of deerskins), enhanced the role of India-based "Moor" merchants (who supplied the court with quality Indian textiles from south India's Coromandel coast), and bestowed the role of royal favorites on Chinese traders, who represented the Thai court's interests in the lucrative "triangular" trade among

What emerges from this revisionist scholarship is a depiction of a period of fluctuation rather than crisis, wherein new regional patterns of exchange emerged to nourish newly integrating societies. The key to this vernacular resiliency was that once the populations of the hinterlands became integrated into externally linked marketing networks, village societies in addition to the urbanized courts became culturally dependent on cotton textiles, which were initially supplied by foreign merchants. When international demand for local pepper and spices dissipated there was no corresponding demise in parochial demand for cloth. Due to widespread cultural change neither court nor countryside desired to return to the premarket existence that favored upper torso nudity and bark cloth, and in which material possessions had little role in determining status. Thus when the international traders could no longer supply sufficient quantities of reasonably priced and high quality Indian textiles, Southeast Asia's populations readily pursued new options. One solution was to circumvent the Europeans, who continued to market India's textiles, to pursue lower priced quality textiles that were yielded by Southeast Asia's new regional weaving centers.[78] Another was to produce their own, by modifying older barkcloth manufacturing techniques. New patterns of textile consumption and production were ultimately a consequence of local judgment relative to existing cultural values as well as efficient use of one's fruitful time.

Southeast Asia's Textile Production: 1400-1800

Southeast Asia did not have to import cotton. Regions with a sufficient dry season, such as east Java, central Sumatra, Bali, Lombok, south Sulawesi, Sumbawa, Luzon, Cebu, and Cambodia produced and sold raw cotton, which was cultivated alongside wet-rice fields. Their market was their wetter neighboring regions: the Malay Peninsula, southern Sumatra, the southern Philippines, Borneo, and Maluku, and the largely barren "Spice Islands" of the eastern Indonesian

Thailand, China, and Japan (D. Pombejra, 1993: 257-270). See also Arasaratnam, 1994, relative to Indic networking in the Bay of Bengal during this era.

78) B.W. Andaya, 1993: 110, reports the Dutch attempt to secure a cloth trade monopoly over the Jambi river basin in the 1680s, wherein the Dutch negotiated a contract with the local ruler that allowed them to be exclusive agents of Indian cloth, to the exclusion of other types of cloth that were locally traded by indigenous and Chinese merchants. As a consequence the upland populations refocused their trade on neighboring Palembang, which remained an openly competitive port. In the 1683-1684 trading season the Dutch trading lodge in Palembang made a profit of 37,570 guilders from pepper purchases and cloth sales, while during the 1684-1685 season the Dutch profit in Jambi was only 2,868 guilders: "The piles of textiles that lay unsold and rotting in the Dutch warehouse told their own story, and native traders fared little better than the VOC ... there were no customers."

Fig. 1. "A Weaver near Todo, West Flores, Indonesia, May 1965" Photograph by
Mattiebelle Gittinger/The Textile Museum, Washington, D.C.

archipelago. By the nineteenth century French visitors reported that Cambodia
nurtured enough cotton along the Mekong north of Phnom Penh to "supply all
of Cochin-China"—the French subsequently constructed textile factories in Vietnam
to furnish this marketplace. Between the thirteenth and seventeenth centuries
some Southeast Asian cotton yarn and cloth was even taken back to China by
returning traders from ports in Java, Luzon, and Vietnam. At least by the seventeenth century there was a large-scale cotton yarn trade from the dry regions
of Burma up the Irrawaddy and along caravan routes into Yunnan.[79] The importance of cotton as a viable cash crop was acknowledged by Europeans, who
made their first demands for colonial tribute in terms of local cloth in Java,
Makassar, and Luzon.[80]

---

79) V. Lieberman, 1993: 226, 232.
80) A. Reid, 1988: 90-92.

The first cotton textiles were produced on simple back-strap tension looms, a two-bar frameless loom with a back strap, belt, or yoke passing around the weaver's back and secured to a breast beam located in front of the weaver. A second beam, called the warp beam, is secured to a tree or a house pole. The thread that is strung between these two beams is called the warp thread; thread woven through the warp threads is called the weft. Back strap looms are usually as wide as the arm span of the weaver, who thus weaves relatively narrow strips of cloth about fifty-five centimeters in width. Larger pieces of cloth are the result of sewing two smaller pieces together.[81] Textiles produced on back strap tension looms are woven in a continuous circular warp; as the cloth is woven it is wound around the breast beam. These cotton cloth cylinders continue the tradition of bark cloth, which is woven on these same simple looms,[82] and symbolize the continuous flow of life itself; cutting of the unwoven ends of the cloth was often ritualized, and could be cut only by those community members (inclusive of the woman producer) with sufficient magical prowess to contain the potentially harmful powers inherent to the cloth.[83] Herein local society adapted technology consistent with culturally defined need.

Indonesian textile weavers were the first to employ warp stripe *lurik* and warp *ikat* production methods. In the warp stripe lurik technique different colored thread is strung between the warp beam and the breast beam to produce stripes. Ikat is a dye-resist method of decorating warp threads, which are laid out length-wise on a frame and then counted into "ikat" sections. Each section contains a group of threads that are bound together as a unit to resist the dye. Several ikat bundles are needed to produce a comprehensive design; multi-colored ikat threads are doubled or quadrupled in a bundle, and thus insure a symmetrical multi-colored woven pattern that is dominated by indigo blue or mordant red. Ikat cloth of Bali and Sumbawa has traditionally been the most colorful.[84]

Jan Wisseman Christie's recent study of the early Javanese textile tradition asserts that an indigenous weaving industry had evolved by the ninth century,

---

81) The first visual representation of the back-strap loom in Indonesia appears in a relief from Towulan, the site associated with the capital of the fourteenth century east Java-based Majapahit state, and shows a girl weaving in an open pavilion. A.J. Bernet Kempers, 1976: 241.

82) The Miao hill tribes of upland Laos continue this tradition, in contrast to the even more simple bark cloth pounding technology among the populations of the eastern Indonesian archipelago. This information was confirmed by Elizabeth Riddle of the Ball State University, Department of English, a Miao specialist, who has studied the transformation of the Miao textile tradition among America-based Miao.

83) R. Maxwell, 1990: 34-58, 66-86, 93-100, 143-147.

84) B. Solyom and G. Solyom, 1984: 21-27; H.I. Jessup, 1990: 141, 144, 149, 151, 153, 272, 273; W. Warming and M. Gaworski, 1981: 53-100.

Fig. 2a. Waxing/Batik Designs: Javanese Batik.

Fig. 2b. Hot wax/Brass Marker: Javanese Batik.

THE TEXTILE INDUSTRY IN SOUTHEAST ASIA, 1400-1800   113

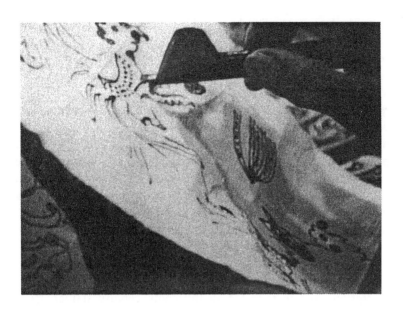

Fig. 2c. Waxing Batik Designs/Patterns prior to Emersion: Javanese Batik.

Fig. 2d. Waxing Design Prior to Dye Emersion: Javanese Batik.

when uniquely Javanese indigo-blue and wungkudu-red ikat cloth is depicted on temple statuary, which is wrapped in cloth that has horizontal decorative bands that are characteristic of ikat textiles.[85]) By the tenth century professional weavers produced high quality cotton cloth on new *cadar* looms, which were a local version of body-tension looms used elsewhere in East Asia during that era. On these looms, which could not produce a continuous warp, a loom reed or comb was used to separate fine threads inserts in the weaving process.[86]) By the eleventh century the continuous warp-ikat process had gained favor; contemporary epigraphy references weft-ikat *songket* cloth, which was decorated with gold and silver thread and colored silk thread inserts,[87]) and the initial plaid designs. *Banaten* cloth also receives initial citation; this was a product of an increasingly specialized textile industry that included master artisans who did not weave, but who bleeched and smoothed the surface of ready-made cloth prior to decoration. This process evolved into the production of free-hand batik (*tulis*, "to draw a line"), which uses wax to prevent dyes from penetrating the cloth and thereby propagates decoration, that is initially reported in twelfth century inscriptions and is reflected in thirteenth century statuary.[88]) From the eleventh century royal charters make special reference to reserved design motifs and colors—in contrast to old reds, blues, and whites—that included distinction between *tulis mas* ("drawing in gold") and *tulis warna* ("drawing in color"). Wisseman Christie highlights the role of foreign trade as the external source for this indigenous evolution of material culture, particularly the initial role as stimuli of Chinese and Indian textile imports.[89])

New dye resist production methods were introduced or developed in the Indonesian archipelago in the fourteenth and fifteenth centuries, in a period coincident to the adoption of Islam among court society.[90]) The market demand of newly converted Islamic societies encouraged these new developments, as well as the stylization of local flora and fauna patterns that replaced depiction of human and animal forms in locally produced dye resist textiles. This was the era in which Indian double ikat *patola* cloth from Gujarat was introduced and became market dominant. Patola cloth was more brightly colored than local cloth, and came in wider widths. Locals eventually responded by producing

---

85) J. Wisseman Christie, 1992: 10-11; 1993.

86) See M. Gittinger, 1979: 229-231.

87) M. Gittinger, 1979: 115-116, argues against woven gold and silver thread inserts, insisting that Java's early craftsmen only pasted gold and silver on their cloth.

88) R. Barnes, 1979: 54-55, documents five types of body-tension looms indigenous to the region.

89) J. Wisseman Christie, 1993, argues that early batik patterns were local expressions inspired by Indic originals.

90) R. Barnes, 1989: 19-20, 82-87, on the adoption and local emulation of patola cloth.

higher quality cloth. Whereas the warp ikat method common to India and Southeast Asia used only cotton threads, new *weft ikat* weaving used silk threads, which were initially imported, to yield competitive woven patterns. Tie-dyeing, wherein cloth was wrapped, tied, or stitched prior to dyeing and bound areas do not absorb the dye, also became popular by the sixteenth century. Javanese weavers refined the *batik* dyeing method. But their batik manufacture (which was sometimes referenced as the production of "painted cloth") proved to be too time consuming to be market competitive against the cotton imports from Gujarat, south India, and Bengal until the late seventeenth century, when Java's batik craftsmen responded to the new market opportunities of that age by interjecting greater pattern and color variety.[91]

Archipelago dress also changed, as Muslim men began to wear pants or trousers and women began to cover their breasts. Tailored skirts, robes, coats, shirts, and jackets became popular among the elite. Most of such stylized cloth was made from imported textiles, due to their high quality and general availability, but also due to continuing fears that locally produced cloth was spiritually possessed; popular belief held that cutting imported cloth rather than locally woven textiles minimized personal danger.[92]

On the mainland the spread of Theravada Buddhism beyond the courts was coincident to new patterns of cloth production and use.[93] An initial issue as Buddhism's popularity spread in Burma and Thailand was the need to distinguish monks from laity.[94] In Buddhist tradition monks were forbidden to adopt the scanty garments and ashes worn by Hindu ascetics. When going to receive alms in a village, The Buddha prescribed that:

> ... a Bhikkhu should put on his waist cloth so as to cover himself all around from above the navel to below the knees, tie his belt round his waist, fold his upper robes and put them on, fasten the block (belt) on, wash [his hands], take his alms-bowl, and

91) M. Gittinger, 1979: 115-137; W. Warming and M. Gaworski, 1981: 101-189; I.M. Elliott, 1984.

92) M. Gittinger, 1979: 28-31; for an overview of the transitions in the use and manufacture of cloth during the era of Islamic conversion see R. Maxwell, 1990: 299-351.

93) M. Gittinger, 1989: 225-239.

94) The most recent studies of fifteenth through eighteenth century Theravada Buddhism on the mainland are V. Lieberman, 1993: 240-249, and Y. Ishii, 1993. Both authors stress the critical role that Buddhism assumed in Burmese and Thai movements toward religious orthodoxy and cultural integration; due to royal initiatives that effectively placed the Sangha in subordination to the state, Buddhist monks became agents of cultural homogenization that paralleled movement toward more centralized polities. The most important vehicle by which royal authority over the monks was asserted was the institution of universal examination systems, which were administered by the king, and which were the acknowledged source of Sangha membership and monastic hierarchy. These examinations stressed a code of acceptable monastic behavior and belief that was in accord with the orthodox teachings of Pali language sacred texts that derived from Sri Lanka.

then slowly and carefully proceed to the village. He is to go amidst the houses properly clad. . . .[95])

Male adepts were subsequently required to wear shawls over their upper body, or, optionally, a single cloth garment that was cut and sewn from multiple "rags." This use of cut cloth was purposeful, and symbolized the separation of the monk from this-worldly allegiances. The emphasis that monks should wear cut cloth garments was highly meaningful to Southeast Asians. In Thailand and Burma, where there was respect for traditional values that discouraged the cutting of cloth, laymen wore whole-cloth skirts, while members of the Sangha wore cut-and-stitched "rag" robes. One exception was when a monk's single-cut robe was produced within a twenty-four hour period prior to donation, symbolic of limited time and involvement by the producer and thus non-attachment to this world. This rationale was cited so that monks could receive imported robes from India, or robes fashioned locally from pieces of imported fabric; similar reasoning allows contemporary monks to receive and wear the ready-to-wear robes woven by modern machinery.

Women's skirts in Burma and Thailand, meanwhile, are made from up to three pieces of cloth. This was because women, who dominated over local matrilocal society, were associated with the world of desire. In local society women are traditionally said to control rice fields, textiles, and sons. Their clothing represents a significant time investment and strong attachment to the things of "this world." In Thailand, traditional *phaa sin* ("with design") women's skirts are decorated with symbols from the natural world and the world of myth, with pythons, watermelons, rice grains. chickens, trees, and mythical *naak* (naga). These designs (*laay*) appear only on women's skirts and on textiles associated with women, especially pillow covers. Often resist-weft dye process upper and lower borders, which are separately produced, are subsequently stitched to the main textile, which may be locally woven or an imported fabric.

Men's skirts, *phaa sarong*, are made of uncut single pieces of cloth that lack elaborate patterns (*laay*) associated with the woman's world of desire, but these may have no motif except for white bands near the weft ends (*phaa chongkrben*) or geometric grids of large rectangles separated by one or more white lines (*phaa ko maa*). This latter patterned style duplicated the plaids that became common in the Indonesian archipelago at the time of Islamic conversion, and were initially imports from India. But unlike the archipelago, where there was general preference for cotton textiles—except in the Muslim courts of the neighboring Malay Peninsula and Sumatra where the elite also extensively wore

---

95) T.W. Rhys Davids and H. Oldenberg, 1965-69, *Kullavagga*, VIII, 4:3.

silk,[96]) high quality silk sarongs gained later favor among the Thai elite.[97]) Young men wear brightly colored *phaa sarong*, but as they grow older darker tones are considered more appropriate to those who are symbolically severing "this worldly" attachments.

Monks and Thai royalty wear cloth that employs minimal design. The robes of monks, which like those of women are supposed to be made from multiple cuttings of cloth, have a specified staggered patchwork motif that symbolizes rice fields with bunds. Only monks and royalty may wear clothing of yellowish ivory, the difference being that a monk's clothing is made of inexpensive cotton and derived from the stitching of multiple pieces of cloth, while that of male royalty is a single unseamed piece of silk.[98])

Silk was less popular than cotton in the island world, even though both mulberry trees and silk worms were indigenous. The noted exception was the Straits of Melaka region, where Malay court elite extensively wore silk to distinguish themselves from commoners, who wore cotton. Pasai in Sumatra was the acknowledged source of the best regional silk. The local ruler was said to have the magical power to convert thread into gold, an allusion to Pasai's yellow-colored silk, which had a rougher texture than Chinese imports.[99]) Pasai exported silk to India until it was annexed by Aceh in the 1520s, and subsequently pepper and rice cash cropping displaced earlier silk production and profits derived from these insured easy access to silk imports. Silk was also produced in south Sulawesi, where production continued in the Bugis state of Wajo into the twentieth century, and provided the colorful Bugis dress sarong.[100]) There was a more developed silk culture on the mainland. Burmese and Thai produced silk, but only in Vietnam, due to its intense Chinese contact, did silk consumption and production take widespread precedence over cotton. Vietnamese silk manufacture was as advanced and meticulous as that of the Chinese and Japanese. Vietnam exported a considerable scale of raw silk to Japan until the Tokugawa

96) The Trengganu region has especially been noted for its traditional silk weaving; Melaka's rulers extensively wore imported silk clothing as a symbol of their status, as did later Malay Peninsula sultans who followed. See *The International Herald-Tribune*, July 2, 1993: 2.

97) D.K. Wyatt, 1984: 63-64, documents early Thai silk production in thirteenth century Sukhothai culture, when Thai were raising silkworms and cultivating mulberry trees, and Thai silk was exported to neighboring Cambodia. Despite the quality of Thai silk, the Thai elite also encouraged import of Chinese silk and Indian cottons. See D. Pombejra, 1993: 254, 263-266.

98) H.L. Lefferts, Jr., 1992. Emphasizing the magnificence of a royal gift, a Thai chronicle explained it was woven entirely of imported silk "without any admixture of Thai thread." *Traibhumikatha c. 1345*, trans. F. Reynolds and M. Reynolds, 1982: 176.

99) A.H. Hill, 1960: 51.

100) W. Warming and M. Gaworski, 1981: 114-120.

banned the trade in 1617. Between 1570-1630, Japanese vessels could not trade directly with China due to Japanese prohibition on the export of gold to pay for Chinese imports, thus Japanese traders voyaged to Southeast Asia to exchange silver for Vietnam's raw silk, as well as Vietnamese and Chinese silk cloth.[101])

The International Textile Market and Southeast Asia: 1500-1800

During the sixteenth and seventeenth centuries the largest single item of Southeast Asian import was Indian cotton cloth. Personal adornment and clothing were the principal items of non-essential expenditure for most Southeast Asians, so that any increase in income was likely to show first in expenditures on cloth:

> ... As one observer pointed out for the Burmese, they were parsimonious in food and housing, but "splendid and extravagant in their dress. They have always in their mouths that their dress is seen by everybody; but one [rarely] comes into their houses to observe what they eat and how they are lodged." Indian cloth was preferred to local cotton because of the much brighter colors Indians could fix in their dyes, the bold designs, and the fine weaving.[102])

The boom in Southeast Asia's pepper and spice exports was thus matched by a rapid increase in cloth imports. Sultan Mahmud (r. 1488-1511), the last and wealthiest ruler of Melaka, is credited in the *Sejarah Melayu* with sending a mission to south India to acquire forty varieties of cloth. Tome Pires, writing shortly after the Portuguese conquest of Melaka in 1511, estimated that cloth imports from Bengal, Coromandel, and Gujarat conservatively totaled 460,000 cruzados a year, equivalent to about nineteen tons of silver.[103]) Between 1620-1650, the Dutch annually carried cloth valued between ten and twenty tons of silver (roughly one to two million guilders) from the Coromandel coast to Batavia.[104]) Indian cloth was traded not only in the great maritime emporia, but also in the tiny spice growing islands of the eastern Indonesian archipelago, and even the land locked region of Laos, where it took at least three months to transport it by bullock carts from the Thai urban center of Ayutthya.[105])

---

101) R.L. Innes, 1980.
102) A. Reid, 1992: 470-471, quoting V. Sangermano, 1966: 159.
103) A. Cortesao, 1944: 269-272.
104) T. Raychaudhuri, 1962: 140-143. Reid estimates the total Southeast Asian imports of Indian cloth to have peaked at fifty tons of silver in value, representing more than twenty million square meters, or almost one meter of cloth per person per year. See A. Reid, 1992: 471.
105) Reid (using Pires figures) calculates that Melaka received fifteen large ships per year from Gujarat, Coromandel, and Bengal worth over 1/2 million cruzados; one-half that number were imported by Aceh in the early seventeenth century; an English factor there believed he could annually sell 4,500 corges (90,000 pieces) of Indian cloth per year, as well as 100

The decline of the Spanish galleon trade from North America to the Philippines in the eighteenth century was due in part to similar increasing popularity of Indian cottons and a decreasing demand for Chinese silk, previously the anchor in the Chinese trade with Manila—Chinese silk had been reexported from Manila to Japan as well as to Europe. Governor Jose Basco y Vargas (1778-1786) established a corporation of Spanish merchants (*consulado*) and formed the Real Compania da Filipinas ("Royal Company of the Philippines") in 1785 to assert a government monopoly over the Indian cotton imports, but backed down when the native Manila merchant community (a mixture of Chinese, mestizo, and Filipinos) resisted his efforts between 1789-1799. While non-Spanish European trade ships were barred, Manila was reopened to Asian ships carrying Asian goods, notably textiles, but Vargas also financed the initiation of a competitive local cotton industry at Iloilo by distributing spinning and weaving machines.[106])

In the mid-seventeenth century declining international market demand for Southeast Asia's spices, the consequence of a combination of local overproduction and the diffusion of spice cultivation to the New World, and Dutch monopoly over the nutmeg and clove exports of the Malukus, diminished the regional flow of trade profits. That there was an economic restructuring is reflected in Dutch trade records. Although the Dutch had a near monopoly over Indonesia's spice exports to the West, their sales of Indian cotton cloth declined by twenty percent between 1652-1703.[107]) Dutch East India Company sales to Indonesian vessels visiting Batavia to buy Indian cloth dropped forty-three percent between 1665-69 and 1679-81, and even more in the next twenty years. Notably, Dutch officials complained that Southeast Asians were not buying the expensive imported cloth because they simply couldn't afford it. Instead, from their perspective, the local populations had fallen back on their own growing and weaving, and updated and expanded upon the small-scale production that had marked the age prior to the widespread prosperity:

> ... since these countries flourished more formerly than now, most of these peoples sought Coromandel and Surat cloths [for everyday use], not as luxuries, and gave large amounts of money for that. ... Now most of the surrounding [Indonesian] countries are impoverished, and the [Coromandel] Coast and Surat cloths have become limited to the use of the wealthy.[108])

---

bihar (17 tons) of raw cotton; Ayutthya was importing 75,000 guilders (30,000 rials) worth of Indian cloth per year in the seventeenth century; Makassar in the 1630s consumed 120,000 rials "at Indian prices," double that at Makassar prices. A. Reid, 1988: 95-96.

106) H. Furber, 1976: 217-220.

107) A. Reid, 1992: 491, citing Ruurdje Laarhoven, who calculates that in 1652 the VOC sold 314,039 pieces of Indian cloth in Indonesia, in contrast to 256,458 in 1703.

108) Governor-General and Council report of 1693 from Batavia, quoted in A. Reid, 1992: 491.

While this report attributes the failure to purchase Indian textiles in quantity to local poverty, the consequence of the failing international spice trade, other Dutch documents from this same era convey the very different reality that while there was less demand for Indian textiles, there was still significant market activity that the Dutch were unable to tap. In several instances the Dutch made a last-ditch attempt to assert a cloth monopoly by imposing restrictions on the cotton growth. Having finally come to an understanding of the cultural importance of cloth, the Dutch hoped that by eliminating commercial cotton cultivation indigenous craftsmen would not be able to weave local cloth, and thereby the archipelago populations would have to make textile purchases exclusively from the Dutch.[109]

This Dutch initiative to assert a textile monopoly demonstrates that the decline in cotton imports was not entirely due to the unfavorable Western trade in spices and textiles. Batik, which had previously been produced in limited quantities because the wax dyeing design process was too labor intensive to be market competitive against Indian imports, was a beneficiary of the Dutch intervention. Batik sales notably escalated in the late seventeenth century when new production techniques allowed Javanese batik producers to duplicate and elaborate the woven designs of the Gujarat patola cloth.[110] Bugis seamen were especially prominent distributors of Bali's popular checked cloth, but also collected raw cotton from the dry limestone soils of Selayar and the adjacent south Sulawesi coast at Bira, and had this woven into the checked sarong designs by the women of Selayar and Wajo. These Bugis traders, who operated outside the Dutch monopoly and penetrated markets throughout the archipelago with minimal capital investment, sold this high quality checked cloth at one-half the price of comparable Indian cloths in V.O.C. hands.[111]

By the nineteenth century, there are reports of widespread spinning and weaving by women in every household in almost every Western traveler's account. Through the nineteenth century, however, the enormous growth in peasant consumption of cheap European manufactured textiles, which were judged to be of acceptable quality, and, since they were produced by impersonal machines, were judged to be of little danger of spiritual possession, changed this.[112] Similar to the pre-seventeenth century age, potential local textile producers once again reacted to the reality of the marketplace. Women found their

---

109) B.W. Andaya, 1993, as cited above.
110) I.M. Elliott, 1984: 36.
111) A. Reid, 1988: 95. See also L.Y. Andaya, 1994.
112) In the Philippines commercial production of textiles initiated by the Spanish at Iloilo and French-financed textile factories at Hanoi and Nam Dinh in the 1890s had similar impact.

production of native textiles to be overly costly in personal time. In turn they ci.ose to purchase the cheap European cloth in the market rather than weave cloth in their own homes. Sumatra's women dropped weaving when opportunities to work in the developing rubber industry became available.[113] In Java, the value of imported textiles rose from 3.8 million guilders in 1830 to 13.1 million in 1840; in Burma by 1930, three-fourths of the country's textiles were imported; in Thailand the nominal value of cotton manufacture imports rose seven times between 1864-1910.[114]

Against this trend toward the import displacement of the indigenous textile industry is the case of Java, where Java producers modified their production technique sufficiently to remain cost competitive. Dutch, Swiss, and English textile imports of machine printed imitation batik sold more cheaply than traditionally produced batik, and, even more, introduced colors that were brighter and more diverse than native dyes would allow. To retain a place in the marketplace, local craftsmen responded by developing the waxing *cap* (waxing handstamp), which largely displaced the time consuming free-hand wax resist *canting* (pen drawing) design method. In the *cap* process fine strips of copper needles were painstakingly assembled to match well-known traditional patterns or to innovate. In some instances, specially in central Java where the *cap* process was adopted but used almost exclusively to mirror old patterns, the tireless efforts to duplicate resist designs of hand-drawn batik limited output. More commonly, however, the waxing *cap* made production quality more consistent, and synthetic dyes allowed new color schemes and finally resolved long-standing consumer complaints over the impermanence and dullness of traditional batik. The new stamping process was faster, more mechanical, and required the strong hands of men rather than women. Significantly, too, since women were not the producers, the new waxing *cap* batik did not hold the same cultural stature—it was less dangerous than the highly priced hand canting batik, with miniaturized and even more ornate style variations of conventional patterns, that Javanese women continued to create for an elite market.[115]

This nineteenth century transition to the popular consumption of inexpensive textiles disrupted and changed the woman's role in society. As had similarly been the case in the earlier age when there was mass dependency upon Indian textile imports, Southeast Asian women could better put their efforts into agricultural cultivation for the market rather than devote an inordinate amount of labor time to textiles. For example, it was estimated that a woman needed one

113) B.W. Andaya, 1989: 33, citing J. Tideman, 1938: 227.
114) R.E. Elson, 1992: II, 178.
115) P. Kitley, 1992: 10-18.

month to spin one pound of cotton thread and another to weave a cloth of ten yards length in the early nineteenth century. Also, increased male labor absence due to forced or contracted labor on plantations, in mines, or in the nurturing of cash crops deprived the village communities of a major labor supply. Women compensated by entering the economy as petty traders, domestic servants, and as factory workers. As cash wages became readily available, and the terms of trade favored cash crop cultivation and ancillary industries, it made economic sense to the household for women to be thus employed, and use the cash return to purchase textiles in the market.[116])

Textiles in the Southeast Asian Present

In the past several years there has been a renewed interest in native textile manufacture in Southeast Asia, due in part to poor employment opportunities in the initial post-colonial age that once again put Western imports beyond the reach of native consumers, but also because of the important role indigenous textiles have always assumed in local definitions of legitimacy and power. In response to indigenous need one of the first postcolonial investments was in locally and foreign owned factories that were capable of supplying popular demand for inexpensive mass-produced textiles.

Because of continuing local sensitivity to historical recreation,[117]) newly independent governments also sponsored the renewal of the labor intensive weaving of high-quality textiles, jointly to find employment for the underemployed as well as to reaffirm traditional values that are supported by native handicrafts. In Indonesia, for example, President Sukarno conceived of batik as a true Indonesian textile tradition. Today the Indonesian government funds weaving schools and workshops; the positive market impact of these government ministry managed shops has spread to the private sector, where there is more freedom to experiment in new productive techniques and patterns.[118]) There has been some positive result from government marketing efforts to promote the consumption of high quality Indonesian textiles among affluent international markets. To ap-

---

116) N. Owen, 1978: 157-170.

117) See B. Anderson, 1990, relative to the importance of historical recreation in twentieth century Indonesian politics.

118) In Indonesia resistance to the government ministry managed shops and schools quickly developed on the grounds that the government's intent was to overly standardize production and to support textile patterns and styles that are consistent with the government's attempts to promote its vision of a cultural homogenous Indonesia, to the detriment of strong regional variants. For a regional perspective of these governmental attempts to promote a unified Indonesian culture see R.W. Heffner, 1985.

peal to this market batik patterns now draw upon a whole new range of motifs and patterns that are derivatives of the decorative style of non batik-making cultures. But the greatest increase in demand has come from the indigenous market. Here native textiles have substantial appeal among the upwardly mobile, whose ability to purchase the high quality batik that was formerly reserved for the court elite is a self-assertive statement of ascendancy.

Finding it inappropriate to use Western dress and decoration as a national standard, the government leaders of maritime Southeast Asia have especially made wearing distinctive native textiles socially fashionable. In Indonesia, long-sleeved batik shirts are preferred men's formal wear (worn draped over Western-style trousers). Women's formal attire consists of batik skirts and cotton or silk jackets. Neighboring Malaysia stresses Malay formal dress, inclusive of traditional trousers and silk or cotton jackets or shirts for men and an assortment of cloth coverings among women. In Malaysia dressing in traditional Malay manner is a statement of ethnicity, with socio-political implications in a nation that has a substantial Chinese ethnic minority. The Chinese counter the Malays by expressing their ethnicity by almost exclusively wearing Western fashions. Singapore's government is currently promoting the image of the "Singapore Airlines Woman" in the national and international media. This feminine "ideal" is portrayed in a *Malay* cotton batik dress, which is intended to express and promote renewed national commitment to traditional non-Western *Chinese* moralistic values among a society that is eighty-percent Chinese and only fifteen-percent Malay. Appropriate Filipino business and formal attire requires the liberal use of lightly colored and locally made silks and cottons.

This reemergence of an indigenous textile industry is countered, however, by growing employment opportunities for women in new labor-intensive as well as high-tech factories. Traditionally assertive Southeast Asian women are also well-suited to compete for new urban commercial and professional positions. Southeast Asian women, who have historically responded to the opportunities of the marketplace, once again find that the labor intensive production of cloth is a prohibitively unrealistic investment of their labor time. In Singapore, for example, traditional craft textiles are exclusively imported from neighboring Malay countries because Singapore women are too busy making money as modern highly educated professionals.

The Body Beneath the Cloth in Seventeenth Century Banjarmasin

In the evidence cited above I have found a pattern of ebb and flow in Southeast Asia's textile production in the pre-colonial era. This pattern is one of local response to the realities of local culture as well as the marketplace. My study of the regional textile trade concludes that at no time between 1400-1800 was Southeast Asia's textile production permanently displaced by higher quality or cheaper foreign imports. Rather, I perceive recurrent cycles in which initial dependency on foreign cloth, for both cultural and economic reasons, resulted in local adjustments in technique that once again made Southeast Asia's textile producers market competitive and able to supply indigenous demand, especially when there were negative alterations in the price, quality, or quantity of foreign textiles. My study of textiles does not lead me to a conclusion that there was an ultimate submission to a Western-dominated global economic system in the seventeenth century. Nor do I comfortably place myself among those Southeast Asia specialists who search for the preeminent "autochthonous base" and diminished the significance of external stimulation and/or regional or subregional networks. Instead I have highlighted an interactive international and internal dynamic that created Southeast Asia's viable present.

It is appropriate to offer a concluding reevaluation of my initial citations from the *Hikayat Banjar* in light of these seventeenth century regional patterns of textile production and exchange. I introduced the *Hikayat* as an internal window on the so-called age of cultural and economic transition, and in doing so I highlighted references to a seventeenth century restructuring of the Banjarmasin state in which the acceptance of Islamic statecraft seemed to be the central theme. There was thus a reediting of the chronicle text, by which the chronicle authors diminished or completely omitted references to formalized cloth exchanges. I proposed that this deemphasis on the role of court reciprocity involving cloth was consistent with the local cultural evolution from the Hindu-Buddhist to the Islamic traditions, which was precipitated by Banjarmasin's new status as a major marketing center for pepper.[119])

In retrospect, I am less convinced that the movement to Islamic statecraft is the singular variable that explains the diminished role of cloth in the reedited chronicle text. When considered in light of the regional patterns of textile manufacture and commerce reported above, I now believe that the intent of the new text's authors was less abstruse. Instead, I am convinced that they were hiding the fact that Banjarmasin's court could no longer acquire distinctive imported textiles in sufficient quantity to sustain the old gifting networks upon which the old system of sovereignty was based. Like Sumatra, a Kalimantan/Borneo-based court's sovereign power depended on upstream-downstream and coast-hinterland relationships between a port-based elite and their upland subordinates.[120]) Early courts tried to discourage hinterland populations from periodically plundering

---

119) I address the details of Banjarmasin's Islamic conversion in K.R. Hall, 1994.
120) R. Nicholl, 1983.10.

the coast by convincing them that there were cultural benefits to regular ritual-ized exchanges of goods and services.[121]) With the incidence of the international demand for pepper the upstream-downstream relationship significantly altered. To guarantee the heightened flow of pepper from upstream producers to inter-national traders the coast-hinterland relationship had to be formalized, wherein there were direct negotiations with hinterland pepper producers to secure pep-per, and inevitably this translated into marketplace exchanges of imported cloth for pepper.[122]) This new mass market made imported cotton textiles readily available to upstream pepper producers, to the detriment of the court, which had maintained a prior monopoly of these for its own conspicuous displays as well as for its numerous ritualized redistributions to loyal subordinates. Prior to the expansion of Banjar's international market royal power was based on the court's virtual monopoly of imported cloth. With the intensified coast-hinterland networking system, the Banjar court faced a predicament similar to that faced

---

121) J.J. Ras, 1968: 240-243, on the normal instability among the hinterland populations and the initiation of tributary gift exchanges with the representatives of upstream "chiefs," inclusive of reciprocal cloth gifts by the court. As phrased in the *Hikayat*: "the various [upstream and highland] communities now live in peace, without killing each other any more, thanks to the effectiveness of [the Banjar monarch's] rule." On the early exchange relation-ships between upland and lowland societies see K.L. Hutterer, 1974, 1977b.

122) During the early seventeenth century, due to an influx of Javanese and Makassar refugee traders with their ships, commercial capital, and trade experience, Banjar's court elite became more conscious that wealth could become the source of personal power. The old sys-tem of power, in which status was a consequence of one's birth, was no longer valid. Seeing new opportunities to acquire wealth and consequently to improve their personal status, Banjar elite extended their control over the upstream populations, by personally promoting pepper cultivation and facilitating the flow of hinterland products to the coast to meet the increas-ing demand for Banjar's pepper among international traders. Replacing the loose political alliances of the past, the seventeenth century Banjar elite assumed personal authority over the pepper-growing regions of the upland by resettling coastal and tribal populations on lands where pepper cultivation was stressed. To maximize pepper production they also discouraged the growth of food staples on this land, depending instead upon rice imports from Java, Makassar, and the neighboring Borneo coast port of Kota Waringin, purchased with profits from the pepper trade, to meet the consumptive needs of their pepper cultivators. Among this Banjar elite deriving their wealth from their control over large plots of pepper-producing lands, a group known as *pangeran* became prominent. This pangeran elite eventually became more powerful than the sultan due to their control over the pepper trade. The interests and powers of the *pangeran* are noted by seventeenth century Dutch merchants, who reports that the Banjar sultan could promise pepper, but could not always deliver it to foreign merchants unless the *pangeran* agreed to cooperate. Banjar's sultan was not even allowed to speak alone among foreign merchants without the presence of a representative of the *pangeran* elite. This new elite acquired hinterland pepper from their own lands or purchased the pepper from peasant cultivators at prices the *pangeran* fixed, among themselves, and then auctioned this pepper off to the highest bidder among visiting merchants. Cloth was the critical commodity in each of these transactions. See K.R. Hall, 1995; records for this era that document these transitions include VOC 2195, fols. 5162-5165, dated 1729-1735.

by the rulers of Sumatra's port-polities: it could no longer dominate access to distinctive textiles. This in turn invalidated the reciprocal gift exchanges that served as the gist of royal authority. There was thus critical need to refocus on a non-material requisite for state polity, and the stress on an efficient administration filled the bill:

> ... [the state was successful because of the] excellent way it was organized, and that was because it was conducted in conformity with the arrangements and procedure followed by the king of Majapahit and in agreement with the Javanese usage. In the way they dressed, too, people followed the Javanese fashion. Everyone in the land ... had given up dressing in the old style. Young and old, male and female alike, dressed in the Javanese way. The king ... once said, when all the dignitaries with their subordinates were sitting before him ..., "let none of you dress like the Malays or the Hollanders or the Chinese of the Siamese or the Acehnese or the Makassarese or the Buginese. Do not imitate any of them. You should not even follow the old customs of dress ... we have ... set up a country of our own following the ways and manners of Majapahit. Therefore we should all dress like the Javanese. According to the stories of olden times handed down by the elders, whenever the inhabitants of a country imitated the clothing of people from elsewhere, misery inevitably fell upon the country that had turned to foreign ways of dressing.... The king's instructions are not carried out because the common people do exactly as they themselves like.... Let not our country plant pepper as an export-crop, for the sake of making money, like Palembang and Jambi. Whenever a country cultivates pepper all food-stuffs will become expensive ... [and this will] cause malice all over the country and even the government will fall into disorder. The rural people will become pretentious towards the townsfolk if pepper is grown for commercial purposes, for the sake of money.... During the reign of the founder of our country many foreigners settled down in the land ... but the people ... did not imitate their clothing. For the people ... it became the tradition to dress in the manner of Majapahit and to follow the Javanese fashion.[123])

This expanded citation goes beyond references to proper and improper dress. Its authors' stress is on a state structure and code of etiquette that is consistent with that of Java, which responds to the very real threats to the court's authority that were consequent to the seventeenth century era. This appeal to "Javanize" focused on a conventional order that was symbolized by the legendary Majapahit, where sanctioned status-based distinctions induced security and prosperity.[124]) But the emphasis on dressing Javanese also acknowledged increased local dependency on Javanese cloth rather than Indian imports.

In the new order of that age Banjarmasin was a member of an eastern archipelago trading network that had ample access to regional textiles; chief among these were Java's batiks. Increased seventeenth century competition between Dutch and indigenous traders in the eastern Indonesian archipelago resulted in the eventual shift of Bugis and Makaserrese trading bases to Banjarmasin. Ban-

---

123) J.J. Ras, 1968: 264-265.
124) On the Majapahit legacy see S. Supomo, 1979: 171-185.

jarmasin thus became a major center in the archipelago-wide Bugis trade network that was based in south Sulawesi, and especially achieved prominence
after the fall of Makassar to the Dutch in 1669. While the Bugis network could
not regularly supply Banjar with "Western" cloth, Bugis seafarers as well as
others among a cosmopolitan community that populated the port did have access to a variety of regional textiles. As reflected in the above citation as well
as others from the *Hikayat* "local" textiles, including imported batiks and ikat
cotton cloth were now the market standards. It was noted above that the Bugis
sold these quality textiles that were woven by Southeast Asian artisans at one-
half the price of Indian textiles.

The *Hikayat* authors warned against behaving like these Bugis, the Makaserrese, and the other market-based communities, which were perceived to be
no better than the Hollanders and Chinese—or even the Malays of the Melaka
Straits region (who were by that time dressing in cotton and silk sarongs instead
of the Javanese kain-style cotton wrap around Banjar's court preferred), who
were all categorized as market-focused societies. It is highly appropriate considering the universal regional importance of cloth by the early seventeenth century that the chronicle's authors should distinguish among these trading communities by citing their differing cloth traditions. It was also apt, in light of the
transitions in Sumatra's society that resulted from the expanded pepper trade,
that the Banjar chronicle's authors alluded to Jambi as a prime example of the
despair that could occur if Banjarmasin began similarly "to imitate those who
are only concerned with making money."[125]

But to return to the "old manners of dress" (i.e., to the wearing of bark cloth)
was equally undesirable. In this old order there was no regular submission to
the downriver court. Dressing in Javanese manner provided a necessary means
by which these otherwise autonomous tribesmen could be drawn into a more
centralized polity. The value of Javanese textiles as the source of ideational
linkage is substantiated by students of textile design, who argue that the heightened consumption of Java's batik was especially important as a source of integrating upstream and downstream in the eastern archipelago, in that batik
designs represented a resurgence of animistic traditions. In wearing Javanese
batik the lower body was wrapped in layers of cloth that contained powerful
symbolic images, as opposed to the designs of Indian textiles that had little

---

125) Barbara Andaya comments on this passage, noting with interest the inclusion of Palembang
as an equal example of a decaying polity. Andaya demonstrates that, while this projection of
Jambi's royal misfortunes was appropriate, Palembang was incorrectly paired. Royal initiatives in the face of the new marketing order heightened the powers of the Palembang court
and brought considerable welfare to its subjects. B.W. Andaya, 1993: 117, n. 61.

local meaning.[126]) As such, Java cloth was not unlike local cloth in that it could *bestow* power, in contrast to other imported cloth that was less likely to be spiritually possessed.

Such promotion of Javanese dress was not unique to seventeenth century Banjar. Barbara Andaya, too, places focus on the "Javanization" of the Jambi court in the same era. But Andaya's stress is on Jambi's desire for economic and/or political alliance with the powerful Mataram court as a balance to increased Dutch presence rather than on the cultural symbolism that seems so much at the heart of the Banjar chronicle references. In 1642, by command of the Jambi sultan only Javanese batik could be worn at court. The Jambi ruler insisted that "the people of Kuamang, Tunjah Kota, and elsewhere" (all of whom resided upriver from Jambi) who had previously been permitted to appear at court in Malay clothes, should now dress in Javanese style. In reaction to these initiatives the upstream Minangkabau populations shifted their trade to the "Malay" king in Inderagiri, a rival marketing center where a less rigid dress code prevailed.[127])

The problem in both societies was the market. To the authors of the *Hikayat Banjar* this move to the material (market) economy was associated with the development of commercial pepper growth, and was especially expressed in their references to inappropriate dress. In the seventeenth century world of the revised *Hikayat* text the old order that was based on status distinctions was in serious jeopardy—due to the revised trading opportunities prevalent in the archipelago at that time. As the old rules changed local cultures might become temporarily unstable as marketplace transactions increasingly dominated society. A new order emerged that was increasingly a consequence of external political and economic ties, especially those to contemporary political or economic—rather than exclusively cultural—centers that could redistribute political favors or material reward to those who became political as well as economic and cultural subordinates. The authors of the *Hikayat Banjar* well-understood the dangerous new potentials:

> ... Let people nowhere in this country plant pepper, as is done in Jambi and Palembang. Perhaps those countries grow pepper for the sake of money, in order to grow wealthy. There is no doubt that in the end they will go to ruin...[128])

---

126) This information derives from discussion with Paul Michael Taylor of the Smithsonian Institution at various times between 1990-1993. See also P.M. Taylor and L.U. Argon, 1991: *passim.*

127) B.W. Andaya, 1993: 101; 1992: 40. See also *idem*, 1994, wherein Andaya asserts that the dominance of coastal groups over upstream population was never inevitable.

128) J.J. Ras, 1968: 330-331.

Yet as new centers emerged there was no desire to withdraw from the market-place; there was instead a corresponding renewal of commitments to traditional values that were supportive of the new order in which the marketplace prevailed.

In the face of significant structural changes elements of the ancestral culture served as the common link between the past and the future. I have highlighted cloth as one such source of linkage. In the new order that was emerging in the seventeenth century, coast and hinterland regularized their interactions and shared in a common cultural bond that was defined by cloth. In this new age cloth was a multi-purpose commodity bearing a rich historical legacy that could serve as the point of reference for revised political, economic, and cultural transactions. Thus the reedited *Hikayat* text reflects a cultural synthesis of internal and external ideational stimuli as symbolized in its references to indigenous usage of cloth. This was a locally meaningful response to the changing economic circumstances of the seventeenth century, and was only in part a reaction to an increasingly assertive European presence in the eastern Indonesian archipelago. The revised *Hikayat* text mirrors the attempts at redefinition by its omission of references to formalized textile exchanges and repeated reminders of the dangers inherent when a society converted to a marketing economy and ignored tradition. These themes were conveyed meaningfully by direct allegations that dressing foreign would initiate local demise.

In the revised text, however, which was a product of the post-Banjarmasin court, there was no question that local society would prevail; its authors' concern is demonstration that the Banjarmasin-based government failed due to its inadequate administrative leadership. Thus in the previously cited episode that portrays Dutch conquest, Banjarmasin's society reasserted itself under a restructured government at the new Martapura port-polity. The Martapura-based state is a success in the minds of the chroniclers because: a) it instituted a more efficient government that convinced the diverse populations to renew their commitments to inherited values (those consistent with an idealized "Javanese" statecraft), and b) it restrained local participation in the international trade, wherein the pursuit of material profit rather than cultural well-being prevailed.

Recent studies of other eastern archipelago port-polities report that in comparable seventeenth century restructuring courts that were based in geographically diverse regions acknowledged that administrative centralization was unworkable. They found that there were other ways to organize disparate ethnic groups than through rigid political and royal autocracy. These "cultural states" highlighted the role of a common myth as the validation for royal power, wherein the "state" was a necessary entity because it was perceived to be the source of the "community's" existence. In such situations a cultural "truth" such as a common spiritual bond or some magically possessed object was more durable than any political or economic entity. It was not uncommon for a ruler to hold several artifacts in trust.[129]) In similar fashion an above citation from the revised Hikayat Banjar explicitly lists the king's sacred paraphernalia. Emphasis on the cloth objects in this enumeration confirms the vital role of textiles as the continuing "cultural truth" that links the upstream and downstream populations of the local riverine network.

BIBLIOGRAPHY

Andaya, B.W.
　　1989　"The Cloth Trade in Jambi and Palembang during the Seventeenth and Eight-eenth Centuries," *Indonesia*, 48 (October 1989): 27-46.
　　1993　"Cash Cropping and Upstream-Downstream Tensions: The Case of Jambi in the Seventeenth and Eighteenth Centuries" in Reid, A., ed., 1993: 91-122.
　　1994　"Raiding Cultures and Interior-Coastal Migration in Early Modern Island South-east Asia" a paper presented at the 13th International Association of Historians of Asia Conference, Tokyo, September 1994.
Andaya, L.Y.
　　1993　"Cultural State Formation in Eastern Indonesia" in Reid, A., ed., 1993: 23-41.
　　1994　"The Bugis-Makassar Diasporas" a paper presented at the 13th International Association of Historians of Asia Conference, Tokyo, September 1994.
Arasaratnam, S.
　　1986　*Merchants, Companies and Commerce on the Coromandel Coast*, 1650-1740. New Delhi: Oxford University Press.
　　1994　*Maritime India in the Seventeenth Century*. New Delhi: Oxford University Press.
Anderson, B.
　　1990　*Language and Power, Exploring Political Cultures in Indonesia*. Ithaca, New York: Cornell University Press.
Atwell, W.S.
　　1986　"Some Observations on the 'Seventeenth Century Crisis' in China and Japan," *Journal of Asian Studies*, 45, 2 (1986): 223-244.
Barnes, R.
　　1979　"An Introduction to the Body-Tension Looms and Single Frame Looms of Southeast Asia" in I. Emery and P. Fiske, eds., 1979: 54-55.
　　1989　*The Ikat Textiles of Lamalera: A Study of an Eastern Indonesian Weaving Tradition*. Leiden: E.J. Brill.
Barnes, R. and Eicher, J.B., eds.
　　1992　*Dress and Gender: Making and Meaning*. New York: St. Martins.
Bernet Kempers, A.J.
　　1976　*Ageless Borobudur*. Wassenaar: Servire.
Boow, J.
　　1988　*Symbol and Status in Javanese Batik*. Nedlands: Asian Studies Centre of West-ern Australia.
Braudel, F.
　　1974　*Capitalism and Material Life*, 1400-1800. Glasgow: Fontana.
　　1976　*The Meditarranean and the Meditarranean World in the Age of Philip II*, trans. S. Reynolds, 2 vols., New York: Harper.

---

129) See I. Andaya, 1993; R. Laarhoven, 1990; and J.F. Warren, 1990.

Brown, C.C.
    1952   "Sejarah Melayu or 'Malay Annals': A Translation of Raffles Ms. 18," *Journal of the Malay Branch of the Royal Asiatic Society*, 25, 2-3 (1952).
Buck, D.D.
    1994   "Dimensions of Ethnic and Cultural Nationalism in Asia—A Symposium: Editor's Introduction," *Journal of Asian Studies*, 53, 1: 3-9.
Casparis, J.G. de
    1956   *Prasasti Indonesia II: Selected Inscriptions from the Seventh to the Ninth Century A.D.*, Bandung: Djawatan Purbakala Republik Indonesia.
Cense, A.A.
    1928   De Kronick van Banjarmasin. Santpoort.
Christie, Jan Wisseman
    1992   "Trade and Value in Pre-Majapahit Java," *Indonesia Circle*, 59 & 60: 3-17.
    1993   "Texts and Textiles in 'Medieval' Java," *BEFEO*, 80, 1: 181-211.
Cortesao, A.
    1944   *The Suma Oriental of Tome Pires* (1515). London: Hakluyt Society.
Das Gupta, A.
    1979   *Indian Merchants and the Decline of Surat c. 1700-1750*. Wiesbaden: Franz Steiner.
Elliott, I.M.
    1984   *Batik: Fabled Cloth of Java*. New York: Clarkson N. Potter.
Elson, R.
    1992   "International Commerce, the State, and Society: Economic and Social Change" in Tarling, N., ed., 1992: II, 131-196.
Emery, I. and Fiske, P., eds.
    1979   *Looms and Their Products. Irene Emery Roundtable on Museum Textiles*. Washington, D.C.: The Textile Museum.
Errington, S.
    1989   *Meaning and Power in a Southeast Asian Realm*. Princeton: Princeton University Press.
Fontein, J.
    1990   *The Sculpture of Indonesia*. Washington, D.C.: National Gallery of Art.
Furber, Holden
    1976   *Rival Empires of Trade in the Orient, 1600-1800*. Minneapolis: University of Minnesota Press.
Geddes, W.R.
    1976   *Migrants of the Mountains: The Cultural Ecology of the Blue Miao of Thailand*. Oxford: Oxford University Press.
Gittinger, M.
    1979   *Splendid Symbols. Textiles and Traditions in Indonesia*. Washington, D.C.: The Textile Museum.
    1989   *To Speak with Cloth. Studies in Indonesian Textiles*. Los Angeles: University of California Museum of Cultural History.
Hall, D.G.E.
    1981   *A History of South-East Asia*, 4th Edition. New York: St. Martins.
Hall, K.R.
    1977   "The Coming of Islam to the Archipelago: A Reassessment" in Hutterer, K.L., ed., 1977a: 213-231.
    1980   *Trade and Statecraft in the Age of the Colas*. Delhi: Abhinav.
    1985   *Maritime Trade and State Development in Early Southeast Asia*. Honolulu: University of Hawaii Press.
    1992   "Economic History of Early Southeast Asia" in Tarling, N., ed., 1992: I, 183-275.

132   KENNETH R. HALL

    1994   "Patterns and Networks of Early Islamic Communication in Southeast Asia Circa 1600 A.D." a paper presented at the 13th International Association of Historians of Asia Conference, Tokyo, September 1994.

    1995   "Upstream and Downstream Networking in Seventeenth Century Banjarmasin" in Horton, A.V.M. and King, V.T., eds., *From Buckfast to Borneo: Essays Presented to Father Robert Nicholl on the 85th Anniversary of His Birth 27 March 1995*, special addition of *Indonesia Circle*.

Heffner, R.W.
    1985   *Hindu-Javanese*. Princeton: Princeton University Press.

Hill, A.H.
    1960   "The Hikayat Raja-Raja Pasai," *Journal of the Malaysian Branch of the Royal Asiatic Society*, 33, 2: 1-215.

Holt, C.
    1967   *Art in Indonesia, Continuities and Change*. Ithaca, New York: Cornell University Press.

Hutterer, K.L.
    1974   "The Evolution of Philippine Lowland Societies," *Mankind*, 9: 287-299.

    1977a   ed., *Economic Exchange and Social Interaction in Southeast Asia: Perspectives from Prehistory, History, and Ethnography*. Ann Arbor: Center for South and Southeast Asian Studies.

    1977b   "Prehistoric Trade and the Evolution of Philippine Societies: A Reconsideration" in Hutterer, K.L., ed., 1977a: 177-196.

Innes, R.
    1980   *The Door Ajar: Japan's Foreign Trade in the Seventeenth Century*. Ann Arbor: Unpublished Ph.D. Dissertation, University of Michigan.

Ishii, Y.
    1993   "Religious Patterns and Economic Change in Siam in the Sixteenth and Seventeenth Centuries" in Reid, A., ed., 1993: 180-194.

Jessup, H.J.
    1990   *Court Arts of Indonesia*. New York: The Asia Society.

Jones, A.B.
    1984   *Early Tenth Century Java from the Inscriptions*. Dordrecht: Floris.

Kahin, G. McT.
    1952   *Nationalism and Revolution in Indonesia*. Ithaca, New York: Cornell University Press.

Kathirithamby-Wells, J.
    1990   "Introduction: An Overview" in Kathirithamby-Wells, J. and Villiers, J., eds., 1990: 1-16.

    1993   "Restraints on the Development of Merchant Capitalism in Southeast Asia before c. 1800" in Reid, A., ed., 1993: 123-148.

Kathirithamby-Wells, J. and Villiers, J., eds.,
    1990   *The Southeast Asian Port and Polity, Rise and Demise*. Singapore: Singapore University Press.

Kitley, P.
    1992   "Ornamentation and Originality: Involution in Javanese Batik," *Indonesia*, 53: 1-19.

Koojman, S.
    1963   *Ornamental Bark Cloth in Indonesia*. Leiden: E.J. Brill.

Laarhoven, R.
    1990   "Lords of the Great River: The Magindanao Port and Polity during the Seventeenth Century" in Kathirithamby-Wells, J. and Villiers, J. eds., 1990: 161-185.

THE TEXTILE INDUSTRY IN SOUTHEAST ASIA, 1400-1800   133

Lefferts, H.L., Jr.
   1992   "Cut and Sewn: The Textiles of Social Organization in Thailand" in Barnes,
           R. and Eicher, J., eds., 1992: 44-55.
Leur, J.C. van
   1955   *Indonesian Trade and Society.* The Hague: van Hoeve.
Lieberman, V.
   1993   "Was the Seventeenth Century in Burma a Watershed?" in Reid, A., ed., 1993:
           214-249.
Manguin, P.-Y.
   1993   "The Vanishing Jong: Insular Southeast Asian Fleets in Trade and War (Fifteen
           to Seventeenth Centuries)" in Reid, A., ed., 1993: 197-213.
Mauss, M.
   1966   *The Gift.* New York: Free Press.
Maxwell, R.
   1990   *Tradition, Trade, and Transformation: Textiles of Southeast Asia.* Canberra:
           Oxford University Press.
Meilink-Roelofsz, M.A.P.
   1962   *Asian Trade and European Influence in the Indonesian Archipelago Between
           1500 and About 1630.* The Hague: Nijhoff.
Nicholl, R.
   1983   "Brunei Rediscovered, A Survey of Early Times," *Journal of Southeast Asian
           Studies,* 14, 1: 32-45.
Owen, N.
   1978   "Textile Displacement and the Status of Women in Southeast Asia" in Means,
           G.P., ed., *The Past in Southeast Asia's Present.* Ottawa: Canadian Society for
           Asian Studies, 157-170.
Pearson, M.N.
   1976   *Merchants and Rulers in Gujarat: The Response to the Portuguese in the Six-
           teenth Century.* Berkeley: University of California Press.
   1991   "Merchants and States" in Tracy, J., ed., 1991: 52-116.
Pigeaud, Th.G.Th.
   1960-1963 *Java in the Fourteenth Century, A Study in Cultural History,* 5 vols. The
           Hague: Nijhoff.
Pombejra, D. na
   1993   "Seventeenth Century Ayutthaya: A Shift to Isolation?" in Reid, A., ed., 1993:
           250-272.
Prakash, O.
   1985   *The Dutch East India Company and the Economy of Bengal 1630-1729.* Prince-
           ton: Princeton University Press.
Ras, J.J.
   1968   *Hikayat Bandjar: A Study in Malay Historiography.* The Hague: Nijhoff.
Raychaudhuri, T.
   1962   *Jan Company in Coromandel 1605-1690.* Leiden: Koninklijk Instituut.
Raychaudhuri, T. and Habib, I., eds.
   1982   *The Cambridge Economic History of India.* Cambridge: Cambridge University
           Press.
Reid, A. and Marr, D., eds.
   1979   *Perceptions of the Past in Southeast Asia.* Singapore: Heinemann.
Reid, A.
   1983   ed., *Slavery, Bondage and Dependency in South-East Asia.* London: Queens-
           land University Press.
   1988   *Southeast Asia in the Age of Commerce, 1450-1680: The Lands Below the
           Winds.* New Haven: Yale University Press.

134   KENNETH R. HALL

1990   "The Seventeenth Century Crisis in Southeast Asia," *Modern Asian Studies*, 24,
        1: 1-30.
1992   "Economic Change and Social Change, c. 1400-1800" in Tarling, N., ed., 1993:
        I, 460-507.
1993a   ed., *Southeast Asia in the Early Modern Era: Trade, Power, and Belief.* Ithaca,
        New York: Cornell University Press.
1993b   "Introduction: A Time and Place" in Reid, A., ed., 1993: 1-19.
1993c   "Islamization and Christianization in Southeast Asia: The Critical Phase,
        1550-1650" in Reid, A., ed., 1993: 151-179.
Robertson, J.A., ed. and trans.
1906   *Magellan's Voyage around the World by Antonio Pigafetta [1524].* 2 vols.
        Cleveland: Arthur H. Clark.
Reynolds, F. and Reynolds, M.
1982   *The Three Worlds according to King Ruang. A Thai Buddhist Cosmology.* Berke-
        ley: Center for South and Southeast Asian Studies.
Rhys Davids, T.W. and Oldenberg, H., trans.
1965-1969 *Vinayapitaka*, multiple volumes. Delhi: Motilal Banarsidass.
Sabloff, J.A. and Lamberg-Karlovsky, C.C., eds.
1975   *Ancient Civilization and Trade.* Albuquerque, New Mexico: University of New
        Mexico Press.
Sangermano, V.
1966   *A Description of the Burmese Empire.* trans. W. Tandy. Rome: 1818, reprint
        London: Susil Gupta.
Solyom, B. and Solyom, G.
1984   *Fabric Traditions of Indonesia.* Pullman, Washington: Washington State Uni-
        versity Press.
Supomo, S.
1979   "The Image of Majapahit in Later Javanese and Indonesian History" in Reid,
        A. and Marr, D., eds., 1979: 171-185.
Tambiah, S.J.
1976   *World Conqueror and World Renouncer: A Study of Buddhism and Polity in
        Thailand against a Historical Background.* Cambridge: Cambridge University
        Press.
Tarling, N., ed.
1992   *The Cambridge History of Southeast Asia.* 2 vols. Cambridge: Cambridge Uni-
        versity Press.
Taylor, K.W.
1992   "The Early Kingdoms" in Tarling, N., ed., 1992: I, 137-182.
Taylor, P.M. and Argon, L.U.
1991   *Beyond the Java Sea: Art of Indonesia's Outer Islands.* New York: Harry N.
        Abrams.
Tideman, J.
1938   *Djambi.* Amsterdam: Koloniaal Instituut.
Tracy, J., ed.
1991   *The Political Economy of Merchant Empires.* Oxford: Oxford University Press.
Wallerstein, I.
1974, 1979 *The Modern World System.* 2 vols. New York: Academic Press.
Warming, W. and Gaworski, M.
1981   *The World of Indonesian Textiles.* Tokyo: Serinda Publications.
Warren, J.F.
1990   "Trade, Slave Raiding and State Formation in the Sulu Sultanate in the Nine-
        teenth Century" in Kathirithamby-Wells, J. and Villiers, J., eds., 1990: 187-211.

THE TEXTILE INDUSTRY IN SOUTHEAST ASIA, 1400-1800   135

Willmott, W.E., ed.
    1972   *Economic Organization in Chinese Society.* Stanford, California: Stanford University Press.
Wheatley, P.
    1975   "Satyanrta in Suvarnadvipa: From Reciprocity to Redistribution in Ancient Southeast Asia" in Sabloff, J.A. and Lamberg-Karlovsky, C.C., eds., 1975: 227-283.
Wolters, O.W.
    1982   *History, Culture and Region in Southeast Asian Perspectives.* Singapore: Institute of Southeast Asian Studies.
Woodward, H.W., Jr.
    1977   "A Chinese Silk Depicted at Candi Sewu" in Hutterer, K.L., ed., 1977: 233-244.
Wyatt, D.K.
    1984   *Thailand.* New Haven: Yale University Press.
Zen Sun, E-tu
    1972   "Sericulture and Silk Textile Production in Ch'ing China" in Willmott, W.E., ed., 1972, pp. 79-108.

11
West African Textiles, 1500–1800
Carolyn Keyes Adenaike

Venturing down the Atlantic coast of Africa in the early fifteenth century, Portuguese mariners were seeking African gold, the trade of the Orient, and the fabled kingdom of Prester John. Finding none of the above, they instead embarked on the trade in human beings. However, Africa's textile resources were as attractive to the early Portuguese as its human resources. From their first encounters with Africa, the Portuguese recognized the lucrative trade possibilities in Africa's textile materials. This wealth in textile resources fueled the early Portuguese attempts at colonization and exploration of Africa, quickly becoming and long remaining a staple of Euro-African commerce.

In meeting Africa, the Portuguese encountered a continent far better endowed than their own with the raw materials necessary for the manufacture of textiles. At the time of the Portuguese arrival, Africa already had an extensive and well-developed industry producing textiles from its own diverse sources of plant and animal fibers. In the northern arid and semi-arid regions of the continent, animal fibers could be obtained from domestic sheep (wool), camels and horses. In the forests of West Africa, an indigenous species of silkworm produced protein fibers from which silk thread could be manufactured. Sources of vegetable fibers included – but were not limited to – flax (linen) and cotton. Throughout the continent, the trees and plants of forests and savannahs provided an array of potential textile materials, culled from leaves and barks, and from the midribs of the raphia palm. If we include as textile materials all the vegetable fibers from which such items as ropes and mats could be twisted, plaited or woven, then the range of potential sources grows to encompass a staggering array of grasses from all but the most arid regions of the continent.[1]

If the ecological diversity of the world's second largest continent can be said to have yielded an abundant variety of textile fibers, its endowment with resources for dyestuffs was even greater. Animal, vegetable and mineral sources from which dyes could be obtained were plentiful. Animal dyes could be harvested from shellfish and insects. Mineral dyes could be procured from elements and compounds occurring naturally in the rocks and soils, particularly from iron ore and certain types of mud. The list of potential sources of vegetable dyestuffs would be the longest of all. Vegetable dyes could be obtained from a plethora of plants, from the leaves, roots, barks, wood, seeds, nuts and fruits of trees, and from shrubs, vines and grasses.[2]

That African technologies permitted the extraction and use of many of these raw materials for the manufacture of textiles before the time the Portuguese arrived cannot be doubted. The Egyptians had manufactured and dyed textiles from the time of the Pharaohs. The emperors of Rome had clothed themselves in gowns rendered purple with North African dyestuffs. In West Africa, archaeological samples of textiles date back to the eighth century

---

[1] J.M. Dalziel, *Useful Plants of West Tropical Africa* (London: Crown Agents for the Colonies, 1937).

[2] Jacques Miege, 'Couleurs, teintures et plantes tinctoriales en Afrique Occidentale', *Bulletin du Centre Génèvois d'Anthropologie* 3 (1991–92), 115–31.

AD in Mali, and to the tenth century in Nigeria.[3] By the eleventh century, when European textile makers were still working with the relatively simpler processes required to manufacture and dye protein fibers, West African producers had already mastered the more difficult procedures required by vegetable fibers, as archaeological records show an extensive and varied production of dyed cotton textiles from that time.[4] From the early days of European contact with the Atlantic coast, travelers accounts spoke consistently and admiringly of the richness and variety of African textiles, considering them superior in quality and color-fastness to those manufactured in Europe.[5] There can be no doubt that on arriving on the West African coast the Portuguese encountered an old and sophisticated textile industry, one well in advance of their own.

This encounter provided impetus for further Portuguese exploration of the coast and motivated the Portuguese to establish their first Atlantic African colonies. First reaching the Canary Islands off the northwest coast in 1312, the Portuguese found dyestuffs there derived from the lichens and resins of the islands. Motivated by the possible profits of trade in this resource to Europe, they sought to control of its trade through the political control of the islands producing it. By the 1330s colonization attempts were under way, their prime objective being the procurement of dyestuffs, and the organization of Canarians to accomplish this end. The island of Madeira was similarly colonized, producing dyestuffs for European trade by the early fifteenth century (c. 1425). These islands provided the gateway for the Portuguese exploration of the Atlantic, both southwards along the African coast and westwards to the Americas. Using these islands as a base and continuing down the African coast, the Portuguese developed a middleman position for themselves in the inter-African textile trade, carrying both cloth and slaves from one port to another. The trade in textile materials was at first was more significant than that in slaves. Only with the establishment of European colonies in the New World would the infamy of the trade in slaves outstrip the fame of the trade in textiles.[6]

Dyes purchased from Africa, for use in Europe's own growing textile industry fueled European commercial and imperial expansion in Africa for many centuries. Although often frustrated in their attempts to rival the colors turned out by African producers, European textile manufacturers continued to import great quantities of African dyestuffs measured in tons until well after 1800.[7] As substantial as this trade in dyes was, the quantity of trade in

---

[3] Jean Devisse, et al. (eds.), *Vallées du Niger* (Paris: Éditions de la Réunion des musées nationaux, 1993), 547–8. Thurstan Shaw, *Igbo Ukwu: An Account of Archaeological Discoveries in Eastern Nigeria*, 2 vols. (Evanston, IL: Northwestern University Press, 1970), vol. 1, 240–44.

[4] Rita Bolland, *Tellem Textiles: Archaeological Finds from Burial Caves in Mali's Bandiagara Cliff*, trans. Patricia Wardle (Amsterdam: Royal Tropical Institute, 1991). For further discussion see Carolyn Keyes, 'Adire: Cloth, Gender and Social Change in Southwestern Nigeria, 1841–1991' (Ph.D. dissertation, University of Wisconsin-Madison, 1993), 1–65.

[5] Some examples are reproduced in Elizabeth Isichei, *A History of Nigeria* (London: Longman, 1983), 59, 73.

[6] John Thornton, *Africa and Africans in the Making of the Atlantic World, 1400–1680* (Oxford: Cambridge University Press, 1992), 23, 28–30, 33. The interested reader will find more about West African textiles in Georgy Brooks, *Landlords and Strangers* (Boulder, CO: Westview, 1993).

[7] C.W. Newbury, *British Policy Towards West Africa: Select Documents, 1786–1874* (London: Oxford University Press, 1965), 104. C.W. Newbury, *British Policy Towards West Africa: Select Documents, 1875–1914* (London: Oxford University Press, 1971), 385, 506, 630.

textile fibers and finished fabrics was also very great. After 1500, the combined growth of European colonization of the Americas and the European expansion of cotton textile manufacturing propelled cotton fiber to the fore. Textiles from Europe and Asia were exchanged for slaves in Africa. The slaves were put to work on plantations in the Americas producing indigo and cotton. Dyestuffs and later also cotton fiber from both the Americas and Africa fed the textile industry of Europe. Dyestuffs and cotton fueled the slave trade in Africa,the growth of industry in the Europe, and European imperial expansion in both America and Africa.

So pervasive and basic was the role played by textiles in the history of Afro-European commercial contact, that this simple truism can all too easily be overlooked, relegated to the position of the 'grass' by scholars more captivated by the 'fight of the elephants'. The wealth of natural resources for the manufacture of textiles in Africa was a fact of which those who traded in and used those resources were well aware. The variety of African textiles was as obvious to European merchants of the time as was their technical superiority over the manufactures of Europe. As one scholar has observed, 'All this was on the record; but the record was forgotten'.[8] African textiles are today conspicuous in most history books primarily by their absence. This very absence has created an image of an Africa denuded of its textile history, deprived of its industry, and stripped of its natural resources. The silence has permitted scholars to argue that cotton was unknown in some places prior to European contact, that dyes other than indigo were also unknown, and that African weavers created their colorful fabrics from threads unravelled from imported European fabrics. The net effect is one of an Africa drably clothed until the Europeans arrived and brought it color. The reverse is closer to the truth.[9]

Few pre-1800 textile samples have survived, but the few survivors give witness to an African past colorfully clothed in a diversity of traditions. From grave goods deposited in Mali's Bandiagara Cliffs between the eleventh and seventeenth centuries, a cultural and political backwater at the time, comes evidence of trade with Coptic Egypt, use of dyes of many colors, tie-dye, weaving of numerous designs, tailoring of garments of many types. From seventeenth-century Ardrah come robes of blue and red, tie-dyed with a different technique, tailored in a unique style, woven in again different designs. Scattered eighteenth-century textiles include sophisticated brocade.[10] The surviving samples are too few across time and space, insufficient evidence in themselves with which to reconstruct a history, but eloquent testimony hinting at the richness and diversity of that forgotten history.

European trade documents often limit themselves to tersely pragmatic lists of quantities and prices of types of textiles. The writers of these documents took it for granted that their readers would know what perpetuanas (European woolens) were, and would properly fill an

---

[8] Basil Davidson, *Africa in Modern History* (London: Penguin, 1981), 32.

[9] This stereotype derives in part from some older scholarship. Marion Johnson, 'Technology, Competition and African Crafts', in *The Imperial Impact: Studies in the Economic History of Africa and India*, University of London Institute of Commonwealth Studies, ed. Clive Dewey and A.G. Hopkins, Commonwealth Papers no. 21 (London: Athlone Press, 1978), 259–69.

[10] Lisa Aronson, 'Akwete Weaving: A Study of Change in Response to the Palm Oil Trade in the Nineteenth Century' (Ph.D. dissertation, Indiana University, 1982), 103, 110. Bolland, *Tellem Textiles*. Adam Jones, 'A Collection of African Art in Seventeenth-Century Germany: Christoph Weickmann's Kunst- und Naturkammer', *African Arts* 27 (1994), 33, 35–6.

order for them. While many of the items on these shopping lists were textiles, the specific types of cloth to which these names referred is not always certain. Descriptions and especially samples are few and far between. Yet these lists make it clear that one piece of cloth was not as good as another. They insisted on certain types obtained from particular places and in specific colors, because they would find ready sale or fetch a fine price in a particular port. They lamented too the whims of fashion, as a ship laden with an item popular in a place but a few months previously would find that item no longer desirable, having been replaced by another. And so we learn that the tastes of the buyers dictated the terms of the trade, but we are left to guess what the objects of those tastes looked like.[11]

Oral traditions on the African side are frequently no more instructive than trade documents and ledgers of Europeans. When they mention textiles at all, it is usually with the assumption that the hearer will understand. Technical names for objects and substances may be employed in poetic verse, unexplained. Names for fabrics and garments, the objects to which they once referred long fallen into disuse and forgotten, may be retained in prose and verse, the verbal equivalent of aerial photographs for the archaeologist, and useful for identifying sites potentially fruitful for investigation. In other cases, specialized names may be known only to certain groups of persons, containing in themselves traces of the past. To piece together these traces, decipher the names and match them with the textiles to which they referred is a task not unlike assembling a jigsaw puzzle without all of the pieces. In the end, sufficient pieces may never be found to put together the whole picture.

Yet these fragments show the picture to have been one of great variety. The unifying factor appears not to have been a common tradition, but innovation. Innovation in fashion and taste, technology and technique. Nowhere is this variety more evident than in the textiles from Tellem – of hundreds of fragments, no two are the same. They vary in color, design, weave and fiber. Continuities between these and samples collected at Ardrah are notably absent.[12] The style and structure of the garments vary as greatly as do the fabrics from which they were made. The obvious conclusion is that fashions and tastes were subject to rapid change, to which both production and trade had to be accomodated. If it is possible to speak of an African textile tradition, then it was a tradition of change.

The history of Africa's technologies is yet to be written, and textile technology is no exception. Diffusionist models (the wheel could only have been invented once, therefore all wheels everywhere derived from one archetypal wheel) fail to account for the diversity of textile technology employed in Africa. Usually applied to looms, these models most often suppose two archetypes – a narrow-loom archetype and a broad-loom archetype – attempting to demonstrate that all weaving in Africa derived from one or the other of two variously

---

[11] Examples may be found in Margaret Makepeace, *Trade on the Guinea Coast, 1657–1666: The Correspondence of the English East India Company* (Madison: African Studies Program, University of Wisconsin, 1991). Kenneth Morgan, *Bristol and the Atlantic Trade in the Eighteenth Century* (Cambridge: Cambridge University Press, 1993), 133–4. David Richardson, 'West African Consumption Patterns and their Influence on the Eighteenth-Century English Slave Trade', in *The Uncommon Market: Essays on the Atlantic Slave Trade*, eds. Henry A. Gemery and Jan S. Hogendorn (New York: Academic Press, 1979), 303–30. John Vogt, 'Notes on the Portuguese Cloth Trade in West Africa, 1480–1540', *International Journal of African Historical Studies* 8 (1975), 623–51, counted 102 types of European cloth from England, Flanders, Italy and Spain marketed to North and West African ports.

[12] Bolland, *Tellem Textiles*. Jones, 'A Collection', 35–6.

AFRICA 255

WEST AFRICAN TEXTILES 5

placed original centers. But this distinction is an artificial one as the size of the loom is less important than the mechanism by which it works, with shape and mechanism being independent variables. Loom size and structure were probably determined more by the type of fiber to be woven and the type of textile desired.[13]

European observers reported a broad range of looms as well as fabrics woven without a loom. Africans employed broad looms and narrow looms, vertical, horizontal and oblique looms. Some looms used continuous warping and others used discrete warping. There were looms with single, double or multiple heddles, or no heddles at all. Some looms had treadles, or foot pedals, in varying numbers, and other looms had none. A history of loom technology would need to account for this variety. Weave structures, fiber types and fiber technologies (spun or unspun, spinning technology, tensile strength, etc.) would also be an essential component of a history of weaving technology. Without the study of fiber technology, no history of weaving technology can be complete.[14]

The study of African garments and tailoring is at an even more rudimentary stage than that of weaving. Buried under generalizations about 'wrappers' and 'robes', the area is waiting for its historians. The history of garments is inseparable from that of weaving and fibers, as cloth was made to be used and the use for which it was intended must in many cases have influenced the means and dimensions of its manufacture.

As of yet, it is possible to do no more than suggest the broad outlines of a history of dyestuffs and dyeing, and even this much is possible only because the technology and the chemistry of dyeing are so closely linked. Although chemical studies of African textiles and dyes are crucial, no attempt has yet been made to study the chemistry of African dyestuffs, and textile samples in museum collections have not been tested for African dyes.[15] Until and unless chemical studies are undertaken, there can be no history of dye technology. Without a history of dye technology, no history of textiles can be complete. To date, of all the numerous African sources of textile dyes, only indigo has been the object of chemical study.[16]

One can suggest that the earliest African dyes should have been the simplest to use, particularly those which require only water and salt to yield the dye (substantive dyes). Also potentially very old are a number of dyestuffs containing high concentrations of tannins; such dyestuffs do not require the addition of mordants, as the tannic acid naturally present in the plant is capable of fulfilling that role. Probably also quite old is the use of compounds of iron oxide as a dye, with the use of iron as a mordant for vegetable dyes probably following afterwards. Logically, dyes requiring more complex processes (vat dyes and mordant dyes) should have developed later. This development may have been complete by the eleventh

---

[13] The argument for the importance of mechanism has been effectively made by John Picton, 'Tradition, Technology and Lurex: Some Comments on Textile History and Design in West Africa', in *History, Design and Craft in West African Strip-Woven Cloth: Papers Presented at a Symposium Organized by the National Museum of African Art, Smithsonian Institution, February 18–19 1988* (Washington DC: National Museum of African Art, 1992), 13–52.

[14] Examples of this variety may be found in Brigitte Menzel, *Textilien aus Westafrika*, 3 vols. (Berlin: Veroffentlichungen des Museums fur Volkerkunde Berlin, Neue Folge 26, 1972).

[15] Bolland, *Tellem Textiles*, 294–5.

[16] O.L. Oke, 'The Chemistry and General History of Dyeing', in *Adire Cloth in Nigeria*, ed. J. Barbour and D. Simmonds (Ibadan: Institute of African Studies, University of Ibadan, 1971), 43–8.

century in West Africa, as archaeological textiles from Mali show that a broad range of dyes was in use at that time.[17] In Africa, the youngest of the natural dyes were probably those derived from plants of foreign introduction, several of which were brought from the Americas between the fifteenth and nineteenth centuries.

In the broadest outlines of a likely development from the simpler substantive dyes to the more complex processes required with vat and mordant dyes, the early progress of dyeing in West Africa was perhaps not completely unlike that of Europe. There, however, the similarity ends, as the industries on the two continents followed separate lines of development. Differences of climate and raw materials, as well as concepts about mordants and dye chemistry, doubtless all played their roles, and African dyers developed very different technologies from those of their European counterparts.[18]

For the history of trade in textiles between Europe and Africa one would expect much greater detail, as the sources available are both more abundant and more conventional in type. Yet in the present state of knowledge the picture remains lamentably incomplete.

Trade in textile goods began almost immediately upon Portuguese arrival in Africa. In addition to purchasing raw materials (mainly dyestuffs) and finished products for export to Europe, the Portuguese were also able to occupy a niche in the inter-African textile trade. They purchased textiles from one part of the coast for re-sale elsewhere along the coast. Whether they created this role for themselves and so stimulated the inter-African cloth trade, or simply fell into the role as supplemental middlemen in an existing trade network is not certain. It may be supposed that their ocean-going vessels complemented African coastal and riverain craft, facilitating or extending the reach of existing African networks of overland or waterborne trade along the coast. Systems of creeks and lagoons existed along many parts, but not all, of the Atlantic coast (Loango, Senegambia, Sierra Leone, Liberia, Ivory Coast and Nigeria), and these as well as extensive riverain systems reaching far inland were navigable by African craft. The larger European ships coasted the deeper waters. This navigational complementarily may have facilitated the extension of water-borne cloth trade, integrating riverain, lagoon, and ocean-borne trade into a single commercial network reaching far inland as well as along thousands of miles of coastline. This commercial integration may have stimulated African textile production. European traders found their role sufficiently profitable to justify continuing their middleman activities in the inter-African cloth trade for several centuries.[19]

The volume of the textile trade was very great. Cloth was doubtless the single largest category of goods which Europe exported to Africa,[20] and the African side of the exchange was no less considerable. Although the data is sketchy, it does indicate the magnitude of the African trade. As an example, eastern Kongo in the early seventeenth century was exporting

---

[17] Bolland, *Tellem Textiles*. The earliest dyed textiles so far recovered in West Africa date from the eighth century and are red, green and blue, Devisse, *Vallées du Niger*, 547–8.

[18] For further discussion, see Keyes, 'Adire', 7–11.

[19] Thornton, *Africa and Africans*, 20. J.E. Inikori, 'Africa in World History: The Export Slave Trade from Africa and the Emergence of the Atlantic Economic Order', in *General History of Africa*, vol. 5, ed. B.A. Ogot (Paris: UNESCO, 1992), 101.

[20] Thornton, *Africa and Africans*, 45. A considerable portion of these were re-exports from Asia. Morgan, *Bristol*, 134.

some 100,000 meters of cloth to Angola. Its exports also went in the other direction along the coast to Loango, where the death of a seventeenth century ruler occasioned a display of wealth that included some 700 meters of cloth imported from eastern Kongo, in addition to a variety of Asian and European fabrics.[21] The Central African trade is presented elsewhere in this volume.

The volume of trade in West Africa was no less impressive than in Central Africa. It has been calculated that the kingdom of Benin exported some 5–10,000 meters of cloth annually to other parts of Africa, mainly the Gold Coast, while also importing Dutch linens and Indian fabrics. In the 1640s, the Dutch were reselling to the Gold Coast 'thousands of cloths' purchased from Allada (on the Slave Coast). In addition, the Gold Coast in the seventeenth century was also importing some 20,000 meters of European and Asian cloth per year.[22] There can be little doubt that the bulk of imported textiles represented only a small fraction of the total cloth consumption at a given place and time, and that many imports were luxury items destined for the elite.[23]

In considering the volume of trade, the role of re-exports should also not be overlooked. Areas with sustained high levels of turnover in both imports and exports of cloth may in fact have been re-exporting some of what they imported. In the cases of Kongo and Benin it is striking that these same regions were both among the largest importers of European cloth and the largest exporters of local cloth. This may have been because these were the major cloth-producing areas and thus commanded pre-existing highly sophisticated marketing systems, into which additional imports from Europe could easily be fed. The influx of imports may have stimulated existing markets. Re-manufacturing should also not be overlooked as a possible factor. In the case of seventeenth-century Allada, European imports were unravelled and rewoven, and then re-exported both in Africa and across the Atlantic, where they fetched a high price. These and other areas may have functioned as major cloth production-distribution centers.[24]

In the fifteenth century, the Portuguese role in the export of African cloth was limited to commerce within Europe and along the Atlantic coast of Africa. In the sixteenth century, it expanded to include the export of African fabrics across the Atlantic. From the sixteenth century, a sort of trans-Atlantic triangular trade in textiles developed. Raw materials (dyes and cotton) were carried by European merchants from the Americas to Europe, where they were used in the manufacture of European textiles. European textiles were carried by sea to Africa, where they were exchanged for African fabrics and raw materials. African raw materials (mostly dyes) went back to Europe. African fabrics went both along the Atlantic coast of Africa and west across the Atlantic.

By the seventeenth century, other European nations had become involved, including the Dutch, Danes, Swedes and Germans. European middlemen purchased fabrics from Asia for

---

[21] Thornton, *Africa and Africans*, 49, 51–2.

[22] Ibid.

[23] Thornton, *Africa and Africans*, 50, estimates that European and Asian imports represented 2 percent of annual cloth consumption on the Gold Coast. There is at present little data about textile use and durability with which to evaluate overall consumption patterns.

[24] Thornton, *Africa and Africans*, 51–2. E. M'Bokolo, 'From the Cameroon Grasslands to the Upper Nile', in *General History of Africa*, vol. 5, ed. B.A. Ogot (Paris: UNESCO, 1992), 527.

resale in Africa, where they found a ready market. This trade was profitable enough that by the eighteenth century the Dutch textile industry sprouted a branch specifically devoted to the manufacture in Holland of imitation Asian fabrics, for sale to Africa. By the eighteenth century the Dutch, British and French had replaced the Portuguese as the leading cloth merchants. Competing with each other to feed their expanding textile industries, they depended both on an African market for the finished products and on the resources of Africa to supply raw materials and labor in the Americas. The British also began to manufacture textiles intended solely for the African market.[25]

By the eighteenth century, the triangular pattern of trade on the Atlantic had become entrenched, and best known for its human cargo. The slave trade was at its peak. Far from being displaced by the slave trade, textiles were a key component of that trade. Together, guns, alcohol and cloth were the three main commodities provided, almost always in combination, to procure slaves. From Africa were sent the human laborers to work the plantations of cotton and sugar in the New World, to produce the raw materials to supply European industry. The finished products of that industry, cloth from cotton, alcohol from sugar cane, and guns, were in turn sold to Africa to obtain more labor. Textiles were an integral part of the classic equation of the slave trade. Although African textiles continued to be exported, their role in the equation is less clear.[26]

Emphasis on the role of European middlemen has tended to obscure the role of Africans in setting the terms of the trade. Slaves were sold because African merchants agreed to sell them, and it was they who fixed the prices, the value and terms of the exchange. While guns and rum can be said to have had the effect of ensuring the supply of slaves for sale, the role of imported textiles in the equation reflected the tastes of the African merchants and consumers. European and Asian textiles were imported mainly as luxury goods, destined for the wealthy elite. Which ones, how many, and at what prices were subject to the fashions and tastes of the Africans who purchased them. Demand was by no means constant, as the fabrics in high demand (and therefore commanding high prices) were subject to sudden changes, as the ledgers of European merchants show, and not infrequently lament.[27]

The impact of the European trade (draining raw materials, some more renewable than others) and especially of the slave trade (draining labor) on textile production in Africa is not yet clear. The drain of human and material resources must have affected production, but to what effect and what extent is uncertain. Similarly, the extent to which this was compensated by the wealth derived from the trade and the import of luxury fabrics is also not

---

[25] M. Malowist, 'The Struggle for International Trade and its Implications for Africa', in *General History of Africa*, vol. 5, ed. B.A. Ogot (Paris: UNESCO, 1992), 1–22. Johannes Postma, *The Dutch in the Atlantic Slave Trade 1600–1815* (Cambridge: Cambridge University Press, 1990), 73–6. Ruth Nielsen, 'The History and Development of Wax-Printed Textiles Intended for West Africa and Zaire', in *The Fabrics of Culture: The Anthropology of Clothing and Adornment*, ed. Justine M. Cordwell and Ronald A. Schwarz (The Hague: Mouton, 1979), 467–98.

[26] Postma, *The Dutch*, 103–5.

[27] Although recent scholarship has re-evaluated the role of Africans in setting the terms of trade (see Thornton, *Africa and Africans*, 52–71), a stereotype still persists of Africa as a passive dumping ground for 'cheap' European textiles (Malowist, 'The Struggle', 3, 12). This too is being re-evaluated, and recent estimates place the proportion of luxury textiles at 50 percent or higher of the fabrics traded to Africa. Postma, *The Dutch*, 104–5. Thornton, *Africa and Africans*, 44–5, 48.

certain. One can speculate that the slave trade must have impacted not only on African production, but also on the uses to which the manufactures of that production were put. Changing social classes, concentrating wealth in the hands of those who controlled the supply of slaves, draining wealth from those among whose communities the slaves were taken, increasing insecurity of both life and property, all of these may be expected to have affected the production and use of textiles in West and Central Africa.

The impact of the slave trade on European perceptions of Africa should not be underestimated. The accounts of European traders in the era of the slave trade often gave contrasting colorations to their depictions of those selling slaves on the one hand and those selling other commodities on the other. The trade in slaves had to be justified, the human beings in question presented as somehow less than human, or else the trade could not have continued. Exporting primarily cloth and pepper in the sixteenth an seventeenth centuries, the kingdom of Benin is one example. European visitors portrayed it in genial terms, in contradistinction to its more heavily slave-trading neighbors. Without belaboring the point, it is well to bear in mind that the descriptions European traders have left us of Africa were to a large extent self-serving descriptions. Thus Benin was long admired, its people described as 'very gentle and loving'. Only on the eve of conquest would it become the 'City of Blood'. Yet its neighbors had long been characterized with negative stereotypes.[28] To recover the history of textiles we must first be aware of, and critical of, the presence in the sources of self-serving misinformation, stereotypical statements that served to justify the gravest of injustices. This is particularly apparent for the history of production.

In the area of production, scholarship has been slow to abandon certain underlying assumptions, among them the stereotypes that African production was generally small in scale, that the technologies used were simple or rudimentary, that the products were inferior.[29] Some studies of African textile production have, however, yielded strong challenges to these notions, demonstrating large–scale, high–volume production employing sophisticated technologies and characterized by high levels of economic and professional specialization, in a manner not unlike the model of industrial production advanced by Isichei.[30]

To accept the supposition that African production was small and unsophisticated would make it easy to accept also the supposition that African production was easily and significantly influenced by contact with the products and methods of European manufacture. But it would be an error to think that African producers could not compete with European producers, thus throwing open the market for European manufactured goods, or that African consumers, once they came in contact with the manufactures of Europe quickly recognized

---

[28] A.F.C. Ryder, *Benin and the Europeans, 1485–1897* (New York: Humanities Press, 1969), 84, 92–3, 247–8, 250–51. Thornton, *Africa and Africans*, 67–9, 110–11.

[29] A.G. Hopkins, *An Economic History of West Africa* (London: Longman, 1973) was one of the more influential proponents of African economic underdevelopment. The critique of economic history has been made by Philip Shea, 'Economies of Scale and the Indigo Dyeing Industry of Precolonial Kano', *Kano Studies* n.s. 2(1) (1974–77): 55–61, and more recently by Thornton, *Africa and Africans*, 1–9, 43–53.

[30] Philip Shea, 'The Development of an Export-Oriented Dyed Cloth Industry in Kano Emirate in the Nineteenth Century' (Ph.D. dissertation, University of Wisconsin-Madison, 1975). Jan Vansina 'Raffia Cloth in West Central Africa 1500–1800', included in the present volume. Keyes, 'Adire', 204–22. Isichei, *A History*, 57–64.

these materials as superior and adopted them in preference to their own.[31] For textiles, the equation was not that simple. African materials continued to be exported, African textiles continued to fetch a high price both in Africa and in the New World, and Europeans continued to recognize the technical superiority of West African cloth until well after 1800.[32] Stereotypical notions combined with the slow accumulation of research on African textiles produced a one-sided view – as if innovation flowed in one direction only, from Europe to Africa. Yet innovation flowed in both directions.

African influence on European production was multi-faceted. The importation and adaptation of African dyestuffs for European industry is one example. But Europe also relied on Africa as an export market for its finished cloth, and African consumers' tastes dictated the market. To maintain marketability European manufacturers tailored their manufactures to this African market. Both Holland and Britian developed branches of their textile industries devoted to producing cloth for African consumption. On the African side, where finished cloth was also exported, special types of cloth were also created for the inter-African and American export markets.[33] African consumers were no passive accepters of whatever Europe sent them, but discriminating buyers whose tastes strongly influenced not only the marketing but also the production of cloth in Europe as well as in Africa.

The social use of textiles in Africa is an essential part of the equation. It is also a remarkably understudied part of the equation. Most pernicious here are stereotypes of Africans as wearing little or no clothing, living in relatively undifferentiated societies, their lives constrained materially and otherwise by the dictates of rigidly unchanging tradition.[34] This image is false. The reality is that the social use of textiles (primarily dress) provided visual expression of complex social differentiation.[35] The social use of dress is inseparable from social history, in Africa as much as in other parts of the world.

Changes in dress went hand in hand with social changes. The social use of textiles (dress) was subject not so much to tradition as to changing fashions and tastes. Dress reflected social status, and fashion as such was the preserve of the elite. Fashionable and expensive fabrics, whether imported or locally made, were by definition a luxury trade. This much is valid as a generalization. Cloth, during the period in question, was often hoarded by the wealthy elite as a form of wealth in itself. This also is clear in broadly general terms. Beyond that the specifics must be studied locally, not in the sense of ethnic traditions but in terms of the styles, fashions and tastes prevailing in a particular town or local area at a

---

[31] For example, Eve de Negri, 'Nigerian Textile Industry Before Independence', *Nigeria Magazine* 89 (1966), 95–101.

[32] Pierre Verger, *Flux et reflux de la traite des nègres entre le Golfe du Bénin et Bahia de Todos os Santos du XVIIe au XVIIIe siecle* (Paris: Mouton, 1968), 526–7, includes a nineteenth century description of the use of expensive imported African cloth in Bahia. Thornton, *Africa and Africans*, 51, 53, notes that some African textiles were among the most costly in the inter-African trade, and mentions a case of a million Senegambian mats being ordered for marketing in Europe in the early eighteenth century.

[33] According to Thornton, *Africa and Africans*, 49, this was the case in Cape Verde.

[34] The description of Harold Bindloss, *In the Niger Country* (London: Frank Cass, 1968), is one example.

[35] This diversity of dress and its social meaning is particularly apparent in traveler's descriptions of Ghana, for example in the eighteenth century account of Paul Erdman Isert, *Voyages en Guinée et dans les îles Caraïbes en Amérique* (Paris: Karthala, 1989). A careful study of such written records would no doubt yield much for the social history of Ghana.

particular point in time, and of their changes through time and across permeable and changing geographic boundaries.[36]

The history of social use is the essential basis for the rest, as trade and production alike were governed by fashion and taste, hence by social use. Fashion and taste governed the price and popularity of textiles. The uses to which they could be put determined the scope of their market. Where certain textiles (such as imported velvets and damasks) were the prerogative of the ruling elite as the insignia of their status, their market was tightly constrained by the size of this elite and the depth of its pockets, as well as its tastes. Where a type of cloth was produced primarily as daily wear for the common man, the market was clearly large, but proportionately humbly priced. Where cultural practices required special cloth for special purposes (such as grave goods, funerals or initiations) the production and marketing of these were probably most tightly circumscribed.

It follows that cloth imported from Europe could not simply flood the African market indiscriminately. Imports of cloth were governed not by European convenience, but by changing African wants and preferences (a situation still commonly lamented by Europeans in the 1800s). This being the situation, European imports destroyed neither African production nor African taste (and certainly not African technology). European imports of cloth were instead controlled and restricted by the uses to which Africans put these textiles. Africans successfully set the terms of the trade, limiting the type, quantity and value of European textile imports until well after the period covered by this volume. In the process they preserved also the greater share of the African market for African producers.

In conclusion, one may well question the prevailing image of European effects on Africa. The reality was not an unchanging, conservative Africa passively accepting changes brought from an innovative Europe. Rather innovation and materials flowed in both directions. African textile production was on a large scale, as were African exports of fabrics and materials. African social use dictated the market for imported fabrics from Europe, and was inextricable from African social history. From future studies of Africa's textiles will no doubt flow a truer picture of the diversity and productivity of African economies and technologies, a more nuanced image of African societies, and a greater appreciation of Africa's relations with the wider world.

---

[36] See Keyes, 'Adire', 267–300.

12

Raffia Cloth in West Central Africa, 1500–1800

Jan Vansina

> In this kingdom of Congo they make some cloth of palmtrees with a surface (skin) like velvet and some worked like velvety satin, so beautiful that those made in Italy do not surpass them in workmanship. And in the whole of the other Guinea there is no other land in which they know how to make these textiles other than in this kingdom of Congo.[1]

In these words, written around 1505–1507, a leading Portuguese cosmographer, well acquainted with the coast of Central Africa reported on raffia cloth as one of the products of the kingdom of Kongo (and of the neighboring Loango coast) that had most struck the imagination of his compatriots since their arrival in these lands. Early visitors were astonished to find excellent cloth 'very well woven and with many colors' made out of raffia. Indeed some of this cloth was ornamented 'in high and low relief like velveted satin among us', and the ability to execute quite naturalistic 'needle work'on such cloth was admired. The return gift of the king of Kongo to the king of Portugal *c.* 1488 comprised many pieces of dyed cloth 'in vivid colours'.[2] Evidently he had a hoard of these cloths in his store houses. Europeans found such cloths desirable. Cushions covered with them and lengths of decorated Kongo *mfula* cloth are already listed in the estate of a Portuguese trader of São Tomé who died in 1507.[3] Nor was this passing praise. The excellence and diversity of raffia textiles from western Central Africa continued to be extolled by Europeans until well into the eighteenth century – including the favorable comparison with Italian fabrics.[4]

Furthermore, various museums still treasure some seventeenth-century raffia textiles from the Loango coast, Kongo and the colony of Angola while others have been documented in

---

[1] D. Pacheco Pereira, *Esmeraldo de situ orbis* (Lisbon 1954), 171 (book 3:2). The original dates from 1505–1507. 'Nesto reino do Congo se fazem uns panos de palma, de pelo como veludo, e deles como lavores como çatim velutado, tão fermoses que a obra deles se não faz melhor, feita em Itália. E em oda a outra Guiné não há terra em que saibam fazer estes pannos senão neste reino do Congo'.

[2] For mentions by the early chroniclers Rui da Pina, Garcia de Resende and Joaõ de Barros see A. Brasio, *Monumental Missionaria Africana. África occidental* (Lisbon 1951), vol. 1, 43, 57, 61, 63, 70, 82, 113, 118. The quotes are taken from them about a royal gift (57, 70): 'e muitos panos de palma bem tecidos e com finas coores'; about a mitre like cap (82) 'com lavores altos e baixos e maneira que ácerca de nós hé a tecedura de cetim avelutado'. On naturalistic needlework 61 'huu carapuça, em que andava hua serpe mui bem lavrada dagulha, e muy natural'.

[3] E. Bassani *Un Cappuccino nell'Africa nera del seicento* (Quaderni Poro 4), (Milan 1987). 86 fn. 52. So common was the use of raffia cloth to cover cushions that some Dutch traders in Loango called them 'cushion-leaves' cf. O. Dapper, *Naukeurige Beschrijvinge der Afrikaensche Gewesten* (Amsterdam, 1676) 2nd edition, Part II, 163, 164, 183. The pagination in the first edition (1668) is different. Dapper was a compiler. On this subject he mostly used Dutch documents from c. 1600 to1650.

[4] E. Bassani, *Un Cappuccino*, 45–6 citing A. Zucchelli da Gradisca *Relazione del viaggio et missione di Congo nell'Ethiopia Inferiore Occidentale* (Venice, 1712), 149. The specimen of luxury cloth kept at the Museum for anthropology in Munich is of 18th or perhaps even early 19th century manufacture. Cf. M. Kecskési *Kunst aus dem Alten Afrika* (Innsbruck, 1982), 279–81, ill. no. 294.

2   JAN VANSINA

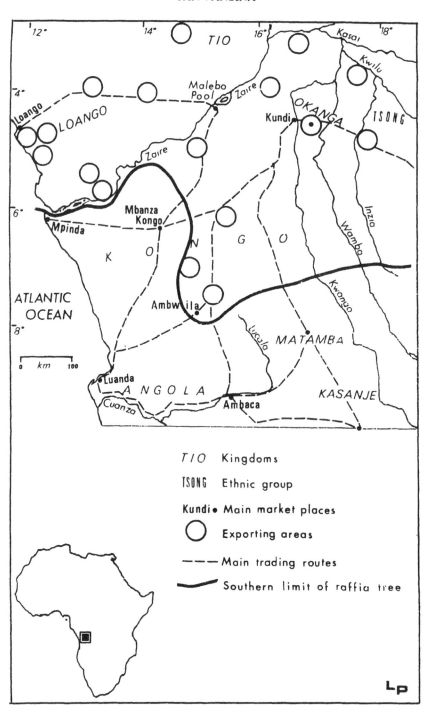

Raaffia Cloth in West Central Africa, 1500–1700

drawings or paintings in seventeenth-century illustrations.[5] They fully confirm the glowing reports about the technical skills and artistic merits of their makers. Last but not least documents from the late sixteenth century onwards give more details about different types and qualities of cloths and report on the extent, complexity, volume and the gains to be made in the raffia cloth trade.

Loango and Kongo moreover are only the tip of an iceberg, for they are the only part of Central Africa that is well documented before the later nineteenth century when data becomes available for the lands further east. At that time considerable amounts of raffia cloth were woven and had apparently been so for centuries in an area stretching from the coast to the edges of lake Tanganyika.[6] This renders a sketch of the major outlines of the history of the manufacturing of raffia cloth and its trade in and around the region of Kongo in earlier centuries even more valuable.[7] Because many readers will be unfamiliar with the technology involved this paper first briefly describes the associated manufacturing processes. It continues with a section on the uses of raffia cloth, followed by a discusion of its trade and use as a currency. The paper concludes with a discussion of the question: how far can the manufacture of raffia in central Africa be called an industry?

1. The Technology of Raffia Manufacturing

Raffia is a fibre derived from the cuticle within the leaflets of raffia leaves.[8] Although this fibre can be obtained from seven varieties of raffia tree Central Africans preferred to use only *Raphia textilis Welw.* and *Raphia Gentilii De Wild.* probably because the fibres obtained from them were longer. In nature raffia trees of all sorts are usually found singly or often in dense stands along brooks, small rivers and swamps.[9] Every single part of the two species of

---

[5] Bassani, *Un Cappuccino* publishes the illustrations made by Cavazzi on the spot in Angola (*c.* 1660) color 1–33) and discusses them, 41–57 (ill. black and white 4, 9–19). A. Jones 'Collection of African Art in Seventeenth-Century Germany', *African Arts* 38 and ill. 23, 24. In all about 50 specimens have been reported from museums in Copenhagen, Rome, London, Ulm, Munich and there are probably others. But none of these textiles have been properly studied.

[6] For a general distribution in what is now Zaire see H. Loir, *Le tissage au Congo Belge* (Tervuren, 1935), map 1. The southern limit of both raffia trees and weaving lies around 7° or 7°30 south, except in what was the kingdom of Kongo. Intensive weaving occurred in the southern part of the distribution area (south of the main rainforests) i.e. roughly south of 3° South.

[7] For an introduction to the sources see especially B. Heintze 'Zur materiellen Kultur der Ambundu nach den Quellen des 16. und 17. Jahrhunderts', *Paideuma* 35 (1989), 119–27; and from an art historical perspective Bassani, *Un Cappucino.* Both these studies focus on Angola. For Kongo J. Thornton, 'Precolonial African Industry and the Atlantic Trade, 1500–1800', *African Economic History* 9–14 focuses on economic aspects. For the Loango coast Phyllis Martin, *The External Trade of the Loango Coast, 1576–1870* (Oxford, 1972), 35–9, 60–65, 106, 165.

[8] The main processes involved are described according to late 19th century practices. Cf Loir, *Le tissage,* 19–47; J. Picton and J. Mack, *African Textiles* (London, 1979), *passim* esp. 32–7; A. Stritzl, *Die Gestickten Raffiaplüsche* (doctoral dissertation, Wien, 1971), especially for dyes. Most of these are confirmed by *c.* 16th and 17th sources..

[9] Picton, Mack, *African Textiles* 32; J.E. Opsomer, 'Les cultures coloniales', *Encyclopédie du Congo Belge* Brussels, 1953, vol. 1, 499; Raponda Walker and R. Sillans, *Les plantes utiles du Gabon* Paris, 1961), 337–40. *Raphia textilis Welw.* was cultivated and used the most for weaving. But see G. Hulstaert, *Notes de botanique mongo* (Brussels, 1966), 134–6 (three raffias: *Raphia gentiliana De Wild.* cultivated, *Raphia Laurentii De Wild.* and *Raphia sese De Wild.* both used but not for weaving).

raffia trees mentioned, not just the leaves, were used by Central Africans[10]. Hence all Central Africans at least spared raffia trees where they found them. In some areas they actually planted them and it was not unheard of to find regular orchards planted near villages where weaving was of major importance.[11]

In the nineteenth century raffia weaving was practiced nearly everywhere where raffia trees grew. The trees require minimal temperatures above 10°C, 1500 mm or more of rain per year, and a dry season shorter than 14 weeks. Hence they occur in the rainforests and their margins – roughly between 6°N. and 7°30 S. – and from the Atlantic Ocean East as far as the high mountains of the western Rift valley. The amount of actual weaving in any region depended primarily on the amount of raffia cloth needed as garments. For raffia was only one of a number of substances like barkcloth, leather and furs, not to mention leaves or grasses that could be used for clothing.[12] In the late nineteenth century most people of the rainforests wore very few clothes and furthermore relied mainly on barkcloth and leaves. Very little raffia was woven there even though some cloth was woven in intricate patterns on the most complex looms known from Central Africa.[13] In contrast in the savannas to the south everyone but small children wore an everyday knee-length raffia skirt, which had to be renewed some three times a year.[14] Costumes for special occasions consisted of several layers of skirts, or plaited skirts many times longer than an ordinary wrapper. Raffia cloth was also used for togas or long coats, bags and accessories. Hence raffia was woven in very large quantities in that region.

The processing from palm leaf to cloth is as follows. To obtain the fibre one cuts the leading fresh topshoot when it is about to unfurl its leaflets from a mature tree, i.e. only one leaf per tree at a time.[15] The many still folded leaflets are then detached from the midrib

---

[10] Walker Sillans, *Plantes utiles* and Hulstaert, *Notes de botanique* . My own fieldnotes (Kuba, Kasai) stress that palmwine, raffia, piassava, construction materials, rooftiles, materials for furniture and even edible grubs and the 'palmcabbage' were all used. Not one part of a raffia tree was wasted.

[11] Laying claim to the ownership of all palmtrees colonial authorities denied that Africans ever cultivated any palmtrees, raffia palms included Hence Loir, *Le tissage*, 19. Yet see Walker, Sillans, *Les plantes utiles*, 339 and Hulstaert, *Notes de botanique*, 134. and around 1610 for Loango S. Brun, *Schiffarten: welche er in etliche newe Laender und Insulen...* (Graz, 1969), 15, 'men tend and plant the wine tree'; E.G. Ravenstein (ed.) *The Strange Adventures of Andrew Battell of Leigh in Angola and Adjoining Regions* (London, 1901), 69, 'Of their palm trees which they keep with watering and cutting every year they make velvets...'. In Kongo c. 1578 W. Bal ed. and translator: *Description du Royaume de Congo et des contrées environnantes par Filippo Pigaffeta et Duarte Lopes (1591)* (Paris, 1965), 37, speaks of careful pruning and lopping. In the 19th century orchards were common in the Kwilu area of Zaire, among the neighboring Lele and Kuba and further east still among the Songye.

[12] In parts of the area people went about almost unclothed, men wearing only a breechcloth and women either a minimal garment made of leaves or tiny aprons. Barkcloth was the main cloth used.

[13] Loir *Le Tissage*, 45–7, 51–3, map 3, Table ill. I and II. Looms such as fig. 41 p. 43 can only be worked by experts.

[14] M. Douglas, 'Raffia cloth Distribution in the Lele Economy', *Africa* 28 (1958), 111 notes that it took at least two woven lengths and 'borders' to fashion an everyday skirt. More elaborate skirts required five to ten lengths.

[15] First observed c. 1578. Cf. Bal, ed. and translator: *Description du Royaume de Congo et des Contrées environnantes par Filippo Pigaffeta et Duarte Lopes (1591)*, (Paris, 1965), 37; Dapper, *Beschrijvinge*, 149; L. Dubois, 'Notes sur les principales plantes à fibres utilisées au Congo belge et au Ruanda-Urundi', *Bulletin agricole du Congo belge* 42 (1951), 881–2; E. Opsomer 'cultures coloniales' A single mature tree produces up to six shoots a year, but cannot be used until it is four years old or older and will last only for four years. The average quantity of raffia produced per leaf remains has not been reported.

which may be up to ten meters long. The skin of each leaflet is incised and peeled off from the translucent fibre within. This dried unfolded fibre is about 1 to 3 cm in width and about one meter long. The fibre can then be used as it is e.g. to make a fringed costume[16] or to twist rope, but most of the fibres are processed further. They are left to dry, sometimes after having been soaked to make them supple.[17] They are then converted into thread by splitting them by hand or more satisfactorily by combing. Only combing allows one to obtain a thin thread. The thinner the thread the tighter the weave the more valuable the cloth.[18] Hence some weavers were not content with combing the fibres once, but did this up to three times.[19] The raffia fibre is then ready for weaving. Central Africans neither twist fibres nor knot them together to make a long continous thread. Hence the length of the fibre, about one meter long dictates the maximum length of fabric that could be woven.[20] Cloth is woven on a single heddle loom, fixed tension either vertical or oblique and set up within a permanent frame of sturdy timbers or stretched between a horizontal roof-pole and a heavy horizontal log on the ground.[21] Operated with one pick it yields a square of cloth measuring well under 1 m by 1 m when in plain weave· Once woven the square of cloth is then cut from the frame and selfedged. By using multiple picks complex designs could be woven.[22]

Lengths of cloth were often sewn together to obtain the size desired for a specific garment, wall hanging or carpet.[23] Raw raffia cloth tends to be stiff, hence it was often softened it by soaking and pounding.[24] The whole garment could then be dyed if and as required.

Dyes were often applied, either to the fibres before weaving or to the whole cloth. The 'painted cloths' of the early Portuguese observers refer both to whole cloths in one color or

---

[16] Dapper, *Beschrijvinge*, 179.

[17] On soaking F. Bontinck ed. and translator *Histoire du royaume du Congo (c. 1624) – Etudes d'histoire africaine* (Paris, 1972), 81; F. Bontinck, ed. and translator, *Jean-François de Rome O.F.M. Cap, , La fondation de la mission des Capucins au Royaume du Congo (1648)* (Paris, 1964), 108.

[18] Ibid., 150 ('de grofte en de fijnte').

[19] Loir, *Le tissage*, 20–22, fig. 3;Picton, Mack, *African Textiles*, 33–7, fig. 26, p. 34; The Lele were reputed for their extra fine cloth. They combed it three times as opposed to the Kuba who combed theirs only once. M. Douglas 'Lele Economy Compared with the Bushong', P. Bohannan and G. Dalton, *Markets in Africa*, 223.

[20] Bal, *Description*, 37; Loir, *Le tissage*, 25; Picton, Mack, *African Textiles*, 37

[21] Loir, *Le tissage*, 22–48 and map 2 (tension). P. I. Darish, 'Dressing for the Next Life', A. Wiener and J. Schneider, *Cloth and Human Experience* (Washington, 1989), 121–3 (Kuba). Early descriptions of looms are so incomplete as to be nearly unusable. Cf. the texts cited in E. Bassani, *Un Capuccino*, who cites the descriptions of Cavazzi (43) and Zucchelli (46) the only two early known descriptions of a loom. Still Zucchelli does report the use of multiple picks. J. Thornton, 'Precolonial' 10, confuses the fabrication of bark cloth and weaving. It is significant that permanent frames were common during the 19th century in most areas where much raffia was produced and that an oblique rather than a vertical loom was used. This allows the weaver to beat the woof in place with less effort.

[22] There were two standard sizes in the 16th and 17th centuries c. 40×40 cm (range 40–45 cm and on the Loango coast only), and c. 52×52 cm (range 50–55 cm). Some lengths for luxury cloth were extra large up to 67×67 cm. These sizes are obtained from estimated sizes mentioned by a dozen sources and from the measurements of a few cloths in museums. These sizes were still the usual ones as late as c. 1900. For instance see A. Mahieu *Numismatique du Congo, 1485–1924* (Brussels, 1925), 13–15.

[23] An apparatus for keeping the two lengths stretched out together for easier sewing has been reported only for some regions and during the nineteenth century.

[24] For recent Kuba procedure P. Darish, 'Dressing for the Next Life', 121. See note 17 for an alternative.

to multiple colors on one cloth. Around 1660 Cavazzi claims 'and as to the range and brilliance of the dyes, they excell those in Europe'. There is evidence for the colours red, yellow, green, blue, brown, and various nuances of these thereof as well as white and black but very little is known as yet about dyestuffs and dyeing techniques.[25] Fibres of different colors used in plain weave yield striped and checkerboard patterns. More complex straight edge geometric designs usually require multiple picks. One cloth can be dyed whole or dyed in one or more patterns by using stitch-dye or tie-dye or stamp dye techniques. All of these have been identified in Central Africa except for stamp dyeing.

The most common additional techniques to embellish cloth were embroidery, sometimes in relief, and the creation of a velvet like pile cloth made by slipping small threads perpendicularly into the fabric – not unlike techniques used to make pile carpets.[26] Open work piqué including quilting is mentioned in two seventeenth-century sources and is also known from nineteenth century Kuba textiles much further east.[27] Appliqué of cloth on cloth is not mentioned in any source before *c.* 1795 although a description of a noble dress in Loango mentions an appliqué of raffia cloth on furs.[28]

A single person did not carry out all these operations. Combing thread, setting up the loom, weaving, sewing lengths together, and tailoring everywhere was the work of adult men weavers, while picking the leaves and obtaining the fibre, among the Kuba at least, was a job for older boys.[29] Beating cloth and embellishing it by any technique was women's work. It is less clear who dyed.[30]

---

[25] Giovanni Antonio Cavazzi de Montecúccolo cited in the edition and translation of Graziano M. de Leguzzano, *Descrição Histórica dos três Reinos Congo Matamba e Angola* (Lisbon, 1965), I. 170 (Book I: 349); Stritzl, *Die Gestickten Raffia Plüsche*, 78–88; Loir, *Le Tissage*, 49–50; Darish 'Dressing for the Next Life', 121, 124 (both genders dye); Heintze, 'Zur materiellen Kultur', 123; Dapper, *Beschrijvinge*, 150 (green); Bassani, *Un Cappucino*, 42–3; Lopes de Lima, *Ensaios sobre a statistica das posessões Portuguezas no ultramar. Livro III. De Angola e Benguella e suas dependencias* (Lisbon, 1846), 54 for indigo (blue) and urzella (red). A substantial range of colors was produced as both seventeenth century illustrations made by Cavazzi and surviving textiles show.

[26] Stritzl, *Die Gestickten Raffia Plüsche*, 72–7. In real carpets the pile is knotted in the fabric.

[27] Dapper, *Beschrijvinge*, 150 mentions Spanish piqué trousers; one can also think of open work like Madeira work. This is the only technique which may have been a 16th or 17th century innovation in imitation of Iberian models. A reference to quilting occurs in G.D. Gibson, C. McGurk, 'High-Status Caps of the Kongo and Mbundu Peoples', *Textile Museum Journal* 4, no. 4, 77 cites G. Merolla, *Breve e succinta relatione del viaggio nel regno di Congo* (Naples, 1692), 77 but in a l ater English translation which may easily have mistranslated such a technical term. Unfortunately I was not able to check the original.

[28] L. Jadin, 'Relation sur le royaume du Congo du P. Raimondo da Dicomano', *Bulletin de l' Académie royale des sciences coloniales* (1957), 323. (A translation but as the action of applying is described there could be no technical error. Dapper, *Beschrijvinge*, 150 (cloth on fur). The naturalistic snake on a 15th century mitre may have been appliqué. Cf. note 2. Appliqué is common on 19th C. Kuba cloth.

[29] Many sources do not specify gender. When they do, they mention men e.g. D. Carli in 1668 for Kongo cited by Thornton, 'Precolonial African Industry', 14. For Loango *c.* 1610 Brun, *Schiffarten*, 18; Ravenstein, *The Strange Adventures*: 50. In the 19th century only men were weavers in Central Africa. Yet in 1701 on the Loango coast. Yet A. Dewar, ed. *The Voyages and Travels of Captain Nathanael Uring* (London, 1928), 39, 40, claims that the weavers were women.

[30] No source directly mentions that women sewed or made pile cloth. But Francesco M. Gioia, *La Maraviglliosa Conversione...della Regina Singa...* (Naples, 1669), 181 has women at Njinga's court spinning cotton and 'sewing country cloth'. Bontinck, 'La fondation', 116 mentions specialist dyers in Kongo, but not their gender. Among the Kuba both genders dyed fibre or cloth as needed. Cf. Darish, 'Dressing for the Next Life', 121 (women) 124 (men).

The best informed estimates about the length of time needed to weave a plain weave piece of cloth hold that one man easily weaves one about 50×50 cm length in one afternoon or three to four per day.[31] Setting up a loom and weaving are included in this estimate, but in addition fibre needed to be obtained, dried, combed, and cloth needed sewing and dyeing, and all these operations were normally not carried out by the weaver. Hence it is difficult to estimate the total amount of labor involved in making a given quantity of cloth. As to luxury cloth, one seventeenth-century estimate claims that it took 15/16 days to produce a luxury garment.[32] But as the embroideries and the pile obviously required more work than weaving, and work was done by persons other than the weaver, an estimation of the total amount of labor involved is difficult.

2. The Uses of Raffia Cloth

According to all the early written reports which mention dress, African men and women dressed daily in plain weave raffia skirts and this was the usual dress from the Loango coast to Angola and from there to areas in the east well beyond the ken of European observers.[33] Such skirts undoubtedly consumed the bulk of raffia produced. For if raffia cloth is in general comparable to fabrics such as cotton it is much more fragile because in washing the cloth, especially by beating and wringing, it breaks its fibres. Although Cavazzi c. 1660 estimated that a raffia skirt would last for six months if well woven and well cared for, the anthropologist Mary Douglas limits this to four months of daily wear, i.e. perhaps as much as a third less than cotton.[34] Therefore at least three skirts per adult are needed each year. Each skirt from waist to knee, the shortest garment reported, required from three to four lengths of raffia hence ever adult consumed nine to twelve lengths per year.[35] In the seventeenth century that meant at least 1,800,000 lengths to as much as 3,000,000 lengths of

---

[31] No older source gives any indication. Various authors strongly disagree in part because they do not specify which operations exactly are measured nor what size cloth was measured. This estimate stems from Kuba and Lele practices and is made by Darish, Douglas and myself (fieldnotes) applying to an average 50×50 cm piece which is at least similar to most older pieces. M. Douglas, 'Raffia Cloth', 111 (five is a maximum); P. Darish, 'Dressing for the Next Life', 121. But E. Dusseljé, *Les Tégués de l'Alima* (Antwerp, 1910), 71 estimates ten lengths of 40×40 while R. De Beaucorps, *Les Basongo de la Luniungu et de la Gobari* (Brussels, 1941), 40 was told that only one length a day could be made.

[32] Dapper, *Beschrijvinge*, 149, *nsaka* 15/16 days. This is the vaguest of estimates. Does it refer to the basic weaving with perhaps a woven-in design or to basic plain weave without adornment ? or to a finished piece of luxury cloth ? Dusselje, *Les Tégués*, 71, counts 'one week' for luxury cloth; Darish 'Dressing for the Next Life', 123–4, 126–7, shows that a full length ceremonial cloth normally took months to finish and that several women might work on the embroidering.

[33] For a general view of Kongo dress: T. Obenga, 'Habillement, cosmétique et parure au royaume de Kongo (xvi e–xviii e Siècles', *Cahiers congolais d'anthropologie et d'histoire* 4 (1979), 23, 25–7 and 33 ill. 33. Also Leguzzano *Descrição* I: 166–170 (book 1: 343–349).

[34] Leguzzano, *Relação* 1, 170 (book 1: 349); Douglas, 'Raffia Cloth Distribution', 112.

[35] Dapper, *Beschrijvinge*, 157, 158, mentions four (of the 40×40 size), 17 four or five (women) and 150: six for second grade ceremonial cloth. Some other sources (*mfula*) also mention four. Cf. B. Heintze, *Fontes para a história de Angola do século XVII*, vol. 1 (Stuttgart, 1985), 310. Given the sizes of waists and hips three lengths of the 50×50 size would do. In 1795 nearly destitute women used only one cut into two parts to serve as front and back aprons Cf. L. Jadin, 'Relation', 336 ('one palm' or. c. 26 cm – Neapolitan measure – for each apron).

plain weave cloth per year just for the kingdom of Kongo.[36] The whole region from the Loango coast to the Cuanza river and inland as far as Malebo Pool Kinshasa and the Kwango river may have used up to twice that amount.

While women's skirts everywhere seem to have been of this length, men's skirts in Loango went from waist to ankle, while in the Tio kingdom men wore a blanket size garment either toga like or wrapped just under the armpits. Local notables or nobles wore more. In the kingdom of Kongo they added a reticulate cloth of raffia in the shape of a cape and their women wore a corsage and several layers of skirts, some down to the ankles others down to the knee.[37] Plain raffia was also used for some hats or caps, belts, shoulder bags, and for large bags in which to carry a headload of *nzimbu* shells[38] while scraps were reused for a variety of humble purposes including packing. The Portuguese used plain raffia to make tents.[39]

Then there were the intricately worked and exquisitely dyed luxury wares. These were used for garments, cushion covers, wallhangings and carpets. Lopes tells us that certain kinds of cloth were reserved for the king of Kongo while Dapper tells us that the king of Loango reserved the most elaborate and finest worked cloth for himself and his favorites, while the nobility dressed in a class of cloth that was nearly as showy but less finely woven. These garments were much larger than ordinary skirts. The luxury piece of cloth now in Ulm for instance includes twelve lengths[40] while the second best quality *nsaka* in Loango included six.[41] Twelve pieces or more were probably common for the luxurious textiles used as wallhangings in Kongo and in Loango. The largest single piece mentioned is the royal carpet of Loango mentioned by Dapper as a monumental 33. 80 meters by 19.78 meters.[42] Lesser amounts of cloth, probably one length per article, went into the fashioning of some of intricately worked caps worn by all chiefs. Cushion or pillow covers required one length of luxury cloth and probably one at least of plain weave but it is not known whether this article

---

[36] A conservative estimation of the kingdom of Kongo's population as calculated by J. Thornton, 'Demography and History in the Kingdom of Kongo', *Journal of African History* 18 (1977), 507–30 is 500,000 inhabitants (526), 200,000 to 250,000 of these being adults needing 9 to 12 lengths a year. I have not included cloth needed for children's dress. Cf. L. Jadin, *L'ancien Congo et l'Angola, 1639–1655* (Rome, 1975), vol. 2, no. 292, 688–97 over two to three years old. The Loango coast area, the Tio kingdom and central Angola together also boasted a substantial population and hence used large amounts of cloth.

[37] W. Bal, 'Description', 118–99; Dapper, *Beschrijvinge*, 150–51, 164, 172, 173, 180, 199, 205, 233; J. Jadin, *L'ancien Congo*, vol. 2, 669, 684, 688–97, 959, 972 and note 31.

[38] O. Dapper, *Beschrijvinge*, 150 (belts), 151 (bags) 151, 172, 199 (hats) 254 (carrying *nzimbu* in headloads of 64 Dutch pounds (c 30 kg ?) each; note 31. Caps were sometimes made out of woven raffia but often made in 'needlework' and in material other than raffia. Cf. Brun, *Schiffarten*, 13 'gestrickte oder geflochtene häublin', Ravenstein, 'The Strange Adventures', 50 'make fine caps of needlework as they go in thestreets'. Gibson, McGurk, 'High Status Caps', Bassano, *Un Cappuccino*, 53–7.

[39] W. Bal (ed.), *Description*, 37. M Alves da Cunha (ed.), *Historia das guerras angolanas por António de Oliveira de Cadornega 1681* (Lisbon, 1942), vol. III, 73. They withstood both wind and water very well.

[40] Of 52.3 cm square each. Cf.. A. Jones, 'A collection', 39 fig. 23.

[41] Dapper, *Beschrijvinge*, 149. His text is far from clear on the number of pieces (of 67×67 cm each) in a *kimbo* cloth. *Nsaka* was either 'more than half less' *in size* of a *kimbo* as P. Martin, *The External Trade*, 37 has it or its *value* was 'more than half less' which fits better with the following comments.

[42] Dapper, *Beschrijvinge*, 164. Battell (1607) mentions 'fifteen fathoms about, of fine *ensacks*' i.e. 27.43 meters (at six feet) or 32.01 (at seven feet). Cf. Ravenstein, *Strange Adventures*, 47 and 44 and A. Dewar, 29 (1701) for other carpets.

existed before the Portuguese arrived. In 1701 an armrest at the court of Loango in the shape of a globe was 'wrought with Silk Grass of several Colours into different Figures of Birds and Beasts'.[43] The Portuguese also used luxury raffia cloth for Mass vestments, quilts backed with damas, and cushion covers.[44]

While the quantities of luxury cloth required per year by the courts and by notable men in villages were but a small fraction of the quantities used for ordinary dress, they absorbed considerably more labor per length than did a plain length of cloth. Estimates range from at least seven to perhaps as much as fifteen or twenty times more – although the weaver only did a fraction of the work involved.[45]

Raffia textiles and garments especially were a marker of socio-political status. The quality and the quantity of the cloth used for a garment, the number of garments, the richness of its design all betrayed the position and power of its wearer. In Loango, Kongo and Matamba certain types of textile were reserved for the king or the right to wear them could only be bestowed by him to a few of his special favorites, while the rich and powerful competed with each other in ostentatious display at public gatherings such as assemblies or dances.[46] Thus the larger the political center the more raffia cloth and the richer the raffia cloth found there. The greatest quantities of and the richest raffia textiles were both treasured and displayed at the courts of the larger kingdoms such as Loango, Kongo, or Matamba. Rulers hoarded all sorts of raffia cloth in their treasury houses along with imported cloth.[47] They collected plain weave cloth as tributes and fines and used it as gifts or stipends to officials and clients.[48] Indeed raffia cloth was in such demand that lengths of plain weave were used as currency in northern and eastern Kongo, on the Loango coast and also in Angola where the Portuguese introduced this usage, a topic which is further developed below.

Still raffia was not without competition. In Loango for instance the highest nobility also wore fur garments. In parts of Kongo and Angola barkcloth obtained from either the baobab or the fig tree was also in use.[49] Some garments were knitted or woven with other materials such as the fibre of pandanus and later pine apple, while cotton was used in

---

[43] Dewar, *Voyages*, 29.

[44] F. Bontinck, ed. and translator, *Histoire du royaume du Congo – Etudes d'histoire Africaine* 4 (1972), 66.

[45] See note 30.

[46] Bal, *Description*, 37; Dapper, *Beschrijvinge*, 149 (royal privileges). All the sources underline the ostentatious displays by rulers of luxury textiles both local and imported. Queen Njinga especially was reputed in this regard. Cf. Gioia, *Maraviglliosa Conversione*, 175, 193; Leguzzano, *Relação* 2, 137 (book 6: 82).

[47] K. Ratelband, *Reizen* 64 (Loango royal warehouses filled with cloth). J. Thornton, 'Precolonial African Industry', 13 (estates of kings of Loango 1624 and Matamba 1663).

[48] Bal, ed. *Description*, 67 (gifts); Dapper, *Beschrijvinge*, 167 (fines); Bontinck, *Histoire*, 66 (tribute); A. Hilton, *The Kingdom of Kongo* (Oxford, 1985), 39, 106–7 and index: 'tribute'. This meant that when the kingdom Kongo and its redistributive system collapsed after 1665 the demand for both plain and luxury raffia cloth plummeted; Alves da Cunha, *História* 3, 195 (stipend s); Taxes (*disimos*) in Angola were also paid in cloth. Cf. Fernão de Sousa – Brasio, *Monumenta* 8 (1632), 171–2 (1632); A. Parreira, *Economia e sociedade em Angola na época da rainha Jingo século XVII* (Lisbon, 1990) 115 (Angola: baptisms); Leguzzano, *Relação* I, 214 (Book, 65) for medical expenses in Kasanje.

[49] Heintze, 'Zur materiellen Kultur', 119–20; Ravenstein, *The Strange Adventures*, 18 (but 31 the Jaga used palm cloth 'as fine as silk' even though none were produced where they then lived; Dapper, *Beschrijvinge*, 244. Indirect evidence suggests that centuries before 1450 raffia cloth had ousted barkcloth as the main fabric for garments.

Kongo for some skullcaps. In Angola cotton for wrappers was also woven but on a quite limited scale.[50]

As time wore on the consumption of raffia varied. At the court of Kongo for instance, the most luxurious of raffia garments were at the latest by the 1570s being replaced by expensive imported cloths and by the mid seventeenth century imported cloth also began to be worn by patrician women.[51] Of course, the total quantity of luxury garments available from all sources also grew so that the decline in demand for raffia luxury textiles was probably still small and it may have been offset by a rising demand from Portuguese settlers as well as demand from newly wealthy courts such as that of Queen Njinga in Matamba. After 1665 Kongo sank into civil war and its capital, the largest market for luxury cloth was destroyed in 1678. On the Loango coast imported luxury textiles also competed with raffia cloths but replaced them at a much slower pace.[52] As to cloth for currency, while exports from eastern Kongo and beyond to Luanda dropped after 1641 and ceased after 1665 exports from Loango actually increased until 1693.[53]

During the eighteenth century the demand for luxury cloth declined further as they were replaced by imports from Europe or India but there was still a demand nevertheless.[54] Indeed, as late as 1824 some luxury cloth was still used in Luanda.[55] Demand for plain weave cloth also declined as first the patricians and then commoners began to adopt cheap imports, especially in that part of Kongo where raffia was not produced locally. Elsewhere, e.g. on the coasts of Loango the mass of the population still wore raffia cloth by the 1770s.[56] In Angola the decline of raffia resulted both from the gradual development of cotton weaving in the major African trading centers such as Ambaca and to a lesser extent by

---

[50] Heintze, 'Zur materiellen Kultur', 127 (Angola, 1583). Her hesitation as to the accuracy of the source is unwarranted given later developments in the colony of Angola, the terminology for cotton in Mbundu and the use of cotton in Kongo for caps. Cf. Dapper, *Beschrijvinge*, 199 and later sources; Brun, *Schiffarten*, 29 (Loango, hammocks in cotton).

[51] Bal, *Description*, 119; and all subsequent sources for Kongo; Dapper, *Beschrijvinge*, 151 (women); Leguzzano, *Descrição* 1, 166–70 (Book 1, 343–9).

[52] Dewar, *Voyages*, 29, 32, 34. By 1701 two or three garments in European cloth had replaced fine raffia cloth as marriage gifts.

[53] Hilton, *Kingdom*, 165 may exaggerate somewhat but not much. Cf. Alves da Cunha, ed. *História*, 187 (no more traffi c to Okango1670's) but 276 (a successfull voyage after 1648).

[54] Kecskési, *Kunst*, 280–81 (Munich's 18th C. raffia velvet). E.A. da Silva Correia, *História de Angola* (Lisbon, 1937), vol. 1, 155–6 under the heading 'Textiles' mentions first cotton cloth both plain and in luxury cloths and paid in lieu of taxes at Ambaca by the 1780's (165). But plain raffia was still in use as currency 'in the interior', and both plain and luxury cloth was still produced in the interior (probably in the Dembos and eastern Kongo) used by Africans, including chiefs and still in demand in Luanda for cushions and blankets as before and now also for pillows, sails and hammock curtains (156–7). Around 1780 the price per length was 80 reis and upwards (321).

[55] Lopes de Lima, *Ensaios*, 54, 82 again mentions cotton first but raffia was still used as currency in the interior at 50 reis a length (1824). Luxury cloth was still made and he mentions two tablecloths in 'cut velours'. C. Jeannest, *Quatre années au Congo* (Paris, 1886), 155 still describes a limited trade in luxury cloth in 1874.

[56] L. Degrandpré, *Voyage à la côte occidentale d'Afrique fait dans les années 1786 et 1787* (Paris, 1801), part I, 71, claims that raffia cloth was no longer used for clothing; also 80–81, but describes the wealthier people 75; 13 on weaving. According to Proyart, *Histoire de Loango, Kakongo et autres royaumes d'Afrique* (Paris, 1776), 107–9 the poor still wore raffia cloth, it was still a currency and there were still weavers making some remarkable luxury cloth. Raffia was further used for hats, bags and some other articles but no longer as tapistries on walls. Luxury matting had taken its place (56).

substitution of European cloth for raffia cloth.[57] Nevertheless even by the later nineteenth century many in the interior of the Angolan colony still dressed in raffia cloth and this at a time when imported cottons were common dress all along the northern coasts.[58] In the raffia producing regions inland, even in Kongo, and even at large markets such as those at Malebo pool, raffia was still daily wear.

A novel demand for raffia as well as imported cloth grew on the Loango coast during the eighteenth century. It became customary to wrap the corpse of a ruler, patrician or rich trader in a huge bale composed of pieces of cloth (some imported, but mostly raffia) from his own estate and cloth donated by his associates or underlings. The custom seems to have originated in an earlier funeral practice reported for the Loango king in the seventeenth century, whereby a small number of textiles were buried with the king.[59] By the 1780s such bale-coffins had become so big on the Loango coast that sometimes waggons and a road had to be built to transport the whole to its last abode.[60] A century later the practice was thriving as far east as Malebo Pool. There, one observer estimated that an average major funeral consumed 9000 lengths of cloth and he mentioned an exceptional one where the bale was so large that the facade of the house in which the corpse rested had to be taken out before the bale could be moved.[61] The practice required large amounts of raffia cloth (of the type also used as currency) which were then destroyed in this process.

Overall, the sources for the period give the impression of an almost insatiable demand for raffia cloth and this despite growing imports from Europe. This great demand clearly left a clear imprint on the production processes of raffia in the area. These differ from those in the northern rainforests in the following ways. Raffia trees were cultivated in orchards, an oblique loom was used at least in eastern Kongo and beyond, and weavers in that area preferred to weave quickly produced plain weave cloth and have that embellished by various processes to produce luxury cloth rather than to produce complex woven-in designs. This preference required fewer skilled specialists than was the case if the designs were woven-in while it also rendered labor inputs more flexible because several persons of both genders could participate in the making of luxury garments.[62]

3. Trade

Different sorts of fabrics and palmcloth are made there [Eastern borders of the kingdom of Kongo].

---

[57] Silva Correia, *História*, 155–6; Lopes de Lima, *Ensaios*, 54.

[58] Jeannest, *Quatre années*, 57, 137, 155 mentions that by 1874 even on the Congo coast some people still wore raffia cloth traded from the interior where it was still the usual costume and that multicoloured cloth was still produced there, undoubtedly in the Soso region.

[59] Dapper, *Beschrijvinghe* 168 (refers to 1624?), further he notes (233) that in Angola a corpse was dressed in new clothes for burial, perhaps a general practice in the area.

[60] Degrandpré, *Voyage*, 147–50, 152–4 ill. One group north of the river turned such coffin-bales into the shape of a huge person, the *niombo*. A neighboring group then miniaturized these as *muzuri*. Cf. R. Widman, *The Niombo Cult among the Babwende* (Stockholm, 1967); B. Söderberg, 'Les figures d'ancêtres chez les Babembé', *Arts d'Afrique noire* 13 (1975), 21–33 and G. Dupré, *Les naisssances d'une société* (Paris, 1985), 248–55.

[61] J. Vansina, *The Tio Kingdom of the Middle Congo, 1880–1892* (London, 1973), 208–13, 305, 308–9.

[62] Darish, 'Dressing', 126.

JAN VANSINA

> And since we are on that topic I have to describe the art with which they weave various sorts of cloth, like velvets with and without pile, brocades, satins, taffetas, damasks, sarcenets and other similar stuffs.[63]
> ...The inhabitants [of Sundi] trade with the neighboring regions. In return they receive cloth from the palm, ivory, sable and marten furs and belts made in palmleaves which are highly esteemed in these regions.[64]

All this according to a Portuguese trader who was in Kongo between 1578 and 1583. A sizeable trade in raffia cloth was to be expected, given the strong demand for raffia cloth allied to the fact that raffia palmtrees do not grow in western Kongo or in most of the then colony of Angola. A list of the exporting regions mentioned by late sixteenth and seventeenth century sources in fact corresponds closely to all the areas where raffia trees grew. One of these lay north of the estuary of the river Zaire and the adjoining lowlands of the Loango coast[65] as well as two more beyond the coastal mountain range between Loango and Malebo Pool.[66] However, most of the traded raffia came from eastern Kongo and beyond. While some cloth was exported from the Inkisi river valley mainly in the Kongo provinces of Nsundi and Mbata[67] most came from the markets of Kundi and Okanga on the Kwango river and beyond.[68] Although neither the Portuguese nor their agents crossed the Kwango river there are clear indications that the trade route ran further east to the region of the Tsong (Songo: *pannos songos*) which lay beyond another sizeable river, probably the Inzia an affluent of the Kwilu river.[69] That route gave access to the very extensive raffia tree stands of the Kwilu river basin. Raffia cloth was also exported from the Ndembu area in the borderlands of Kongo and Angola and one report of 1668 mentions a single village in the

---

[63] Bal, *Description*, 37.

[64] Bal, *Description*, 67.

[65] Dapper, *Beschrijvinge*, 143 (Loangidi, Lovangomongo)184 (Ngoi) among many sources; Ravenstein, *Strange Adventures*, 52 (Bongo=Vungu), Heintze, 'Zur materiellen Kultur', 120.

[66] Dapper, *Beschrijvinghe*, 217 (Bokke meale or lower Niari valley), 218 (Makoko or Tio) 219 Pombo (Malebo Pool probably from Tio); Bal, *Description*, 37 and Sardinha in Brasio, *Monumenta* 6, 104 (Anziko or Tio). The main Tio producing area was Sese and Njinju. Cf. J. Vansina, *Tio*, 10, 145

[67] Eastern Kongo generally Bal, *Description*, 36–8, J. Thornton, 'Precolonial African Industry', 12 note 49 citing Brasio, *Monumenta* 15 (1988), 534 (Mumbwadi was all of eastern Kongo and beyond eastwards). Hilton, *Kingdom*, 39 (Mbata), Heintze, 'Zur materiellen Kultur', 120 (Mbata) Sardinha in Brasio, Monumenta 6, 52 (Mbata)104 (Mbata, Nsundi, but according to Bal, *Description*, 67 Nsundi was an importer).

[68] Okanga is very often mentioned from 1595 to 1680 usually for its trade in palm cloth and slaves. Kundi was its major market place. Cf. Sardinha in Brasio, *Monumenta* 6, 52–3, 104 Songa (Tsong or Songo in Kikongo), Cundi, Okanga, and Ibar (Ebale). Dapper, *Beschrijvinge*, 217 (Okango, Konde (Kundi), Fungeno (Mfuninga); Heintze, 'Zur materiellen Kultur', 120. The cloth was bought on the important market of Kundi as well as at the capital of Okanga. The names of regions mentioned in this area all liearound Kundi and Okanga.

[69] 'Songo' appears on maps from c. 1642 onwards as in Brasio, *Monumenta*, 8, opp. 16 as Monsongo (map dating 1643–1646) and in Dapper's book as Songo: it lies one river beyond the Wamba. F. Bontinck, *Histoire*, 56–7 specifies that it lay well beyond Okanga, i.e. beyond the Wamba river. He correctly refutes Brasio's erroneous identification (note 10). A certain Rafael de Castro had traveled on this remote route c. 1619–1620. Cf Brasio, *Monumenta* 6, 491–2. Oral tradition remembers the route from Kundi (Takundi) to near Tsong country and associates it with traders now called Hungaan. C. F. Lamal, *Basuku et Bayaka des districts Kwango et Kwilu au Congo* (Brussels, 1965), 88–9. This route linked the vast palm tree regions of the Kwilu river basin to Okanga and its market at Kundi which helps to explain why by far the largest proportion of raffia cloth from eastern Kongo came from 'Okanga'.

province of Mbamba, near the southwestern limit where raffia palm trees grew, in which all the men were so busy weaving that even the arrival of a missionary did not distract them.[70]

Raffia cloth was traded to Loango from its environs and from the Niari valley on the road to Malebo Pool. The capital of Kongo, San Salvador or Mbanza Kongo, imported its cloth from Mbata Malebo Pool and from *c.* 1590 onwards from Okango. Between 1575 and 1600 Luanda and the new colony of Angola generated a new demand in which the adjoining regions to the east took part. Before 1640 most of the supplies came overland from Mbanza Kongo, although quantities of raffia cloth were also shipped directly from the Loango coast to Luanda by Portuguese ships under a monopoly contracted in Lisbon.[71] After 1648 a new route from Luanda to Okanga was developed which completely bypassed the heartland of Kongo to the East and which also provided the then flourishing capitals of Matamba and Cassange further southeast with raffia cloth.[72] In addition to all this, one should not underestimate modest local exports from places where raffia trees grew to neighbors beyond the growing areas. That was the case for example for exports from the palm rich area just north of the estuary of the Zaire to the capital of Soyo on the southern bank.

The raffia trade routes mentioned were also used for slave trade. Caravans to Okanga or Malebo Pool brought both raffia and slaves to the coast. Cloth was packed in oblong baskets or *mutete*. One full basket weighed about thirty kilograms and constituted a headload.[73] However, precious cloth was apparently also carried in boxes.[74] Raffia textiles were measured by the number of 'leaves' they comprised. These individual 'leaves' or lengths came in two standard sizes *c.* 40×40 cm (only used on the Loango coast) and *c.* 52 × 52cm (used everywhere) although extra large lengths of up to 67 × 67 cm were sometimes made for luxury cloth.[75] To calculate value one counted the number of lengths per cloth, the degree and type of ornamentation and the tightness of the weave. Luxury cloths were also valued differently according to difference in decor which varied according to origin. The luxury market therefore absorbed raffia products from different origins as well as overseas imports from Europe or from West Africa none of which directly replaced another.[76] There are some

---

[70] B. Heintze, 'Zur materiellen Kultur', 122 and her fn. 21 and 22 (citing Cadornega); J. Thornton, 'Precolonial African Industry', 14 and Hilton, *Kingdom*, 107 citing, Dionigio Carli (1668).

[71] Sardinha in Brasio, *Monumenta* 6, 53, 104; Bento Banha Cardoso (1611) and King to Luis da Silva (1616) in Brasio, 6, 18 and 260. Also a relation about Loango from 1620 in Brasio, 6, 479–80; Heintze 'Zur materiellen Kultur', 120 and her note 16; Ratelband, Reizen, 45.

[72] Hilton, *Kingdom*, 75–8, 164–5; Bassani, Un Cappuccino, ill. 17 (probably Kasanje); ill 27 (Njinga of Matamba) 46–7; For Matamba also Francesco M. Gioia, *Maravigliosa conversione*, e.g. 175, 181, 183, 193 (luxury 'country cloth') and Jadin, *L'ancien Congo* 1, 346, 349 (trade) Cloth came to Matamba from eastern Kongo to its north.

[73] A headload of *nzimbu* shells was a bag of 2 arrobes at 32 (Dutch) pounds per arrobe (Dapper *Naukeurige Beschrijvinge*, 234) or about 30 kg (64 lbs); Heintze, *Fontes* I, 310 for counting by mutete as a measure of quantity each one containing 240 Kundi and 250 half Kundi lengths of cloth.

[74] Bassani, *Un Cappuccino*, ill. 17.

[75] Cf. fn. 22. The averages stem from all the estimates of size given in numbers which could be found in the sources and some published measures of surviving lengths of cloth. The ranges around each standard average are small and the standards do not overlap with each other. They confirm the claim in Bal, *Description*, 65 (*c.* 1580!) that Loango cloth was smaller than cloth from elsewhere.

[76] J. Thornton, 'Precolonial African Industry' on the hoards of the king of Loango (1624) and Njinga (1663). Gioia, *Maravigliosa Conversione*, 331 (bridewealth paid to Njinga for her sister); Heintze, 'Zur materiellen Kultur, 123, citing Cavazzi among many other indications.

indications that producers ornamented their cloth according to the taste of the consumers. Most surviving textiles are ornamented in a straightedged geometric style typical in general for Kongo or Loango artefacts, but seventeenth-century illustrations from Matamba show a different style of ornament, curvilinear arabesques, the so-called *sona* which were favored in areas east of the Kwango river.[77] Yet to a large extent these cloths came from the same areas in Okanga which also produced the Kongo type cloths.

The available contemporary sources both about quantities and value of cloth traded stem from Angola. A fiscal official twice informed the council of State in Lisbon about this matter *c.* 1611/1612. He listed the average quantities of cloth coming into Luanda city anually as follows[78]:

From Kongo:
12, 500 'painted' cloths at 640 reis each;
45,000 *songa* (i.e. from Songo east of Okanga) cloths at 200 reis each;
35,000 half *cundi* (i.e. from Kundi in Okanga) cloths at 100 reis each.
From Loango:
15,000 *exfula* (*mfula*) cloth at 200 reis each, only exported by a royal contractor;
333[79] *ensaca* (*nsaka*) cloth at 1200 reis each.

First one notices that only 15,333 items came from Loango as opposed to 92,000 from Okango, that is only 14.2 per cent of the total 107,333 cloths. Secondly the numbers allow for a tentative calculation about the number of woven lengths that can be made. Half Kundi's are certainly one length only at 52 cm., m*fula* four at 40 cm and *nsaka* are six at 52 cm.[80] The other lengths are unknown, probably *songa* were three, and 'painted 'cloths four or more both at 52 cm. Reckoning painted cloth at four lengths, a probable underestimate, one obtains 61, 998 lengths for Loango and 220,000 for Kongo or a total of 281, 998 lengths or 22 per cent of the total. Converting this into meters yields 25,038 meters for Loango and 114, 400 meters for Kongo or 139, 438 meters a year.[81]

The second indication about quantity occurs in the treaty of April 13 between Portugal and Kongo. Kongo undertakes to pay within one year 900 loads of cloth as payment for war damages.[82] This is equal to 250 half *cundi*.[83] The total amount in question was 225,000 lengths, or 117,000 meters to be paid within one year, an amount comparable to the annual imports from Kongo into Angola (*c.* 1611) and to the annual production at a sixteenth century textile centre such as Leiden. Yet the amounts traded annually say *c.* 220,000 lengths, were only *c.* 11 per cent of the 2,000,000 estimated lengths (or 1,040,000 meters) or so needed to clothe the population of Kongo. The inescapable conclusion from all this is that raffia cloth around Kongo was manufactured on a grand scale, an industrial scale.

---

[77] *Contra* Heintze, 'Zur materiellen Kultur', 123–6 who believes that the *sona* patterns were added in Matamba.

[78] Sardinha in Brasio, *Monumenta*, 6, 52–4.

[79] The text has 'few' but he reckons the total value at $400 000.

[80] *Mfula* were the ones used in Angola as *libongo* currency. Cf. B. Heintze, *Fontes*, 310 each *mfula* contains four *libongo*. For *nsaka* Dapper, *Beschrijvinge*, 149–50 (*sokka*).

[81] Thornton, 'Precolonial African Industry', 12 estimated '100,000' meters for exports from Kongo.

[82] Hilton, *Kingdom*, 163–4. L. Jadin, *L'ancien Congo* 2, 1120 (article 2). This was reduced from 1500 loads asked for by the Portuguese governor of Angola (1154).

[83] Heintze, *Fontes*, 310.

Portuguese merchants were deeply involved in this trade. In Lisbon one merchant held the contract monopoly the trade with Loango which was conducted there by his agent.[84] Sardinha, perhaps with some exaggeration, claimed that the raffia trade to Loango yielded 1200 per cent 'or at least 1000' per cent profit, while the trade to Okanga yielded some 800 per cent, profits far higher than those then made in the slave trade.[85] But Cadornega who arrived in 1639, also confirms that traders to Okanga made huge profits before 1640 and that the raffia trade was far more profitable then than the slave trade.[86]

The heyday of the Portuguese trade to Okanga lasted until 1641. After an hiatus in trade due to the Dutch conquest of the colony, traders once more went to the Okanga regions but from late1648 onwards they found the going over Mbanza Kongo increasingly difficult. They pioneered a new road which avoided Mbanza Kongo but found then that even along this new route local rulers in eastern Kongo levied more taxes than had been the case earlier. The fabulous profits of earlier days it seems, could no longer be achieved.[87] The Portuguese trade then declined to the point that neither the name Okanga nor those of its constituent areas recurs in sources after c. 1680. The trade to Okanga continued however but was taken over by local African traders (the Soso) and written sources no longer mention it directly. At first, the official export of cloth from Loango to Luanda grew to compensate but it also came to an end in 1693 when the colony abandoned its raffia currency for a copper one, although raffia remained a currency among Africans in the colony for about a century after that date.[88] The decline of demand during the eighteenth century also naturally implies a decline in trade. But even by the last quarter of the nineteenth century – and despite the now widespread use of cloth imported from Europe – plain raphia cloth was still brought from the interior to the coastal area of Kongo and into Angola.[89]

Was raffia cloth ever exported to Europe or the Americas? After all, as has been told, there was a market for raffia among the Portuguese in Angola. But apart from scattered references to individuals eager to acquire specimens of luxury cloth as souvenirs, there is no indication of any such trade during the sixteenth and seventeenth centuries. However, in the late eighteenth century ships from La Rochelle are said to have imported raffia cloth from Benin to France and the New World.[90] This raffia may well have come from the Loango coasts where La Rochelle ships were active in the slave trade. Yet no European source there mentions any trade in this article.

---

[84] Cf. note 70. The monopoly trade continued until 1692.

[85] Sardinha in Brasio, *Monumenta* 6, 104.

[86] Allves da Cunha, *História* 3, 273–5.

[87] Alves da Cunha, *História* 3, 275–80; Jadin, *L'ancien Congo* II, 1121 (art 8 on tolls).

[88] Proposals to introduce copper coins were already made in 1648 but rejected because of the huge profit the Portuguese Crown made on the raffia currency. Cf. Jadin, *L'ancien Congo* 2, 1103–5, 1177–9. In the interior of Angola however, raffia remained a currency throughout the 18th century. Raffia was still used as currency on the Loango coast c. 1860 according to all sources e.g. J.J. Monteiro, *Angola and the River Congo* (London, 1875), 169.

[89] Cloth currency was still flourishing in the cataracts area of lower Zaire by the end of the century (Mahieu, *Numismatique*, 13–17) and could still be bought as late as 1959 on the left bank of the Kwango south of the border between the Belgian Congo and Angola (A. Rijckmans, *Ngonge* (1960), 2 cited by Bassani, *Un Cappuccino*, 85 n. 37).

[90] S.B. Alpern, 'What Africans got for their Slaves: A Master List of European Trade Goods', 1 – *History in Africa* 22 (1995), 10 (for summer petticoats).

4. Raffia Cloth as Currency

The kingdom of Kongo had two currencies. One was a shell, the *nzimbu* obtained from the island of Luanda. This was used as the sole object for exchange and as a standard of value in all the coastal provinces of Kongo from Luanda to the mouth of the river Zaire as well as at Kongo's capital and in its surrounding province. The Kongo kings controlled its output and used it as official money for their income from tribute, tolls and fines. They also used it to pay expenses such as the wages to foreigners in their service (e.g. clerics) and to pay their main functionaries.[91] But on the Loango coast standard lengths of plain raffia of an average 40 × 40 cm continued to be used as currency and as a standard for value and in eastern Kongo and in the interior beyond raffia lengths of *c.* 52 × 52 cm were used. The money was carried in single lengths or in 'books' of lengths sown together at a corner.[92] Raffia was an obligatory means of exchange. For instance when the Dutch arrived on the Loango coast they could only sell their imports for local raffia cloth and only buy the products of the land with this cloth.[93] In Kongo and eastwards raffia cloth was bought for shells. The African kingdom of the *ngola* used still another currency although raffia cloth was traded there. However, once the Portuguese founded their colony they also introduced lengths of raffia as 'money' a usage speedily adopted by Africans even in the areas eastwards beyond the colony.[94] The Portuguese controlled the amount of currency in circulation by stamping *libongo* cloth imported from Loango with their royal seal twice and the cheaper *mpusu* cloth imported from Kongo once. Only these *pannos marcados* or 'marked cloth' were currency while the unmarked cloth (*pannos limpos*) were but merchandise.[95]

Over time the situation changed as the Portuguese began to import shells similar to *nzimbu* from Rio de Janeiro and thus devalued the currency. Then in 1649 they obtained control over the Kongo 'mint' on Luanda island. As a result the court of Kongo practically abandoned the shell standard in favor of the raffia standard although shells continued to be bought in eastern Kongo and beyond to function there as one of multiple currencies.[96] In Angola unmarked raffia lengths continued to circulate as currency among Africans even after 1693 when copper coins replaced raffia as an official currency.[97]

---

[91] See note 48.

[92] Dapper, *Beschrijvinge*, 233 (45×45 cm); Loir, *Le tissage*, 59 (45×42. cm). The sizes mentioned from the lower Zaire or to its north are smaller than those from the east, at least since the 1570s. Cf. Bal, *Description*, 65. For 'books' Moortamer in Jadin, *L'ancien Congo*, vol 1, 357–8; Loir, *Le tissage*, 59 fig. 49; Mahieu *Numismatique*, 16; Picton and Mack, *African Textiles*, 15 ill. 10.

[93] Dapper, *Beschrijvinge*, 157–8, a situation similar to that encountered by M. . Douglas among the Lele in 1949 where she had to first obtain raffia cloth paid from the local courts which accepted them as payment of fines before she could buy any Lele manufactures. Cf. Douglas, 'Raffia Cloth', 116.

[94] Hilton, *Kingdom*, 77, 107, 116, 164–5; J. Cuvelier, *L'ancien royaume de Congo* (Brussels, 1946), 310–12.

[95] Hilton, *Kingdom*, 77 citing Moortamer (1643) and Cadornega (1670s) Cf. Jadin, *L'ancien Congo* I, 357–8 (Moortamer to the chamber of Zeeland 29 June 1643) and Alves Da Cunha, *História* 3, 195–6. For an earlier mention cf. Heintze, *Fontes* 1, 310 (*panos sujos marcados*). The amount of raffia currency in circulation elsewhere remained uncontrolled.

[96] Hilton, *Kingdom*, 165 (king Antonio carried raffia cloth for his army's expenses and stipends in Kongo were now paid in such cloth. Cf. Alves da Cunha *História* 3, 196. On relations between currencies on a major market in the 1880s cf. Vansina, *Tio*, 282–96.

[97] Ralph Delgado, *Historia de Angola* (Lobito, 1955), vol 4 (a), 176–8.

In some ways raffia cloth was 'money'.[98] Its unit was cheap and light, although like paper money it wore out[99] and 'everything could be bought with it'.[100] This was not strictly true. The scanty evidence concerning actual transactions suggests that while raffia was used for buying manufactured goods in the markets, rights over persons (slaves, bridewealth, medical services) and was used to settle dues of any sorts (social, political, legal) it was not used for buying food and there was no market for it at all in wage labor, land, or even houses. The currency was not fully fungible and a fully fledged raffia money-economy did not exist.[101]

While the sphere of circulation for this currency was limited, it is still remarkable that it did not devalue over time, even though the supply of currency was uncontrolled except in Angola. One would expect inflation with subsequent devaluation but that simply did not happen. Cloth was more than a currency, it was also a much needed commodity. The intrinsic exchange-value of a length of cloth was equal to its use-value. Moreover at any given time the largest volume of production, perhaps nine tenths of it was destined for clothing, not for currency nor for hoarding. The currency was not sufficiently fungible. Neither could it exchanged for European currencies. All of this explains the stability of its value. In the Angolan colony however 'marked' cloth operated within a market economy and was money like. Still the currency was not acceptable outside of the colony. Hence the Portuguese there 'thought' of this currency in terms of gold and silver coins and converted it 'up' into metallic money of universal value whenever possible. As expected in such a case cloth did devalue over time against the reis.[102]

5. How far was Raffia Manufacturing an Industry?

Impressed by the quantity of cloth traded annually from eastern Kongo to Angola J. Thornton and A. Parreira claim that Kongo textile production was an industry and they compared its output to the contemporary cottage industry in Leiden. Thornton converted the numbers given by Sardinha into meters of cloth, multiplied the resulting figure by three or by four to obtain total production in eastern Kongo and adjacent regions and thus derives production

---

[98] Leguzzano, *Relação* 1, 350 (book 4, 2): Capuchins refused gifts in cloth as contrary to their regulations because it was 'money'.

[99] Jadin, *L'ancien Congo* 2, 1177–8 about 'used up' cloth. Hilton, *Kingdom*, 77 attributes the drop in value of *libongo* cloth from 12 *reis* and more in1641 when the Dutch conquest interrupted the supply to 5 *reis* after the reconquest in 1648 to their ragged condition. Cf also J. Cuvelier, 'L'ancien royaume, 311. If so this shows that cloth did not only have value as a currency but a latent use value as well.

[100] Dapper, *Beschrijvinge*, 149 (Loango 'om daer alles voor te kopen') but 217 limits this to 'op hun merkten' i. e. on their markets (Angola).

[101] Vansina, *Tio*, 282–96 discusses spheres of currencies and currency conversion on the huge market at Malebo Pool in the 1880s. Spheres of currency imply limited fungibility. Under those circumstances currency conversion means a permanent loss or access to a portion of the available market in goods and services. This situation clearly operated in the 17th century. For instance the king of Portugal (and sometimes his agents) gained hugely from their ability to convert raffia cloth in fungible specie.

[102] Jadin, *L'ancien Congo* 3, 1472–3 about the 100% gains made when the financial officials in Luanda asked for taxes paid in slaves, which they then credited on the state ledgers as in raffia money. The recommendation of the royal council (2: 1177–9 in 1649 not to replace raffia cloth with copper coin also stresses the 'double profit' made on cloth currency.

per capita figures comparable to data for Leiden.[103] But this similarity only means that commodity production may have reached proto-industrial levels, not that the production was *organised* or *functioned* like an industry.

To begin with no entrepreneurs were involved in the production process itself and there was no putting out system. No capital was invested in equipment nor in the acquisition of raw raffia which was not traded. Contemporary sources only tell us that men wove. Therefore raw lengths of cloth produced by a single male weaver from his own palm trees may well have belonged to that person. But we dont know if the palm trees could in fact be owned by single persons or only by groups e.g. a kin group. We dont know for certain who did the later needle work like embroidering or making pile in the case of luxury cloth although in the last century this was women's work everywhere in Central Africa. Indeed work on a single garment often involved several women.[104] While direct inferences from much later practices and in a neighboring area cannot be valid evidence, it is still worthy to note that nowhere then did a single producer fully own raffia cloth of any kind although the last producer could exchange cloth. Even so, others held some rights over the goods or services acquired with it. At the very least this situation strongly suggests that ownership in in earlier centuries was also a complicated issue.

There were no central African entrepreneurs placing orders or buying the production of captive producership, except for kings to a limited degree.[105] Normally producers decided whether or not to sell cloth and they sold on an open weekly market.[106] Even the thought of capitalistic entrepreneurship did not exist. Unlike Sardinha for example no central African thought in terms of interest or return on capital, although he or she was well aware of the profit to be made. The underlying reason for this attitude simply is that there was no fully developed money economy in Central Africa. Basic requirements from food to houses, land, labor, and even medical assistance were not evaluated in terms of any currency, nor could they be acquired with currency. Ordinary people did not need much currency for daily living. When they had to acquire some tools that could not be made locally (e.g. ceramics, metal tools or cloth) they obtained these objects in return for specialties of their own. The *nzimbu* or raffia currencies basically only facilitated the underlying barter. As to social payments (e.g. fines, tribute, bridewealth) these were communal affairs and they were likely to be settled from a raffia currency hoard held by the representative of a community. In the absence of a universal standard of value, and a universal fully fungible currency there was no market economy. That is why the manufacture of raffia cloth was a system of commodity production, not an industry. It stands in sharp contrast to a cottage industry, which developed precisely because rural folk needed significant amounts of money, and could no longer avoid incorporation into a capitalist market economy of which Holland after1500 was the prime example.

---

[103] Parreira, *Economia*, 53; Thornton, 'Precolonial African Industry', 12–13.

[104] Darish, 'Dressing for the Next Life', 124, 126. Unfortunately no early source clearly mentions that women and only women did this work.

[105] Leguzzano, *Relação* 1, 170 (book 1, 349). Kings and nobles kept groups of weavers who worked only for them and as they desired. See also 84 (book 1, 159) where city dwellers in Mbanza Kongo commissioned weavers and then sold their products on the market.

[106] J. Cuvelier, L. Jadin, *L'ancien Congo d'après les archives romaines, 1518–1640* (Brussels 1954), 135; Leguzzano, *Relação* 1, 84 (book 1, 159).

As to the large volume of textile production this by itself is not so remarkable. The output of each weaver per year might amount to no more than a few dozen lengths of cloth a year, but the joint output of thousands of part-time weavers spread out over a huge area and using raffia from tens of thousands of trees easily accounts for the estimated volumes of production, at least for plain weave.[107] What it is remarkable though is the capacity of the political administration to transfer and concentrate large quantities of raffia at central points. Large amounts of cloth produced beyond immediate needs were used as payments for tributes, tolls and fines. They traveled up the political ladder, and thus went from the countryside to the capital.[108] The long distance trade of cloth in bulk probably emerged only c. 1525 when Portuguese traders began to finance the first caravans trading for slaves. Even in the mid seventeenth century the quantities traded annually seem to have been about the same or a little higher than the amount transferred through administrative channels.[109]

The Kongo and their neighbors produced surprisingly large quantities of raffia cloth and did this with considerable know-how and artistic skill. They also produced other manufactures such as metalware (men), basketry and matting (men), and ceramics (women). For each of these activities there were specialists as well as casual workers. Local trade in these products sustained well developed markets where transactions were eased by recourse to currencies. Village life then was much more diversified than scholars have imagined hitherto and the economic, social and political implications of this situation still remain to be explored.

[107] There are too many little-known variables to calculate the number of weavers or the number of trees required annually with any precision. Still tentative calculations show that the main constraint on large scale production was the number of trees rather than the number of weavers required.

[108] Indeed even as late as the 1650s there were many Kongo traders but they were only involved in small transactions, not long distance trade. Cf. Dapper, *Beschrijvinge*, 201. F. Bontinck, *Jean-François de Rome*, 115, stressing that even the wealthy and the nobles 'are not too concerned to ammass wealth'. By then African traders on the Loango coast working with foreign credit began to fit out caravans of their own.

[109] In 1649 the 225,000 lengths of cloth to be paid by Kongo were a little higher than the annual amount procured by trade from there before 1641. The 1649–1650 obligation however was an exceptional demand, *in addition* to the usual annual requirements, showing that the annual production for the market could be doubled if necessary.

Index

Please note: Page numbers which appear in italics are references to tables or illustrations

putting-out system
in India, 170–3; historiographic
considerations, 177
in Latin America, 78

Qianjiaqiaozhen, textile industry in, 131
Qing dynasty (China), textile industry in,
public versus private control of, 127
Querétaro, textile production in, 81–2, 84
Quito, textile production in, 83

raffia cloth, 263–81
annual consumption of, 269–70, 272
area of production, 264
as currency, 271–2, 278–9
production of, 265–9; as industry, 279–81
quality of, 263–5
trade in, 273–7
uses of, 266, 269–73
valuation of, 275–6
raffia trees, 265–6, 273
ramie, 126, 140, 144, 149, 150, 152
range of, 264, 266, 274
Raychaudhuri, T., historian, 171
Real Compania da Filipinas, 232
Reid, Anthony, historian, 202–5, 222
religion, in Southeast Asia, cloth and, 206–7
Rio de Janeiro, textile industry in, 99
Rock, Margaret, spinner, 51
rope production, in West Africa, 251
Russia
relations with Iran, 31, 41
silk trade in, 34
Russo, Jean, historian, 47

Sadleir, Anthony, Resident of Injiram, 193
Sadraspatnam, textile industry in, 180
Safavid state (Iran)
collapse of, 43
silk trade and, 27, 35–7, 39
Saint-Hilaire, Auguste de, naturalist, 99
Salis, weaving caste, 165–6, 178–9
Salonica, wool industry in, 3, 10–11
salt
in China, public versus private development
of, 124
and Indian textile trade, 156
Santos, Ignacio Alvares dos, loom owner, 106
Sardinha, P., accountant, 277, 279
satin, 126–7
Schlumbohm, Jürgen, historian, 75, 78, 82
self-consumption, comparison to market-
oriented production, 213
Seniyar, weaving caste, 178–9

Shaanxi, textile industry in, 138
Shandong, textile industry in, 138
Shanghai, textile industry in, 135
Shanxi, textile industry in, 127–8, 138
Sharp, Mary, testator, 50
sheep, see also wool
in West Africa, 251
Shen, writer, 129–30
Shenyang, textile industry in, 135
Sherley, Robert, adventurer, 29
shipbuilding, in China, 123
Shirvan, silk production in, 28, 38
Shortledge, Hannah, loom owner, 59
Sichuan, textile industry in, 126–7, 133, 138
Sicily, silk exports of, 39–40
silk
Iranian export to Europe, 27–43
Ottoman exports to Europe, 4–5
in Southeast Asia, 231–2
in West Africa, 251
silk crepe weaving, in Tokugawa Japan, 147–8
silk production
in Aleppo, 12, 12–15, 28–9, 38; volume of,
32
in Anatolia, 8, 8–9
in Bursa, 2, 4, 11, 12, 12–15, 20, 28; cost
of, 7
in China, 119, 126–9, 133; decline of,
128–9; historiographic considerations,
123; labour and, 126
in Iran, 35–6
and Iranian economy, 35–9
in Italy, 27–8
monetization of, 37
in Ottoman Empire, 8, 8–9, 9; development
of, 20
quality control in, 42
in Southeast Asia, 201, 217–18, 233
in Tokat, 13, 13–14, 14
in Venice, 13
silkworm, in West Africa, 251
silver
in British-Iranian trade, 35
mining of, in China, 124
minting of, in Iran, 37
Simcock, Benjamin, weaver, 55
Simontown, Jean, testator, 50
Singapore, dress in, 237
Skardon, John, Resident of Cuddalore, 195
Sketchely, John, weaver, 55
slavery, and textile industry
in Brazil, 108, 112, 115
in China, 123
in North America, 65–6